CHICAGO PUBLIC LIBRARY
SULZER REGIONAL
4455 N. LINCOLN AVE. 60625

Chicago Lincoln Statue, Lincoln Square

The John and Mary Jane Hoellen
Chicago History Collection
Chicago Public Library

The Dawning Place

The Dawning Place

The Building of a Temple, the Forging of the North American Bahá'í Community

by
Bruce W. Whitmore

BAHÁ'Í PUBLISHING TRUST
WILMETTE, ILLINOIS

Bahá'í Publishing Trust, Wilmette, Illinois 60091

Copyright © 1984 by the National Spiritual Assembly
of the Bahá'ís of the United States. All rights reserved.
Printed in the United States of America
88 87 86 85 84   5 4 3 2 1

Photo credits: pp. 37, 39, 63, 105, 107, 116, 118, 119, 151, 156, 175, 177, 184 top and bottom right, 187, 195, 207, 213, 231—Bahá'í House of Worship Activities Office; front cover, pp. 51, 125 bottom, 189, 201, 217, 218, 219, 221, 222, 223, 225, 235, 239, back cover bottom right—Bahá'í Publishing Trust; pp. 45, 91—Bahá'í World Center; pp. 43, 142, 209—Bruce W. Whitmore; p. 19—Edna M. True; pp. 13, 27, 29, 30, 33, 47, 78, 85, 90, 93, 106, 109, 117, 125 top, 127, 128, 134, 144, 146, 147, 148, 149, 152, 154, 155, 167, 168, 169, 170, 171, 172, 176, 184 bottom left, 185, 186, 214, 215, 216, 229, 230, back cover top left, top right, and bottom left—National Bahá'í Archives; p. 79—Northwestern University Library; p. 162—Portland Cement Association.

Note on translations: It is Bahá'í practice that texts of Bahá'u'lláh, the Báb, and 'Abdu'l-Bahá in translation are not considered authoritative unless the translation is undertaken under the supervision or with the approval of the Bahá'í World Center. Passages from Bahá'í sacred writings quoted from standard Bahá'í texts, such as *The Promulgation of Universal Peace* and *God Passes By*, are authoritative. However, many of the translations used in the present work were made early in the century by individuals whose knowledge of Persian, Arabic, and English varied. Moreover, there was during much of the period covered in this book no requirement or even mechanism for review or authorization such as now exists. Therefore, when many early translations are quoted, they are to be considered historic documents since they were the only ones available at the time, even if they did not render the Persian or Arabic exactly.

Library of Congress Cataloging in Publication Data

Whitmore, Bruce W., 1944–
    The dawning place.

    Includes bibliographical references and index.
    1. Bahá'í Temple (Wilmette, Ill.) 2. Wilmette (Ill.)—Temples. 3. Bahaism—United States. I. Title.
    NA5235.W483W5 1984   726'.1789'097731   83-25852
    ISBN 0-87743-192-2
    ISBN 0-87743-193-0 (pbk.)

Cover design by John Solarz

*With gratitude
to my father, Lorin A. Whitmore,
my grandmother, Katrina J. Valentine,
and the many other Bahá'ís throughout
the world whose unacclaimed efforts
played such a vital role in transforming
the dream of the Bahá'í Temple
into reality*

CHICAGO PUBLIC LIBRARY
SULZER REGIONAL
4455 N. LINCOLN AVE. 60625

CONTENTS

Preface / ix

1. Prologue / 3
2. The Bahá'í Faith Comes to America / 7
3. Mother of the Temple / 18
4. Corinne True Goes to Akka / 24
5. The Search / 36
6. Nettie Tobin's Stone / 42
7. Birth of the Bahai Temple Unity / 49
8. The Ceremony / 53
9. The First Long Wait / 66
10. The Quest for a Design / 76
11. Day of Decision / 87
12. The Agony of Victory / 101
13. The Second Long Wait / 121
14. Skyward / 143
15. The Master Craftsman / 158
16. The Temple's Beauty Emerges / 174
17. The Fame of the Temple Spreads / 192
18. The Final Years / 200
19. The Dedication / 227
20. Epilogue / 237

Appendices / 243
    1 The Bahá'í Faith / 245
    2 Ashkhabad, the City of Love / 248

3 Brief Biographies of Some Bahá'ís
  Associated with the Temple Project / 252
4 Tables and Other Miscellaneous Information / 259

Notes / 273
Index / 321

PREFACE

MY FIRST visit to the Bahá'í Temple in Wilmette occurred in 1953 when I was not quite nine years old. In the company of my parents I journeyed by train from Los Angeles to attend the dedication of the building. Most of my personal recollections of that historic event and the activities surrounding it are vague, with the exception of two occurrences. On the day following the public dedication I remember entering the auditorium of the Temple for a program and being anointed on the forehead with attar of rose by Amatu'l-Bahá Rúḥíyyih Khánum, the wife of the Guardian of the Bahá'í Faith, Shoghi Effendi. I also remember accompanying my parents and some other Bahá'ís to the Temple on our last day in Chicago before catching our train home. Having become quite bored, another boy and I wandered outside, where we encountered the grounds keeper, Wyatt Cooper, in the gardens. We were delighted when Mr. Cooper told us that the canal flowing past the Temple was teeming with small marine life. Sensing our excitement, he offered to loan us a large jar for exploration. By the time our parents located us, our clothes were drenched. Our parents did not share our delight!

Exactly two decades later I returned to the environs of the Temple to work for the National Spiritual Assembly of the Bahá'ís of the United States. Like many other Bahá'ís, I loved the Temple but knew little of its history or its significance. When I became a member of the Temple's staff, I discovered that even the historical information in the office's files was limited and often inaccurate.

Encouraged by the late Charlotte Linfoot, who was the assistant secretary of the National Assembly during my first years in Wilmette, I undertook, in mid-1974, a cursory research of the history of the Temple. That effort resulted in an article that was printed in *Bahá'í News*, a monthly publication, in November 1974.

Within weeks of the appearance of the article dozens of Bahá'ís expressed

Preface

to me their excitement and pleasure at learning "all about the Temple," a reaction I had never anticipated. What I sensed most from their comments was their need to know more about their Bahá'í heritage, to feel a closer bond with their spiritual predecessors. The story of the Temple seemed a perfect vehicle for helping fulfill this need since the struggle to erect the building had touched the lives of nearly every early Bahá'í in North America.

Encouraged again by Charlotte Linfoot, as well as by many other Bahá'ís, I decided, in spite of my strong feelings of inadequacy, to write a book about the Bahá'í Temple in Wilmette. The research that took place during 1975 and 1976 resulted in four additional articles, which appeared in *Bahá'í News* (April, July 1975; January, February, November, December 1976). During the next five years the project moved forward in spurts as other obligations took precedence. It was not until 1981 that the book truly began to take form.

Since the history of the Temple spans nearly every decade of the existence of the Bahá'í Faith in North America, the National Bahá'í Archives of the United States proved a rich source of information. The collections that were most important to this work are those of Thornton Chase, Helen Goodall, and Albert Windust; the records of the Chicago House of Spirituality, the Bahai Temple Unity, and *Star of the West* magazine; and several of the transcripts of national Bahá'í conventions during the 1910s and 1920s.

Two other primary sources also provided valuable information. The first is a collection of documents assembled by Corinne True, one of the most important figures in the history of the Temple project; these documents were made available to me by her daughter, Edna True. The second is a collection of materials that belonged to another early American Bahá'í, Louise Waite. Following Mrs. Waite's death these materials came into the possession of my grandmother, Katrina J. Valentine, and, eventually, of myself.

Also critical to this endeavor are the issues spanning the first fifteen years of *Star of the West* magazine, the first thirteen volumes of *The Bahá'í World*, numerous issues of *Bahá'í News* from its inception in 1924 to 1953, and selected early issues of *World Order* magazine. Several other Bahá'í and non-Bahá'í books, as well as newspaper and magazine articles, provided additional glimpses.

The Bahá'í Faith is unique among religions in that its early history has been recorded and preserved in millions of documents. Yet many of these records are still in the possession of individual Bahá'ís, and many more repose in the small archival collections of thousands of local Bahá'í communities throughout the world. It must be left to future historians to mine the rich gems contained within these documents. The present work, therefore, is not a defini-

Preface

tive history of the Bahá'í Temple at Wilmette. The unique story of this fifty-year enterprise warrants a series of volumes, albeit sometime in the future.

Another limiting aspect of this book is that it concentrates on but a few of the many Bahá'ís who struggled to help rear the Temple; these few have been chosen primarily because of the amount of available documentation on their involvement. Future works will be able to explore in greater detail the vital contributions of the many who are not recorded in these pages.

To assist the reader in locating towns and villages in Palestine, Russian Turkistan, and Persia that are discussed in the book, I have used spellings common in atlases and geographic dictionaries published in Western, English-speaking countries. Hence this book uses neither indigenous spellings nor the transliterations of Persian and Arabic names commonly found in most Bahá'í publications. However, transliterations within quotations have been left in their original form. Thus terms such as *Mashriqu'l-Adhkár* and *Bahá'í* are spelled several different ways throughout the book.

For the reader unfamiliar with the Bahá'í Faith, basic background material on the history and teachings of the religion can be found in appendix 1.

In addition to the great debt of gratitude that I owe Charlotte Linfoot and Edna True, I wish to convey my deep appreciation to Archivist Roger Dahl, who provided support and guidance during the several years I carried out my research in the National Bahá'í Archives; to Dr. Magdalene Carney, who was also a prime source of support and encouragement and who reviewed the first draft of this work; to Amatu'l-Bahá Rúḥíyyih Khánum and Arna Perron, who shared remembrances of their involvement with the project; to Robert Stockman and R. Jackson Armstrong-Ingram, who provided invaluable critiques of important events related herein; to Isabelle Windust, who provided copies of several documents originally belonging to her father, Albert Windust; to the National Spiritual Assembly of the Bahá'ís of Canada, which provided biographical information on Louis Bourgeois; to Nancy McFadden, who translated the information on Mr. Bourgeois from French to English; to Helen Burt Potteiger, who provided biographical information on her father, Major Henry Burt; to Roy Solfisburg of the architectural firm Holabird and Root, who helped me gain a basic understanding of the architectural importance of the building; to Frances Worthington and Frances Sadler, for their help in indexing the book; to Dr. Betty J. Fisher and Richard Hill, editors, who lovingly and expertly guided and counseled this novice writer; and, finally, to my precious wife, Patricia, who contributed untold hours in reviewing these pages and offering advice.

THE DAWNING PLACE

Chapter One
PROLOGUE

A NEW age dawned in 1903 when the Wright brothers flew their airplane above the sands of Kitty Hawk for the first time. That moment marks far more than a technical triumph, for air travel would soon draw people everywhere closer together, effectively shrinking this planet to the size of a neighborhood.

The year 1903 also marks the birth of another human triumph—one not nearly so well known, but one that may prove to be far more significant to the future of humanity. The events leading to this achievement began on a Saturday evening, 7 March, when eleven men sat around a large table in a downtown Chicago office. All were members of a relatively new and almost unknown religion, the Bahá'í Faith. This religion, they believed, would guide mankind into an era of unity and harmony never before thought possible.[1]

During the meeting a letter from a Persian Bahá'í, Mírzá Asadu'lláh, was read. The arrival of such letters was not uncommon. Several of the men at the table periodically corresponded with Bahá'ís in India, Turkey, Egypt, Persia, Russia, and elsewhere. Thornton Chase, one of the group's members, noted in a letter to another Persian Bahá'í that

> By means of these letters from different countries and widely separated nations, we learn of the penetrating power with which the Word of God is spreading around the world. . . . Its power is such that it not only enters the individual hearts, but from each centre it sends forth a wonderful power of attraction, which draws all those hearts together and causes them, although unseen by each other, to love one another as the children of One Father. . . .[2]

Mírzá Asadu'lláh's letter was unique, however, in that it would launch the eleven men, members of the governing board of the Chicago Bahá'í community, on a course of action most people would have considered foolhardy; for enclosed with the letter was an account, dated 10 December 1902, of the

Prologue

beginning of construction in Ashkhabad, Russian Turkistan, of the world's first Bahá'í Temple. The account described how the governor of Turkistan, escorted by a sizable honor guard in dress uniform, came to the building site and, after being greeted by nearly eight hundred Bahá'ís, proceeded to lay the cornerstone. During the ceremony the governor declared, " 'It gives me great pleasure to realize that the House of Worship . . . of the Bahais is being erected in my days, and my hope is that I will see it when it is finished.' "[3]

Although the eleven Americans had briefly learned of the project two weeks earlier, they were now impressed by the governor's seemingly uninspired comments. They were equally impressed by Mírzá Asadu'lláh's suggestion that they consider building a similar Temple in the United States. A lively discussion ensued, resulting in a petition's being drafted, edited, adopted, and mailed to Palestine to 'Abdu'l-Bahá 'Abbás, the leader of the Bahá'í Faith at that time.* In part the petition stated:

"we are enkindled with the fire of the love of God that burnt and melted all other thoughts and desires into one great desire:—

"That in these parts and regions there may arise a Mashrak-el-Azkar, built in the Name of the Glorious God, and that there may go forth from the shelter of its beauty, rays of brilliant light. . . .†

". . . permit us to begin the blessed undertaking of the erection of the Mashrak-el-Azkar in Chicago. We pray for wisdom and strength; we pray for thy

---

*'Abdu'l-Bahá 'Abbás was the eldest son of Bahá'u'lláh, Prophet-Founder of the Bahá'í Faith. Although 'Abdu'l-Bahá was originally named 'Abbás Effendi, He later assumed the title of 'Abdu'l-Bahá, which means "Servant of Bahá." He became Bahá'u'lláh's closest companion and protector and constantly aided Bahá'u'lláh in many ways. Bahá'u'lláh specified that following His own death, 'Abdu'l-Bahá was to function as the head of the Faith and the authoritative interpreter of Bahá'u'lláh's teachings.

†The Temple is one part of a Bahá'í institution known as the Mas͟hriqu'l-Ad͟hkár, which means "the dawning place of the mention of God." This institution also consists of educational, social, and humanitarian agencies. (See chapter 20 for additional information about the Mas͟hriqu'l-Ad͟hkár.)

Although within the Bahá'í community the building is still called the Temple, the term House of Worship has been used to describe the building since the early 1930s. Shoghi Effendi preferred House of Worship but approved of the use of both terms. (See Shoghi Effendi [letter written on his behalf] to National Spiritual Assembly of the Bahá'ís of the United States and Canada, 25 August 1931, Original Letters of Shoghi Effendi, microfilm reel 8, National Bahá'í Archives, Wilmette, Ill.)

Prologue

mighty assistance, knowing that thou art the helper, and in that help, God makes us strong.

"In joy and hope that thou wilt grant our supplication, the eleven members present raised among themselves, a starting fund of eleven hundred dollars."

In a letter written to Mírzá Asadu'lláh two days after the petition was drafted, the eleven Americans reported that his letter was read at a gathering of all Chicago Bahá'ís and prompted an additional $150 in contributions for the Temple in America.[4]

Since everything traveled by ship, intercontinental mail service at the turn of the century took several weeks. 'Abdu'l-Bahá's reply, therefore, was not received until late May:

> I was rejoiced through your endeavors in this glorious Cause, made with joy and good interest. I pray God to aid ye in exalting His Word, and in establishing the Temple of Worship, through His Grace and ancient Mercy. Verily, ye are the first to arise for this glorious Cause in that vast region. Soon will ye see the spread of this enterprise in the world, and its resounding voice shall go through the ears of the people in all parts.
>
> Exert your energy in accomplishing what ye have undertaken, so that this glorious Temple may be built, that the beloved of God may assemble therein, and that they may pray and offer glory to God for guiding them to His Kingdom.

Three other letters containing statements about the Temple were received from 'Abdu'l-Bahá during the next several weeks. In one of these He declared:

> O friends of Abdul-Baha, and His co-sharers and partners in the servitude of the Lord of Hosts! Verily, the greatest affair and the most important matter today is to establish a Mashrek-el-Azkar and to found a Temple, from which the voices of praise may rise to the Kingdom of the Majestic Lord. Blessings be upon ye for having thought to . . . erect such an edifice, advancing all in devoting your wealth in this great purpose and in this splendid work. You will soon see the angels of confirmation succeeding you, and the hosts of reinforcement crowding before you.[5]

Only nine years had passed since the first Americans had learned of Bahá'u'lláh, whom they believed to be the most recent of many prophets or divine teachers that God has sent to mankind. In their investigation the new

Prologue

Bahá'ís discovered that, according to Bahá'u'lláh, the fundamental truths of all major world religions are identical and come from one and the same God. The Bahá'ís found that Bahá'u'lláh's teachings provided not only spiritual guidance for individuals and families but also a set of progressive social teachings to help all humanity solve its global problems. Furthermore, the Bahá'ís saw in the Bahá'í Faith a future in which peace and unity could be permanently established on earth. For them the Temple would represent to humanity a symbol of Bahá'í beliefs—that there is only one God, that all religions share a common foundation, and that people of all races, nations, economic groups, and religious backgrounds are equal in the sight of God.* Now a project had been born that would keep the few and scattered Bahá'ís in the United States and Canada busy for the next half century.

---

*Bahá'í Temples are not only centers of worship for Bahá'ís but are also places where everyone may worship God irrespective of religious background or cultural or racial heritage.

Chapter Two

THE BAHÁ'Í FAITH COMES TO AMERICA

THE FIRST Americans had become adherents of the Bahá'í religion in Chicago in 1894. Their conversion came less than a year after the Bahá'í teachings were first mentioned publicly in the United States at a meeting of adherents of many religions held in conjunction with the 1893 World's Columbian Exposition.

The United States Congress had selected Chicago as the location for the mighty exposition, which was intended to commemorate the New World's discovery by Christopher Columbus four centuries earlier. One site under consideration was a desolate stretch of Lake Michigan's beach a few miles south of downtown Chicago. It was a gray and windy day in January 1891 when a group of architects and city officials went to inspect the site at the invitation of Daniel H. Burnham, one of the men who had rebuilt Chicago after the Great Fire of 1871. He had gathered the group together at this remote spot to convince them that this was where they should erect the exposition.

From its beginnings the project was plagued with problems. It took seven thousand men to build the canals, islands, roadways, and 150 buildings that sprawled across the nearly seven-hundred-acre site Mr. Burnham had selected. In 1891 alone eighteen workers were killed, seven hundred injured. The weather that winter was unusually severe. Heavy snows collapsed roofs; torrential rains washed away equipment and, in some cases, entire buildings; mud surrounded nearly everything else. It was not until 1 May 1893, the 401st anniversary of Columbus' discovery, that President Grover Cleveland was able to open the exposition formally.

More than twenty-seven million people were attracted to the glittering fair during the six months it was open. Many architects claimed that the imaginative designs of the buildings dramatically advanced the field of architecture. Others, such as Louis Sullivan and Frank Lloyd Wright, strongly disagreed. Sullivan declared that the exposition set back architecture by at least a half century. Nonetheless, the huge plaster buildings (one reportedly covered thirty-one acres), the art galleries, the Ferris wheel that accommodated more than seven hundred people at a time, the palaces, and the lagoons—all created a world of fantasy never before experienced in the United States.

There was, however, a less desirable environment within the exposition—the infamous amusement area known as the Midway Plaisance, infested by "confidence men, all sorts of fakers, pea-shell and three card monte men, harpies, floozies, and thieves of all kind." One newspaper reported that murders, robberies, and burglaries were so frequent that the police began ignoring them. " 'The horde of malefactors that have literally taken possession of the town,' " the paper said, " 'are absolutely fearless.' "[1]

Contrasting the exposition's celebration of material achievement, with its plethora of somewhat-less-than-noble pursuits, was a series of two hundred congresses presented as an auxiliary to the exposition to "set forth the social, political, artistic, and religious aspirations of the age. . . ." In announcing these congresses the United States government expected that a number of issues of international significance would be considered:

> "The grounds of fraternal union in the language, literature, domestic life, religion, science, art, and civil institutions of different peoples; the economic, industrial, and financial problems of the age; educational systems, their advantages and their defects, and the means by which they may best be adapted to the recent enormous increase in all departments of knowledge; the practicability of a common language for use in the commercial relations in the civilized world; international copyright and the laws of intellectual property and commerce; immigration and naturalization laws and the proper international privileges of alien governments and subjects and citizens; the most efficient and advisable means of preventing or decreasing pauperism, insanity, and crime, and of increasing productive ability, prosperity, and virtue throughout the world; international law as a bond of union and a means of mutual protection, and how it may best be enlarged, perfected, and authoritatively expressed; the establishment of the principles of judicial justice as the supreme law of international relations and the general substitution of arbitration for war in the settlement of international controversies."[2]

One of the most heralded of these congresses, the World's Parliament of Religions, opened on 11 September 1893 in the Hall of Columbus of the Art Institute of Chicago. Never before had representatives of such diverse religious elements assembled to share ideas and philosophies:

"At the appointed hour . . . the crowds in the right-hand aisle of the auditorium parted in quiet step, and two and two the royal delegates of the one Great King, escorted by the managers of the parliament, came slowly into view . . . men of many tongues, of many lands, of many races; disciples of Christ, of Mohammed, of Buddha, of Brahma, of Confucius, in the name of the common God, for the glorification of the Father. The sight was most remarkable. There were strange robes, turbans and tunics, crosses and crescents, flowing hair and tonsured heads. The representatives marched down the center aisle, and amid the cheer that welled up from the hearts of 4,000 men and women, took their seats in triple rows upon the platform, beneath the waving flags of many nations."[3]

The parliament met for seventeen days and freely discussed widely divergent ideas on the incarnation of God, revelation, immortality, the universal elements in religion, and other themes, in "a spirit of harmony, or at least of tolerance." As the parliament drew to a close, its participants began to recognize a common purpose among the religions represented. One delegate observed that

"By this parliament the city of Chicago has placed herself far away above all the cities of the earth. In this school you have learned what no other town or city in the world yet knows. The conventional idea of religion which obtains among Christians the world over is that Christianity is true, all other religions false. . . . You know better, and with clear light and strong assurance can testify that there may be friendship instead of antagonism between religion and religion, that so surely as God is our common Father, our hearts alike have yearned for Him, and our souls in devoutest moods have caught whispers of grace dropped from His throne."

Another added: " 'Fathers of the contemplative East; sons of the executive West—behold how good and how pleasant it is for brethren to dwell together in unity. The New Jerusalem, the city of God, is descending, heaven and earth chanting the eternal hallelujah chorus.' "[4] The parliament served to instill an awareness among some of the delegates of the compelling need for humanity to unify itself. Yet the parliament failed to discover a universal mechanism that mankind could employ to achieve such a goal.

A brief intimation that such a mechanism might exist can be found in the parliament's transcript of the thirteenth day, in a paper entitled "The Religious Mission of the English-Speaking Nations." It was one of two papers sent from the Middle East by Rev. Henry H. Jessup, D.D., director of Presbyterian Missionary Operations in North Syria. Rev. Jessup had lived in the Middle East for more than forty years and had once declined appointment as the United States ambassador to Persia. Like many missionaries he failed to understand that the Bahá'í Faith is an independent world religion; he believed instead that it was a "liberating" force within Islám destined to result in mass conversion of Muslims to Christianity. In an attempt to prove his incorrect concepts, Rev. Jessup closed his paper with an extract from E. G. Browne's account of an interview with Bahá'u'lláh, the Prophet-Founder of the Bahá'í Faith:

> This then is our mission: that we who are made in the image of God, should remember that all men are made in God's image. To this divine knowledge we owe all we are, all we hope for. We are rising gradually towards that image, and we owe to our fellow men to aid them in returning to it in the glory of God and the beauty of holiness. It is a celestial privilege and with it comes a high responsibility, from which there is no escape.
>
> In the palace of Behjeh [Bahjí], or Delight, just outside the fortress of Acre [Akka], on the Syrian coast, there died a few months since a famous Persian sage, the Babi saint, named Behâ Allah [Bahá'u'lláh]—the "Glory of God"—the head of that vast reform party of Persian Moslems, who accept the New Testament as the Word of God and Christ as the deliverer of men, who regard all nations as one, and all men as brothers. Three years ago he was visited by a Cambridge scholar [E. G. Browne], and gave utterances to sentiments so noble, so Christ-like, that we repeat them as our closing words:
>
> "That all nations should become one in faith and all men as brothers; that the bonds of affection and unity between the sons of men should be strengthened; that diversity of religion should cease and differences of race be annulled; what harm is there in this? Yet so it shall be. These fruitless strifes, these ruinous wars shall pass away, and the 'Most Great Peace' shall come. Do not you in Europe need this also? Let not a man glory in this, that he loves his country; let him rather glory in this, that he loves his kind."[5]

In commenting on Rev. Jessup's reference to Bahá'u'lláh, Shoghi Effendi, the great-grandson of Bahá'u'lláh and the appointed successor to 'Abdu'l-Bahá, wrote four decades later:

> Strange indeed must appear to every observer, pondering in his heart the significance of so great a landmark in the spiritual history of the great American

Republic, the circumstances which have attended this first public reference to the Author of our beloved Faith. Stranger still must seem the associations which the brief words uttered on that historic occasion must have evoked in the minds of those who heard them.

Of pomp and circumstance, of any manifestations of public rejoicing or of popular applause, there were none to greet this first intimation to America's citizens of the existence and purpose of the Revelation proclaimed by Bahá'u'lláh.[6]

The teachings of Bahá'u'lláh reached beyond the parliament, for portions of Rev. Jessup's talk were reprinted in at least two Chicago newspapers. There is no indication, however, that the speech or its publication generated any interest in the Bahá'í Faith.

Ibráhím Khayru'lláh, the man who would teach the first Americans about the Bahá'í Faith, and whom 'Abdu'l-Bahá would call " 'the second Columbus,' " was already in the United States and journeying toward Chicago when the World's Parliament of Religions ended.[7] It would be nine months, however, before a functioning religious community would be founded.

Syrian by birth, Ibráhím Khayru'lláh had moved to Egypt after graduating from college. He became a Bahá'í in that country in 1890. In 1892 he left Cairo and traveled to Russia in order to sell an invention to the Russian government. His mission unsuccessful, he continued his journey to Europe and then to American in order to market another invention. Although he was a grain and cotton merchant in Egypt, he at least partially earned a living in America as a spiritual healer. While several Chicagoans were attending his classes on the Bahá'í Faith in mid-1894, Mr. Khayru'lláh sparked the first interest in Bahá'u'lláh's teachings. Four of his students declared themselves believers in the new religion.* The following year 6 more Chicagoans joined, 1 of whom moved to New York. Two years later, in 1897, there were 238 people in Chicago who had either become members or were interested in the Faith. New York had 9 members, and a third city, Kenosha, Wisconsin, soon had 18 Bahá'í residents as well.[8]

Ibráhím Khayru'lláh devised a series of about twelve lessons to teach the fundamental tenets of the Faith. Only toward the end of the series did a student learn of Bahá'u'lláh. This secretiveness, coupled with Mr. Khayru'lláh's insist-

---

*According to a membership list maintained in Chicago between 1894 and 1899, the first four individuals to enter the Bahá'í Faith in the United States were William F. James, Marian A. Miller, Edward W. Dennis, and James B. Thornton Chase.

The Bahá'í Faith Comes to America

ence that the Faith be taught only through his classes or by his approved teachers, attracted many who were intrigued by the Faith's seeming mysteriousness as well as its obscurity. But the general public regarded the " 'Truthknowers' " and " 'Truthseekers' " with suspicion.[9]

Ibráhím Khayru'lláh's distorted approach was doomed to failure, for he was presenting a religion whose fundamental principles include an unfettered search for truth. When he accompanied the first group of American Bahá'ís to the Holy Land to meet 'Abdu'l-Bahá, Mr. Khayru'lláh boldly sought 'Abdu'l-Bahá's approval for several erroneous doctrines he had been promulgating in America. "Not content with having taught the falsehood that 'Abdu'l-Bahá was Jesus Christ incarnate . . . ," William Collins has written, "Khayru'lláh sought the Master's ['Abdu'l-Bahá's] approval of a book he had written which advocated the doctrine of reincarnation.* When 'Abdu'l-Bahá attempted to correct . . . Khayru'lláh's mistaken notions of Bahá'í teachings, he [Mr. Khayru'lláh] developed a burning antagonism which was to smolder for several more months before bursting forth in the gravest test to be faced by that early band of American Bahá'ís."[10]

Early in 1900 Ibráhím Khayru'lláh renounced his allegiance to 'Abdu'l-Bahá, Who, Mr. Khayru'lláh claimed, had distorted Bahá'u'lláh's teachings. Since most Bahá'ís in America had only a minimal and oftentimes inaccurate understanding of even the most fundamental of Bahá'u'lláh's teachings, many became agitated and confused. As a result, many "fell away like the leaves from the trees in Autumn," completely disavowing their relationship with the Faith.[11] A few continued to support Mr. Khayru'lláh and assisted him to form the National Association of the Universal Religion. However, the group and their misguided leader soon faded into oblivion.

One of the few who remained steadfast in the Faith was James B. Thornton Chase, a member of the first group to become Bahá'ís in Chicago. Born on 22 February 1847 in Springfield, Massachusetts, Thornton Chase had been a pupil of Rev. Samuel F. Smith, the composer of "America," and had served as a Union army captain during the Civil War. Later, after studying at Brown University, he spent some years in Colorado and eventually began working in the insurance business. According to Carl Scheffler, a Bahá'í and a contemporary of Thornton Chase, Mr. Chase's

---

*Bahá'u'lláh often referred to 'Abdu'l-Bahá as "the Master," a title that denoted the unique position 'Abdu'l-Bahá was to assume as Bahá'u'lláh's successor. Many of the early Bahá'ís used the title to express their love and respect for 'Abdu'l-Bahá.

JAMES B. THORNTON CHASE
one of the first Bahá'ís in the United States.
He was surnamed "Thábit" (Steadfast)
by 'Abdu'l-Bahá.

interest in religion was a life-long one. A profound student of comparative religion, he was, he said, convinced that this undoubtedly was the "Day of God", and he neglected no avenue in his search for the Truth of God. Not only did he study the existing great organizations in the religious world but no new sect that sprung up was likely to escape his scholarly scrutiny. A few years previous to his contact with the Faith of Bahá'u'lláh he became a follower of Emanuel Swedenborg, without, however[,] dropping his indefatigable search for a greater light which he felt must surely appear in this age.

He was of a deeply mystical nature, as well as an exact and methodical student whose appraisal of ideas and facts was most searching and critical. Logical, kindly, even sympathetic, he was certainly not easily led in his religious life by the many voices that clamored for recognition in that day of cults and "isms".[12]

Thornton Chase was a high-level executive of the Union Mutual Life

The Bahá'í Faith Comes to America

Insurance Company when he became a student of Ibráhím Khayru'lláh and accepted the Bahá'í Faith in 1894. According to the earliest membership roster, he was the fourth person in America to become a Bahá'í; yet 'Abdu'l-Bahá later referred to him as " 'the first American believer.' "[13] It is probable that 'Abdu'l-Bahá conferred the designation upon him because, of the first four Bahá'ís in America, he was the only one who remained steadfast in the Faith after Mr. Khayru'lláh's defection. Thornton Chase was also a source of strength and encouragement, a father figure, for those who maintained their loyalty to Bahá'u'lláh.

Having an unusually clear comprehension of Bahá'u'lláh's teachings, Mr. Chase went on to play a major role in the expansion of the Bahá'í community. In a letter to 'Abdu'l-Bahá four years after the crisis precipitated by Ibráhím Khayru'lláh, Mr. Chase described with marked clarity the external forces that continued to slow the expansion of the Faith:

> Everywhere I go, at home and abroad, I strive to find listening ears, but they are so few, so very few. The "freedom" in this Country causes every "new thing" to be looked at with suspicion, because there are so many of them. In this city of Chicago are hundreds of sects, "fads", "movements", religions, etc[.], of all grades and degrees. . . . There are a few hungry hearts among the people, and even they are deceived by appearances, and are fearful of all things. Nearly all are roaming here and there, seeking for some new thing that will confer personal benefits such as healing the body, material riches or occult powers. The Truth of God, if it bring not personal, worldly advantage, is not attractive to many.[14]

The Bahá'í community, Thornton Chase continued, was also troubled by internal difficulties:

> The false teaching of ignorance, and the enthusiasm of teaching without wisdom (or even knowledge) has done measureless harm, and hindered the growth of the Cause. Even now, some of the dear friends, with hearts of gold, are teaching in such a way that Truth is clouded rather than revealed. The great proportion of American believers today are those who had abandoned the churches and followed after many things, devices of modern minds and old and new forms of "occultism", and at least found a resting place in Bahaism; but the greater portion of them have not cast away the former things, and have simply added to them a belief in the fact of the Manifestation, and thus their teachings are a mixture of many things.

Furthermore, the attempts to educate and unify the Bahá'í community were thwarted by a difficulty in arranging meetings: "The work is very much scattered," Mr. Chase observed, "and we have found it impossible to learn how many and who are all the believers in this one city."[15]

One unified effort to spread Bahá'u'lláh's teachings was the result of several Bahá'ís' membership in New Thought, a nationwide group of societies "of those who claim to desire to obtain a closer association with the Power of God, and who have abandoned all connection with their former churches."[16] Thornton Chase and a few other Bahá'ís served on the Chicago executive committee. When the committee invited Mr. Chase and another Bahá'í to address one of the trimonthly meetings at which all of the Chicago societies gathered, several hundred people were introduced to the Bahá'í teachings.

Another unifying force within the Bahá'í community was the arrival of several Bahá'í scholars sent to America by 'Abdu'l-Bahá. These scholars, Shoghi Effendi has written, "succeeded in rapidly dispelling the doubts, and in deepening the understanding, of the believers, in holding the community together, and in forming the nucleus of those administrative institutions which, two decades later, were to be formally inaugurated through the explicit provisions of 'Abdu'l-Bahá's Will and Testament."[17]

The early Bahá'í communities had very little of the Bahá'í sacred writings in published translation. Thornton Chase, a prolific writer himself, began encouraging the publication of new materials shortly before the turn of the century. Although he felt that the available materials had been "sufficient to establish us in a firm faith and to fill our hearts with love to God," his interest was sparked by the shoddy printing of a small pamphlet by some Bahá'ís who had accompanied Ibráhím Khayru'lláh to the Holy Land in 1898. Arthur Agnew recorded Mr. Chase's reaction:

> It was poorly gotten up with a crinkly paper cover, with a large figure 9 on the cover.* Mr. Chase brought a copy to me at lunch. He seemed disturbed in some way. He appreciated the effort made to get out some of the literature of the Cause,

---

*The number 9 is a symbol of the Bahá'í Faith. Shoghi Effendi has explained that 9 is the highest single digit in the decimal system, " 'hence symbolizes comprehensiveness, culmination,' " as well as " 'perfection' " and " 'unity.' " Shoghi Effendi has also noted that " '9 has the exact numerical value of 'Bahá' [in the numerology connected with the Arabic alphabet] and 'Bahá' is the name of the Revealer of our Faith, Bahá'u'lláh.' " (Shoghi Effendi [letter written on his behalf] to Nina Matthisen, 28 October 1949, quoted in "Messages from the Guardian," Bahá'í News, no. 228 [Feb. 1950], p. 4)

but he deplored the style it was gotten up in. Said these Holy Utterances should have the best possible dress. He had a copy of the translation of the Hidden Words [of Bahá'u'lláh] and asked me to see what I could do about getting it printed in good style. This was the beginning of the Bahai Publishing Society.

In Thornton Chase's subsequent meetings with translators he demanded painstaking accuracy and always searched for "words that might adequately express the meanings that were concealed in the Persian."[18]

The manner in which the earliest American Bahá'í communities organized themselves is still unknown. However, it appears that Thornton Chase helped to form an elementary governing structure in 1900 to handle some of the basic needs of the Bahá'í community in Chicago. In 1901 he played a pivotal role in establishing Chicago's "House of Justice," an elected governing board based primarily on rudimentary instructions, given by the Persian scholars sent by 'Abdu'l-Bahá, regarding how a Bahá'í community should function. The House of Justice—changed in 1902 to the "House of Spirituality"—and similar Bahá'í institutions in other American cities would undergo great changes in the decades that followed as 'Abdu'l-Bahá, and later Shoghi Effendi, guided and nurtured them.

Thornton Chase always manifested a highly developed sense of order in his writings, and he eagerly accepted the principles of Bahá'í community administration that 'Abdu'l-Baha taught. Several years later he would write:

> Just as sure as man lives, as the sun shines, as the earth is formed and revolves; so sure is it that ORGANIZATION is the base of UNITY and of all accomplishment, materially or spiritually, as long as souls dwell in human bodies. Disorganization means death, scattering, disunity and decay.[19]

He worked tirelessly to keep the Chicago House of Spirituality functioning, despite violent opposition from those who were adverse to the whole idea of organization. Through such nascent directive bodies, and with the painstaking guidance and nurturing of 'Abdu'l-Bahá, an organized Bahá'í administration in America was born.

But the infant American communities tended to reflect current social values and standards, rather than those taught by Bahá'u'lláh, because of the Bahá'ís' still limited understanding of Bahá'í principles. The notion of male supremacy and authoritarianism, contrary to Bahá'u'lláh's teachings on the equality of the sexes, was widespread in the Chicago Bahá'í community, where only men were permitted to serve on the House of Spirituality.

'Abdu'l-Bahá tolerated the condition of male dominance with respect to governing the community until the Bahá'ís had collectively achieved the level of maturity necessary for women to participate fully in that process. For the time being 'Abdu'l-Bahá focused the attention of the women on teaching the Faith. At the turn of the century the women in Chicago organized a group called the "Women's Assembly of Teaching." 'Abdu'l-Bahá declared that they would "set such a flame to the regions as will kindle the heart of the universe, and will cause the pillars of the world to tremble." "But all of their mention and thought in their meeting," He warned, "should be confined to teaching the truth, and to constantly persuade people in pure and divine brilliancy and in absolute godlike spirituality. They should not interfere with the affairs which have regard to the Board of Consultation [House of Spirituality]." Nevertheless, 'Abdu'l-Bahá noted in a letter reprinted in a 1910 edition of *Bahai News* that " 'Today the women in the West lead the men in the service of the Cause. . . .' " The editors of the magazine added: "Nine-tenths of the active workers in the Cause in the West are women. This should . . . awaken the men of the West to their duty in the field of service."[20]

Both the Women's Assembly of Teaching and the House of Spirituality would prove indispensable in realizing the dream of those earliest Chicago Bahá'ís to build a Temple. The Temple project itself would provide, in just a few years, the first opportunity for the women to serve equally with the men in an administrative capacity. Together they would guide the course of the most significant enterprise the Bahá'ís of the Western Hemisphere would attempt during the first half of the twentieth century.

Chapter Three

MOTHER OF THE TEMPLE

ONE OF the founders and the first president of the Women's Assembly of Teaching was Corinne Knight True. Although she expended untold energy in sharing Bahá'u'lláh's message with countless people, Corinne True's greatest contribution to the Bahá'í Faith was that, more than any other American believer, she was responsible for motivating the Bahá'ís to build the first Bahá'í Temple in North America.

Corinne True was born on a plantation near Louisville, Kentucky, on 1 November 1861. Her father, Moses Green Knight, was a Presbyterian minister but, due to a throat ailment, was forced to retire when quite young. He married Martha Thomas, an only child who had inherited the plantation along with thirty slaves. Since being a slave owner was morally intolerable to Mr. Knight, he declared that the slaves must be given their liberty. Yet Mrs. Knight's family had always treated their slaves well, and the majority did not want to leave their plantation home. Moses Knight agreed that they could remain in his employ as free people. He constructed several new houses, erected a school, hired a teacher, and provided for every need of his employees.

It is ironic that Corinne's earliest recollection was of an incident generated in part by racial hatred, an incident that would haunt her for the remainder of her nearly one hundred years of life. Although the Civil War had raged for more than three years, it had little effect upon the life of the Knight family until one afternoon when Union troops, unexpectedly and without provocation, plundered its home. Held tightly in her grandmother's arms, three-year-old Corinne was horrified as she gazed down from a second-story balcony and watched the soldiers pillage the only world she had ever known.

Corinne's parents reared her in an environment that reflected all of the culture and charm associated with the South. Her early education was provided by tutors, and she proved to be an excellent student. She possessed an extensive

Mother of the Temple

CORINNE KNIGHT TRUE
the "Mother" of the Bahá'í Temple in Wilmette,
Illinois, and one of its most ardent supporters

knowledge of the Bible, primarily because of her father's demand that it be studied constantly. Moses Knight, with his orthodox ministerial background, was a strict father; yet the lives of his six children were filled with happiness and gaiety.

In the mid-1870s, when Corinne was in her early teens, life on the plantation ended abruptly when the family moved to Chicago. There they purchased a house on the city's west side and began a new way of life. After completing high school, Corinne returned to the South to attend a noted finishing school. While home during a recess, she fell in love with the new boy next door, Moses True. Not long afterward they married. Chicago remained their home until the birth of their first daughter, at which time they moved to Michigan. After enlarging their family with four more children over the next several years, Mr. and Mrs. True returned to Chicago in the early 1890s to be close to Mrs. True's family once again.

Soon after their return tragedy dramatically altered the course of Mrs. True's life. Nine-year-old Harriet, her eldest daughter, a girl with a warm personality and an intense love of life, fell down the basement stairs and died shortly thereafter. Unable to understand the reason for this loss, Corinne True's faith in God was severely shaken. Serious questions about the meaning of her life haunted her and sent her searching for answers.

For almost seven years Mrs. True devoted considerable time to several religious movements, including Christian Science. At first she felt that the spiritual chasm that had developed in her life had been bridged; but when misfortune again entered the True household in 1898, that spiritual support vanished quickly. One of the three children born since the Trues' return to Chicago, their youngest son, Nathaniel, contracted diphtheria. Near death, he was given an injection of a newly discovered drug that seemed to cure him miraculously. Yet several weeks later, on 3 May 1899, he died of heart failure.

During the time Corinne True was grieving over Nathaniel's death, a close friend told her one day about a lecture given by some Persians on the previous evening. Mrs. True's curiosity was piqued by her friend's brief description of a new Eastern religion, and she eagerly agreed to attend one of the lectures to learn more. She accepted the Bahá'í Faith almost immediately.[1]

It was 'Abdu'l-Bahá's first letter to Corinne True, written after He learned of her suffering, that finally brought peace and comfort to her:

> *O thou who art tested with a great calamity!*
> Be not grieved nor troubled because of the loss which hath befallen thee—a loss which caused the tears to flow, sighs to be produced, sorrow to exist and hearts to burn in great agony; but know, this hath reference only to the physical body . . . , for separation belongeth to the characteristics of the body. But concerning the spirit, know that thy pure son shall be with thee in the Kingdom of God and thou shalt witness his smiling face, illumined brow, handsome spirit and real happiness. Accordingly, thou wilt then be comforted and thank God for His favor upon thee.[2]

Corinne True's strength was tested again within weeks of the arrival of 'Abdu'l-Bahá's letter: Kenneth, one of her young twins, also caught diphtheria. Like his brother before him, Kenneth's condition seemed to improve following an injection of the new drug. But he, too, died of heart failure. The drug, it was later discovered, had a side effect that weakened the heart. Again 'Abdu'l-Bahá consoled Mrs. True:

Mother of the Temple

> *O thou who art patient and resigning thyself to the judgment (of God)!*
> Be not grieved at the calamity which hath unexpectedly come upon thee and for the misfortune which heavily weigheth upon thee. It behooveth one like thee to endure every trial, to be pleased with the decree and to commit all thy affairs to God, so that thou mayest be a calm, approved and pleasing soul before God.
> Know thou, that thy beloved son hath soared . . . up to the loftiest height which is never-ending in the Kingdom of God. . . . Truly, I say unto thee, wert thou informed of the position in which is thy son, thy face would be illuminated by the lights of happiness and thou wouldst . . . long for ascending to that praiseworthy position.[3]

Calmed by these words, Corinne True turned her attention to teaching the Bahá'í Faith to people who had not yet encountered it. Unlike most other Bahá'ís before the turn of the century who still attended church, she renounced church going and taught constantly both at and away from home. Because she possessed a thorough knowledge of the Bible, she was able to convince many of her audiences that the coming of Bahá'u'lláh had fulfilled many biblical prophecies. She often traveled to Michigan and Wisconsin, where she met with old friends and lectured to small groups. As a result she became instrumental in establishing several Bahá'í communities within the two states.[4]

Despite sadness over the loss of three children, Moses and Corinne True made their family one of the happiest imaginable. The Trues were devoted to their children and spent every spare moment with them. The ambience in the True household became magnetic and drew large numbers of neighborhood children into constant activity. 'Abdu'l-Bahá encouraged the Trues' devotion to children in a letter to Mrs. True in April 1902:

> It is incumbent upon thee to nurture them from the breast of the love of God, to urge them towards spiritual matters, to turn unto God and to acquire good manners, best characteristics and praiseworthy virtues and qualities in the world of humanity, and to study sciences with the utmost diligence; so that they may become spiritual, heavenly and attracted to the fragrances of sanctity from their childhood and be reared in a religious, spiritual and heavenly training.[5]

Corinne True studied the Bahá'í writings constantly and continued for over twenty years to be educated by 'Abdu'l-Bahá, Who sent more than fifty letters of guidance to her before His death in 1921. Addressing her in 1902 as a "loving torch, flaming by the fire of the Love of God!" He warned, "How many souls advanced unto God, entered the shadow of the Word of God and became celebrated in the world, as Judas Iscariot. Then, when the tests became severe and trials great, their feet turned from the path; turned from confession to denial; changed from love and affection to severe enmity. Then the power of tests, whereby the foundations shake, were manifested."[6] Corinne True's degree of understanding of the Bahá'í teachings proved vital to rebuilding the Chicago Bahá'í community after Ibráhím Khayru'lláh's defection in 1900.

Mrs. True was not at first interested in the Chicago House of Spirituality's plans to build the Temple. It was to her "utter astonishment," therefore, when 'Abdu'l-Bahá wrote to her shortly after He granted permission to the House of Spirituality to construct the building:

> Now the day has arrived in which the edifice of God, the divine sanctuary, the spiritual temple, shall be erected in America! I entreat God to assist the confirmed believers in accomplishing this great service and with entire zeal to rear this mighty structure which shall be renowned throughout the world. The support of God will be with those believers in that district that they may be successful in their undertaking, for the Cause is great . . . because this is the first Mashrak-el-Azcar in that country and from it the praise of God shall ascend to the Kingdom of Mystery and the tumult of His exaltation and greetings from the whole world shall be heard!
>
> Whosoever arises for the service of this building shall be assisted with a great power from His Supreme Kingdom and upon him spiritual and heavenly blessings shall descend, which shall fill his heart with wonderful consolation and enlighten his eyes by beholding the glorious and eternal God![7]

As president of the Women's Assembly of Teaching, Corinne True shared the letter with the other women, who contributed a small sum of money for deposit in a savings account. Yet it would be years before Mrs. True would realize the extent of her responsibility in promoting the project.

In 1911 Albert Windust, publisher of a monthly Bahá'í magazine called *Star of the West*, wrote a reply to one Bahá'í's complaint about the seeming dominance of some Bahá'í women in several of the Faith's affairs:

> The Cause of God needs women—especially spiritually poised women—free from "desire and hope". Man is the seed sower; woman the seed grower. A glance at the growing institutions of the Cause reveals the especial devotion of

women. . . . It is a sign that the Cause has taken root in America; that it is being "mothered" now.

It seems, therefore, that the Temple project has found a devoted "mother" in Mrs. True. . . . If this "mothering" is misinterpreted as "having control", why then it must be admitted they have control.

It was some time before I saw this aspect of things. Man-like, I rebelled against the *seeming* open-handed kidnapping (pardon the expression) of the various institutions of the Cause by women; but now, I realize (being a father myself) that a man is more or less useless in the presence of an infant, and that a mothers' love and care are divinely appointed agencies to preserve the life of the child.[8]

Corinne True's dedication and perseverence would eventually prompt Bahá'ís throughout the world to call her, with affection, "Mother of the Temple."

Chapter Four

CORINNE TRUE GOES TO AKKA

RELATIVELY little was done between 1903 and 1906 to plan for the construction of the Temple, for a number of conditions impeded a whole-hearted effort. In Chicago there was confusion among many of the Bahá'ís as to whether 'Abdu'l-Bahá meant specifically to erect a physical structure. As a result, the Bahá'ís devoted their time to other spheres of activity, such as teaching, conducting classes to study the Bahá'í teachings, and publishing Bahá'í materials. Even if the Chicago Bahá'ís had undertaken the project in earnest, the size of their community probably would have prevented any significant progress.

By 1906 Bahá'ís resided in approximately 150 cities in North America, and twenty-four governing institutions had been formed in cities in eleven states; Washington, D.C.; Honolulu; and Montreal. The majority of these communities were too small and inexperienced to have responded in a meaningful way to any requests for support from Chicago. Of the larger communities, New York at first desired to erect a Temple of its own. Other large communities, such as Washington, D.C., apparently remained unaware of progress in the project until 1906.

There are only a few references to the Temple in the minutes of the Chicago House of Spirituality before 1906. Nevertheless, the House of Spirituality, after securing technical information from the builders of Ashkhabad's Temple, did initiate a search for possible sites in 1904. One of the members of the House of Spirituality, Albert Windust, located a beautiful tract of land just south of Jackson Park, the site of the Columbian Exposition. For a long time many felt that Mr. Windust's site would be the chosen location.[1]

There were other sporadic efforts that called attention to the Temple project. In December 1904, for example, a Chicago Bahá'í, Louise Waite, coordinated a musical performance with her husband, Edgar, that raised $103 for the new "Bahai Temple Fund." Among the performers were "the very foremost and most expensive artists in the city," who provided their services without charge to the Bahá'ís.[2] The event served not only to raise money for the fund but also to generate interest in the Faith's teachings. One performer, a talented pianist and organist, eventually became a Bahá'í.

Widespread enthusiasm would not be aroused until an unfortunate incident brought the Temple project to the forefront of Bahá'í activity. In the spring of 1906 the Chicago House of Spirituality decided to help care for three children who had recently been orphaned. It was not unusual for the community to assist members; in one instance a family who had moved from Illinois lost everything in a flood and received considerable aid from the House of Spirituality. What was unusual in the case of the children was that their deceased mother, a Mrs. Holcomb, had not been a Bahá'í. Having no one to assist her except the children's grandmother, Mrs. Holcomb had appealed to the Chicago Bahá'ís for help shortly before her death because she had heard that the Bahá'ís were loving, caring people.

By the end of September 1906 nearly seven hundred dollars was spent caring for the Holcomb children. The following week, on 6 October, the Women's Assembly of Teaching proposed to the House of Spirituality that a house be purchased for the children in Muskegon, Michigan, since the grandmother lived in that community and had petitioned for permanent custody of the children. The House of Spirituality agreed to the plan on 13 October. It was the women's decision to contribute their Temple Fund savings toward the purchase of the house, Corinne True later wrote, that "led to the revival of the Temple subject which had been snowed under for some little time."[3]

By November 1906 the project was gaining momentum rapidly. The Temple was a major topic of consultation at each meeting of the House of Spirituality. The notion among Chicago Bahá'ís that building the Temple would be a strictly local endeavor—an attitude Corinne True considered the "limitation which rendered us powerless" in earlier years—began to fade quickly when the Bahá'í communities of Washington, D.C., and Cincinnati wrote that they "were united in favor of the project." On 31 December George Lesch, secretary of the House of Spirituality, wrote the Kenosha Bahai Men's Board that the House of Spirituality did not have any information that led them to believe that the Temple project "has been specialized to any particular locality." He also noted that "the conditions existing at present seem to strengthen us in the conviction that it is a general work for the good of the whole body of American believers." "In this connection . . . ," he added, "there is a movement on foot to give impetus to this very idea."[4]

A letter dated six weeks earlier (16 November 1906) from Corinne True to the Chicago House of Spirituality reveals that the "movement" came from a proposal of the Women's Assembly of Teaching. A petition regarding the Temple, the women suggested, should "be sent throughout America to be signed by every Bahai who can be reached" and then forwarded to 'Abdu'l-Bahá so that "He may bless the united Arising for the Mash-rek-el-Azkar." In early December the House of Spirituality approved the proposal and contracted for the printing of a pamphlet containing letters from 'Abdu'l-Bahá regarding the Temple. With this pamphlet the Bahá'ís could be better acquainted with 'Abdu'l-Bahá's directives for the project. The petition, which accompanied the pamphlet, said in part, "We, the undersigned, desire to arise for the erection of the FIRST MASHRUGAL-ASKAR in America, in compliance with the Tablets revealed in behalf of this Great Spiritual Edifice." A letter that also accompanied the pamphlet revealed the vigor of their new resolve: "Recognizing the Oneness of the Bahai Kingdom we feel this a vital movement to bring that Oneness into manifestation." As the simple sheets of notepaper were returned, Moses True glued them together to form a long scroll. By the time the scroll was complete, it bore nearly eight hundred signatures of people residing in twenty-eight states, the District of Columbia, the Canadian province of Ontario, the Hawaiian Islands, and the city of Paris.[5]

The Chicago House of Spirituality decided that one of its members, Arthur Agnew, should take the petition to 'Abdu'l-Bahá. But Mr. Agnew's trip to the Holy Land had to be postponed when one of his children contracted scarlet fever. At about the same time Corinne True had also requested permission from 'Abdu'l-Bahá to visit Him. Another tragedy in her family had prompted the need to make the journey; for her oldest son, Laurence, who would soon have completed his education at the University of Michigan, had drowned toward the end of the summer of 1906. His death occurred during the year's most important sailboat race on Saginaw Bay in Lake Huron, known for its treacherous winds. About midway through the race, as Laurence made his way forward along the sailboat's deck to adjust the jib, a sudden gust of wind whipped the sail across the deck. The impact knocked Laurence, apparently unconscious, into the water. It was nearly a week before his body was recovered.

Still mourning Laurence's death, and carrying the petition, which had been placed in a tin cylinder for protection, Corinne True and her daughter Arna sailed from Boston aboard the S.S. *Republic* and arrived in Palestine on Monday, 25 February 1907. They were required to land at Haifa, where they would wait until it was safe to make the short journey north to 'Abdu'l-Bahá's home in Akka. Visiting 'Abdu'l-Bahá was somewhat of a risk, for He was often

Corinne True Goes to Akka

Haifa, Palestine, 1900, much as it looked when Corinne True visited 'Abdu'l-Bahá in the Holy Land in 1907. Rising above the harbor is Mount Carmel, the "mountain of the Lord."

troubled by Islamic clergymen and government officials who considered Him to be a heretic.

Disembarking at Haifa was a memorable experience for Corinne True. Since the harbor was too shallow to permit large ships to dock, passengers had to transfer to large rowboats. The travelers would climb down steps, which were usually slippery, to reach a platform on the side of the ship. There they would wait until a wave lifted one of the boats high enough so that the Arab boatmen could grab them and lift them across to a seat. Once all the passengers were seated, the boats were rowed to the dock.

After arriving on shore, Corinne and Arna True were escorted to the Hospice of the Little Child, an inn located in Haifa's German Templar Colony. 'Abdu'l-Bahá's wife, Munírih Khánum, had driven from Akka to greet them. "We were almost beside ourselves," Mrs. True later wrote, "with the joy of realizing that actually and truly we were in Haifa, with Acca just across the bay ever in sight. . . . We fell asleep on our pillows perfectly intoxicated with the realization that at last we were to visit the One upon whose Holy Utterances we had been feeding our souls for the past eight years. Sleep was very sweet that night and upon arising the next morning we looked out of our bedroom windows to see Acca across the blue sea and Carmel's point bathed in the new morning's sunshine—a veritable landscape dream almost too beautiful to belong to earth."[6]

'Abdu'l-Bahá's summons came two days later. After hiring a carriage with three horses, the Trues started for Akka at 10 A.M. The route the carriage took gave the Trues a glimpse of the narrow streets of old Haifa before they turned their gaze toward Akka and the shores of the Mediterranean. Traveling north past scores of fishermen, the Trues and their driver rode along the edge of the Mediterranean's waters, for the sand there was firmer for the horses' footing. In front of them were the walls of Akka, which seemed to rise slowly and mysteriously out of the water.

Akka: the city "ancient beyond the knowledge of man," Thornton Chase would write a few months later, "a point of vantage and of strife and . . . renowned for its desperate seiges and defences." "It has witnessed," he continued, "many scenes of war and seige, of hunger and thirst, of torture and death." Bahá'u'lláh and 'Abdu'l-Bahá had been imprisoned there in 1868 after successive banishments from Tehran to Baghdad, then to Constantinople (now Istanbul) and Adrianople (now Edirne). In Akka Bahá'u'lláh and 'Abdu'l-Bahá were to suffer the "strictest confinement," Shoghi Effendi has written, and were forbidden to associate for many years with their Bahá'í companions and the local inhabitants.[7]

The house where 'Abdu'l-Bahá had lived since 1896 had been built by a former governor of Akka, 'Abdu'lláh Páshá, and had been the governor's official residence while in office from 1820 to 1832. 'Abdu'l-Bahá had rented a portion of the property, which actually consisted of several structures, after His earlier residence, known as the House of 'Abbúd, became too small for His family. Corinne True and her daughter entered the house through an archway of red brick. After crossing an open courtyard, they continued their walk up a weatherbeaten flight of steps to a small, whitewashed court. Their guest room was nearby, furnished with two small beds, a wooden bench, a straw mat over a stone floor, and a table that was always adorned with fresh flowers. From the window they could see the old sea wall and the waters of the Mediterranean.

After a few minutes 'Abdu'l-Bahá arrived at their room with a handful of purple and pink hyacinths. He spoke many words of welcome and, Corinne

House of 'Abdu'lláh Páshá, Akka, Palestine, where 'Abdu'l-Bahá resided for fourteen years and received many early pilgrims from the West

True recalled, "said it made him so happy to see the east and the west becoming so united. . . ." She immediately felt humbled by His presence: "I really was not prepared for such a Manifestation of Power. I expected the Love but pictured Abdul Baha as the Christian does the meek, humble Nazareen. I found Him to be a powerful Dynamo—A Lion—as well as the Most Majestic Personage I ever hope to see."[8]

It soon became clear to Corinne True that every action of 'Abdu'l-Bahá and the members of His household was monitored and controlled by the Turkish authorities; yet the outpouring of love within those walls made the suffering of a troubled world seem far away. Some time earlier 'Abdu'l-Bahá had written a letter allaying Corinne True's concern for His well-being: "This prison is indeed more precious and sweet than a garden to me, this fetter is greater than any

'ABDU'L-BAHÁ
son of Bahá'u'lláh and head of the Bahá'í Faith from 1892 to 1921. Corinne True found Him to be "a powerful Dynamo—A Lion" and "the Most Majestic Personage" she ever hoped to see.

liberty and the confinement is broader than the most spacious wilderness. Therefore, grieve not on this account."[9] At last she understood His words.

The early Bahá'ís felt a close, personal relationship with 'Abdu'l-Bahá. They often regarded Him as they would their own father, yet they revered Him as their Lord. Many of those who lived in the Chicago area had asked Corinne True to take gifts to 'Abdu'l-Bahá as an expression of their devotion. By the time she departed from Chicago, her luggage included a large suitcase full of presents—pictures of children, a shawl, a fruitcake, a crocheted mat—as well as several letters.

On the morning of her second day in Akka, 'Abdu'l-Bahá sent for Corinne True. "I gave him the numerous letters," she later wrote, "and then the photographs which he enjoyed greatly.... The roll of names for the Temple lay beside me, wrapped in a piece of wrapping paper, and before I had gotten to it to give it to him, he said that was for the Mashrek-el-Askar. After I had explained the long list of names to him, he patted me on the back and said I had done well and ever after this I was to be his daughter just as if I were Monevah Khanum, his own daughter." "His satisfaction at the work we have done toward the Temple," she continued, "seemed to fill him with great joy."[10]

She described to Him the terrain around Chicago, after which He advised that the Temple be located away from the business district of the city. It must be near the lakeshore, He added, as the location would be more beautiful there, and the Bahá'ís must build it on as large a piece of land as could be obtained. He then left the room for a moment and brought out a ground plan: "First the building, with nine sides, in the middle; then a circular court about that; leading from this circle were to be nine avenues; between each a garden, and in the middle of each garden a fountain of water." Building the Temple, He made clear to her, was the greatest matter for the progress of the Faith at that time. Her work toward successful completion of the project, He said, would cause her to suffer and be misunderstood; yet she must pray in order to gain the strength she would need.[11] She would do exactly that.

While Corinne True was being immersed in a vast outpouring of knowledge from 'Abdu'l-Bahá, Arna's young spirit was quite restless. The journey had been an exhausting experience, and the first morning Arna failed to rise for prayers, which greatly displeased her mother. At lunch that day 'Abdu'l-Bahá asked her if she was happy, and she candidly replied, "'Well, yes, but not very.'"[12] As Corinne True paled over the presumptuous response of her daughter, a smile spread across 'Abdu'l-Bahá's face. He leaned forward slightly and asked Arna if she would be happier playing with the Persian children in another part of the house. Arna was delighted; it was not long before all of the children of the household, including ten-year-old Shoghi Effendi, knew every American game she could remember.

Despite 'Abdu'l-Bahá's gracious hospitality, Corinne True felt a little uncomfortable in the Holy Land because of the differences in culture and language. This was most evident at times when 'Abdu'l-Bahá was absent and those who were present spoke no English. One particularly disquieting experience occurred one afternoon as she sat alone in her room writing letters. Responding to a knock at the door, she opened it to find a veiled Persian girl. Smiling sweetly, she motioned the girl into the room, and they sat down facing each other. As one minute faded into another and the silence grew more pronounced, her uneasiness mounted; then her emotions changed swiftly, first to shock, then to relief, and finally to a fury of which only a mother is capable, as Arna, bursting into uncontrollable laughter, threw back her borrowed veil.[13]

Several other events deeply affected Corinne True, albeit in an entirely different way. She was particularly impressed by 'Abdu'l-Bahá's daily routine and observed that it was His deeds, rather than His preaching, that truly distinguished Him as a Bahá'í. On Friday morning she looked on as He distributed alms to about one hundred poor men, women, and children, many of them crippled and blind, who had assembled in the courtyard of His home, as they did each week. He moved quickly from one to another, "stopping sometimes to leave a word of sympathy and encouragement," Mrs. True later said, "dropping small coins into each eager outstretched palm, touching the face of a child, taking the hand of an old woman who held fast to the hem of his garment as he passed along, speaking holy words of light to old men with sightless eyes, inquiring after those too feeble and wretched to come after their pittance of help and sending them their portion with a message of love and uplift. . . ." Later in her visit, while Corinne True was preparing to drive to the tomb of Bahá'u'lláh with 'Abdu'l-Bahá's wife, 'Abdu'l-Bahá came to Mrs. True's door and, in deepest humility and sincerity, begged a favor of her: Would she kiss the threshold of the tomb for Him, as He had not been permitted to visit it for three or four years. Of that moment she later recalled, "If ever in my life I felt broken-hearted, it was at this."[14]

There was one other person in 'Abdu'l-Bahá's family with whom Corinne True was enchanted—His sister, Bahíyyih Khánum. Known to Bahá'ís as the Greatest Holy Leaf, Bahíyyih Khánum was only six years old when Bahá'u'lláh was first imprisoned in 1852. She later accompanied her Father into exile and was a constant source of solace for both Bahá'u'lláh and 'Abdu'l-Bahá during their lifetimes. The task of managing 'Abdu'l-Bahá's unique household occupied each of Bahíyyih Khánum's days from 6:00 A.M. to midnight as she saw to the needs of the many Bahá'í pilgrims who sought 'Abdu'l-Bahá's presence. The members of His family "instinctively accepted" her authority and constantly "sought her wise and loving counsel," as Bahá'ís eventually would do from all over the world.[15]

Bahíyyih Khánum spent many hours with Corinne True and shared her recollections of Bahá'u'lláh and of the tremendous hardships endured by the family after Bahá'u'lláh was banished from Persia. She told of their great joy

BAHÍYYIH KHÁNUM
*the Greatest Holy Leaf, daughter of Bahá'u'lláh.
She had unfailing admiration for the Temple work
and " 'centered her brightest hopes' " on its completion.*

when they were cast into the prison cell at Akka and heard the door being locked, for then they knew they would not be separated from Him. No one, however, felt any malice toward their Turkish captors; in fact, Corinne True recalled, "No one [in 'Abdu'l-Bahá's home] ever criticises or finds fault with anyone—they only see the good in everyone. . . ."16

During the last afternoon of the Trues' visit, 'Abdu'l-Bahá encouraged Mrs. True to develop the same attitude. Gently taking her hand, He described to her the kind of love, a universal love, that extends beyond a few personal friendships to embrace all humanity. "He said it was like a lover receiving a letter . . . from his beloved and the letter arrives torn, soiled and almost destroyed but it is infinitely precious because it was from his beloved—That is the way you must look upon everyone, no matter what. You love them because they are creatures of God." When the time came to say good-bye, after six days in 'Abdu'l-Bahá's home, Corinne True fought desperately to hold back her tears. She feared the return trip, having had frightening experiences in Naples and Alexandria on the voyage to Haifa. Yet 'Abdu'l-Bahá's comforting words the previous day had done much to allay those fears.[17]

While Mrs. True and her daughter waited for the driver who would take them back to Haifa, one of the women of the household came to the carriage and said that 'Abdu'l-Bahá would like to see "Mamselle Arna." Arna recounted:

> When I got into His room, He went to His bureau and got a large handful of lovely silver Persian coins which were very small and gave them to me. I was delighted, said good-bye, and went back to the carriage. I showed mother what the Master had given me, and she said, "To keep?" And I said, "Yes!" With that she grabbed them out of my hand, saying how wonderful it would be for all of her Bahá'í sisters and put them into one of the suitcases. . . . Again one of the women appeared and again I was taken to the Master's room. This time he got a handful of silk handkerchiefs and gave me them. When I returned to the carriage mother was really excited because these were things of 'Abdu'l-Bahá's and again she grabbed them and put them quickly into the suitcase. Again one of the women appeared and again I was led to the Master. This time He gave me several stones with the [Bahá'í] symbol engraved on them and then he took my other hand and placed a lovely white stone in it and folded my fingers over it and said, "For you!" He hadn't seen mother take all of these things, but each time it raised her spirits. She got the one handful of stones, but I always kept the white stone. . . . Mother was hardly back on the shores of America before she was giving away these items to the early believers.[18]

Leaving Haifa, Corinne and Arna True sailed to Naples, where a letter from Moses True awaited them: Arthur Agnew's son had quickly recovered, and the family would be arriving shortly in Naples en route to visit 'Abdu'l-Bahá. Mrs. True decided to wait for the Agnews' ship. Two days later she received notification that it was docking. At the boat landing she was surprised to find that Carl Scheffler and Thornton Chase had accompanied the Agnews on their trip. They all found rooms at the Trues' hotel, where they "ate cake and drank lemonade like a lot of boys and girls. . . ." "Isn't this too good to be true," Corinne True wrote later, "that five of us from our home Assembly sat together there, some going to the Blessed Master and some returning from the Holy Visit!"[19]

From Naples the Trues traveled to Paris and London at 'Abdu'l-Bahá's request, there to convey His love and develop some new Bahá'í friendships. They arrived home in the United States in early April 1907, and Mrs. True immediately began writing letters to Bahá'ís throughout the country. In the letters she described her experiences in Akka and implored the Bahá'ís to contribute to the construction of the Temple. She also helped to dispel the misunderstanding that the Temple was being built by and for the Chicago Bahá'ís alone: It was an *American* Temple, "and therefore the responsibility rests at the door of every Bahá'í in this land to Arise with all the powers of his or her being to further this Work." Within weeks of her first appeal, contributions were being sent from many parts of the country and were deposited in the Women's Assembly of Teaching savings account. "In reality this marks the beginning of our nationality," Mrs. True wrote. "If Baha-Ollah does not raise up a people . . . with a national life created by following His Laws and Ordinances, then He is less than even Abraham or Moses. Shall we not push forward with untold energy to prove Baha-Ollah is the Lord of Lords and the King of Kings and show to the world the greatness of His Word?"[20]

Chapter Five

THE SEARCH

ALTHOUGH there was close cooperation between the Chicago House of Spirituality and the Women's Assembly of Teaching during the planning and distribution of the petition, some of the men felt the women had exerted too much authority. Thornton Chase, despite his close friendship with Corinne True, was frustrated with her "interference." It was a shock to him during his stay in Akka when, in response to his questions about building the Temple, 'Abdu'l-Bahá replied, " 'When you return consult with Mrs. True—I have given her complete instructions.' "[1]

'Abdu'l-Bahá's statement may have challenged Thornton Chase's attitude toward the work of the Bahá'í women for the Faith. According to Carl Scheffler, who accompanied Mr. Chase to the Holy Land, "In the presence of the Master he [Mr. Chase] seemed completely melted and overcome by the love of 'Abdu'l-Bahá, and the love and kindness of the believers. Not all of the experiences in that Holy Household were purely pleasurable, for 'Abdu'l-Bahá in his kindly manner corrected many concepts that, in spite of a broad vision and deep understanding, still were wrong. That 'Abdu'l-Bahá loved him dearly was obvious, and his response was that of a loving trusting son."[2]

Moments before Thornton Chase's departure from Akka, 'Abdu'l-Bahá urged him to see that the construction begin as soon as possible. " 'After centuries it is not so important as it is now,' " He said, as recorded by Arthur Agnew, " 'but now it is very important. . . . This building will be the cause of unity and prosperity. . . . You have only to begin; everything will be all right.' "[3] 'Abdu'l-Bahá commanded Thornton Chase to convey this urgency to the Chicago House of Spirituality. He said that it was not necessary to build in the city where land was expensive, but He repeated that it was desirable to have the Temple located near Lake Michigan.

Corinne True, after returning from Akka, had launched her own search for suitable land. For many weeks, sometimes every day, she donned heavy

CORINNE TRUE (left) and CECILIA HARRISON
at the Grosse Pointe site after it was located late in the summer
of 1907. Mrs. Harrison often accompanied Mrs. True as she
searched for a suitable Temple site.

work shoes and traveled by horsecar to the relatively undeveloped areas north of Chicago. She was often accompanied by Cecilia Harrison, a Bahá'í and the widow of an Anglican clergyman. Corinne True's unrelenting search eventually caused her to collapse from exhaustion, and she traveled south to recuperate. Yet before becoming ill, she had discovered a thickly wooded tract at Grosse Pointe—a bluff overlooking Lake Michigan in what is now the village of Wilmette—that she felt "was the chosen place."[4]

Several other sites were located by other Bahá'ís, including two more near

The Search

Jackson Park in Chicago (one was selling for $85,000) and three in Evanston, immediately north of Chicago (one was selling for $4,500). The Chicago House of Spirituality also seriously considered a twenty-acre site near Evanston that it felt "could be subdivided and sold to [the] believers for sufficient profit to eventually cover [the] cost of erecting [the] Temple."[5]

On 30 June 1907, in preparation to build the Temple, the House of Spirituality formed a legal agency, the " 'Bahai Assembly,' " which was vested with the authority to "have the care, custody and control of the real and personal property" of the Bahá'í community and to "erect houses or buildings." Four weeks later, on 29 July, the House of Spirituality organized its affairs further by requesting that all Temple funds held by the Women's Assembly of Teaching and all future contributions be deposited with its own treasurer. It also appointed Corinne True the secretary for its Temple Fund to take advantage of "the good work" she had "already done in that direction," and for which the House of Spirituality wished "to express our sincere appreciation."[6]

During the late summer or early fall of 1907 the House of Spirituality sent a letter to approximately two dozen Bahá'í communities calling for a national meeting, the first of its kind, to consult on the project. Nine delegates were sent to Chicago, including representatives from Wisconsin, Michigan, California, and the state of Washington. They joined several Chicago Bahá'ís on 26 November, the "Fête Day of 'Abdu'l-Bahá," and visited potential sites for the future Temple.* The first one they examined was on the south side of the city near Jackson Park, recommended four years earlier by Albert Windust. Afterward they stopped at the home of Grace Foster for a "sumptuous" dinner, which nearly "incapacitated the delegates to visit the north shore" in the afternoon.[7]

Later that day the delegates traveled to Grosse Pointe (the site recommended by Corinne True) and to at least one other site in nearby Evanston at the corner of Sheridan Road and Hill Street (now Maple Street). In the evening they

---

*The Fête Day of 'Abdu'l-Bahá was the inspiration of the Bahá'í community of Ashkhabad, Russian Turkistan, which "thought there should be a day set aside for the Center of the Covenant, Abdul-Baha, in which all the believers should gather together, chant the prayers, remember His life, His deeds, His actions, and, above all, remember His example and servitude, His example of evanescence and love and unity with the world. A supplication was sent and He accepted it. He accepted this day and, therefore, annually this day has been celebrated by them." (Dr. Ameen'u'llah Fareed, quoted in Minutes of meeting held in the home of Mr. and Mrs. M. A. True, 26 November 1907, p. 5, Bahá'í Temple Unity Records, National Bahá'í Archives, Wilmette, Ill.)

The Search

Grosse Pointe (ca. 1907), the wooded bluff overlooking Lake Michigan that Corinne True felt was "the chosen place" for the first Bahá'í Temple in North America

gathered at Corinne True's home on Adams Street, Chicago, to make their decision. Thornton Chase opened the meeting with a prayer for unity, after which Corinne True shared a greeting she had composed for the occasion:

"We are assembled here to-night under the great Banner of Unity; we are celebrating a thanksgiving day—The Thanksgiving Day of the nations. . . .

"The wisdom of calling delegates to expend money and time in traveling, especially just now, has been deeply questioned. In answer I will quote . . . [from 'Abdu'l-Bahá]:

" 'It has been decided by the Desire of God that union and harmony may, day by day, increase among the friends of God . . . in the west. Not until this is realized will the affairs advance by any means whatever. And the *greatest means*

The Search

for the union and harmony of all is Spiritual Meetings. . . . If . . . UNITY of believers . . . does appear . . . it is certain that those countries will, in a short time, become the Paradise of ABHA [the Most Glorious], and the Light of Unity . . . and singleness will shine upon the *whole world from the west*.'

"To bring this into manifestation is the one sole object of calling this Spiritual Meeting. . . . Abdul-Baha says: . . . 'When man is associated with that Transcendent Power emanating from the Word of God, the tree of his existence becomes so well rooted in the soil of assurance that it laughs at the violent hurricanes of skepticism which attempt its eradication. . . .'

"Having assembled here through the transcendent Power emanating from the Word of God, as a united body, . . . let us devote this evening to consultation over the Temple, so that it may be upbuilt."[8]

The visiting delegates then greeted the assembled Bahá'ís on behalf of their respective communities and assured the Chicago Bahá'ís of their communities' commitment to the project. Several letters and telegrams were read that had been received from communities unable to send delegates; two of the letters, from Philadelphia and Seattle, contained contributions for purchasing the land.

The ensuing consultation dealt with whether the sites to the north of Chicago were more desirable than the Jackson Park area to the south. Speaking in favor of the north, Byron Lane of Bangor, Michigan, felt that " 'any one' " of the spots they looked at " 'would be more beautiful . . . because the surroundings are much nicer and it is more quiet. It is for the rest of the soul and if we go there to pray we do not want the turmoil of the world interfering or interrupting us.' " Albert Hall, a Bahá'í lawyer from Minneapolis who had sent his opinion a few days earlier, favored a site like Jackson Park that was near "the homes of the poor, whose hearts the Infinite has tried in the crucible of affliction and made them readier to see the light of His truth."[9]

Thornton Chase found the discussion premature, for he felt it was impossible to make a decision until the money was nearly in hand: " 'I hope the friends who have come here will go home and work for money—that is what we need, not to choose a site but to raise the money to get a site, and when that money is raised, when we see the money, we can find a site that will suit everybody.' "[10]

A Persian Bahá'í disagreed with Thornton Chase, saying, " 'If we depend upon having the money in sight, we shall never build the Temple.' " He urged the Bahá'ís to summon the spiritual support of God and, coupled with the " 'mental support' " of the Bahá'ís, proceed with confidence that the money would be found. Their efforts must become unified, he continued, for " 'The reason why the believers in Ishkabad were able to build a Temple was because they were first united themselves. . . . If you are united you have no reason to doubt the confirmation, strength and power of God.' "[11]

The choice had been narrowed. Most of the assembled Bahá'ís favored recommending the north side to the House of Spirituality. Within one week the House of Spirituality would decide to seriously consider the property at Sheridan Road and Hill Street. But their attention would soon shift to the Grosse Pointe site with its commanding view of the lake and the vast expanse of undeveloped land adjacent to it for gardens and additional buildings. As the Bahá'ís departed the convention, the words uttered earlier that day by Bernard Jacobsen, of Kenosha, Wisconsin, echoed as a call to action:

> "Each and every one of our delegates are going back to our different centers and we are going to enthuse and fill them with ambition to put the shoulder to the wheel and see that this Temple is brought to a completion."[12]

Chapter Six
NETTIE TOBIN'S STONE

IN VARIOUS cities the Bahá'ís began holding meetings to increase support for the Temple, and several communities formed local treasuries to gather money for the project. 'Abdu'l-Bahá continued to send letters of encouragement, expressing His wish "that all the beloved of God, collectively, in the continent of America, men and women, will strive night and day, until the Mashrak-el-Azkar be erected in the utmost solidity and beauty." He wrote a special letter to the New York Bahá'ís, who still dreamt of building a Temple in their own city, and admonished them to devote their talents and resources to the Chicago project: "for should (the believers) undertake (the erection of the Temple) in many places," He said, "it will not become completed anywhere. And, as in Chicago they have preceded every other place to plan the erection of the Temple, undoubtedly, to co-operate and help them is nobler and a necessity."[1]

The Chicago House of Spirituality explored the possibility of purchasing the Grosse Pointe site and learned that the owners of the various parcels of land were willing to sell them. Yet despite 'Abdu'l-Bahá's encouragement and the sentiments of the delegates who had recommended the site, as well as the House of Spirituality's own declaration in December 1907 that it was "ready to serve the Cause of God in this most important matter," it was decided not to proceed because of inadequate funds.[2]

The House of Spirituality's reluctance to act probably stimulated the Bahai Assembly of Washington, D.C., in February 1908 to propose the formation of the "Bahai Temple Association of America." The association would be "composed of local branches throughout the country," working "to unite" the Bahá'ís, "to receive voluntary offerings," and therewith to "purchase suitable land, and to erect thereon the Temple."[3] The proposal, however, did not attract sufficient support.

In late March a Temple business meeting, most likely organized by the Women's Assembly of Teaching and open to all Bahá'ís, was held in Chicago. It

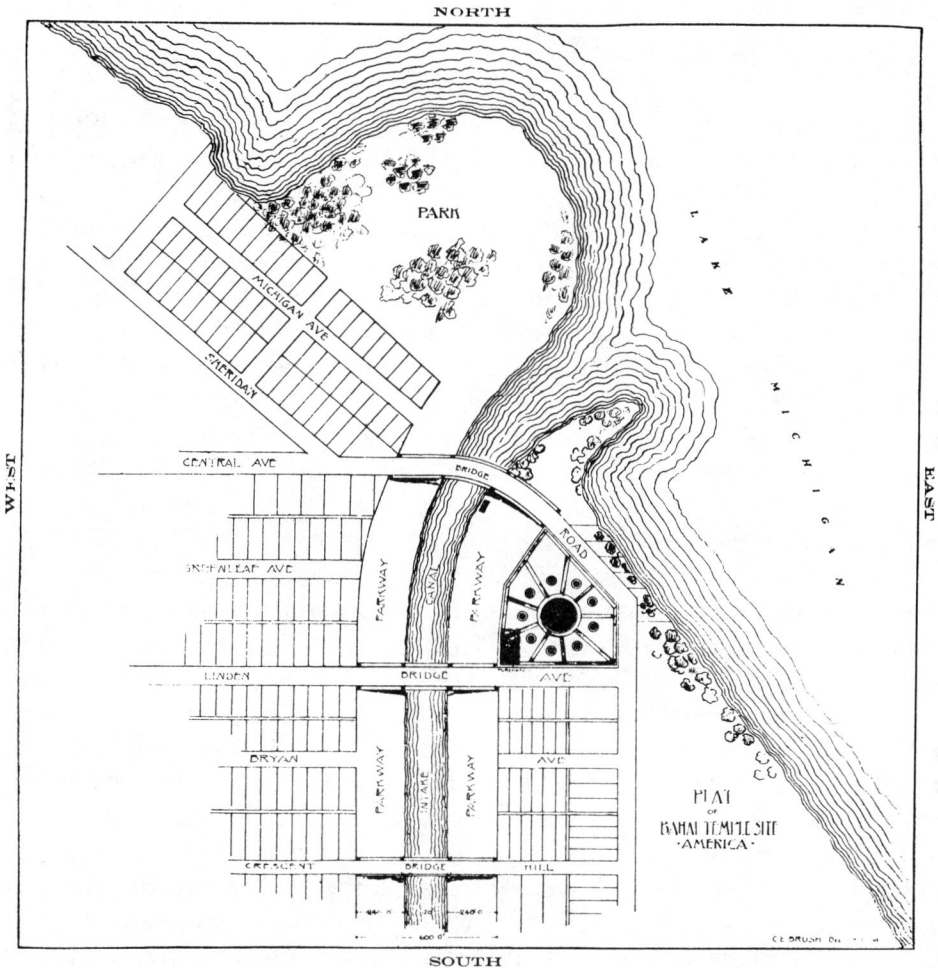

A plat of the Temple site showing the two lots (black rectangle) purchased by the Chicago House of Spirituality in 1908

was decided to recommend to the House of Spirituality that it purchase a small portion of the site with the funds it already had. This action, it was hoped, would inspire Bahá'ís everywhere to begin contributing the funds required for the rest of the land. The House of Spirituality, troubled by unrest in the financial community and a severe tightening of withdrawal policies by area banks, and wishing to appease those Bahá'ís who wanted them to take further action, seized upon the recommendation as a promising solution. On 9 April they purchased for two thousand dollars two small lots, each fifty feet wide and 196 feet deep, located in the southwest corner of the nearly seven acres that eventually would be acquired. The four-month delay by the House of Spirituality, however, proved beneficial, for the purchase price was considerably less than the Sanitary District of Chicago had paid for adjacent land a short time before.

The two lots, which comprised nearly a half acre, were located near the former site of a Potawatomie Indian village. In 1790 a French Canadian fur trader, Antoinne Ouilmette, arrived in the area. In the village he met Archange Chevallier, whose father was a French trader and whose mother was part Indian.[4] A few years later Antoinne and Archange were married among the trees of Grosse Pointe.

By the 1820s white settlers could be found throughout northern Illinois and southern Wisconsin. But the increasing white population created tremendous resentment among the Indians. In July 1829 the Treaty of Prairie du Chien was signed, which became the first step in a plan by the United States government to force the Indians out of Illinois and Wisconsin. In recognition of the Ouilmettes' help in persuading the Potawatomies to agree to the treaty, the government awarded the Ouilmettes a land grant of 1,280 acres, including Grosse Pointe. They lived on the land until shortly before Archange's death in 1840. Antoinne died the following year.

Land speculators, founders of the village of Wilmette, purchased various sections of the land from the Ouilmette children in 1844, the year that witnessed the birth of the Bahá'í Faith. Wilmette grew steadily during the next several decades and became one of the most prominent communities in northeastern Illinois. By the time the two lots were purchased for the Temple, the village's population had grown to approximately twenty-three hundred. Wilmette possessed, however, only six miles of paved roadways, which were regulated by a posted speed limit of twelve miles per hour. The village boasted of an innovative method of imparting justice to speeders: "the law-enforcement cadre would douse the hapless driver with a high-pressure stream of water."[5]

Soon after the first portion of the Temple site was acquired, Bahá'ís began to gather there often. On 23 May 1908 they celebrated the sixty-fourth anniversary of the Declaration of the Báb, the Prophet-Forerunner of Bahá'u'lláh. Upon hearing of the celebration 'Abdu'l-Bahá expressed the "utmost joy" because "the friends of the merciful passed some time on that Day joyous and singing in the land of the Mashrak El Azkar. . . ." Prayer meetings were also common. During one gathering several Bahá'ís, including Corinne True, placed nine

Nettie Tobin's Stone

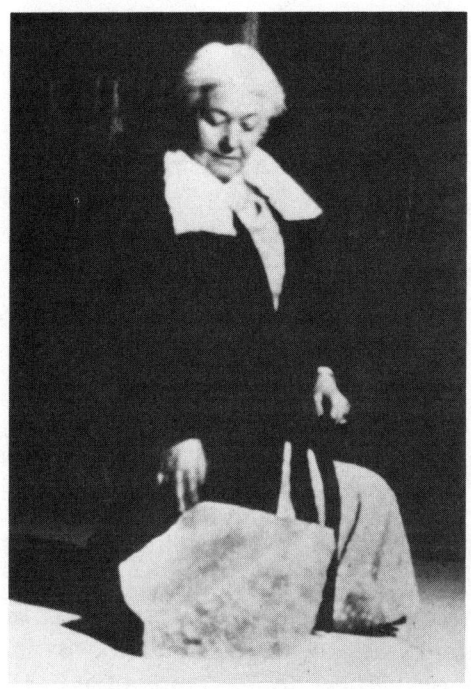

ESTHER "NETTIE" TOBIN
and the stone she brought to the Temple site in September 1908. This photograph was taken many years after Foundation Hall was completed in 1922.

stones in a circle and anointed them with attar of rose, water, and olive oil.[6]

After 'Abdu'l-Bahá received a map of the site, He affirmed that it was a "delightful spot worthy of this edifice and building." He recommended, however, that the site be enlarged "yet a little more, so that spacious ground around the Mashrak-el-Azkar may afford ample room for a rose garden." "Thank God!" He added, "the people of God made such a sincere resolution and exerted such a great effort. It is hoped that all the friends . . . , from all regions and directions,—will assist the erection of this building, so that in a short time a wonderful edifice may arise in the name of God and prove the reason whereby the people may examine and investigate the Cause of God. . . ."[7]

The Chicago House of Spirituality was reluctant, however, to purchase additional land because many Bahá'ís were bothered by the fact that Grosse Pointe was eight miles north of the center of Chicago, and they assumed that the land would probably be traded for a site nearer the city. The controversy would continue for several more months.

One Bahá'í who made a unique contribution to the Temple project in 1908 was Esther Tobin, known to her friends as Nettie. She was a loving, humble

45

woman who earned a meager living as a seamstress. After her husband's death in Detroit in 1892, she moved to Chicago with her two small sons, brother, and half-sister. Yet once there she could barely support her children; oftentimes she would buy groceries for the evening meal with money she earned during the same day. She had not attended school, which may account for her peculiar habit of using words out of context, a trait that often sent herself and her friends into fits of laughter. Paul Dealy, an early Bahá'í, invited her to several Bahá'í meetings, including those at the True home. It was in that home that she became a Bahá'í, probably in 1903. Shortly thereafter, she was employed by Corinne True as a dressmaker and visited the True home one or two days each week.

Although Nettie Tobin worked actively as a member of the Women's Assembly of Teaching, she was troubled by her financial inability to contribute to the building of the Temple. After praying often that God send her something to offer as a gift, she reportedly heard a voice on several occasions that told her to find a stone. Her inspiration most likely came from a letter written in June 1908 to the American Bahá'ís by Mírzá Asadu'lláh, the Persian Bahá'í who had proposed the project to the Chicago House of Spirituality in 1903. In the letter Mírzá Asadu'lláh wrote, "Now is the time for expending energy and power in the erection of the edifice, be it a mere stone, laid in the name of the Bahai Mashrak-el-Azkar. For the glory and honor of the first stone is equivalent to all the stones and implements which will later be used there."[8]

Shortly after the letter arrived, Nettie Tobin visited a construction site near her home, just north of downtown Chicago. She sought out the project's foreman, told him about the Temple, and asked if he could offer her an inexpensive building stone. The foreman, enchanted with Nettie Tobin, showed her a small pile of limestone rocks, damaged and unfit for use, and invited her to take one. Later that day she and her neighbor wrapped one of the stones in a piece of carpet, tied clothesline around it, and dragged the bundle home, where they deposited it in the front hall.[9]

On Labor Day 1908, two days after acquiring the stone, Nettie Tobin requested assistance from Mírzá Mazlúm, an elderly Persian friend who had become a Bahá'í after seeing a number of Bahá'í prisoners martyred.[10] Along with Mrs. Tobin's brother, Leo Leadroot, they would take the stone to Grosse Pointe, where they would meet Cecilia Harrison and Corinne True.

The threesome had difficulty convincing the conductor of the State Street horsecar to allow the stone on board. Yet Mrs. Tobin insisted, he gave in, and they placed the stone, still tied in the carpet, on the back platform. After traveling through Chicago to the north side of the city, they transferred to

A gathering of Chicago Bahá'ís at the Temple site on 2 May 1909, presumably to celebrate the Twelfth Day of Riḍván, a Bahá'í holy day. Thornton Chase is the tall man on the left.

another car and rode to the corner of Central and Ridge avenues in Evanston, probably the station closest to the Temple site at that time.[11] Because they were still six blocks away from the site, the stone would have to be carried the rest of the way by hand. But once they had gone about three blocks, the stone became too heavy to carry any farther, and they began dragging it along the ground.

The trip took much longer than Nettie Tobin had anticipated. Corinne True and Cecilia Harrison, who had been waiting at the site, became worried and started back toward the station. They soon came upon Mrs. Tobin's group. At this point Mírzá Mazlúm, apparently inspired by photographs showing young men carrying stones from the quarry at Ashkhabad for the Bahá'í Temple there, begged his companions to place the stone on his back. He managed to progress another half block to an old, unoccupied farmhouse, where they left the stone in the yard overnight.

Very early the next morning Nettie Tobin returned alone to the farmhouse with a homemade cart and a fire shovel. When she tried to lift the stone into the

Nettie Tobin's Stone

cart, she broke the cart's handle and, in so doing, injured her wrist. A man nearby, responding to her difficulties, helped her to replace the stone in the cart and fixed the handle for her. After resuming her trek for a half block, she enlisted the aid of a newsboy, who helped her reach the west corner of the land. As they dragged the cart across the two lots, it fell apart, leaving the stone sitting amidst the rubble. Her deed accomplished, Nettie Tobin said some prayers and left for home.[12]

In the months ahead the stone provided a focal point for Bahá'í gatherings. Not everyone, however, was enchanted with the new addition, particularly Thornton Chase. In a letter dated 2 October 1908 he wrote, "I presume if the members of the H. of S. [House of Spirituality] should each do a similar thing, quite a number of persons would be delighted, taking it as an evidence that the House of Spirituality was really 'doing something.'"[13]

'Abdu'l-Bahá had already sent a stone marker for the Temple site. The stone was possibly of the same material as the Báb's marble sarcophagus, a gift of the Bahá'ís of Rangoon, Burma. Other stones were reportedly sent by Bahá'ís from various parts of the world. Yet none of these ever reached the Temple grounds. Only Nettie Tobin's contribution, "the stone which the builders refused," would be available to serve as the marker dedicated by 'Abdu'l-Bahá in 1912.[14]

Chapter Seven
BIRTH OF THE BAHAI TEMPLE UNITY

IN 1909, the year after Henry Ford introduced the Model T, Bahá'ís representing many communities gathered again in Chicago to consult about the Temple project. Corinne True had been instrumental in arranging for this meeting. Feeling disappointed by the Chicago House of Spirituality's reluctance to purchase additional land, and fearing that the Chicago Bahá'í community lacked the capacity to administer successfully such a large project, she wrote to 'Abdu'l-Bahá in late spring 1908 to suggest a plan: that the project be directed by an organization representing Bahá'í communities throughout America. Corinne True's idea may have been inspired by the Washington Bahai Assembly's proposal in February. Yet her own plan would request each community in America to appoint a delegate to a national organization. Hence the Chicago House of Spirituality would no longer control the project.

'Abdu'l-Bahá, pleased with the plan, responded that it "will become the cause of harmony in the Word in all America." His reply set in motion events that would provide an arena within which a national Bahá'í administration would evolve, and He placed the Temple at the focal point of this evolution. His letter also marked an important step in the recognition of the equality of men and women, for He directed that "ladies are also to be members" of the organization.[1] Because of the Temple, Corinne True later affirmed, woman would "take her stand side by side with man and both work as one soul to accomplish this mighty edifice. . . ."[2]

In response to 'Abdu'l-Bahá's letter the Chicago House of Spirituality called for a meeting "representing as far as possible all the American Believers." It was to take place between 20 and 23 March 1909 in Chicago. "Can you not see," wrote Corinne True to a friend, "what a glorious gathering that will be. . . . It fairly thrills one's soul to meditate upon that meeting. . . . I do hope every Assembly will realize the great importance of this convention and send us their delegates, for it is the laying of the foundation of the Mashrak-el-Azkar. We must become a united band in order to do so stupendous a work. . . ."[3] Thirty-nine delegates, representing thirty-five cities in fourteen states, Hawaii, and the District of Columbia, were sent to Chicago. Some cities were represented by several delegates—there were four, for example, from New York. San Francisco, Oakland, Los Angeles, and Pasadena, California, and Honolulu, Hawaii, together sent one delegate, John Bosch.

On the first evening, 20 March, the delegates attended a reception given in their honor at the home of Grace Foster. The next morning, 21 March, they celebrated the Bahá'í New Year in Chicago at the Masonic Temple's Corinthian Hall.[4] Later that day they were escorted to Wilmette to examine the site at Grosse Pointe.

The first business session was held on 22 March at the Northwestern University Assembly Hall at Lake and Dearborn streets in downtown Chicago. Thornton Chase, then chairman of the Chicago House of Spirituality, called the convention to order at 10 A.M. and greeted the delegates:

> "This is a Bahai assembly; that means much. Abdul-Baha has written that when one enters a meeting . . . all personal desires or ambitions should vanish. Although opinions may differ, they should be like ripples on the waving sea and be lost in the ocean of love. We should put ourselves entirely under the guidance of the Spirit of God, and as there is but one Spirit of God, every action in its completion should be unanimous; there should never be a minority in a Bahai Convention."[5]

'Abdu'l-Bahá sent a letter to the delegates, which was read at the convention by Corinne True:

> "Among the most important affairs is the founding of the Mashrek-el-Azkar, although weak minds may not grasp its importance; nay, perchance, they imagine this (Mashrek-el-Azkar) to be a temple like other temples. They may say to themselves: 'Every nation has a hundred thousand gigantic temples; what result have they yielded that now this one Mashrek-el-Azkar (is said) to cause the manifestation of signs and prove a source of lights?' But they are ignorant of the fact that the founding of this Mashrek-el-Azkar is to be the inception of the organization of the Kingdom. Therefore it is important and is an expression of the upraising of the Evident Standard, which is waving in the center of that continent, and the results and effects of which will become manifest in the hearts and spirits. . . .

Birth of the Bahai Temple Unity

Delegates to the first Bahai Temple Unity convention, 20–23 March 1909, assembled on the front porch of Corinne True's home in Chicago. Mrs. True is in the middle of the top row. Thornton Chase is diagonally below her to the left.

"Now ye who have convened in that center, (coming) from other cities in America with sincere intentions and lofty endeavor, have ye proposed to undertake this mighty affair? Know ye for certainty . . . that ye will render the Kingdom of God a distinguished service, whereby ye will become dear in both realms and will shine forth as morning stars from the horizon of the love of God.

"This organization of the Mashrek-el-Azkar will be a sample for the coming centuries and will hold the station of the mother, and thus later in other cities many Mashrek-el-Azkars will be its offspring."[6]

Descriptions of several sites, including detailed information on Grosse Pointe, were provided to the delegates. In addition to the two lots already purchased, an option on twelve adjacent lots had been secured for Corinne True by Albert Hall of Minneapolis for $500. The decision of the delegates was unanimous: they would build at Grosse Pointe.

On the final day of the convention, 23 March, the delegates gathered at Corinne True's home and convened in the attic billiard room. There they formed the Bahai Temple Unity, the "permanent national organization for the construction of the Mashriqu'l-Adhkár," and adopted its constitution, hammered out the previous day.[7] A nine-member Executive Board, including six men and three women, was chosen: Mountfort Mills (president), Anna Parmerton (vice-president), Bernard Jacobsen (secretary), Corinne True (financial secretary), Arthur Agnew (treasurer), Helen Goodall, Albert Hall, William Hoar, and Charles Mason Remey.

Before adjourning, the delegates arose and joined hands, facing east, while Bernard Jacobsen led a prayer of thanksgiving. In unison they repeated nine times the Greatest Name, then stood for a moment in silent prayer.* "The 'ecstasies of eternal joy,'" Corinne True remembered, "were greater at this Convention than I have known them to be anywhere outside of Acca . . . [and] Haifa."[8]

The convention was not the only event of great importance to occur in the Bahá'í world during that week. On 21 March in the Holy Land, 'Abdu'l-Bahá laid to rest the body of the Báb in the Shrine built for His remains on Mount Carmel. " 'By a strange coincidence,' " 'Abdu'l-Bahá wrote, " 'on that same day . . . a cablegram was received from Chicago, announcing that the believers in each of the American centers had elected a delegate and sent to that city . . . and definitely decided on the site and construction of the Mashriqu'l-Adhkár.' "[9]

Henceforth the building of the Temple would be directed by the Bahai Temple Unity. Through its subsequent activity it would encourage cohesion, dedication, and determination among the Bahá'ís and would become the predecessor of today's national Bahá'í administration, not only in the United States but also in countries throughout the world.

---

*The Greatest Name, *Alláh-u-Abhá*, is a greeting among Bahá'ís that means "God the All-Glorious." It was first used during Bahá'u'lláh's exile in Adrianople.

Chapter Eight

THE CEREMONY

WITHIN DAYS of the close of the 1909 convention a committee of the Executive Board—consisting of Albert Hall, Bernard Jacobsen, and Mountfort Mills—began working on the purchase of the twelve lots for which Corinne True held option.[1] On 17 May the Bahá'ís purchased that land from Silas Crandall for a reported $32,500. The *Chicago Examiner*, mixing fact and fiction, reported that

> While none of those interested in the movement can give any definite date, it is believed work will be started within the next two months.
>
> The work is to be accompanied by unique ceremonies. Many members of the local cult, it is said, will give up their homes and live on the sacred grounds while the work is going on. With their own hands they will construct the temple, men and women alike carrying brick and mortar. . . .
>
> The temple will be built to symbolize the new man—the perfected man—to justify the perfected world. It will have nine outer walls and nine fountains, each fountain representing a world religion and a world Messiah, all meeting and unifying through to the latter day revelation of truth made through triune manifestations of God through the three great Bahai messengers. The temple will be erected on a triangular plot and will represent the trinity of teachers* who brought to the world the gospel of Bahaism.[2]

Since 'Abdu'l-Bahá had already indicated that the gardens should be circular, the Executive Board was not pleased with the triangular shape. In an effort to make the plot more circular the Executive Board convinced the village

---

*The Bahá'í Faith has only one founder, Bahá'u'lláh. The *Chicago Examiner* may be referring to 'Abdu'l-Bahá and to the Báb, Prophet-Forerunner of Bahá'u'lláh, as the two other teachers.—ED.

The Ceremony

of Wilmette to eliminate roadways running through the property. The board also negotiated with the Sanitary District Board of Chicago, which was building a canal along the western boundary, in order to straighten out that boundary.[3] But a misunderstanding between the Executive Board and the Sanitary Board almost caused the negotiations to fail. When the Sanitary Board did not hear from the Executive Board—because the Executive Board was waiting to hear from the Sanitary Board—the Sanitary Board assumed that the Bahá'ís were no longer interested in the site modifications, and workers were ordered to begin construction of the canal. On the day the digging was to start, a fierce storm broke out that prevented work on the canal for four days. Communications were reestablished during that time, and the land transactions were completed. By April 1910 Honore Jaxon, negotiator for the Executive Board, reported, "As the matter is now agreed upon, by all the parties in interest, our holdings are so consolidated that on our own land we can draw a circle of nearly five hundred feet diameter. . . ."[4]

Payment for the land seemed formidable at first. Although the Chicago House of Spirituality had given a Temple Fund of $3,666.44 to the Bahai Temple Unity, along with the title to the two lots, the amount in the fund was far short of what was needed, for the contract on the land required the payment of $5,000 every six months, plus interest. Corinne True, as the new financial secretary of the Executive Board, wrote to Helen Goodall that "every effort will need to be made to meet" the payments and that "all must unite in sacrificing." The initial response of the Bahá'ís was heart-warming: "The Contributions to the Fund came in so fast," Mrs. True recalled, "that I was rushed to death receipting for them."[5]

During the first year of the Bahai Temple Unity, several methods for collecting money were devised, including a Widow's Quilt Fund, the use of thirty-five hundred "blessing boxes," and the private sale of Bahá'í hymn books. Children in Bahá'í Sunday school groups nationwide sent in their offerings—sometimes only a few pennies, but often several dollars. In Washington, D.C., a variety of programs were begun, including one in which Bahá'ís performed odd jobs for other Bahá'ís and then contributed their wages. One woman from Greenwich, Connecticut, convinced that the Temple would be completed with unusual swiftness, sent her donation of nineteen dollars and wrote, " 'I hope that I am not too late!' " By the end of the year, contributions had been received from sixty-one cities in twenty-two states. Although the amount received from North America (Canada, Mexico, the Hawaiian Islands, and the United States) and Europe (England, France, and Germany) totaled $7,638.66, this sum was nearly equaled by gifts totaling $7,092.85 from Bahá'ís in India, Turkey, Syria, Palestine, Russia, Egypt, and Persia.[6]

These contributions from the East were encouraged by 'Abdu'l-Bahá, Who bade the Oriental Bahá'ís to " 'strive to gather these funds to be sent to the Occident that it may become known and evident throughout the universe that the Bahais of the East and West are as members of one household and the children of the one Lord.' " In reference to the particularly large contributions from Persia, He wrote:

> "From the inception of the world until now there has been no uniting bond between Persia and America. . . . Now consider what a joy and bliss have united these two regions in the shortest space of time! . . .
>
> "The beloved in the East are striving with heart and soul to contribute to the best of their ability, although the internal conditions of Persia have, during the last few years, been exceedingly disturbed. . . . There has been no agriculture, no trade and no commerce; nay, rather, in all the provinces there have been political disputes and quarrels. . . . Thus, they have been wholly occupied with their own affairs. Notwithstanding this, they have striven to contribute to the Mashrak-el-Azkar in Chicago according to their best ability, and they will never be found wanting! If Persia should obtain order, the beloved there will make a worthy contribution."[7]

Referring to the contributions from the East, Corinne True wrote to Helen Goodall, "My soul is thrilled and thrilled [and] I see the marvellous work of Union of the whole world being done by the Mashrakel Azkar."[8]

During October 1909, when Louise Waite, an early Bahá'í from Chicago, visited 'Abdu'l-Bahá in Akka, He said to her, "You must tell the believers in the West that they must work equally hard, with great love and zeal, to show the East their appreciation." Mrs. Waite described to 'Abdu'l-Bahá the many sacrifices being made for the project all over America. When He heard about the work of the children, she recalled, "All would have felt a thousand times repaid could they have seen His face so illumined with love and real joy. 'Very good! very good!' He said over and over."[9]

Another visitor to Akka in 1909, Isabella Brittingham from New York, asked 'Abdu'l-Bahá if He would visit America. After forty years of imprisonment in Akka, 'Abdu'l-Bahá regained His liberty in 1909 as a result of the Young Turks revolt. Now that He was no longer a prisoner, the Bahá'ís in America hoped that He would visit them. Corinne True recorded that conversation later,

The Ceremony

writing, " 'He laughed very joyously ... emphasizing the first word *"If they build the Mashrakel Azkar." ' "* When Mrs. Brittingham asked Him again, " 'His face grew very serious and a great majesty came upon it. After a second or two He continued "If the ground in America is well prepared so that much work can be done for the Cause. . . . The building of the Mashrakel Azkar will prepare that ground." ' "[10]

Many requests were sent in the following months, to which 'Abdu'l-Bahá replied:

> If ye are yearning for my meeting, and if in reality ye are seeking my visit, ye must close the doors of difference and open the gates of affection, love and friendship. Ye must pulsate as one heart, and throb as one spirit. . . .
>
> Verily, verily, I say unto you, were it not for this difference amongst you, the inhabitants of America in all those regions would have, by now, been attracted to the Kingdom of God, and would have constituted themselves your helpers and assisters. Is it meet that you sacrifice this most glorious Bounty for worthless imaginations? No, by God! Should you reflect for one moment, you shall become enabled to destroy instantly the foundation of this difference by absolutely refraining from backbiting and faultfinding amongst yourselves. Adorn with infinite love and concord the assemblage of beatitude, bring about the meeting of happiness, establish the banquet of the oneness of the realm of humanity, loosen your tongues in praising each other, and then anticipate the presence of Abdul-Baha in your midst.[11]

In August 1910 'Abdu'l-Bahá left the Holy Land and traveled to Egypt, where He remained for nearly a year. From Egypt He sailed for Europe, a trip that greatly raised the expectations of the Bahá'ís in America that He would journey to their shores. Their hopes, however, were soon extinguished. Writing to them again, He said, "With great love you have asked for the presence of Abdul-Baha in America, I also greatly wish to go to the friends and see their interesting faces. But during this journey I have no time. I must go back to the East, this is according to wisdom. Therefore with great regret and sorrow at separation I am obliged to return. If it pleases God next year I will take a journey towards the West so that I may engage myself in seeing the faces of the friends, in proclaiming the Word of God and in spreading the Divine Fragrance and the calling of the Kingdom of God in the great meetings and assemblies."[12]

After hearing 'Abdu'l-Bahá's letter, Corinne True wrote to Helen Goodall, "At first my heart went down to my boots but in a moment a great strength

The Ceremony

came to me and I saw it was of His Great Mercy to us. We have slumbered over the Mashrakel Azkar work and now we can make atonement if we will, and get the land paid for and prepare the building." In an earlier letter she had written, "I feel like mounting the housetops . . . [and] shouting to the people to Arise for the Temple—because if you do this Abdul Baha will bless the Land of America with His Holy Presence."[13] Many Bahá'ís did increase their efforts. The Executive Board succeeded in retiring $24,500 of the mortgage on the land, which left only $10,000 still to pay. Eventually, the momentous news arrived, and the Bahá'ís rejoiced: 'Abdu'l-Bahá was coming to America.

He arrived in New York aboard the S.S. *Cedric* on 11 April 1912 and spent the next two-and-one-half weeks in New York and Washington, D.C. The purpose of His visit was " 'to set forth in America the fundamental principles of the revelation and teachings of Bahá'u'lláh.' "[14] While in New York and Washington He gave addresses daily in the homes of various Bahá'ís and at several churches and educational institutions, including Columbia and Howard universities. Late in the afternoon of 28 April He departed for Chicago.

The fourth Bahai Temple Unity convention opened the following morning in the Corinthian Hall of Chicago's Masonic Temple. The most stirring aspect of the gathering was the announcement on the third line of the printed program: "Guest of honor Abdul Baha Abbas." The delegates expected 'Abdu'l-Bahá to arrive in Chicago early on the twenty-ninth and "passed an anxious morning and afternoon meeting inward-bound trains. . . ." The second page of the *Chicago Daily News'* evening edition reported: "Bahaist Chief Missing: Abdul Baha, Head of Cult, Disappears on His Way to Convention in Chicago: Puzzles His Followers." The train reached Chicago that night. "The moment the friends saw the Beloved," Mírzá Maḥmúd-i-Zarqání recorded, "they cried out 'Allah-O-Abha' and 'Ya Abdul Baha', and the whole station resounded with their voices."[15]

On the following morning, 30 April, the delegates learned that the Executive Board had purchased 292 feet of lake frontage on the east side of Sheridan Road, which thereby allowed for an unobstructed view of the lake.[16] Corinne True reported that contributions had been received during the past year from Bahá'ís in eighty-eight cities located in twenty-seven states, and from Bahá'ís in Canada, England, Egypt, France, Germany, Hawaii, Italy, Persia, and South Africa.

That same day several Chicago Bahá'ís and newspaper reporters crowded into 'Abdu'l-Bahá's suite at the Plaza Hotel. After an interview 'Abdu'l-Bahá, accompanied by Dr. Zia Bagdadi, traveled north to Corinne True's Kenmore

The Ceremony

Avenue home to visit Davis, her critically ill son.[17] The young man, a star athlete at the University of Michigan, had injured his knee during a pole vaulting competition shortly after his father, Moses True, had died of a heart attack in December 1909. For several months the knee bothered Davis, and, at the invitation of one of his classmates, he decided to spend the summer at a lumber camp in Oregon, where he hoped his knee would have a chance to heal. Rather than live at the camp's main house with the rest of his friend's family, the two boys decided to stay in one of the worker's cabins. Several weeks later they learned that one of the former occupants of the cabin had since contracted tuberculosis and died. By the time Davis returned to school he was not feeling well, and in November his doctor determined that he, too, had the disease. The doctors felt that the attack was mild and sent him east to a sanatorium. Nevertheless, his condition deteriorated. In April 1911 Corinne True took him to a sanatorium in Denver, Colorado, where the doctors hoped that he would benefit from the climate. As the summer months passed, Davis seemed to improve, but by the end of the year his condition again worsened. In March 1912 the doctors determined that he had only a few weeks to live. He returned home from the sanatorium shortly before 'Abdu'l-Bahá arrived in Chicago.

After visiting Davis, 'Abdu'l-Bahá came downstairs and told Corinne True that her son was a wonderful young man and that He found him much better than expected. She was overjoyed and confident that 'Abdu'l-Bahá's presence would cause Davis to recover. Hence she joyously accepted 'Abdu'l-Bahá's invitation to accompany Him to the lectures He was scheduled to give that afternoon. Shortly after they left, Davis died. His final words were that he was happy 'Abdu'l-Bahá was present to comfort his mother. Only later did Mrs. True realize that 'Abdu'l-Bahá had been referring to Davis' spiritual rather than physical condition.

'Abdu'l-Bahá and Corinne True had driven to Hull House, the civic center founded by scholar and philanthropist Jane Addams in 1889 to provide "the ignorant, inarticulate immigrant tenement-dwellers of Chicago's congested slum areas" with "a center for a higher civic and social life."[18] After 'Abdu'l-Bahá was introduced, He urged the several hundred people there to promote unity among the races:

> In the human kingdom itself there are points of contact, properties common to all mankind; likewise, there are points of distinction which separate race from race, individual from individual. If the points of contact, which are the common properties of humanity, overcome the peculiar points of distinction, unity is

assured. On the other hand, if the points of differentiation overcome the points of agreement, disunion and weakness result. One of the important questions which affect the unity and the solidarity of mankind is the fellowship and equality of the white and colored races. Between these two races certain points of agreement and points of distinction exist which warrant just and mutual consideration. . . . In fact numerous points of partnership and agreement exist between the two races; whereas the one point of distinction is that of color. Shall this, the least of all distinctions, be allowed to separate you as races and individuals? In physical bodies, in the law of growth, in sense endowment, intelligence, patriotism, language, citizenship, civilization and religion you are one and the same. A single point of distinction exists—that of racial color. God is not pleased with—neither should any reasonable or intelligent man be willing to recognize—inequality in the races because of this distinction.[19]

Following the talk He spoke on the same subject to the Fourth Annual Convention of the National Association for the Advancement of Colored People at Handel Hall in downtown Chicago.

More than one thousand persons gathered that night to hear 'Abdu'l-Bahá speak at the closing public session of the Bahai Temple Unity convention in the Masonic Temple's Drill Hall. After a choir had sung several selections, and Albert Hall, Mountfort Mills, and Lua Getsinger had given talks, 'Abdu'l-Bahá was introduced. "At once, the vast concourse, as one person, arose," Joseph Hannen recalled, "and in a breathless silence the one awaited by many there for years, entered and proceeded to the platform."[20] The theme of 'Abdu'l-Bahá's talk was the building of America's Temple:

> Among the institutes of the Holy Books is that of the foundation of places of worship. That is to say, an edifice or temple is to be built in order that humanity might find a place of meeting, and this is to be conducive to unity and fellowship among them. The real temple is the very Word of God; for to it all humanity must turn, and it is the center of unity for all mankind. It is the collective center, the cause of accord and communion of hearts, the sign of the solidarity of the human race, the source of eternal life. Temples are the symbols of the divine uniting force so that when the people gather there in the House of God they may recall the fact that the law has been revealed for them and that the law is to unite them. They will realize that just as this temple was founded for the unification of mankind, the law preceding and creating it came forth in the manifest Word. Jesus Christ, addressing Peter, said, "Thou art Peter, and upon this rock I will build my

The Ceremony

church." This utterance was indicative of the faith of Peter, signifying: This faith of thine, O Peter, is the very cause and message of unity to the nations; it shall be the bond of union between the hearts of men and the foundation of the oneness of the world of humanity. In brief, the original purpose of temples and houses of worship is simply that of unity—places of meeting where various peoples, different races and souls of every capacity may come together in order that love and agreement should be manifest between them. That is why Bahá'u'lláh has commanded that a place of worship be built for all the religionists of the world; that all religions, races and sects may come together within its universal shelter; that the proclamation of the oneness of mankind shall go forth from its open courts of holiness—the announcement that humanity is the servant of God and that all are submerged in the ocean of His mercy. . . .[21]

At the conclusion of the talk the audience sang Louise Waite's "Temple Song." Before returning to the Plaza Hotel, 'Abdu'l-Bahá presented two thousand francs as a personal gift to the Temple Fund.[22]

The following day, 1 May, dawned chilly and overcast. Amid the trees at Grosse Pointe stood a large tent, erected for the dedication by 'Abdu'l-Bahá of the Temple site. The day was coincidentally the nineteenth anniversary of the dedication ceremony for the World's Columbian Exposition. Nearly four hundred Bahá'ís traveled to Wilmette via automobile or the Northwestern Elevated Railroad and gathered at the corner of Linden Avenue and Sheridan Road. Standing along a wide pathway leading toward the tent, they patiently awaited 'Abdu'l-Bahá's arrival at 11:00 A.M.[23]

One of those unable to be present was Thornton Chase. Two and one-half years earlier his company had transferred him to Los Angeles in an attempt to redirect his ever-expanding concentration upon the affairs of the Faith and his concurrent decrease of attention to company duties. Yet the company failed to alter his allegiance. His duties as a supervisor required that he make frequent business trips, usually to western coastal cities and sometimes as far north as Canada. At every stop he spoke about Bahá'u'lláh; during one trip he conducted thirteen public meetings in fourteen evenings. When in Los Angeles he held meetings each Sunday afternoon in a hall he rented for four dollars. Although he no longer lived in Chicago, he never ceased to consider himself a member of the Chicago House of Spirituality, and he continued to correspond frequently with members of that institution. It is ironic that Thornton Chase, the first American Bahá'í and a devoted teacher and leader of the nascent American Bahá'í community, never lived to see 'Abdu'l-Bahá during His trip through

The Ceremony

America; for Mr. Chase died on 30 September 1912, less than twenty-four hours before 'Abdu'l-Bahá's train would cross into California several months after the dedication in Wilmette. When visiting his gravesite a few weeks after his death, 'Abdu'l-Bahá said, as reported by Mírzá Aḥmad Sohráb:

> "Mr. Chase was of the blessed souls. The best time of his life was spent in the path of God. He had no other aim except the good pleasure of the Lord and no other desire except the attainment to the Kingdom of God. . . . He summoned the people to the religion of God; he suffered them to enter into the Kingdom of God; he wrote books and epistles. . . . In reality he has left behind him certain signs which will never be forgotten throughout ages and cycles. . . . The traces of this personage will ever shine. This is a personage who will not be forgotten. For the present his worth is not known but in the future it will be inestimably dear. . . .[24]

With the dedication of the Temple site imminent, Thornton Chase's nine-year-long effort was beginning to bear its hard-won fruit. But the Bahá'ís began to wonder if the dedication was going to take place at all when 'Abdu'l-Bahá did not arrive at the appointed time. He did not come down from His room at the Plaza Hotel until 10:30 A.M., the time already uncomfortably close to the scheduled beginning of the ceremony at 11:00. Because several Bahá'ís and other people were waiting to see Him in the lobby, He spoke at length before departing. "Mounted in a modern taxicab," He arrived at the dedication site a few minutes before 1:00 P.M. "after mystifying his followers by unexpected delay," reported the *Chicago Daily News*. "He had been counted on to arrive two hours before and was 'lost' between the Plaza hotel and this village."[25]

The Bahá'ís were even more mystified when the taxicab stopped in the center of the road, where one of the Persians accompanying 'Abdu'l-Bahá called for Corinne True. Despite her grief over Davis' death, she had felt duty-bound to be present at the dedication. She stepped forward and was directed to enter the car. The driver then continued north on Sheridan Road and stopped at the bridge over the canal. One account of this event stated that 'Abdu'l-Bahá wanted to see the new bridge and canal locks at the end of Wilmette Harbor. Another indicated He wanted to inspect the boundaries of the property. It is more likely that the loving and compassionate 'Abdu'l-Bahá wanted a few minutes to comfort His bereaved daughter.

The trees made it difficult to see where the taxicab had gone. Nevertheless, some of the children spotted 'Abdu'l-Bahá and Corinne True on the other side of the property and went running toward them. Surrounded by this happy

The Ceremony

group of youngsters, all of whom He lovingly patted, 'Abdu'l-Bahá walked toward the northern side of the tent.

Nearly three hundred people took seats inside "in three concentric circles, with a broad open space in the center across which the friends could read the love in each other's eyes. . . ." Around the outside of the seating area stood many more people who could not be accommodated. A committee had been formed to plan a program for the dedication, but it soon realized that 'Abdu'l-Bahá "needed no guidance other than that of the Holy Spirit."[26] After walking down one of the nine aisles, 'Abdu'l-Bahá stood in the center of the tent and began His address:

> The power which has gathered you here today notwithstanding the cold and windy weather is, indeed, mighty and wonderful. It is the power of God, the divine favor of Bahá'u'lláh which has drawn you together. We praise God that through His constraining love human souls are assembled and associated in this way.
>
> Thousands of Mashriqu'l-Adhkárs, dawning points of praise and mention of God for all religionists will be built in the East and in the West, but this, being the first one erected in the Occident, has great importance. In the future there will be many here and elsewhere—in Asia, Europe, even in Africa, New Zealand and Australia—but this edifice in Chicago is of especial significance. It has the same importance as the Mashriqu'l-Adhkár in 'Ishqábád [Ashkhabad], Caucasus, Russia, the first one built there. In Persia there are many; some are houses which have been utilized for the purpose, others are homes entirely devoted to the divine Cause, and in some places temporary structures have been erected. In all the cities of Persia there are Mashriqu'l-Adhkárs, but the great dawning point was founded in 'Ishqábád. It possesses superlative importance because it was the first Mashriqu'l-Adhkár built. All the Bahá'í friends agreed and contributed their utmost assistance and effort. . . . From such a mighty and combined effort a beautiful edifice arose. Notwithstanding their contributions to that building, they have assisted the fund here in Chicago as well. The Mashriqu'l-Adhkár in 'Ishqábád is almost completed. It is centrally located, nine avenues leading into it, nine gardens, nine fountains; all the arrangement and construction is according to the principle and proportion of the number nine. It is like a beautiful bouquet. Imagine a very lofty, imposing edifice surrounded completely by gardens of variegated flowers, with nine avenues leading through them, nine fountains and pools of water. Such is its matchless, beautiful design. Now they are building a

Above: 'ABDU'L-BAHÁ (standing, center) in the tent set up for the ground-breaking ceremony for the Temple, 1 May 1912. Below: 'ABDU'L-BAHÁ (seated, second from right) and people of many races and nationalities participating in the ground breaking

> hospital, a school for orphans, a home for cripples, a hospice and a large dispensary. God willing, when it is fully completed, it will be a paradise.
>
> I hope the Mashriqu'l-Adhkár in Chicago will be like this. Endeavor to have the grounds circular in shape. If possible, adjust and exchange the plots in order to make the dimensions and boundaries circular. The Mashriqu'l-Adhkár cannot be triangular in shape. It must be in the form of a circle.[27]

After the talk 'Abdu'l-Bahá, followed by His audience, left the tent and requested that Nettie Tobin's stone be brought to Him. The stone had been lying several feet northwest of the tent and had probably been pointed out to Him by Corinne True earlier. He walked back and forth on the property and, after asking where the center of the land would be, turned to someone who showed Him the approximate point.

As the stone was being carried to where 'Abdu'l-Bahá stood, Irene Holmes of New York stepped forward and handed Him a leather case. Inside was a golden trowel she had hoped would be used for laying a cornerstone within the foundation of the building. 'Abdu'l-Bahá tried to use the trowel to dig a resting place for the dedication stone, but it was too dull to cut through the spring grass. He placed the trowel in its case and asked for more practical tools. When it was discovered that plans had not been made to have such tools available, one of the young men ran to a nearby house to borrow an ax. "Like an athlete" 'Abdu'l-Bahá took it and "swung it high in the air." "After several blows," wrote Louise Waite, He "cut through the resisting turf and reached the earth below."[28] The scene inspired the Bahá'ís to sing—first the "Benediction" and then "Tell the Wondrous Story," both written by Mrs. Waite.

In the meantime another young man, Herbert Anderson of Chicago, had run west on Linden Avenue in search of a shovel. He found a work crew on the Northwestern Elevated tracks about four blocks south of Linden Avenue, near Isabella Street, and convinced them to loan him one of their shovels, which he whisked back to the ceremony. As the shovel was handed to 'Abdu'l-Bahá, Corinne True reportedly stepped forward and encouraged Him to let a woman participate in the ceremony.[29] Turning to Lua Getsinger, He bade her to come forward despite her resistance. It was not until He called her a second time that she responded, grasped the shovel, and turned the first earth. Following her was Corinne True, after which, one by one, individuals of many races and nationalities—Persian, Syrian, Egyptian, Indian, North American Indian, Japanese, South African, English, French, German, Dutch, Norwegian, Swedish, Danish, Jewish—were called forward to participate in the digging.

The Ceremony

Now that a rather large hole had been dug, 'Abdu'l-Bahá reached down and scooped up handfuls of dirt, which He shared with several individuals. Then He "consigned the stone to its excavation, on behalf of *all* the people of the world." After retrieving the golden trowel, He pushed the earth back around the stone and declared: "The Temple is already built."[30]

Chapter Nine

THE FIRST LONG WAIT

'ABDU'L-BAHÁ left Chicago on 5 May 1912 and returned to New York via Cleveland and Pittsburgh. In New York He spoke in many churches and homes and occasionally took short trips to Boston and Philadelphia. On 23 July He left New York for a short stay in New England and Canada and then crossed the continent to San Francisco. During His eight-month stay in North America He gave scores of talks and attracted untold numbers of people to His Father's revelation.

Before returning to Palestine on 5 December, 'Abdu'l-Bahá had the opportunity to visit Chicago on two other occasions. During one meeting in Chicago He greeted a cleaning woman who had desired very much to meet Him but had been too embarrassed by her rough hands to enter the reception line. Upon Corinne True's urging she decided to go before Him with the intention of touching quickly the hem of His robe, after which she would move away so that He could not see her hands. Yet as she bent over, He reached out, took one of her hands, and gently pulled her back up. Intently studying her hand, He turned it from one side to the other and with deep love and understanding gazed into her eyes. " 'Sacrifice!' " He uttered simply.[1]

'Abdu'l-Bahá was twice a guest in Corinne True's home, where He attracted large crowds at her meetings. At one lecture the people filled three rooms and crowded the staircase. Mrs. True wrote to Helen Goodall:

> He told us this, "It is stated in certain Prophecies in the East, that when the Standard of God appears in the East, its Tokens will become evident in the West. This is truly good news—this is great glad-tidings for you. I hope that you may be able to fulfill this Prophecy. Thus may all testify to the veracity of this Prophecy, saying, 'Verily, the . . . [Standard] of God did appear in the East, but its Tokens became resplendent in the West.[']"——Could there be a more resplendent Token in the West than the Mashrakel Azkar? He . . . [says] "Its building is the

Most Important of all things. This is the *Spiritual Foundation*. For that reason it is the most important of all foundations. From that spiritual foundation will come forth all manner of advancement and progress in the world of humanity. Therefore, how great is its importance."[2]

In the next eight years, 1912 through 1920, the Bahá'ís were preoccupied with raising money, first to complete payments on the property, then to acquire a fund adequate to begin construction. The Executive Board had hoped to complete payment of the main tract of land before 'Abdu'l-Bahá's arrival in the United States. But the purchase of the lakeshore property had made this impractical hope even more remote. The delegates at the 1912 convention, responding to 'Abdu'l-Bahá's instructions to pay the remaining debt on the main tract as quickly as possible, and wanting this goal to be achieved before He left the United States, had instructed the Executive Board not to proceed with its plan of extending the mortgage for the remaining $10,000. This meant it must be paid with interest by 24 June 1912. The Executive Board also had a $3,000 payment on the lakeshore property due on 1 September. Every Bahá'í community promised to support the effort to achieve this monumental goal. As 24 June neared, however, it became obvious the goal would not be met. The Executive Board considered two options: borrowing the necessary funds from Chicago financial institutions, or selling the lakeshore property. Both were rejected. Negotiations with the mortgage-holder resulted in half the payment's being made as scheduled and a short extention's being granted for the remaining half. In addition, a six-month extension was granted on the payment for the lakeshore property. On 1 October the Executive Board was able to make the final payment on the main tract.

There were many other financial crises during this period. When one of the mortgage payments came due and the funds were found to be inadequate, Corinne True recalled that "We were beside ourselves. We opened our purses and counted up our net capital, trying to find a way to somehow meet the emergency. All seemed lost...." At that time contributions from Bahá'ís in Persia were sent first to 'Abdu'l-Bahá. After a sizable amount had been received, He would forward the money to the United States. The arrival at the last moment of one of these collective gifts permitted the Executive Board to make the payment. "At every turn in the road," continued Mrs. True, "we were protected in this way and the Temple is another of the miracles that prove the power in the Cause."[3]

Most of the contributions from the Eastern Hemisphere were very small.

The First Long Wait

Often a Persian Bahá'í would sell a handkerchief or some other personal item in order to earn a few pennies to send. One Persian Bahá'í, "a poor widow . . . who [earned] a few pennies a day by baking and selling coarse bread," sold one of her earrings and contributed the proceeds. " 'See!' " she said, " 'The good God in His bounty gives us all something we can spare.' " 'Abdu'l-Bahá told one American Bahá'í that another widow, who supported her two children by knitting socks, sent the profit from one sock of each pair to the Temple Fund. The Bahá'í quoted 'Abdu'l-Bahá as saying, " 'These are the things that will build the Mashrak-el-Azkar in America.' "[4]

Numerous contributions also came from India. 'Abdu'l-Bahá was a partner in one of several successful restaurants operated by a group of Bahá'ís in Bombay, and "they have supplicated to him," Bernard Jacobsen reported, "to apply the profits of that store to the purposes of the Revelation. . . . [A] considerable sum has come from this store and from other stores in Bombay for the payment of the land. . . ."[5]

The 1913 Bahai Temple Unity convention, held in New York, dealt almost exclusively with the problem of raising money. Roy Wilhelm, a New York coffee importer and a member of the Executive Board since 1910, noted that, even though " 'what we have accomplished is not bad under the circumstances,' " he " 'could see a trace of disappointment on . . . ['Abdu'l-Bahá's] face on more than one occasion, that we had not done a great deal more.' " The convention decided to implement a contribution system that would be uniform for every Bahá'í community in the United States, and that would use "numbered triplicate receipts for all offerings made to the Mashrak-el-Azkar." The delegates hoped that the new system would encourage "systematic and regular giving" and that "Through this method, collective and unified effort will be assured: the countless rills of pure offerings will become the great river of accomplishment, and the Divine Edifice will be speedily begun and completed."[6]

Each local community was also encouraged to hold monthly meetings to draw attention to the project. 'Abdu'l-Bahá was requested to choose a day for these meetings, which, He directed, should be held on the ninth day of each month. The idea of the Temple meetings soon spread to other countries. In England, Daniel Jenkyn of St. Ives, Cornwall, was "one of the pioneers in England of the Mashrek El Azkar meetings which he always held on the ninth of each month, at this little fishing settlement on the West coast of England. These meetings were inaugurated and kept up through the efforts of Daniel Jenkyn no matter how small the attendance, which sometimes consisted only of himself and a lone fisherman of St. Ives."⁷ The meetings inspired other collective efforts, such as the formation of the Temple Builder's Fellowship, established to raise money and also help individuals internalize spiritual principles through social interaction.

The uniform system for encouraging and acknowledging contributions, supported by the monthly meetings, increased contributions significantly. Corinne True continued to maintain her energetic fund-raising activities, in part because she and many other Bahá'ís believed that 'Abdu'l-Bahá would travel again to America to lay an actual cornerstone once construction was begun. In responding to the many appeals to return to the United States, 'Abdu'l-Bahá wrote, " 'If the believers of God be enkindled and attracted to a superlative degree, perchance this object will again be obtained.' " " 'It is in God's hands. Pray for me to return. . . .' "⁸

Corinne True was so determined to push forward with the project despite all obstacles that she entreated 'Abdu'l-Bahá to send her some specifications for the dome. She felt that with His specifications in hand they could begin constructing the foundation, even though a design had not been selected. She urged every believer with whom she corresponded "not to let the year 1913 close upon us without having wiped out that sum [a debt of $6,000 still remained] so that 1914 rises radiantly as the year for actual activities."⁹

The final payment on the lakeshore property was due 1 September 1915. On 24 December 1913, twenty months before the due date, contributions adequate to make the final payment had been received. 'Abdu'l-Bahá cabled that this accomplishment "caused joy and happiness." Addressing the delegates at the 1914 convention, Corinne True remarked, "This is the 50th year since Baha'o'llah made His declaration of His Manifestation . . . and it certainly looks as though there was some connection between this wonderful fifty year period and the fact that our land was all paid for in America. . . ." In a statement drafted for *Star of the West* shortly after the convention Mrs. True asked the Bahá'ís across the country, "Where can you show a tract of land bought by voluntary contributions sent in from nearly every country of the globe—from the former adherents of all the seven great religions? Literally 'from Greenland's icy mountains to India's coral strand' have the contributions been sent."¹⁰

It had taken nearly six years and $63,716.13 to purchase the land. The task of acquiring funds for the actual construction would be far more difficult: 'Abdu'l-Bahá had requested that they not contract any further debt, and He said that they would need "at least two or three hundred thousand dollars" just to

The First Long Wait

begin building. "And, most assuredly," He added, "if it be built in the days of the Covenant,* it will be more joyful and more heart-rejoicing; but this is difficult."[11]

One of the most trying periods experienced by the Bahá'ís came after the outbreak of the First World War, when communication with 'Abdu'l-Bahá virtually ceased. On the day that Germany declared war on France, 'Abdu'l-Bahá, according to a Bahá'í present, spoke to a large group of Bahá'ís in the Holy Land and recalled His talks in the United States two years earlier:

"While in America, I spoke before many Peace Societies, Churches and Conventions, and foretold the fearful consequences of armed peace in Europe. I said Europe is like unto an arsenal and one tiny spark will cause a universal combustion. *'O men! Come ye together and as far as possible try to extinguish this world-raging fire; do your utmost to prevent the occurrence of this general conflict; make ye an effort so that this flood-gate of human butchery may not be set loose!'* I found no one to listen to my advice. I searched, but there were no hearing ears. I cried out at the top of my voice, I pleaded, I enunciated the evils of war, but people were self-occupied, self-centered. And now *this* is the *result*. They have witnessed . . . that war is conducive to the destruction of the foundation of the edifice of humanity, the cause of devastation of the world of commerce, industry, arts and trade. The combatants—the conqueror and the conquered—are both *losers*. . . .

"So many wars have taken place! So many countries are devastated, so many cities ruined; and yet people are not satisfied with human butchery, are not satisfied with carnage and bloodshed. Still the hearts are stiff and unfeeling! Still the souls are callous and cold, still the minds are dark and frigid, still the people are unsusceptible and unyielding, still they are in deep sleep! Oh! When will they be awakened? When will they become merciful? When will they practice the Golden Rule? This hatred and animosity destroys the basis of the structure of humanity, while love and amity are conducive to the well-being and prosperity of mankind.

". . . Extraordinary exertion must be put forward by the civilized govern-

---

*Bahá'u'lláh stipulated that, following His death, 'Abdu'l-Bahá was to be the authorized interpreter of His teachings and the leader of the Bahá'í Faith. Bahá'u'lláh bestowed several titles upon 'Abdu'l-Bahá that denoted this unique and unparalleled station in religious history. One of these titles was "the Center of My Covenant." Building the Temple "in the days of the Covenant," therefore, meant building it during 'Abdu'l-Bahá's lifetime.

ments to organize . . . an influential, international organization, before which all their quarrels may be arbitrated. What better plan can be conceived by man? What harm is there in this?"[12]

During His trip to America, 'Abdu'l-Bahá had also forecast a dramatic drop in the rate of contributions for the Temple project; but the drop, He said, would be followed by a " 'sudden' " increase. " 'This is necessary, this is wisdom, this is ordained.' "[13] Contributions in 1914 were only half the previous year's level. In 1915 the amount of received funds dropped further. In January 1916 the Executive Board made an appeal through *Star of the West* to all American Bahá'ís for help:

> The world is sick. The European tragedy grows in horror. In America we hear rumors of war. To the Bahais of the world has been given the remedy for the world's ills.
> Do we in America believe it with a realization so deep and powerful that, before another year has passed away, all obstacles shall be overcome and the walls of the first Mashrak-el-Azkar in America, the Mother Institution, shall rise triumphantly, in proclamation to all humanity that the "Most Great Peace" has come?
> Unresting, let us strive for this prodigious achievement. . . .[14]

Shortly after the magazine was issued, the Executive Board sent a letter to every American Bahá'í setting forth a plan to raise $200,000 in two years. As 'Abdu'l-Bahá had predicted, contributions increased dramatically. By the time the 1916 convention was convened, the Bahá'ís had pledged $54,000, although a large portion of that amount would be paid over the two-year period. The delegates, obviously inspired by this turn of events, resolved to accelerate the program of the Executive Board and "raise by a great universal pledge the required $200,000 so that it may be ready for use by November 12, 1917," the one hundredth anniversary of the birth of Bahá'u'lláh. When 'Abdu'l-Bahá learned of the plan, He wrote to Roy Wilhelm:

> You have given the glad news that the foundation of the Mashrak-el-Azkar will be laid next year. This is also my hope that this Temple may become fully constructed and the holy verse of the Koran: "We have given thee a great victory," become realized. For the building of this Temple is a most great triumph.[15]

The First Long Wait

With the United States' entry into the war on 6 April 1917, many Bahá'ís were beset with economic hardship. Fifteen months later, when only $90,000 had been received, the Executive Board, in session at Green Acre, Eliot, Maine, decided to inspire the community by its own example:

> With unchanging faith in the divine resolve of the American friends to make good their compact the members of the Executive Board here assembled ... pledge one-ninth of all their possessions as of this date to the redemption of a portion of the balance yet remaining due.[16]

Many Bahá'ís continued to make notable sacrifices. Contributions included stocks, liberty bonds, jewelry, and one Bahá'í's inheritance of $14,000. Among the other contributors was a woman living in rural Ohio who sent a twenty-five-cent piece on behalf of her dead mother. The mother had "constantly begged her husband to contribute to the Mashrek El Azkar. He refused. After the wife and mother died, the daughter found this quarter in her mother's purse...." Another contributor, a noted musician, arranged testimonial concerts for the fund and sent $1,000 as a "war offering toward our Bahai Temple of Peace."[17]

Roy Williams, a dedicated black Bahá'í, spent several months proclaiming Bahá'u'lláh's message to blacks throughout the southern United States. To each audience he always spoke of the Temple and how it would be open to all peoples. This made his audiences very happy, and even though they were not Bahá'ís and were "very poor and sometimes very old," they would "slip some small offering of their sincerity into the hand of this servant ... dimes or nickels or sometimes quarters ... purely an expression of their hearts...." He accumulated the gifts and sent them to the Temple Fund in their name in order that "the blessing of helping to build the temple might fall upon them...."[18]

The difficulties of fund-raising experienced by the Executive Board were augmented by additional difficulties in caring for the Temple site. A prime motivation for purchasing the lakeshore property had been to prevent the view of the lake from being marred by the construction of a restaurant and gas station. Several "obnoxious huts" were already situated along the beach and were inhabited by vagabonds. One hut was occupied by a fisherman not anxious to leave. The Board charged him rent of one dollar per month, "to prevent his laying claim to any ownership of grounds," but later had to evict him.[19] Over the next six years the Board dealt periodically with individuals attempting to take up residency on the land. Another problem emerged when it was discovered from a survey that four neighbors were encroaching upon the land. One neighbor to the south had erected a fence long before the land was purchased by the Bahá'ís. The Executive Board negotiated for several years in and out of court in order to reclaim the property.

Although Bahá'ís visited the site constantly, often taking acquaintances with them, it was not long before the Executive Board became concerned with the "growing numbers of people visiting the grounds, especially during hot summers . . . when thousands of people come there to find breathing space." On weekends the site attracted countless picnics, ball games, and bathers. Many Wilmette residents began complaining about the situation. Two fishermen were hired as custodians, but they devoted more time to selling trinkets and the fish they caught than to protecting the grounds. The Executive Board dismissed them and hired another custodian, Chris Wagner. When Mr. Wagner found it difficult to make a living, he petitioned the Executive Board for permission to install "temporary equipment" at the site "for the sale of gasoline to automobiles passing said location."[20] The Executive Board approved.

In mid-1916, after a particularly exasperating Sunday afternoon when "two rival sectarian preachers held forth against each other, each group within hearing of each other," the Executive Board decided to recruit a volunteer corps of Bahá'ís who could assist in handling problems and "extend a real Bahai welcome to any inquirers."[21] Yet these forerunners of today's volunteer Temple guides did not fully solve the problem. In August 1917 the Executive Board, faced with the continuing crowd-control problems and feeling that the dispensing of gasoline at the site was inappropriate, decided to terminate its agreement with Mr. Wagner and prohibit any future commercial enterprises on the land. It also ordered the destruction of all remaining huts and other structures and erected a wire fence around the property. Serenity once again settled over Grosse Pointe.

Various governmental agencies made several improvements around the land during the 1910s. A sidewalk was constructed around the property, a beautiful bridge was erected across the canal at Sheridan Road, and trees and shrubs were planted along the banks of the canal. Northeast of the Temple site, a recreational area called Ouilmette Park (now Gillson Park) was created, greatly increasing the area around the site that was protected from other building projects.[22]

In addition to its work on behalf of the Temple project, the Executive Board became more active after 1912 in organizing efforts to spread the Faith's teachings throughout America. One significant event planned by the Executive

Board was an International Bahai Congress at the Panama-Pacific International Exposition in San Francisco. The congress was held in conjunction with the April 1915 Bahai Temple Unity convention. Bahá'í participation in the exposition had been encouraged by 'Abdu'l-Bahá in 1914: "Everyone goes to the Exposition either for amusement or recreation, or in hope of obtaining commercial benefits. But you, who are the believers of God, enter the Exposition with the desire to summon the people to the divine Kingdom...."[23]

The Bahá'ís held a large reception on 24 April at the exposition's Festival Hall. Among the guests was the director of the exposition, John A. Britton, who presented the Bahá'ís with a large bronze medallion in " 'recognition of true worth' " for the " 'gathering together of people such as you, whose sole purpose ... is the unification and solidarity of the people of the world....' " Mr. Britton also told the Bahá'ís, " 'Let me say to you, in all honesty and candor of mind, that in the many times I have, in my official capacity, given, to those who have come here, recognition of our appreciation of their participation in our affairs, none has afforded me the extreme pleasure I am afforded today by the privilege of giving this to you, who represent so much to humanity.' "[24]

The medallion was accepted by Dr. Frederick W. D'Evelyn, president of the congress and a frequent delegate to the Bahai Temple Unity conventions. In appreciation for the medallion, Dr. D'Evelyn replied:

> "This humble bronze is symbolic of a broader measure, the token of that birthmark which divinity has predestined to herald ... that universal manhood which a unified humanity alone can consummate. Thus dedicated, this token shall start upon its mission. It will travel to the land of the cradle song, where shepherds watched their flocks by night.... It will voyage to India.... To China, to Japan, to Africa, to the Isles of the Sea ... and to the broken brotherhood of Europe ... it will tell of a better and a brighter day, of a kindlier and a nobler kinship. And, sir, when at last its mission is complete, it will come back to rest beneath that dome where a unified humanity shall make mention of God; the Mashrak-el-Azkar.
>
> "The bell [Liberty Bell], in its mission, sounded the liberty of the nation. This, in its fulness, tells of the freedom of the world. This may seem a measure too broad, an estimate too great, but it could not be otherwise, for it bears the Bahai message of unity...."[25]

In an effort to step up Bahá'í teaching activity, the delegates at the concurrent 1915 Bahai Temple Unity convention authorized the Executive Board to "select teachers, and under the wisest programme that it can arrange, circulate this [Bahá'u'lláh's] Message throughout the world. . . ." The delegates also directed the Executive Board to establish a special fund "for the necessary expenses" of increased teaching work. Although the results were far less than anticipated, the program significantly stimulated teaching activities. One Bahá'í who became active as a traveling teacher was Louis Gregory, an eminent black lawyer. In describing his activities to the Bahá'í community in 1917, he reported that "more than fifteen thousand [people] were reached directly" in the southern states, "most of them students, representing many sections and communities."26

The effort to spread the teachings was given additional guidance beginning in 1916 when 'Abdu'l-Bahá, despite His difficulty in communicating with Bahá'ís during the First World War, succeeded in sending the American Bahá'ís the first five of an eventual fourteen letters that outlined a systematic plan for spreading Bahá'u'lláh's teachings to the peoples of the world. Known as the Tablets of the Divine Plan, the letters delineated 120 territories and islands to which the Americans should carry the message of Bahá'u'lláh.27

One American who brought the message to royalty, statesmen, and commoners alike in country after country was the incomparable Martha Root. A former school teacher, she was a member of the *Pittsburgh Post* editorial staff and in her mid-thirties when she dined with Roy Wilhelm in Pittsburgh on 23 January 1909. Although she had met Mr. Wilhelm several months before, he explained Bahá'u'lláh's revelation more fully to her that day, and she accepted the Bahá'í Faith shortly thereafter. In response to 'Abdu'l-Bahá's summons in the Tablets of the Divine Plan, Martha Root made a commitment to travel throughout the world to proclaim the Faith. She informed 'Abdu'l-Bahá of this decision, to which He promised that her labors would witness "great results" and "extraordinary confirmations."28 As more and more Americans like Martha Root left their homeland over the next several decades, the American Bahá'í community found itself with a new responsibility, that of guiding and encouraging these scores of emigrating Americans. Never before had any Bahá'í community been asked to undertake such a monumental world mission.

When 12 November 1917 arrived, the day on which the Executive Board had hoped to have raised $200,000 for the construction of the Temple, only $133,000 had been contributed; $40,000 of that amount was still uncollected. Despite the rising enthusiasm that the Executive Board had tried to cultivate, their goal proved unrealistic. They would wait for another three years, until 1920, before the goal was finally met.

Chapter Ten

THE QUEST FOR A DESIGN

AMONG THE architects who were giving serious thought to a design for the Temple was Louis Bourgeois. A French Canadian, Mr. Bourgeois was introduced to the Bahá'í Faith in or near New York City probably as a result of the New York Bahá'ís' search for an architect to design their own Temple. For several months Mr. Bourgeois' attraction to Bahá'u'lláh's teachings was slowly nurtured by Marie Watson, Eaton Moses, Roy Wilhelm, and other Bahá'ís living in the area. During the winter of 1906–07 Mr. Bourgeois became a Bahá'í and moved to West Englewood (now Teaneck), New Jersey, to help Roy Wilhelm expand the Bahá'í community there.[1]

Louis Bourgeois was a direct descendent of the Acadians who had settled Nova Scotia, as was Antoinne Ouilmette, the early pioneer after whom the village of Wilmette is named. Mr. Bourgeois accredited his mother, Magdelaine, with nurturing his artistic creativity and boundless curiosity. She, too, had been interested in art. He once reminisced that she often walked into the woods to observe the changing seasons and to gather flowers and grasses, with which she scented and decorated their home.

One of Louis Bourgeois' earliest recollections as an artist was making a drawing of a steam locomotive near his boyhood home when he was eight years old. His eyes had widened as he gazed at "the great chariot," and he knew he would be in serious trouble, for he had disobeyed his father by stealing away from the farm to watch the new railroad being built. But this was the first locomotive he had ever seen, and the sight was worth any punishment.

It was not the enormousness of the metal monster that transfixed him, but the intricacy of its many parts. Compelled by his artistic nature, he attempted to capture that complexity by drawing an outline of the engine on his school slate. One of the several railroad officials and local dignitaries who were discussing the inauguration ceremony scheduled for the following week noticed Louis and walked over to view his efforts. Greatly impressed by the ability of the young

The Quest for a Design

child, the man asked if he could have the picture. Louis, already worried about the punishment he was likely to receive, was frightened by the thought of the consequences if he came home without his slate. He jumped up to run away, but the official coaxed him to stay. He convinced Louis to transfer the drawing to paper and then present his work to the president of the Grand Trunk Railway Company during the inauguration ceremony.

Early the following Saturday Louis arrived at the new train station in his hometown of Saint-Célestin de Nicolet, Quebec, by running through four miles of fields to avoid the roadway and his father's carriage. François Bourgeois, needless to say, was dismayed when he arrived at the ceremony and discovered the youngest of his ten children prominently participating in the most important event to occur in the town in a long time.

Louis Bourgeois' drawing ability eventually found expression in architecture. His first job was as a clerk with a hometown company that specialized in building churches. He later left home, took up residence in the cramped attic of a store in which he worked, and began saving money for his architectural studies. His first design, the church of Saint-Wenceslas in the diocese of Nicolet, was completed when he was twenty-one.[2]

Two years later Mr. Bourgeois married, but his wife, a distinguished musician, died not long after the birth of their third child. Following her death he worked for a time in a studio with one of his cousins. With the assistance of their employer both men were able to move to Paris to continue their architectural studies at the famed École des Beaux Arts. After Mr. Bourgeois' cousin returned to Canada, Mr. Bourgeois traveled extensively throughout Italy, Greece, Egypt, Persia, Turkey, and other countries.[3] His wanderlust was motivated in part by his desire to study first hand the different architectural styles of the world. It was also for him the beginning of a long spiritual quest, for he at last had the opportunity to investigate many of the world's religions.

In 1886 Louis Bourgeois settled in Chicago. After spending the next several years in the Midwest, he moved to California in the mid-1890s. Although he planned several commercial structures there, he primarily designed private residences, one of which was a large estate in Hollywood for the famed floral artist Paul De Longpre. This structure, as well as the Gray Hotel in Los Angeles, was noted in particular "for the touches of intricate tracery and elaborate ornamentation which characterize the Bourgeois style."[4] While working on the estate, Mr. Bourgeois was attracted to De Longpre's daughter, Alice, whom he would marry fifteen years later.

A close friend of Louis Bourgeois', L. B. Pemberton, recalled a walk he

The Quest for a Design

LOUIS BOURGEOIS
the French-Canadian architect of the Temple

took with Mr. Bourgeois one spring morning in 1901 through the Mission Hills in Santa Barbara, California. "He related at some length," wrote Mr. Pemberton, "that his mission in life was to build a large temple to be dedicated to Truth, which was to be surrounded by other buildings devoted to Art and Science and the welfare of humanity. Just where these buildings would be located he was not sure, but . . . [he] hoped it might be somewhere in sunny California." Louis Bourgeois later reflected on his early inspiration:

> "I had a strong psychic feeling that the Christ spirit was astir in the world and that I should design the temple for this spirit. I had been something of an amateur astronomer and had thought with wonder of the beautiful spiral curves which the heavenly bodies trace in the sky as they circle the sun in their elliptical orbits that cut each other in different planes and that move forward as the whole solar system moves.
>
> "I was standing by the seaside, and, as an inspiration made me see how these pure mathematical lines of astronomy could be worked into designs of wonderful beauty, I traced on the sand of the seashore such figures as I have wrought into the dome of that temple. Although when I began to work no wave

The Quest for a Design

The Bourgeois-Blumenstein design for the Permanent Court of Arbitration's Peace Palace and Library at The Hague. Many features are similar to those of Bourgeois' design for the Wilmette Temple.

was in sight, all of a sudden a great wave came up and washed out my design, as if some unseen power wished to hide this yet undiscovered secret of nature. . . ."[5]

In 1901 Louis Bourgeois left California and traveled to Pittsburgh. The De Longpres were heartbroken not long afterward when they learned through Associated Press dispatches that he "had been taken to a sanitarium near Pittsburgh with pneumonia and three days later had passed on." The report, however, was premature, and before the end of 1901 Mr. Bourgeois settled in New York. There he collaborated with another architect, Paul Blumenstein, to prepare a competitive design for the Permanent Court of Arbitration's Peace Palace and Library at The Hague. The Permanent Court of Arbitration had been established in The Netherlands in 1899 for the peaceful settlement of international disputes. The Bourgeois-Blumenstein design attempted to express in architectural terms the Court's goal of peace and, as such, avoided any suggestion of castles, citadels, or other historically warlike structures. The circle was used extensively in the building and gardens to express unity and harmony; the

The Quest for a Design

eight points of the building's octagon exterior represented the eight nations that formed the tribunal.[6]

During 1904 Louis Bourgeois and Paul Blumenstein were both introduced to the Bahá'í Faith. After becoming a Bahá'í about two years later, Mr. Bourgeois decided to send his eight-sided design for the Permanent Court of Arbitration to 'Abdu'l-Bahá when Roy Wilhelm visited Him in 1907; it was one of at least two designs that were sent to 'Abdu'l-Bahá before 1909. Mr. Wilhelm recalled that 'Abdu'l-Bahá looked at the Bourgeois design "casually & passing . . . [it] back to me commented—'The Bahai Temple will have nine sides.' "[7]

The Executive Board of the Bahai Temple Unity, immediately after its April 1909 election, invited architects in the United States and Canada to submit designs for the Temple before August. Louis Bourgeois seized the opportunity, but he found the three-month time limit too short to prepare a completed design. Instead, he submitted " 'preliminary sketches,' " which, he regretted, " 'were not satisfactory to me. I could get only the general outline. The inverted circle I had chosen for the form of a nine-pointed star was my ideal in symbol as an open circle is a magnet, but the feeling of the space for windows and doors was not satisfactory.' "[8]

Although six designs had been submitted by October, Louis Bourgeois discovered that he still had time to solve the problems in his design long after the August deadline, as 'Abdu'l-Bahá had told the American Bahá'ís not to choose definite architectural plans until they had raised a sizable portion of the money for construction. Between 1909 and 1917 Mr. Bourgeois reworked the design but still could not develop an adequate architectural arrangement for the windows and doors. " 'Nothing seemed to fit in those circles,' " he said, " 'so I decided to wait for a new light.' "[9]

In 1917 Mr. Bourgeois, at Roy Wilhelm's urging, attended the Bahai Temple Unity convention in Boston, where Bourgeois' 1909 sketches were among the designs viewed by the delegates. " 'I was no more satisfied with my design of three months' work than I was when I delivered the sketches in 1909,' " he recalled, " 'but in the basic principle of the symbolization I could not find anything to alter. Only the details were not my ideal.' " Alfred Lunt, president of the Bahai Temple Unity's Executive Board, and a lawyer, approached Louis Bourgeois after the convention to ask him if he " 'could not put a more Oriental feeling' " into the design. Agreeing that he could, Mr. Bourgeois left the convention " 'with a new fire in my heart and the desire to do something worthy of the cause.' "[10]

Because the world war had decreased the demand for architects, Louis

Bourgeois could find no work that would support himself and his family and enable him to continue refining the Temple design. " 'Mrs. Bourgeois proposed to buy a small general store that was for sale near us,' " he wrote, " 'which she was willing to take care of. This was generous, but I had no money to buy the store with. After thinking it over a great deal, we decided that we would mortgage our home in order to get the money with which to buy the store.' "[11] His wife set aside her own career as an artist and devoted her energies to waiting on customers, thus providing the meager income on which they lived.

Louis Bourgeois initially anticipated that the design would require three months to complete. Instead, he struggled for more than two years, during which time he often worked for sixteen hours a day. " 'As soon as I started [the first floor],' " he said, " 'I felt a powerful influence within me, a thrilling sensation that gave me courage. Inspiration came to me without interruption how to use the wonderful space which I had tried to design for eight years without success.' "[12]

The architect felt that the form of the building could not be completely understood by presenting a " 'simple drawing.' " " 'The only way to present it,' " he decided, " 'should be as a model, but how to make a model? I had no money for a model maker and I never had made one before. I had never done carving on a jewelry scale which takes an expert.' " Mr. Bourgeois had built, however, a much simpler model twenty years before in California for one of his design assignments. " 'I remembered the spiritual dictation of twenty years ago, "Go and do it." I made up my mind that I would attempt it.' "[13]

His immediate obstacle was finding money to buy the plaster. As a source of income he turned to his flower garden. The garden had been planted in the shape of a large bell, which, he explained, " 'was the greatest musical instrument we have; it is the conveyor of sound to the greatest distance. . . . [It] conveys our sorrows and our joys. . . . and as the world was in distress I hung out this great bell.' " In the midst of the garden was a " 'small summer house covered with beautiful Perkins roses.' "[14] He cut enough roses to fill his wife's laundry basket and sold them in New York for five dollars, which was enough money to buy his first barrel of plaster.

Modeling in solid plaster was a new experience for Louis Bourgeois, and the work was complicated by the miniature detail it required. To get help he wrote to a French friend, J. A. Meliodon, who was a prominent sculptor, and asked him to come for a visit. After watching his friend work, Mr. Bourgeois began his own carving:

The Quest for a Design

"I worked at this first floor of the Temple a long time. In classic training we were taught to design first the floor plan[,] the mass for the elevation, then work up the details, but I tried this persistently without success. I got that first floor thought out and could not see anything above, so I decided that if it was the work of inspiration, I could trust that power and work according to my leading. I started to carve the first floor. It was a great deal of work but I started early in the morning and kept at it till dark till it was accomplished. I then started to draw the second floor and to my surprise it came to me at once. I tried to draw the third but could not get anything, then I proceeded to carve it [the second floor] in that unusual way and when it was finished, I got the idea for the third. I could not get the dome design until the third was carved . . . I then had all those separate pieces and was very anxious to see what the result would be when they all were put together."[15]

In another account Louis Bourgeois noted that it took him three months to find a dome that would be in satisfactory proportion to the structure below it. " 'I became impatient,' " he lamented, " 'and was almost frantic trying to complete this design. Then one morning I had about given up hope when, in a flash of light, I was awakened and saw the dome of this building. It was *on* the building. I got up and snatched a piece of wrapping paper and made a sketch of the building and the dome and then went back to bed. I arose the next morning and there I found my temple.' "[16]

Rather than carving the entire model, Mr. Bourgeois made models for various sections of the design (such as the main pylon), from which he would cast duplicate pieces to be assembled into the final model. Having no money to cast the pieces, he visited a Mr. Jacobson of Jacobson and Company, one of the largest ornamental plaster makers in America, and explained what he needed. Mr. Jacobson, an old acquaintance of Mr. Bourgeois', offered to cast the pieces free of charge. They began with the casting of the first floor, " 'twelve pieces of towers and twelve pieces for the walls.' "[17]

After three months Mr. Bourgeois brought the models for the second floor:

"Mr. Jacobson said to me: 'What is this casting for now?' I answered: 'The second floor of the Temple.' He answered me: 'I never thought that it was an enormous work like this. I thought what you brought to me three months ago was all there was to it. As this is a company I must explain where the money comes from to pay for the labor.' "

The Quest for a Design

The architect explained that he still had no money, but he promised to pay for the work as soon as he could. " 'He generously accepted . . . [my] offer,' " Mr. Bourgeois recalled, " 'and the work kept on till completion.' "[18]

One afternoon a visiting union steward noticed that a group of the newly cast pieces did not bear the required sculptor's union stamp. Refusing to listen to Mr. Jacobson's explanations, the steward ordered all work to cease. Louis Bourgeois was notified that if the model was to be cast unblemished, special permission would have to be obtained from the union's executive council.

Meeting with the council, the architect explained the purpose of the model and convinced the council to grant permission to forego the union stamp. But they were willing to overlook the stamp " 'only for the pieces that are in Jacobson's shop now.' " In reply, Mr. Bourgeois insisted that the permission was worthless to him unless he could cast all of the pieces without the stamp. " 'Then, after more argument on both sides they decided that that was all they could do at that time and they would argue later about the rest.' " " 'I do not know if they ever argued about it again,' " Mr. Bourgeois wrote, " 'all I know is that I never had any more interference and got all the casting I needed.' "[19]

Despite the settlement of the union problem, Mr. Jacobson continued to complain that he could not complete all of the work Louis Bourgeois required. After refusing a request for 513 columns, he offered to construct a mold so that Mr. Bourgeois could do the casting himself. " 'I accepted the offer,' " recounted Mr. Bourgeois, " 'but found in trying that I could cast about five columns in a day of very arduous work and with great loss of plaster, for it was so delicate that most of the columns broke while I was pulling them out of the mould.' "[20]

Undaunted, he again visited Mr. Jacobson and persuaded him to cast twenty-five columns. Much later he returned to ask for fifty more. " 'I kept at it at different intervals, passing by the back door to the foreman's headquarters, always asking for no more than seventy-five columns at a time, until I managed to get all I needed for three-fourths of the temple which is all one can see from a given point.' "[21]

The completed model was more than twelve feet in diameter, nine feet tall, and several hundred pounds in weight. It represented a structure of gigantic proportions, 360 feet high and 450 feet in diameter, measurements that were chosen as multiples of nine. In determining the Temple's size, Louis Bourgeois may have been influenced by the attitude of one of his former employers, Daniel Burnham, the chief architect of the Columbian Exposition: " 'Make no little plans . . . ,' " he once had said, " 'they have no magic to stir men's blood. . . .' "[22]

The Quest for a Design

The most dominant feature of the model is its symmetry. The use of exact proportions throughout a building was a hallmark of the École des Beaux Arts, where Louis Bourgeois had studied, and whose influence had dominated the architecture of the Columbian Exposition in Chicago. The school's interest in symmetry was inspired by the Neoclassical style that flourished in the early 1800s. Louis Bourgeois envisioned a Temple with nine equal sides crowned in the middle by an Early Renaissance dome, a type constructed in Italy during the fifteenth and sixteenth centuries. For architects of the Renaissance, symmetry was a way to express the concept of unity. Contrasting with the general Occidental configuration of the Bourgeois dome, however, is an Oriental element—a skin of arabesque tracery commonly found in Islamic architecture.

The ribs above the dome are reminiscent of the Gothic ribbing found on some Early Renaissance domes, such as that of the cathedral in Florence. However, the ribs of the Bourgeois design differ from those of Early Renaissance domes in that they continue downward to the base of the clerestory, a level commonly found directly below the dome. The presence of a clerestory is a feature of both Renaissance and Romanesque architecture; yet the most prominent feature of the Bourgeois clerestory, the scalloped arches with arabesque tracery above the windows, is similar to the interior arches of the eighth-century Moorish mosque in Cordova, Spain.

The large windows of the gallery, immediately below the clerestory, reflect an arabesque influence in their overlying tracery and interlacing arches. The small windows at the base of the gallery, however, are Romanesque because of their unornamented arches and their positioning deep in the masonry.

Arabesque tracery again predominates at the main level. Louis Bourgeois used scalloped arches over the windows, as in the clerestory, and chose the same style of arches to decorate the entrances. Nine pylons stand at the nine points of both the main level and gallery. Ornamented with the symbols of the world's great religions, the pylons evoke the minarets of the great Muslim mosques.[23]

The silhouette of the Temple model, like Mr. Bourgeois' flower garden, resembles a bell, "the conveyor of sound to the greatest distance." "This Temple," he later wrote, "coming from the realm of Baha . . . is the Great Bell, calling to America. Will they hear it?"[24]

Louis Bourgeois claimed emphatically that the design was the result of spiritual inspiration. This notion gained popularity within the Bahá'í community during the early months of 1920 when many people came to the Bourgeois home to view the model. The showing had about it an air of mystery: Everyone

The Quest for a Design

Louis Bourgeois' completed Temple model, featuring ornate light standards on top of each gallery pylon. Note the size of the people in relation to the size of the building.

would gather in a room partitioned in half by a large, dark curtain. After silent prayers were offered, the curtain would slowly part to reveal the model illuminated from within.

Mr. Bourgeois' claim, however, would be challenged during the next several years by Charles Mason Remey, who pointed out that the design was very similar to the Bourgeois-Blumenstein plan for the Peace Palace at The Hague.[25] The shape of the dome was different; there were nine sides instead of the Peace Palace's eight; the clerestory was added immediately below the dome; but there is no denying that the Temple is a modification of the Peace Palace design.

Moreover, it is clear from photographic and pictorial evidence too volumi-

The Quest for a Design

nous to be adduced here that Mr. Bourgeois, like most architects, was subject to the influence not only of his own earlier works but of the works of other architects. A lengthy study now in progress shows, for example, that Louis Bourgeois borrowed details from the noted architect Louis Sullivan. In addition, details from Bahá'í architects, such as Mason Remey, appear in Mr. Bourgeois' post-Boston design and solve problems he admitted not having been able to solve between 1909 and 1917. Mr. Bourgeois' drawings, unchanged since 1909, were on view at the 1917 convention in Boston, along with other designs submitted to the Bahai Temple Unity in 1909 and 1910. New additions at the convention were designs prepared by Mr. Remey—designs he published in a book in the summer of 1917. Among the drawings were Romanesque and Gothic designs that helped Mr. Bourgeois solve the architectural problems of the first floor, particularly problems in the window and door spaces, and a Renaissance design that influenced the development of the silhouette of the building.[26]

Mr. Bourgeois has written that when he began to work on the Temple design after he returned from the Boston convention " 'Inspiration came to me without interruption how to use the wonderful space which I had tried to design for eight years without success.' "[27] That inspiration, after one examines the dates involved and the photographic and pictorial evidence, was the inspiration of synthesizing details into a new, magnificent design that transcended his own previous work and the works of other architects who influenced him. Indeed, this unique and harmonious synthesis was further elaborated in Mr. Bourgeois' design of the ornamentation, through which he expressed symbolically the unity of religions he had sought throughout his lifetime. 'All the religious symbols of the world . . . crosses, circles, triangles, pyramids . . . the Greek and Roman cross, the swastika, the five-, six-, seven-, eight-, and . . . nine-pointed star . . . the serpent, the sun, the fire—everything which man has once used to suggest the Deity or infinity," observed Mary Hanford Ford, can be found in the ornamentation.[28] Furthermore, a series of ellipses in the dome, inspired by Mr. Bourgeois' thoughts of the planets orbiting the sun, symbolizes a unity beyond this planet—a unity that encompasses the entire universe.

Louis Bourgeois' eleven-year endeavor was over. But his was neither the only design nor the only struggle. It remained to be seen whether his creation would fulfill the requirements for the Bahá'í Temple in America, or whether the imaginative design would be rejected and remain forever only a vision, only a dream.

Chapter Eleven
DAY OF DECISION

THE EMERGENCE of the League of Nations gave new hope to a war-torn world in the early days of 1920. Yet within weeks the optimism diminished when the United States Senate rejected both the Treaty of Versailles and the League. Whether the organization could have promoted universal peace and prevented another world war, had it been supported by the United States, is difficult to tell. Nonetheless, this attempt at worldwide unity had failed.

At the same time, the Bahá'ís' seventeen-year struggle to raise their majestic symbol of unity reached a new plateau. The Executive Board, in its annual call for delegates to the 1920 Bahai Temple Unity convention, disclosed that "Abdul Baha . . . has granted permission that at this Convention the delegates should choose the building plan for the Mashrekol-Azkar. . . ."[1]

As in previous years, a Bahá'í congress was held in conjunction with the annual convention. The congress opened with a reception at the Aldine Club in New York City during the afternoon of 24 April. In his introductory remarks Mountfort Mills, who would be elected chairman of the convention, alluded to the United States' failure to support the League of Nations:

> "Just a year ago we gathered in a feast similar to this. It was then in our hearts to realize the Most Great Peace among the nations. We fear the full realization of this is still far away. But far be it from me to sound a note of sorrow or depression. It is rather to emphasize our hopes and expectations, for great is our joy that we have been shown the path that leads to the ultimate goal."[2]

Most of the lectures addressed the promotion of world unity and the role of religion in securing and safeguarding it. Among the other speakers was Corinne True, who said:

> "Jesus told of the Great Day that was to come. As a sign of the coming bounty he revealed the Lord's prayer. Now we are realizing this bounty in a new creation. . . .

Day of Decision

> The Mashrek-ol-Azkar, to be erected on Lake Michigan, is the greatest sign that the blessed hope and promise have been fulfilled."[3]

The convention itself opened on Monday, 26 April, at the Engineering Societies' Building on 39th Street. After organizing the convention and discussing procedural matters in the morning, the delegates turned their attention to the Temple.[4] To begin, Harry (William H.) Randall, treasurer of the Executive Board, was asked to read a collection of notes he had taken while in Haifa and that had been reviewed by 'Abdu'l-Bahá. The notes revealed that 'Abdu'l-Bahá refused to express a preference for any particular Temple design; to do so might have caused disunity among the Bahá'ís. 'Abdu'l-Bahá suggested that the delegates choose one design that was " 'in agreement with the sentiment or opinion of the delegates' " and send it to Him for approval and suggestions. If the delegates could not agree unanimously, He said, they must " 'accept the vote of the majority.' " When told there was only $150,000 on hand to begin building, He responded, " 'That is enough only to begin the foundation, you must get more money'."[5]

At least fifteen designs were displayed at the 1920 convention, although only three of the architects were present—Louis Bourgeois, Charles Mason Remey, and William Sutherland Maxwell, known to Bahá'ís as Sutherland. The delegates decided to allow each of the designers twenty minutes to explain his concept. Mr. Bourgeois, now sixty-four years old, told the delegates that he believed Bahá'u'lláh had alluded in His Hidden Words to the evolution of a new art form. Thus Mr. Bourgeois had attempted to avoid any specific style of the past. Since Bahá'u'lláh's teachings unified and fulfilled former religious teachings, Mr. Bourgeois added, and since religious thought had expressed itself through various forms of architecture, Mr. Bourgeois had tried to blend elements of many architectural styles into a new whole.

The delegates expressed concern about the structural stability of Louis Bourgeois' creation, to which he responded, " 'No building of that shape has ever been made but I have had the best engineer in New York visit it [the model] and he told me that this building is the strongest building that the world has ever seen; it has got to be.' " Applause greeted his statement, which prompted the chairman to urge impartiality among the delegates until they had listened to all of the presentations. Yet Mr. Bourgeois' confidence was bolstered by their expression of support. Earlier he had boldly stated, " 'I don't care if you take it or don't take it, this building will be built somewhere.' " Commenting on the reaction of a fellow architect, Mr. Bourgeois later added, " '[The architect] studied it three hours, and I don't think I will tell you what he said about it because it is too good.' "⁶

In addressing the delegates' further concern that the model represented a building too large and costly, Louis Bourgeois explained that his design could be reduced to half size without losing its architectural integrity. The smaller foundation level, he said, could be constructed for approximately $200,000. " 'You can use that for your meeting and wait until you have more money for another floor,' " he noted. " 'And keep on going, and then you will have a monument that will draw the world, otherwise you will have a chapel.' "⁷

Another of the architects, Charles Mason Remey, recounted the long years he had spent preparing nine designs, each based on a different style of architecture. Although he displayed all nine, he recommended only one for the delegates' consideration—a design in an Indian style, presented as a landscaped model—because he felt its size and cost were reasonable. Sutherland Maxwell exhibited his own plans in a series of colored drawings. The Maxwell design expressed the Bahá'í symbolism of the number *nine* by incorporating nine fountains in the gardens, each nine feet in diameter; nine steps leading to the entrances; a central auditorium eighty-one feet in diameter; meditation areas surrounded by nine columns; and a dome lighted by twenty-seven glass mosaic windows. Mr. Maxwell explained to the delegates that he had attempted to find "a point in construction where the East and West would contact."⁸

The four remaining designs were by Charles E. Brush of Chicago (then deceased), Charles L. Lincoln of New York City, Myron Potter of Cleveland, and Fred J. Woodward of Washington, D.C. Mr. Potter's design was apparently the largest, for he estimated it would cost $20,000,000 to construct. Mr. Remey's Indian model would have cost less than $600,000; Mr. Maxwell's plan, approximately $1,000,000; and Mr. Bourgeois' half-size plan, $1,500,000.

Midway through the session on the following morning, 27 April, the delegates assembled in one of two rooms used for displaying the designs on an upper floor of the Engineering Societies' Building. At the close of the previous day's session it had been decided, after considerable discussion, that an expert architect and engineer be invited to confer with the delegates before making the final selection. Waiting to speak to the delegates was H. Van Buren Magonigle, president of the Architectural League of New York City, and " 'one of the best known architects in the country.' " Mountfort Mills, the chairman of the convention, briefly explained to Mr. Magonigle that the delegates wanted to choose a design that would " 'symbolize unity between the East and the West—the idea is that it does not represent any locality, it is universal.' "⁹

Day of Decision

Charles Mason Remey's Indian-style design, displayed at the 1920 Bahai Temple Unity convention, held in New York City

With that information in mind, Mr. Magonigle addressed the convention:

"The problem before me is rather a difficult one, because I am forced to consider these various designs, not from your point of view at all, but from the point of view of an architect who knows only what he has gathered this morning . . . of your tenets, and of the scope of your particular belief, and so, as I say, I can only judge of these things from the purely technical standpoint."

He then commented on each of the exhibited designs in the first room:

"taking that structure there at the end of the room, which has a certain curious blend of the Oriental and the Western [it is unknown to which design he was referring]; it does not satisfy me in its proportions or in its outlines. . . .
"The next is rather a confused composition, which after all, has no beauty, and that is the first test that you have to apply in any work of art, I don't care what it is, a painting or a building, the test you must apply is that of beauty, and I think that test might apply to a religious structure as well. . . .

Day of Decision

William Sutherland Maxwell's Temple design, which foreshadowed many of the details in his later design for the Shrine of the Báb, Haifa, Israel

"This one (Mr. Remey's design and model) here, I am frank to say I do not care very much for. It hasn't any particular beauty of silhouette. . . .

"That one leaves me quite cold[;] if a design does not give me a thrill, it isn't any use, and that doesn't thrill me a bit."[10]

Only two designs drew favorable comments, one merely because Mr. Magonigle felt the " 'great orb resting on the top of the construction' " to be " 'extremely attractive.' " He then commented on Louis Bourgeois' large plaster model, which was displayed in an adjoining room:

"Now, the design in the other room has some tremendous possibilities. It is very very curious, it is like nothing that I have ever seen before. It has that quality of universality which Mr. Mills has talked about—it is rather something new, to which Mr. Mills has referred, and it is very difficult for me to refer it to any known period of architecture except possibly the modern note that has growth [sic] up in Chicago under Louis Sullivan. Yet, there are certain structural features about it which are more than questionable. I think the whole upper part should be revolved for a part on its axis so as to bring those buttresses down. At the present time these buttresses come down over the very openings through which you go. It does not satisfy the eye when these huge weights come down apparently to a void. Void over void, and solid over solid, is the principle of construction and is as old as the world, and however new the architecture may be, it has to keep its feet on the ground, and they must come all the way down to the ground although its head may be in the clouds. It is a tremendously imaginative work. It has elements of great beauty. There are certain things about it that are really extraordinary. This idea of a perfect dome, with a glass dome inside, and then a perforrated [sic] dome with lights between, inside of that, so that at night this thing would be lighted—the use of light, in itself, is a very wonderful and a very modern thing in architecture. From a practical point of view whether the snow and ice along Lake Michigan will reach into these crevices and ultimately tear it to pieces is a serious question; I am not at all sure that there are not certain features which in execution would have to be modified from a practical point of view, but as I said, the shape of the building is perfect, if you want a work of pure imagination—I think that of all the designs I have seen this design in the other room . . . is better than any of these other ones."[11]

Next Mountfort Mills introduced a Mr. Abbott, an engineer employed by the Fuller Construction Company, which a decade later would build the Temple superstructure. Mr. Abbott had been invited to the meeting to give information about the cost of each design. Despite his difficulty in determining costs without knowing the final dimensions of the building and the materials to be used, he was able to provide several rough estimates. With reference to Louis Bourgeois' design he agreed with the architect's suggestion to build the structure in stages. The foundation, he estimated, would cost between $100,000 and $200,000, depending on the type of ground upon which it was constructed.

During the afternoon session the delegates became enmeshed in controversy over the appropriate amount of money that should be spent. Corinne True noted that 'Abdu'l-Bahá had not provided specific guidance on this point:

"The only thing we ever had from Abdul Baha regarding costs happened one morning in New York in 1912 when Mr. Roy Wilhelm and I were talking with Abdul Baha and . . . Abdul Baha remarked at that time, 'Do you know how much this will cost—it will cost over a million dollars. . . .' "[12]

Day of Decision

Louis Bourgeois' drawing of the Bahá'í Temple, exhibited with his plaster model at the 1920 annual Bahá'í convention. Some of the details in the drawing differ from those in the model.

Day of Decision

The delegates felt an urgent need to initiate construction; for they still hoped 'Abdu'l-Bahá would return to lay a cornerstone, and they wanted to finish the building during His lifetime. Hence they did not want to wait for a significant increase in contributions before the design they selected could be started. Perhaps their sense of urgency inspired them the following morning to contribute nearly $13,000 to the Temple Fund.

Many letters from 'Abdu'l-Bahá about the Temple were reread and discussed, for the delegates wanted to be certain their decision would be in conformity with His guidance. One delegate suggested that an "informal ballot" be taken to give everyone an insight into the collective sentiments of the delegates. Roll call was taken, everyone joined in a prayer for divine guidance, and the votes were cast:

> The chairman of the ballot committee, Mr. McConaughy, reporting upon the vote, announced the result as follows: For Mr. Remey's model plan, seven votes; for Mr. Remey's No. 5 plan, the so-called Indian or Persian model, thirteen votes; Mr. Maxwell's plan, one vote; Mr. Bourgeois' plan, twenty-eight votes—making total of forty-nine votes cast [nine delegates had already departed from the convention]. The chair announced that by this informal ballot the majority of the votes had been cast for Mr. Bourgeois' plan and that the situation was now cleared for the formal action of the Convention.
>
> Upon motion, it was duly moved, seconded and voted that the Convention now proceed to a formal ballot.[13]

One of the delegates asked for recognition and suggested that " 'nothing would please Abdul Baha more, in this present deliberation, than if we could make it a unanimous vote for Mr. Bourgeois's model.' " Thunderous applause filled the room. When Mountfort Mills asked that " 'all those in favor of this motion will please rise,' " every delegate rose to their feet.[14]

The major New York newspapers immediately printed articles about the Bourgeois design. A columnist for the *New York Times* suggested that " 'Americans will have to pause and study it long enough to find that an artist has wrought into this building the conception of a religious League of Nations.' " An art critic for the *New York American* wrote, under a banner that proclaimed "Bahai Temple Strikes New Art Note":

> Many persons who have seen the model for this building . . . say that the great Temple will be the most beautiful modern structure in the world. Some go so far as to say that it will be the most beautiful structure ever erected. . . .

The Bahai Temple of Peace combines within itself all the lovely elements of all the types of architecture that man has ever devised. This may at first sound rather discouraging to students of art who know how inspirationless eclectic works usually are. If a painter tries to combine all the good points of all the schools of painting he invariably gets a picture that is tame and uninteresting. It is the individual method that counts.

But, after looking at Mr. Bourgeois' model for his beautiful Temple, listen to him explain, in a voice trembling with enthusiasm, just how he came to combine all styles of architecture in his design:

"The Bahai Movement," says Mr. Bourgeois, "is a fusing of the essential spiritual elements of all religions and all philosophies. . . . All the teachings that have held the minds of men and ennobled them are found to be very much alike in essence. The doctrines of Christ, of Buddha and of Mohammed greatly resemble each other. As with religions so it is with architecture. If you resolve the different architectural systems to their idealistic basis, laying aside all extreme forms, you will see that they harmonize so perfectly that they can be blended without one discordant note. That is what I have tried to do in the Temple of Peace—to combine all architectural modes into a symbol of the Bahai Movement."[15]

The news of the Temple design spread quickly to other cities. The *Washington Post,* under an impressive second-page banner entitled "An Architect Who Was Inspired By the Stars," printed an extensive article that began, "Half the history of the world is written in the temples that men have erected in honor of their gods." The article went on to give an historical overview of the world's religious structures. Listed were the "more notable of the American religious edifices. . . . These are constructions singular and marvelous: But now a temple more singular and more marvelous than any of them is about to arise in the city of Chicago." The closing paragraph of the article contained a puzzling and amusing statement: "It is expected, too, that the venerable prophet, Abdul Baha, will come from Syria and take up his residence in the great nine-sided temple to be built in Chicago."[16]

Photographs of the model and news releases were issued by the Underwood Press (also known as Underwood and Underwood), a news service akin to the present-day Associated Press. These releases appeared in the majority of daily and weekly newspapers throughout the country. Several magazines and special interest publications also reported on the Temple and the religion that gave it birth. The Unitarian Church's *Christian Register,* for example, said,

Day of Decision

" 'Wonderful as the architectural design of the Temple is, those most concerned in its erection see in the universal service it will render to mankind its supreme importance. The Bahai message is primarily a message of unity. It recognizes the divine elements which underlie all great world religions.' "[17]

By autumn 1920 the story of the Temple had reached the shores of Europe and Asia. One of the longest of the published statements appeared in newspapers in several distant cities, including Tokyo and Honolulu:

> A new creation of transcendent beauty has dawned upon the horizon of the architectural world. The model of the great Bahai Temple . . . is being visited by increased throngs, and it has been the object of professional, artistic and general interest. . . . Like many—indeed most—of the great art productions, this has come from one who has endured the struggle, against discouraging deprivation and deferred hopes, but the universality of the praise bestowed upon the model finally evolved must bring the fullest degree of recompense for years of battling against depressing odds. . . .
>
> It is to be a temple of peace, whose broad portals of welcome and encouragement to devotees of any and every religion shall be always open. . . .
>
> . . . [Compared with] its spiritual appeal the famed beauties of the Taj Mahal and the Alhambra grow strangely pale.[18]

The Temple design evoked countless enthusiastic reactions from individuals. The brilliant Persian Bahá'í scholar Jináb-i-Fáḍil, sent to America by 'Abdu'l-Bahá to visit every known Bahá'í community, and lecturing to thousands of people in churches, universities, and organizations, discovered that the Temple had become "one of the greatest teachers" of the Faith. As soon as every one of his lectures was concluded, "innumerable souls rushed to the platform and with joy in their faces said, Oh, yes, we have read in our papers, in our magazines, in our Literary Digest[,] in the art paper, all about this international temple and we are heart and soul with this idea and hope that it may be founded in the speediest possible manner."[19]

One woman, the president of a local chapter of the Theosophical Society, attended an introductory Bahá'í meeting at Louise Waite's home and "sat spellbound, her eyes fixed upon the picture of the Temple which hung on the wall." Although the building had not been mentioned by the speaker, she asked:

> "O, do tell me what building that is a picture of; is it not a Temple?" "Yes", was the reply. "Where? Where is it?" she eagerly asked. When told it was a picture of

the model of the Baha'i Temple, . . . she arose and went up to the picture and stood in silence with clasped hands and bowed head before it. Soon the tears ran down her cheeks; for a moment or two there was absolute silence in the room, then she turned and with a radiant smile, . . . [exclaimed]: "I never was so deeply moved in all my life. As I sat looking at the picture a great SOMETHING seemed to flow forth from it. . . . The Essence of Unity and Peace, such Peace as I have never felt before but dreamed of."[20]

Not all opinions were positive. Some felt the design was confusing, while others found it grotesque. Many religious groups seized the opportunity to attack the claims of the Faith and the principles it advocates. A writer for *Leaves of Healing,* a sectarian publication from Zion, Illinois, attempted to foresee what he thought to be the fate of the Temple:

> All the medical libraries, all the museums—everything that man has worked to collect, day and night, through all the centuries—will be burned up! Wonderful (?) man! The Masonic Temple in Chicago will have to go! The Bahai Temple being erected at Wilmette will have to go! All the great colleges and all the great libraries will be burned to ashes! The earth will be ABSOLUTELY CLEANSED, and then will come the Perfect Age, when the New Jerusalem will descend to the earth.[21]

It is ironic that the writer included the Temple in his forecast, for Bahá'ís believe the Temple heralds the establishment of the "New Jerusalem" for which the writer was waiting.

The Executive Board of the Bahai Temple Unity created an Ideas Committee in 1920 to utilize the Temple project in order to expand the public's awareness of Bahá'í principles and to increase contributions from Bahá'ís. The enthusiastic chairperson of the nine-member committee was Martha Root, who had recently returned from a three-month trip to South America, where she had made scores of friends in city after city and had secured editorials about the Bahá'í Faith in many influential newspapers. After her appointment to the committee she sent to every Bahá'í community letters that encouraged her co-workers to strive for creativity:

> Abdul Baha will give inspirations for His Temple. The treasuries of ideas and treasuries of funds to put those ideas into being are waiting to be revealed, only it requires faith and severed hearts. . . . "wrestle with God" for one idea every day for the Temple. . . . If you begin tomorrow it may be too late. This letter

for ideas is sent to you to ask you to reply . . . with the first best idea that comes to you—and then please keep right on sending them.

Soon a variety of activities was under way, and several special subcommittees were operating, including: Certain Money Plan Ideas; Advertising Committee; Children's Group Plans; Publicity Group; "Hands of Service"; Moving Picture Group; Music Committee; Stereopticon Slides; Circular Letters to Other Organizations Group; Plays Committee; Bulletin News; and a Prayer Group Committee.[22]

In March 1921 Martha Root launched a project of her own in which she addressed letters to several prominent citizens in many nations:

> My dear Brother in the Service to Humanity:—
> Acting on the principle that great humanitarians are always interested in what other successful uplift men think of Universal Movements, this letter is to ask you if you will write in a few words what effect you think the basic principles of the Bahai Cause (enclosed herewith) are having in the spiritual emancipation of humanity.

The letter then sketched briefly the life of Bahá'u'lláh, stated the principles of the Bahá'í Faith, described the Temple and its purpose, and concluded with an invitation:

> The book that I, as a world newspaper and magazine writer, and an ardent Bahai, am writing to promote this Cause, and as a pure gift to the Temple, is just the setting forth of the basic Bahai principles, a vivid history of the Bahai Movement, and letters from Kings, governors, heads of the greatest business firms, architects, philanthropists. The object is to show what you and other successful men of affairs think of this Bahai Cause as a means to bring the spiritual emancipation of the races.
> Would you not consider it a privilege to send me a few lines telling what these principles are doing. Your word, united to the tremendous power of the great ocean of Creative Thought will help the multitudes. God gives you opportunity to be a means through whom this Universal plan can come into operation.[23]

The audaciousness of Martha Root was remarkable. It would serve both the Temple and the Faith well in years to come.

Shortly after the 1920 convention, the Bourgeois model was placed on public display at the Kevorkian Gallery, a Persian rug center in New York. Thousands came to view it. As one newspaper noted, "Musicians, artists, poets and editors have fallen victim to the lure of its spiritual beauty and masses of the lay public have been enthralled by its magnetism." "Mr. Bourgeois' model of the Temple . . . ," recorded one Bahá'í, "has created quite a sensation. All sorts of big people go there to see it. I hear it whispered around down there that some rich people want to build it here in New York." Among the prominent visitors to the model was George Grey Barnard, a famous American sculptor, who " 'pronounced it "the greatest creation since the Gothic period." ' " Mary Hanford Ford, a Bahá'í who was a widely respected authority on literature, art, and music, wrote, " '[Barnard] believes it will be built not only in Chicago, but in its full size on Fort Washington Heights in New York, where a group of millionaires will place it as an illustration of what religion has become to humanity.' "[24]

Another visitor to the gallery was Luigi Quaglino, a former professor of architecture from Turin, Italy, who intended to make a " 'brief survey.' " After studying the model for three hours, "and for two hours without speaking," he said, " 'This is a new creation which will revolutionize architecture in the world, and it is the most beautiful I have ever seen. Without doubt it will have a lasting page in history. It was a revelation from another world.' "[25]

One well-known writer on religious drama, Mozo Samuel, remarked that " 'Prior to this time no architecture has made any deep impression upon me, but this Temple model has thrilled me, and I desire to visit it again and be alone with this marvelous creation.' " Another writer, a theatrical magazine editor, criticized the model as " ' "decidedly over-decorated" ' " and " ' "an . . . [absurdity] in its full size." ' " " 'He was something of a scoffer,' " Mary Ford recorded, " 'and had evidently heard unpleasant things about the Baha'i movement.' " When the usher explained the " 'significance of the decoration,—how each line and curve was an expression of a great thought or a noble principle, so that all the spiritual tradition and future aspiration of the human race seemed embedded in this Temple,' " his attitude softened. " 'His eyes began to shine . . . and though he came to stay five minutes, he was in the heavenly presence two hours and left it regretfully. Now he has opened his magazine to a monthly article on the Baha'i Movement.' "[26]

In early 1921 the model was transported west to be exhibited with a model of the soon-to-be-famous Wrigley Building at an architectural exhibition at Chicago's Art Institute. The exhibition was held in the same building that, in 1893, had housed the World's Parliament of Religions, where the Bahá'í Faith was first mentioned publicly in North America. In the first week the model was seen by thirty-four thousand people, who "crowded around the glorious model, spellbound." A Bahá'í who "saw it for the first time in the quiet peace of the evening" said, " 'That Temple came from Heaven. What marvelous lines! What celestial Beauty! Just to stand before it is a Spiritual Experience. It is so Pure! So Holy! like the Worlds of God!' "[27]

An artist from Paris was "awed as by a heavenly vision" and thought that it was "the most beautiful building I have ever seen in all the world." One woman suggested that it reminded her of "our dreams of fairyland, its tracery is so ethereal." Another said, " 'Just to enter the Temple will bring the Peace that passeth understanding.' " Some of the visitors studied the details for hours and were moved to ask, " 'What does it stand for? Tell us about it.' " The interest in the Bahá'í Faith aroused by the Temple model was perhaps surpassed only by the attention given to 'Abdu'l-Bahá during His American visit. "If the model so gloriously proclaims the Cause of Unity...," wrote Louise Waite, "what will the Temple itself accomplish? It will attract the people by tens of thousands to the New Kingdom of GOD which has descended among the nations."[28]

The American Bahá'ís still needed to seek 'Abdu'l-Bahá's approval for the Bourgeois design. Hundreds of thousands of dollars would have to be raised. And the methods for constructing the building had to be determined. Nonetheless, seventeen years after the project began, the Bahá'ís had a design for their Temple.

Chapter Twelve
THE AGONY OF VICTORY

A FEW months after the 1920 convention, Mountfort Mills journeyed to the Holy Land. There he discovered that 'Abdu'l-Bahá had been seriously ill and was, in Mr. Mill's words, "so weak that your hearts could not but have been touched, as ours were, and moved to the point of expressing our hope that he would be careful of his health for the sake of those in the world who love him so dearly."[1]

'Abdu'l-Bahá, according to Mr. Mills, said:

> "In one prayer I could have health the remainder of my life, but it is necessary for me to suffer to show to others that these things can be borne and overcome. I must first undergo all hardships. Then you will be able to undergo them. I must experience every difficulty that I may teach you to do likewise. I must be an example that you may learn to do the same, resisting all difficulties, that firmness and steadfastness may be shown. Strength will be given to sustain work for God if the purpose is to aid him."[2]

At that moment no American Bahá'í had any idea of the ordeals soon to be faced. None could anticipate the great difficulties that would nearly crush the dream of the Temple. And none knew of the developments that would challenge the Bahá'í community in America to grow in strength and administrative skill.

The Temple project moved forward rapidly at first. 'Abdu'l-Bahá had seen the Bourgeois drawings just before the 1920 convention but had suggested that " 'a smaller one would be better.' "[3] After the convention He approved of the selection but again cautioned that the original plan was too large. The Executive Board, obeying instructions from the delegates, had already asked Louis Bourgeois to reduce the design to one-half its original size. Mr. Bourgeois was also directed to prepare a sketch showing the upper pylons placed directly above the lower ones, as Mr. Magonigle, the architectural consultant at the convention, had advised. But the rotation of the upper level robbed the Temple of much of its beauty, leaving it " 'a rigid structure' " that " 'lacked motion.' "[4] Mr. Bourgeois' original concept prevailed and was adopted.

The quick ratification of the delegates' decision by 'Abdu'l-Bahá caused some people to believe that He had approved the larger design, despite His recommendations to the contrary. Attempting to eliminate the confusion, the Executive Board sent a cable to Haifa on 4 August 1920:

> "Understanding recent tablets approve Bourgeois design have adopted model reduced preserving original beauty, estimated cost million and a half. Proceeding construct foundation and increase fund. Supplicate divine assistance."[5]

Four days later 'Abdu'l-Bahá responded, " 'Your news imparted great joy. Assuredly, friends, exercise greatest effort in this service.' " Before the cables were exchanged 'Abdu'l-Bahá had written a letter to the Executive Board that did not arrive until a few days later. In it He expressed His hope that the size would be such that " 'one million dollars may suffice for its construction. This should be reconsidered only if possible.' "[6] The Executive Board, feeling obligated to limit their expenditures accordingly, sent Louis Bourgeois back to his drawing table. Although he spent countless hours modifying the design, the estimated cost could only be lowered to $1,200,000.

On 11 January 1921 Mr. Bourgeois sailed for Palestine via Europe aboard the German liner *Imperatur*, perhaps the largest steamer afloat at that time. He was accompanied by his wife, Alice, his friend L. B. Pemberton, and a carefully guarded four-foot cylinder that contained three drawings: one, the detailed colored rendering of the design that was submitted to the 1920 convention; the other two, a front elevation and a cross section of the redesigned Temple. The width of the upper auditorium had been reduced from 450 to 152 feet, the height from 360 to 191 feet. The most noticeable changes were fewer windows on the main level and loss of the original design's squatty appearance.

When Louis Bourgeois reached Haifa two months later, 'Abdu'l-Bahá was in the town of Tiberias, on the Sea of Galilee, recovering from His illness. Upon reaching Tiberias, Mr. Bourgeois was received by 'Abdu'l-Bahá for one hour on each of four days:

> "What was said about the Temple did not take more than fifteen minutes. I showed him the design of the large Temple in color. He examined it carefully and

said, 'It is very beautiful, very beautiful.' Many times he repeated these words, 'Very beautiful.' 'The most beautiful in the world. It was given to you from the Kingdom,' he said, and I answered that I felt in my heart it was from the Kingdom and that it made me very happy to hear it from his lips. He added, 'All the troubles around you will be removed. You have been confirmed in this work.' In another visit he said that BAHA'O'LLAH had conferred a great favor upon me.

"He looked at the Chicago design [the reduced plan] which had no ornaments on the drawing and said, 'It is not like the other one showing the large design.' I explained to him that I had no time to draw the ornaments and that the engineer would not need them for his work. He replied, 'Do it just like this one,' pointing to the large design, and I replied that I would.

"Then we looked at the floor plans. After looking them over he asked me, 'What are you going to do with the rooms around the dome?' I told him that that was the reason of my visit to him and asked him what he would like to have done with them. He said, 'What did you have in mind when you planned those rooms?' and I told him that they could be used for the teaching of the message, a room for each language and opening the screen, throwing all into one large audience for service. He said, 'No, you will give a room to every religion so that each may worship in its own way.' This made me very happy."[7]

Louis Bourgeois apparently misunderstood 'Abdu'l-Bahá's last statement, perhaps because they were speaking through an interpreter. For the next decade the Bahá'ís perpetuated the idea that several small chapels around the perimeter of the central auditorium would be used to hold services for other religions. The Bahá'ís, they believed, would worship only in the central auditorium. It is more likely that 'Abdu'l-Bahá wanted to correct Mr. Bourgeois' erroneous notion and emphasize that the building must be open not for services of other faiths, but for unfettered worship by all people.

A few months before Louis Bourgeois' trip, in the late summer of 1920, the Executive Board had encountered the first of many difficulties they would experience in the next few months: The village planners in Wilmette wished to change the curve in Sheridan Road at the point where it passed the Temple site. The proposed change would have significantly reduced the size of the Temple land. When the Executive Board met with a citizen's committee, they decided to recommend to the Village Board of Trustees the exchange of small sections of land bordering the roadway. Not only were the Wilmette officials happy, but the Executive Board was able to make the grounds nearly circular, fulfilling a wish expressed by 'Abdu'l-Bahá during His visit in 1912.

The Agony of Victory

The Bahá'ís raised an additional $25,000 during the summer months of 1920. Boring began on 24 September to determine the depth of bedrock. Soon thereafter the Executive Board called for bids to construct the caissons—the foundations that would rise from the bedrock to support the Temple's massive dome. The Board also secured the services of Major Henry J. Burt, chief structural engineer of the noted architectural firm Holabird and Roche. Major Burt's professional experiences included surveying and constructing railroads, designing and supervising construction of steel buildings and bridges, teaching civil engineering at Iowa State College, and authoring a widely used college textbook, *Steel Construction*. He joined Holabird and Roche in 1911 and supervised the design and construction of many notable Chicago buildings—the Palmer House hotel, the Tribune Tower, and Soldier's Field stadium among them. Yet the Temple would, according to his daughter, become "his most important commission."[8]

On 6 January 1921 Major Burt and Alfred Lunt applied to the village of Wilmette for a construction permit. Mr. Lunt recalled, " 'You all know you can't erect even a hen house anywhere in any community without a permit of the governing body of the village or community or city. The village of Wilmette has a very arduous and exhaustive ordinance . . . which is in very great detail and requires a lot of plans and drawings to be placed on file. . . .' " The Executive Board expected the permit to be granted quickly. Yet they discovered that the village trustees had wished to protect the residents of Wilmette by changing their ordinance to accommodate a building the magnitude of the Temple. Mr. Lunt noted that " 'they passed . . . two or three amendments to the long ordinance they already had, which carried over several months, because those ordinances all had to be published in the papers in order to become effective, and they would not do anything until they had become effective.' "[9]

Within days of the original filing, a small group of citizens vociferously opposed the construction of the Temple. Newspaper articles appeared, some in Wilmette's *Lake Shore News*, "which assailed Bahai principles, which assailed the purposes of the Temple, which misrepresented the whole idea of the Bahai Temple Unity and its objects and its ideals. . . ." On 20 January 1921 the *Chicago Herald and Examiner* reported that "The temple, proposed by the Bahaists as a place of worship for members of all religions, is denounced by the villagers as an enemy to Christianity." 'Abdu'l-Bahá, upon learning of the opposition, told Mountfort Mills that He was happy "the Bahais had found a little trouble because he said now the cause will begin to grow. . . ."[10]

The Agony of Victory

Bahá'ís and workmen gathered on the Temple grounds when the drilling to locate bedrock was begun on 24 September 1920. Louis Bourgeois (front row, standing under scaffold) is holding a drawing of the Temple.

Public unrest was partially stilled by a detailed statement Alfred Lunt submitted to the *Lake Shore News* in response to earlier attacks. His statement occupied more than fifty column inches in the newspaper's 4 February 1921 issue, refuting the accusations, outlining the Bahá'í concept of progressive revelation, and describing the fundamental purposes of the Temple.* In responding to one critic, who found the building "mysterious, and therefore imbued with some dreadful menace," Mr. Lunt pointed out that

---

*The Bahá'í concept of progressive revelation teaches that God has always provided guidance for humankind through a series of prophets or divine teachers. Among them are Christ, Moses, Zoroaster, Buddha, Krishna, Muḥammad, the Báb, and Bahá'u'lláh. Each of these prophets, according to Bahá'u'lláh, has taught the same fundamental spiritual truths. Differences among their teachings are due to the changing needs of humankind. Each of their revelations, therefore, represents a different stage in the constantly unfolding religion of God.

The Agony of Victory

ALFRED EASTMAN LUNT
a member of the Executive Board of the Bahai Temple Unity for eleven years and its secretary from 1919 to 1924. He put to rest much of the early public opposition to the Temple project.

it is just as mysterious, and no more so than any place of congregation where the hearts are uplifted to Almighty God. On this basis, every true place of prayer is a place of mystery. Yes, a place where the mystery of the human heart is uncovered before its Maker. Let not Mr. Stafford question or look askance at so sacred a function as this, nor liken to fools . . . those who merely seek the privilege in free America of worshipping God as their hearts dictate.[11]

An investigating committee appointed by the Village Board of Trustees examined the Executive Board's application for a construction permit and decided that adequate specifications had not been submitted. The committee was also concerned by the possibility that Bahá'ís might lack adequate funds to complete the building quickly. Wishing to protect the village from an "unsightly and incomplete structure," the committee proposed that the "structure be completed or removed within a fixed time." This concern, and the widespread feeling that "the Temple [would] fall into disuse and ruin because of lack of maintenance," prompted Alfred Lunt to write that "thousands of Roman Catholic, Protestant, and other churches and cathedrals in America would today

The Agony of Victory

Bahá'ís inaugurating construction of Foundation Hall, 21 March 1921. Dr. Zia Bagdadi is holding the shovel; Corinne True is the first woman to his left.

be non-existent" if such restrictions were imposed upon them. "Churches fulfilling today a noble place of service in the community would never have been begun" if it were necessary that "the entire cost was at hand" before building. "This is not the case with Bahais," he explained, "but if it were, it should not have the slightest weight. Faith, sacrifice and real enthusiasm, are greater than fear and prejudice, and are pre-requisites of every great success."[12]

The application was resubmitted on 4 March 1921 and contained all of the required plans, specifications, and drawings. Because the Bahá'ís had hired Holabird and Roche, which had an outstanding reputation, the village officials were reasonably assured that the Bahá'ís would not " 'have an audience there of three or four thousand and then have the Temple fall down. . . .' " Feeling that they had discharged their duty " 'to guard the city against a holocaust,' " the Wilmette village board issued the permit within two weeks. In announcing this success to the American Bahá'í community, the Executive Board wrote, "These attacks have been met and answered in a Bahai spirit, and your Board has been in almost constant session for months, to do everything within its power to meet the requirements. Now, Praise be to God, victory has come. . . . It is as if the storm and the menacing waves of that sea were quieted in an instant by His Word, 'Peace, be still.' "[13]

On 21 March, the first day of both spring and the Bahá'í year, the workmen arrived with their equipment and drove the stakes that positioned the nine caissons. At 2:30 P.M. a group of Bahá'ís, including Corinne True and Dr. Zia Bagdadi, gathered to inaugurate the construction work. After a short devotional service they each turned a shovelful of earth at the spot where the first caisson would be dug.

The contract for constructing the nine great caissons had been awarded to the Avery Brundage Company, whose bid of $47,000 was the lowest of the eight received. The Executive Board had signed the contract during the third week of December 1920. With the building permit in hand, the Bahá'ís watched the work proceed rapidly. For each caisson a well was dug until bedrock was reached, approximately 120 feet below the surface of the land. The wood-lined shafts were then filled with concrete to create massive six-foot-diameter foundation columns.

Six of the caissons were constructed with little difficulty, but the remaining three created a problem that the Brundage Company had not encountered before. Eighty-five feet below the ground, the drills reached water-bearing sand. The workers attempted to bail out the water by hand, but it soon became obvious that they needed to install steam-driven pumping equipment. Unfortunately, the necessary equipment was hard to find because of a " 'shortage of such apparatus in Chicago due to the demand of the oil fields.' " Their first boiler was " 'defective and too small, and the second was unwieldy and had to be taken from an inaccessible location, thus making the cost of hauling and handling a considerable item.' " In order to keep the rising water from damaging the completed work, they also had to continue the expensive hand bailing. " 'The water would gush in so suddenly at times,' " wrote one of the Executive Board's representatives, " 'that the pumps themselves would be flooded and the men would have to climb up the lagging in order to save their lives.' "[14]

The Brundage Company installed an extensive lighting system to allow the bailing to continue around the clock. During the evening of 23 April, the opening day of the 1921 annual Bahá'í convention, the lights inexplicably failed. William Gorman, a young electrician who had recently married, began searching for the problem. The night was particularly dark, and as he traced the cables along the edge of the canal, he slipped and plunged down the steep embankment into the cold water. The other workmen, hearing his cries for help, tried

Construction of the nine caissons by the Avery Brundage Company, 30 April 1921. The contract for the work had been let in December 1920.

desperately to locate him; but as they stumbled through the darkness, the screaming ceased. Mr. Gorman's body was recovered from the canal the following morning.

According to their contract with the Brundage Company, the Executive Board was responsible for the equipment and labor costs for pumping the water. Thus the Brundage Company presented the Executive Board with an additional bill of $42,679.43, of which $19,000 would pay for more than twenty-five hundred man-hours of hand bailing. But the Executive Board felt that the contractor had been negligent by permitting excessive time to elapse before securing pumping equipment. They also suspected that the company had overcharged them on several items. After lengthy negotiations the company and the Executive Board agreed on an additional payment of $30,000.

The Agony of Victory

At the 1921 convention several delegates objected to the seemingly excessive fee the Executive Board had agreed to pay Louis Bourgeois for his design. During negotiations the previous December, Mr. Bourgeois had requested a fee of 7½ percent of the total cost of the building. Since at that time the cost was expected to be $1,200,000, the fee would have amounted to $90,000. From this amount, however, Mr. Bourgeois would have been responsible for all costs relating to the production of drawings and the supervision of the project, including fees for a structural engineer. The Executive Board, feeling this amount was excessive, made a counterproposal that Mr. Bourgeois accepted: he would be paid a flat fee of $50,000 for his architectural services plus $5,000 for the Temple model; $1,500 for his January 1921 visit to 'Abdu'l-Bahá; and up to $6,000 for draftsmen to complete the detailed drawings of the design. The Executive Board had contracted separately with Major Burt for structural-engineering services.[15]

In defense of his fee Mr. Bourgeois explained to the 1921 convention delegates that an architect can usually supervise several projects at once because of the basic similarities of most buildings, which only require small-scale engineering drawings and little communication with contractors. Yet the detail of the Temple needed to be drawn " 'full size, not only the profile.' " " 'There ... [are] more ornaments on this building than any building that was ever built,' " Mr. Bourgeois added, and " 'more work of a detail nature on this temple than there is on ten buildings that I have done during my forty years.' " He explained that he had not been able to employ superintendents to guide the contractors. Therefore, it had been necessary for him to move from New York to Chicago in order to devote his full attention to the Temple, leaving him no time for other work.[16]

Nevertheless, several of the delegates submitted a paper outlining their disapproval of the fee:

> "The question of salary for the Bahai architect is distinctive, apparently, to this convention, and to some of the friends the sum of $50,000 as fixed compensation seems calamitous in scope. The fund for this universal edifice has been contributed to by Bahais in all parts of the world, from sections of the world where a short time ago conditions were well nigh intolerable and from there contributions have been sent in. The suffering in these regions was indescribable. Women and children climbed mountain sides and plucked the grass to boil and eat. All night long in the streets the cry from the surging crowds of "hungry, hungry" reached to the very apex of heaven.

"From every corner and remote village of Persia and other eastern countries, believers, living in the utmost deprivation and abject poverty, sold their household effects, denied themselves the very means of continuance of life . . . in order to contribute to this wonderful temple. Now we are faced with the problem of taking from the fund contributed to by the very life of the believers a large sum of money as salary for architectural designs of a temple made only possible through the Bahai revelation and the fact that the designer had lived and is basking in the rays of the sun of reality."[17]

The Executive Board had carefully considered " 'a standard of sacrifice on the part of Mr. Bourgeois' " when negotiating his fee but had decided that it was inappropriate to do so because " 'if any one else felt coerced into accepting our standards of sacrifice there would be no sacrifice on their part. . . .' " Louis Bourgeois' compensation was also defended by Horace Holley, another delegate to the 1921 convention. The design, Mr. Holley said, had been " 'given an amount of publicity by the press in all parts of the world of incalculable value to this cause.' " Even though Mr. Holley recognized that $50,000 seemed large in proportion to their total present savings of $171,000, he did not feel that the fee was too large considering the value of Mr. Bourgeois' contribution to the growth of the Bahá'í Faith. Mr. Holley continued:

"Now it is apparent that this temple is a great magnet. Mr. Bourgeois was prepared probably all through his life to work out this temple. The future of his life will be entirely dedicated to the developing of the model in an actual material at Wilmette. . . . Therefore, it is one man's entire life, and in return for this dedicated life, dedicated in unconsciousness before, and in consciousness now, he asks this body of delegates for an amount equivalent to an income of $50.00 a week. My friends, I submit to this body that it is not an excessive amount and that if we cut it down or pare it or divide it or subtract it, it would not be acting in the larger spirit of wisdom and confidence which we as the Bahais of this country have in our cause."

A few minutes later another delegate, Grace Krug, reminded the others:

"As . . . Bahais what have we more than the majority of people on the face of the earth? It is love. When His Holiness, Abdul Baha, was asked for the definition of spirituality he said, and I will quote his blessed words, 'It is love in action.' . . . I move, Mr. Chairman, that we act in love in this regard toward our blessed brother,

Mr. Bourgeois. I know his life. I know his sacrifices. I know his ill-health from giving every ounce of energy that he had in his physical nature towards this glorious temple. . . . I hope we will take this vote to protect Mr. Bourgeois for the rest of his life for what I consider is nothing more than the attitude of spirituality, and that is love in action."[18]

The controversy over Mr. Bourgeois' fee subsided for the remainder of the convention, but a second aspect of the contract caused equal concern. Alfred Lunt explained to the delegates that the contract provided for payment of the $50,000 as follows: " 'In 1921 there should be $10,000 paid in quarterly payments. From that time on only ten per cent of the gross amount expended in construction in any one year should be paid him under his contract. That is, if we only spent for example $50,000 in any one year after that he would at the outside receive $5,000. . . . If nothing was spent there would be nothing paid. In other words, we were trying to protect the treasury and at the same time to do what seemed to be fair and right on a contractural basis . . . with the architect.' "[19]

The problem with this arrangement was that it would have been possible for Louis Bourgeois to collect his entire fee before the Temple was completed. Several Bahá'ís had complained to the Executive Board before the convention. A few had even written to 'Abdu'l-Bahá, Who responded that the matter should be clarified at the convention.[20] The Executive Board had already provided for such a contingency and had stipulated in the Bourgeois contract that it was subject to ratification by the convention.

At the recommendation of Corinne True, the convention delegates appointed Sutherland Maxwell to chair a committee—the membership of which he was to choose—to review the Bourgeois contract in its entirety during the convention. The committee was also instructed to review the contract with Major Burt even though the convention had no authority to revoke that agreement. Mr. Maxwell invited Howard Struven, Kingsley White, Hills Cole, Mountfort Mills, George Latimer, and Harry Randall to join him. After carefully reviewing the contract and consulting with Louis Bourgeois, the committee reported to the convention several minor problems in addition to the larger problem of the payment schedule. As a result, the committee recommended that the contract as written be rejected. Following a lengthy discussion by the delegates, they decided to annul the contract, and they offered numerous recommendations to the Executive Board for incorporation into a new contract.

Another issue troubling many of the delegates was the failure of the contractor to center the foundation around the dedication stone laid by 'Abdu'l-Bahá. The unhappy delegates erroneously believed that the stone sat at the exact center of the land. Yet the Bahá'ís at the ceremony in 1912, unprepared for 'Abdu'l-Bahá's question about the center of the property, only could approximate at that time where the center was.[21] Major Burt and Corinne True were unable to pacify the delegates' concerns when they explained that the building was positioned to allow for the greatest amount of circular land around it. One woman became upset and left sobbing. Another delegate exclaimed:

> "I have no doubt that it will be a terrible blow to many, many tender and heroic souls in this country. . . . I, for myself, would just as soon set it right on the corner of the street and have a little archway at the street to go under if we thought that that center there which Abdul Baha established could possibly be maintained. . . . I view as a calamity that that building is not put on that center."[22]

Alfred Lunt, in an effort to clarify the situation, asked Major Burt about the location of the stone in relation to the building. Although Major Burt was unable to give him an accurate answer, he did estimate that the stone " 'lies very close to the outer wall of the basement.' " He then revealed that the stone had been removed and its location " 'marked by a growing bush.' "[23] This created more excitement among the delegates, who demanded that a survey be conducted immediately to ensure that the stone would be replaced in its original location. In an attempt to appease those distressed by the stone's location, the Executive Board later ordered that a chapel be designed to surround it. Plans for the chapel were circulated among the Bahá'ís, but eventually the idea was abandoned.

If the Bahá'ís were concerned by some of the Executive Board's decisions, they certainly could not claim a corresponding dissatisfaction with the efforts of that institution to keep them informed. The Executive Board often distributed lengthy descriptions of events and details of contracts through letters to the Bahá'ís. In their communications they attempted to stimulate support for the project and to expand the Bahá'ís' appreciation for the Temple's importance. One letter said:

> To administer the healing remedy to the nations today is admittedly the highest service. To build the Temple of GOD and open its doors to all men is the present greatest form of that service. Are we resolved upon this? Do we question the continued emphasis the Master lays upon the building of the Temple? Are we

conscious of the vital relation this Eternal Symbol of Unity (the Temple) bears to the present disordered state of human society? That it is the elevation of the Word and Law of GOD, and that *through it*, the people will enter the Religion of GOD "in troops", as He has said? To build the Temple in this time of humanity's need is, at once, the glory and privilege of the Bahais of America.[24]

On 24 August 1921 the Executive Board signed a contract with the McCarty Brothers, another Chicago contracting firm, for the construction of the foundation. The 202 foot wide, 27 foot tall circular structure was referred to as "Foundation Hall" and would become the base from which the Temple would rise. The McCarty Brothers had submitted a bid much lower than the anticipated cost, and it appeared that the excess fees paid the Avery Brundage Company would be completely offset. On 12 September the work began. Soon the ground was "excavated for the driving of the secondary pilings, and the true, majestic proportions of the Temple [could] now be realized by an observer."[25]

In a report sent to 'Abdu'l-Bahá three weeks later the Executive Board again mentioned to Him " 'that hope which dwells in the innermost part of our breasts, which is our longing for Thy Presence in America next Spring . . . , or at such other time as seems to Thee best, to dedicate and bless the Corner-stone of Mashreq'Ul-Azkar. . . . [The] hearts of the friends in America do intensely long for the fulfillment of this great historic event. . . .' "[26] In anticipation of His coming, an indentation had been designed into the interior surface of the outer wall, adjacent to the dedication stone, into which 'Abdu'l-Bahá could set an actual cornerstone. The stone He had laid in 1912 would be placed inside the new stone. Their dream, however, would not be fulfilled. On Monday, 28 November 1921, a cablegram conveyed the crushing news that the heart of the beloved 'Abdu'l-Bahá had stilled.

At the funeral held the following day, the sorrow-stricken residents of Haifa jammed the street along which the casket was born toward the summit of Mount Carmel. At the tomb of the Báb several prominent personages addressed the huge crowd. As part of his remarks, Ibráhím Naṣṣár, a noted Christian writer, declared:

"In the passing away of the great Master, Abdul Baha, the mountain of charity and generosity has tumbled! The echo of his departure sounded in all parts of the world. Therefore humanity is painfully suffering, the tongues are repeating the mentioning of his abundant bounties, the eyes are weeping and the hearts are bleeding! Ah me!"

The Agony of Victory

Naṣṣár's remarks were followed by those of the Muslim muftí, or jurist, of Haifa, Muḥammad Murád:

> "When nations lose one of their great men, whether he is great in his knowledge or great in his generosity or great in his politics or great in his principles and his benevolence, they comfort themselves in this, that there must come out from among their sons a genius who would become a successor to that great departed man. But the calamity of the world of humanity in the loss of the benevolent Abdul Baha cannot be compared to any other calamity, because his vacancy will never be filled by any of the people."

One of the Jewish leaders of Haifa, Salomon Bouzaglo, added:

> "Since the days of Aristotle until this day all philosophers and social reformers have been fanatically using every means to uphold their own sectarian and limited theories, and woe unto whomsoever disagrees with them. But here, with Abdul Baha, there is no prejudice of any kind. All men are brothers."[27]

On 7 January 1922, forty days after 'Abdu'l-Bahá's passing, memorial services were held in Bahá'í communities throughout the world. In the United States one of the most eloquent eulogies for 'Abdu'l-Bahá was written by Albert Windust and published in the *Star of the West* in December 1921:

> Some years ago His Holiness Abdul-Baha said: "These great days are swiftly passing and once gone can never be recalled, so while the rays of the Sun of Truth are still shining and the Center of the Covenant of God is manifest, let us go forth to work, for after awhile the night will come and the way to the Vineyard will not then be so easy to find."
> In this world the night has come—
> And with it—weeping.
> And in the heavenly world?
> O for the pen of a Milton, the brush of a Doré and the music of a Handel, to convey a fleeting glimpse of what is transpiring!
> If it were according to Divine Wisdom that such a scene be pictured, only the vision and Word of Him who has ascended could describe it!
> But His utterance is stilled—
> And our pen is broken.[28]

A few weeks before 'Abdu'l-Bahá's death, building activities at the Temple

The Agony of Victory

An early stage in the construction of Foundation Hall, 1922, showing steel columns for supporting the dome of the Temple and wooden forms for the outer wall and for the ceiling of the central meeting room

faltered when construction workers in the Chicago area went on strike to protest the use of nonunion laborers.[29] A streetcar strike at another time made it difficult for most of the workers to reach the construction site. These problems were minor, however, compared with other difficulties: Tests were performed to guarantee that the new foundation pilings for the outer walls of the building would support the weight for which they had been designed. But the pilings, constructed by the MacArthur Concrete Pile and Foundation Company, failed the tests, and Major Burt demanded that they be replaced. Controversy over what should be done and who was responsible resulted in the postponement of any further work.

The Bahá'ís' confidence in their Executive Board was now completely eroded. No one could understand how the miscalculations had been allowed to

The Agony of Victory

The top of Foundation Hall as it appeared in late spring 1922. In the foreground is the slope that eventually would support eighteen circular steps leading to the upstairs auditorium.

happen. The project seemed doomed to difficulty after difficulty, and no one knew how to reverse the situation. On 9 February 1922 Dr. Zia Bagdadi, a member of the Executive Board, penned a letter to his fellow board members:

> Think of them[—]all are condemned! Some of us may say "well we will not pay the contractor. We will hold them responsible." This means the contractors and workers will fight to the finish. It means loss of materials, delay upon delay of the building, and perhaps a hot battle in the courts!

Dr. Bagdadi noted that Louis Bourgeois, Corinne True, and he had visited the building site as often as possible but inferred that such intermittent inspections were inadequate. He explained that 'Abdu'l-Bahá, for each of the many struc-

The Agony of Victory

Foundation Hall's central meeting room, with temporary skylight, under construction in 1922

tures He had built, had employed a Bahá'í who possessed at least a basic knowledge of construction. "That Bahai supervisor attended the building from start to finish," said Dr. Bagdadi. "He was on the job before the workers reported and he left the place after the workers went home. His presence only made the workers efficient and his open eyes reminded them always to do the right thing." Dr. Bagdadi pleaded "for the appointment of a Bahai supervisor whose duty shall be to be present on the temple ground from this moment until the building is completed." The Executive Board recognized the wisdom of his proposal and a few weeks later appointed Alfred Anderson as the first of several Bahá'í supervisors. The "open eyes" of these supervisors would, for the next three decades, ensure that the Temple was not left to "the mercy of strangers."[30]

Digging up several of the pilings for examination revealed they had been improperly constructed. They were replaced, and the McCarty Brothers agreed to sink several additional pilings as a safety measure. Construction of Foundation Hall at last began to move forward swiftly. The huge structure required

The Agony of Victory

The Bahá'ís' first meeting in Foundation Hall, 9 July 1922, the anniversary of the martyrdom of the Báb

3,100 cubic yards of cement and 114 tons of steel. Although not quite finished, it served as a meeting place for the first time on 9 July 1922, when the Bahá'ís celebrated the seventy-second anniversary of the martyrdom of the Báb. In the following months the Temple site was visited by thousands of curious onlookers from Chicago and other midwestern cities. "They remark," wrote one Bahá'í, "on the great size of the foundations, on the magnificence of the location overlooking Lake Michigan, on the wonder of a Temple open to all sects and religions."[31]

The McCarty Brothers claimed that the faulty foundations had cost them an additional $21,621, and they wanted this amount added to their contract. After two months of negotiations they agreed upon a settlement of less than $6,000 above the original contract. Even with the large extra payment to Avery Brundage, total construction cost for the caissons and basement was $40,150 less than the original estimate of $225,000.

The setbacks at the construction site, coupled with the disputes over Louis Bourgeois' contract and the centering of the building upon the dedication stone,

119

The Agony of Victory

caused many Bahá'ís to lose interest in the project. In spite of appeals for "between $200,000 and $300,000" so that construction could continue uninterrupted, and admonitions that many people throughout the world were "watching, expectant to see what this body of brotherhood, the Bahais, shall accomplish," contributions dwindled to almost nothing.[32]

For a brief moment it seemed to some that success was within reach, that the project would advance swiftly toward completion. But the gray, saucer-shaped foundation would lie cold and barren for a long time, giving no indication of the exquisite structure Louis Bourgeois had envisioned. The Bahá'ís still had many lessons to learn and many problems to solve.

Chapter Thirteen
THE SECOND LONG WAIT

PERHAPS the most ardent supporter of the Temple during the 1920s was 'Abdu'l-Bahá's grandson Shoghi Effendi. Shortly after 'Abdu'l-Bahá's death in November 1921, twenty-four-year-old Shoghi Effendi was appointed by his grandfather's Will and Testament the head, or Guardian, of the worldwide Bahá'í community.[1] But 'Abdu'l-Bahá's Will did more than ensure the continuity of leadership; in it 'Abdu'l-Bahá also consoled the Bahá'ís, counseled them to reflect the highest standards in their behavior; and commanded them to remain firm in their beliefs, to allow no trace of disunity to permeate their ranks, to be loyal and obedient to Shoghi Effendi, and to share Bahá'u'lláh's teachings with all people. The Will also outlined the framework by which the Bahá'í communities throughout the world were to be administered, including the establishment of national governing bodies known today as National Spiritual Assemblies.

Despite the existence of the Will and Testament, which served to ensure unity and the continuity of leadership in the Bahá'í community, 'Abdu'l-Bahá's death shattered the faith of many Bahá'ís. A few even challenged Shoghi Effendi's authority and attempted, unsuccessfully, to harm the Faith. Yet Shoghi Effendi remained determined to carry out 'Abdu'l-Bahá's final directives. In early 1922 Shoghi Effendi summoned to Haifa several Bahá'ís from both the East and the West. Among the Americans who went were Corinne True, Mountfort Mills, and Roy Wilhelm. After they arrived in Haifa, Shoghi Effendi discussed with them the provisions of the Will and instructed them to replace the Executive Board with the first National Spiritual Assembly in North America. The new National Spiritual Assembly would become the national authority for the Bahá'ís in the United States and Canada rather than merely a governing committee for the Bahai Temple Unity.

The election of this new administrative institution was held on 25 April

The Second Long Wait

1922 in Chicago. The electoral process was far removed from that of today's Bahá'í elections, for it involved nominating, electioneering, and a straw vote to narrow the field of candidates. Nevertheless, sixty-three delegates elected nine members to the first National Spiritual Assembly of the Bahá'ís of the United States and Canada. Corinne True received the highest number of votes. The other eight members were: Dr. Zia Bagdadi, Ella Cooper, Louis Gregory, Alfred Lunt, Mountfort Mills, Harry Randall, Charles Mason Remey, and Roy Wilhelm.

Initially, the difference between the National Spiritual Assembly and its forerunner, the Executive Board, amounted to little more than a change in name. The nine members continued to function as the governing board for the Bahai Temple Unity, the fundamental objective of which remained the erection of the Temple. Three years of guidance by Shoghi Effendi were required before the National Spiritual Assembly was able to assume all of the "powers, responsibilities, rights, privileges and obligations" delineated by Bahá'u'lláh and 'Abdu'l-Bahá.[2] Election procedures were also restructured between 1922 and 1925 so that they would be in accordance with Bahá'í principles. Thus Shoghi Effendi designated 1925 rather than 1922 as the year of the formation of the first National Spiritual Assembly in North America.*

Progress in administrative growth did not necessarily ensure progress at the Temple site. Foundation Hall, covered with tar for waterproofing, continued to stand silently and mysteriously alongside Wilmette Harbor. "I would feel indeed disheartened," wrote Shoghi Effendi in November 1923, "were the friends to think for a moment, that its work should fall into abeyance, nay, rather they should do all in their power . . . to provide for the steady and uninterrupted progress of the work, until the day may come when this sublime Edifice, raised in its majestic splendor in the very heart of the continent, may be yet another evidence of the triumph and vitality of the Cause."[3]

In spite of this and other appeals, contributions continued to be negligible. As month after month passed, and further building did not occur, a significant portion of the local residents, many occupying stately homes recently erected,

---

*Because of legal considerations the structure of the Executive Board was retained until 1924 to deal with matters exclusive to the Temple. The National Spiritual Assembly handled all non-Temple matters with which the Executive Board had dealt. Although the Executive Board was dissolved in 1924, it was necessary to maintain the Bahai Temple Unity because the Unity held title to the Temple property. Delegates to the annual Bahá'í conventions (at which the National Spiritual Assembly was elected) also served as delegates to the annual convention of the Bahai Temple Unity, held at a different time during the year.

became greatly displeased. Many others delighted in exchanging stories about the 202-foot-diameter eyesore.

One favorite rumor told that the building contained a gigantic fish tank in which Bahá'ís kept a live white whale, considered by Bahá'ís to be sacred and the object of their prayers. Another rumor suggested that the building was a secret Masonic lodge. Others thought that Foundation Hall was a huge fuel tank, a rumor undoubtedly inspired by the fuel pumps that Chris Wagner had operated between 1916 and 1917. Some carried the rumor further and speculated that the fuel tank served as a secret refueling depot for German submarines. It was feared that these submarines would attempt to rekindle the First World War by harassing shipping on the Great Lakes. The vessels reportedly entered Foundation Hall through a long tunnel connecting it with Lake Michigan.

The submarine rumor was probably prompted by an unusual event on 21 June 1921. That day a German submarine, the *UC-97*, was towed to a point approximately seventeen miles east of Wilmette Harbor, where the gunboat U.S.S. *Wilmette* sent it to the bottom of Lake Michigan. The *UC-97* had been captured during the First World War after sinking seven Allied ships and had been brought to the United States in 1919 to promote the sale of government Victory Bonds. Because the Treaty of Versailles stipulated that all seized combat vessels were to be returned to their country of origin or be destroyed, the Department of the Navy ordered the *UC-97* sunk.

The National Spiritual Assembly, concerned about the impressions being created by the dismal appearance of Foundation Hall, wrote to the Bahá'ís in early 1925:

> Not until the Foundation Hall and grounds have been made dignified and beautiful; not until they have been placed in condition such as not merely to remove all source of criticism on the part of non-Bahá'ís, but to become the object of admiring and friendly interest among the thoughtful people of this country—will the Cause in America progress one single step *in any direction*.
>
> We have accepted the Message as a power—as the only power—capable of bringing order and harmony into the world. In the construction of a material Temple we have consciously or unconsciously undertaken to prove to the world what effect this Cause can have upon those who enter the circle of its influence. Step by step as the Temple arises to the fullness of its glorious beauty we can prove more eloquently than by any words what a new unifying spirit has come to earth in this age. Nothing could ever counteract the evidence of indifference or

neglect in this Baha'i enterprise so many years publicly proclaimed in every part of the world.[4]

In the first issue of the *Baha'i News Letter*, dated December 1924, the National Spiritual Assembly announced that it would spend slightly over $7,000 to make the interior of Foundation Hall usable. Cloak rooms and toilets would be installed, the central core would be partitioned to serve as a meeting room, and other minor improvements would be made. The National Spiritual Assembly also planned to improve the unsightly condition of the grounds by planting a large number of trees and plants. When even such minor work as this could not be started because of a continuing lack of funds, Shoghi Effendi cabled the Bahá'ís and urged them "to realize supreme necessity of immediate universal response to recent Temple appeal." He also told them he was sending "ninety-five pounds sterling" to further the work.[5]

By April 1925 the interior modifications were under way. Among the Bahá'í communities that helped was Chicago, whose members paid for part of the concrete floor and contributed the first piece of furniture—a conference table that is still being used. The exterior improvements began in the early summer. Many Bahá'ís living in the immediate area of the Temple contributed a significant amount of time to grading portions of the land, spreading fertilizer, and planting 372 trees and a variety of shrubs and vines. Unfortunately, the project was not entirely successful. Of 250 castor bean plants, for example, only one survived. The trees grew and the vines climbed the walls; but Foundation Hall still looked far from beautiful, and the public remained displeased.

Dissatisfaction with Louis Bourgeois' design and fee continued to stifle contributions and was one of the main causes of disunity in the American Bahá'í community during the 1920s. Many Bahá'ís remembered H. Van Buren Magonigle's warning at the 1920 convention—that snow and ice might tear the dome to pieces—and felt that a new design should be selected. But Shoghi Effendi made it clear that the issue of the basic design was settled: " 'The matter of the design is a definite thing and cannot be changed,' " Corinne True wrote to the Temple Committee from Haifa at Shoghi Effendi's request. " 'That must be thoroughly understood because it was confirmed by the Master.' "[6]

Charles Mason Remey, the architect who displayed nine designs at the 1920 convention, suggested that modifications be made in the Bourgeois design to render it more durable and less expensive to build. He recommended that the design be submitted for review to an impartial board of architects and civil engineers who were experienced in large building projects. Shoghi Effendi

Above: *A 1930 view of the exterior of Foundation Hall showing trees and vines planted in 1925.*
Below: *The central meeting room of Foundation Hall after improvements made in 1925. The table was a gift from the Bahá'ís of Chicago.*

agreed that it was desirable to use such consultants.[7] Various technical advisory committees appointed by the National Spiritual Assembly during the next three decades would make significant contributions to the successful completion of the project.

Difficulties with Louis Bourgeois' contract also added to the disunity. By early 1922 Alfred Lunt had prepared several new versions of a contract based on the recommendations from the 1921 convention. None were acceptable to Mr. Bourgeois. In the interim Louis Bourgeois was paid according to the proposed changes from the convention even though, technically, a valid contract did not exist. By March 1925 nearly 75 percent of the $50,000 had already been paid. Later that summer a contract was finally negotiated in which the remaining 25 percent ($12,500) would be paid at a rate of $1\frac{1}{4}$ percent of the amount of the construction contracts once work on the building resumed.

Yet another problem resulted from a clause in the annulled 1920 contract that stipulated Louis Bourgeois would be provided working space within the vicinity of the Temple. Through the generosity of Major Burt, a loft in a downtown Chicago building belonging to Holabird and Roche was secured for Mr. Bourgeois at no cost. It was there that he completed all of his large, full-size drawings in 1921. Holabird and Roche then asked to have the loft back so that they could rent it out.

Periodically during late 1921 and 1922 the matter of working space for Mr. Bourgeois was discussed first by the Executive Board and then by its successor, the National Spiritual Assembly. Mr. Bourgeois prepared a design for a building, but the estimated cost was $35,000. This plan was rejected, and a maximum of $5,000 was approved for a facility. Mr. Bourgeois then offered to build a studio on the Temple site at his own expense. Harry Randall, the president and treasurer of the 1923 National Spiritual Assembly, informed Louis Bourgeois on 2 July that the institution had accepted his proposal and that official notice of the decision would be issued later by Alfred Lunt, the National Spiritual Assembly's secretary. On the strength of Harry Randall's letter, Mr. Bourgeois began constructing the studio, which would also contain his living quarters, on the lakeshore property (now 536 Sheridan Road) across the street from Foundation Hall. When Alfred Lunt's letter finally arrived, it included a contract with conditions that Louis Bourgeois had difficulty accepting. The matter remained unresolved for several years.

Many Bahá'ís believed that the studio was constructed without permission, and they incorrectly assumed that the National Spiritual Assembly had paid for it. Furthermore, the classic design adopted for the front of the studio gave many

Studio of Louis Bourgeois, 536 Sheridan Road, Wilmette, across the street from the Temple

the impression that the building was grand and palatial. The building was actually quite modest in size and was constructed of inferior materials. Much of the wood framework, for example, came from the discarded concrete forms that had been used to construct Foundation Hall. The exterior stucco was unusually thin. The plasterboard for the inside walls was the type commonly used in temporary buildings at fairs and expositions. The large windows in front, which contributed significantly to the aura of grandeur, were designed so that Louis Bourgeois would have ample light for working on the architectural drawings.

To help settle the controversy, the National Spiritual Assembly issued a statement in August 1924 explaining that the studio was temporary, "involving no title to any portion of the land," and that it would remain there only until construction was completed or "until the permission of the National Spiritual Assembly is withdrawn." "This structure," the National Assembly clarified, "serves a very useful purpose in connection with the work of the architect, and by its erection the National Fund was saved the expense of providing the usual quarters for drafting, etc."[8]

The Second Long Wait

Inside his studio at 536 Sheridan Road Mr. Bourgeois holds several drawings. Another large one hangs from the top of the wall and continues in sections across the floor.

Over the next few years Louis Bourgeois hosted a number of visitors in the new studio, including the editor of the Scottish publication *John O'Groat Journal*. Recalling his visit, the editor wrote:

"I have no hesitation in saying that when completed this Temple will be one of the most beautiful pieces of architecture in the world. I had the privilege of an introduction to the architect. . . . We spent a considerable time with him in his beautiful studio overlooking the Lake, and he did me the honour of showing me the plans of the Temple, drawings which cost him years of toil, and they are far beyond anything I could have imagined in beauty and spiritual significance. M. Bourgeois, who is well advanced in years, is a genius and mystic—a gentleman of charming personality. In all that I had the pleasure of seeing in his studio I had a privilege that is given to few. My signature is in his personal book, which contains the names of some of the great ones of the earth!"[9]

Despite widespread interest in the Temple, the National Spiritual Assembly continued to find itself without money. Therefore, in December 1925 it devised a plan to "accumulate, in response to the request of Shoghi Effendi, a fund of $400,000.00 [within three years] to construct the first unit of the superstructure." The plan became known as the "Plan of Unified Action" and was based upon recommendations from convention delegates and local Bahá'í administrative institutions, or "Local Spiritual Assemblies," in the United States and Canada.* The National Assembly had also made a detailed study of all instructions Shoghi Effendi had sent since becoming Guardian. In addition to the monetary goals, the Plan of Unified Action had two other objectives—to "unify the efforts and enlarge the numbers of the Cause in North America" and to "penetrate the consciousness of the public with the spirit of Bahá'u'lláh."[10]

At the request of Shoghi Effendi, the Temple Fund had been consolidated in June 1924 into a single National Bahá'í Fund that included all the various funds received from earmarked contributions. Spending could now be allocated according to the priorities established by the National Spiritual Assembly. Thus the $486,000 budget for the Plan of Unified Action, in addition to allowing money for resuming the Temple's construction, provided for the operation of a national office, support of the teaching work, publication of a national news bulletin, subsidization of part of the publication costs of *Star of the West*, and maintenance of the Temple and grounds. "This Budget system is far superior to the method of irregular labeled contributions employed up to this time," the National Assembly noted. "It has never been possible to plan definite methods of service either in the teaching or Temple field more than a few weeks ahead. . . . [Only] by supporting the Budget as a whole can we hope to prepare for the larger responsibilities of the future, while increasing our capacity to serve every requirement of the Cause at the present time." The National Assembly calculated that if each of the fifteen hundred "loyal and active believers" contributed an average of $9 a month, the goal would be reached. Even though

---

*During the mid-1920s all local Bahá'í administrative institutions began to be called "Spiritual Assemblies." Hence the Chicago House of Spirituality became the "Spiritual Assembly of the Bahá'ís of Chicago."

the $400,000 allocation for the Temple was a portion of the National Fund budget, it was still referred to as the Temple Fund. Money for the Temple Fund would be accumulated from contributions "over and above the amount required to meet the fixed monthly and yearly charges itemized" in the National Fund budget.[11]

The heart of the Plan of Unified Action's "immensely extended" teaching activities was the creation of several teaching circuits. "Linking up every Baha'i group in the land," these circuits would provide for regular visits by qualified Bahá'ís who would help organize teaching efforts in each city. The National Assembly also called on each Local Spiritual Assembly to redouble their own efforts to teach, irrespective of the presence of the circuit teachers, and to make the significance of the Temple one of their "foremost subjects for public addresses." In this way the National Assembly hoped that "general interest and support for the Temple will also be directly secured."[12]

Shoghi Effendi wholeheartedly supported the concept of the Plan of Unified Action and sent a cable in January 1926: "Congratulate National Assembly on Plan. Noble in conception, sound in method, forceful in its appeal. Fully endorse it. Commend it to every declared believer, joyously pledging ninety-five dollars a month as my humble share."[13]

Four months after the announcement of the plan, in April 1926, the delegates at the annual convention sensed a new capacity for "effective action" aroused by the new plan, "action capable of conveying the Baha'i spirit into concrete effect." "The power manifest in this Convention," wrote the National Spiritual Assembly, "would seem to betoken a new era in the Cause as a whole. . . . The transition has been from negative loyalty to positive devotion; from the irresolution and gloom of sickness to the exhilaration and vigor of health. A certain period may still be required for the new spirit to penetrate to every atom of the body, but we may be assured that this spirit is both rapid in action and irresistible in effect."[14]

Yet the "period . . . required for the new spirit to penetrate" was somewhat longer than the Bahá'ís had hoped. The Temple Fund—the barometer for the progress of the entire plan—was not growing as quickly as anticipated. In October 1926 Shoghi Effendi wrote:

> the result has by no means exceeded our expectations, nay has considerably fallen below what I confidently expected it to achieve. I earnestly renew my plea and appeal to you . . . to realize, while there is yet time, the far-reaching possibilities with which the present situation is fraught. I am firmly convinced that this

Plan combines, embodies, and serves the two-fold purpose of the present-day Baha'i administration in the United States and Canada, namely the promotion of the vitally needed Teaching work, and the provision for the gradual completion of the Mashriqu'l-Adhkár, both wishes so near and dear to our beloved Master's heart.[15]

The amount of money in the Temple Fund was still relatively small by the end of the year. Only $51,039, which was $110,961 short of the first year's goal, had been contributed to the National Fund. Moreover, expenses had exceeded the National Assembly's total budget by $13,332. Instead of the anticipated first year's $133,000 in the Temple Fund, there was only $3,750. The National Spiritual Assembly, wishing to renew "its devotion to the success of the Temple building fund," pledged in June 1927 to deposit "as much as possible into that fund from the amount on hand."[16] But 1927 proved to be as disappointing as 1926: Only $5,566 was transferred to the Temple Fund.*

At the 1928 convention the chairman of the National Spiritual Assembly, Allen McDaniel, described a recent conversation with Shoghi Effendi in the Holy Land. "Shoghi Effendi . . . told him," reported Louise Waite, "that the believers in America had lost confidence in their N.S.A. . . . That the new N.S.A. must make a Covenant with the friends that from now on they would not exceed their budget and every penny over it received would be placed in the bank for the Temple Building Fund."[17] The statement was greeted by the delegates with great approval. A Canadian Bahá'í businessman in attendance, Siegfried (Fred) Schopflocher, announced that he would make a special contribution of $25,000. Inspired by his gift, the other delegates pledged an additional $15,000. The National Spiritual Assembly, elated by this show of support, voted at its 29 June meeting to transfer $25,000 to the Temple Fund account.

---

*The National Spiritual Assembly, in its Plan of Unified Action budget, allotted $2,745 per month for fixed expenditures (office operation, teaching expenses, Assembly meetings). This, plus an annual cost of $500 for the National Convention, amounted to $33,440 per year, or $100,320 for the three years of the Plan. Added to the $400,000 for Temple construction, the total is $14,000 more than the reported $486,000 three-year budget. The National Assembly had calculated, however, that it would earn approximately $16,000 in interest from the Temple-Fund savings account. Since very little was allocated to the account in 1926 and 1927, the interest was likewise negligible.

Capital expenditures accounted for a significant portion of the budget overrun. Although only two items of $1,550 were initially anticipated, eventually fourteen categories of expenditures, which totaled $29,228, were recorded. Budget and capital expenditures during the three years totaled $135,906—$34,036 in excess of the original budget.

The Second Long Wait

Contributions increased sharply. In July $10,000 more was deposited into the account, and in September another $5,000 was added. By the beginning of March 1929 the Temple Fund had a balance of $87,000. Even though the Plan of Unified Action officially ended at the close of 1928, its spirit continued to pervade the Bahá'í community. "Everywhere the building of the Temple seems uppermost in the minds of the believers," wrote one Bahá'í. "It would be a great stimulus if every Bahá'í might stand for a short time on Sheridan Drive beside the Temple grounds and watch the tens of thousands of automobiles pass from every part of the continent. He would then realize what a powerful asset for teaching the Cause a completed Temple will be."[18]

In early 1929 Siegfried Schopflocher's wife, Lorol, arrived in Haifa after an extended trip to India. As Shoghi Effendi greeted her, he handed her a cable from her husband. Although the following account may not be exact in every detail, since it was written by Lorol Schopflocher three decades after the events transpired, it conveys the spirit of what took place. The cable reportedly read:

> "Are you willing contribute $50,000 to Temple which may mean you do not get a new Cadillac this year?" I laughed out loud and Shoghi Effendi grinned as he said: "What do you think of this?" I laughed again and said "Why not $100,000?" I scribbled a cable on a table napkin and sent Fugeta, the Master's old Japanese servant, off to the telegraph office.... The reply came back "You win, love to Shoghi Effendi, love, Fred."[19]

On 16 March the National Spiritual Assembly voted to deposit $110,000 more in the Temple Fund. In recognition of Siegfried Schopflocher's generosity Shoghi Effendi designated him "the Chief Temple Builder."[20]

Most of the contributions during the Plan of Unified Action came from a few people making large gifts. For example, 80 percent of the funds received between 1 April and 31 July 1928 came from fifty-one contributors. Nevertheless, Bahá'ís were sending money at an unprecedented rate from 344 cities in forty-three states, and the $400,000 mark drew ever nearer.

One Bahá'í who encouraged many contributions before and during the years of the Plan of Unified Action was Victoria Bedikian. Rendered deaf while still a young girl, she decided to pursue a career in art. She later married an Armenian who owned an Oriental art shop in Montclair, New Jersey. 'Abdu'l-Bahá visited the shop on a number of occasions during His American travels in 1912 and encouraged her to devote her artistic abilities to furthering the aims of the Bahá'í Faith.

Victoria Bedikian never bore any children, but she loved all children, especially those suffering from physical disabilities. Inspired by a dream, she decided to purchase a barn, surrounded by nineteen acres of woodland, and transform it into an orphanage that she eventually named the "Garden of Friendship." The project grew rapidly, a small school was built, and by 1921 the orphanage had more than forty boys and girls. 'Abdu'l-Bahá wrote to her that among the Bahá'ís at that time "there is nobody more favored than thee, because thou art busy in the service of the orphans and in the education of the destitute, helpless children. Thou hast no desire but to please God. . . . May thou be a hundred thousand times applauded for this service thou art rendering!"[21]

The orphans were the first to call her "Auntie Victoria," an endearment by which she became known to Bahá'ís everywhere. Their love for her enkindled within her a desire to express her love for all Bahá'í children. Hence she decided to publish a small magazine, *Bahá'í World Fellowship,* and to foster the formation of Bahá'í children's groups, known as "Fellowship Gardens." By the mid-twenties there were several hundred of these groups, nearly half of them outside of the United States.[22]

Auntie Victoria wrote letters constantly to other Bahá'ís in which she encouraged them to contribute toward the construction of the Temple. The volume of her letters, adorned with her artwork, became considerable. It was later written that the only material belongings possessing any meaning for her were "a tiny typewriter and her art materials and addresses of Bahá'ís all over the world which she guarded with her life."[23]

Her motives were wholly pure, but her persistence offended some Bahá'ís. The apparent administrative autonomy of the gardens made some Bahá'í communities uneasy. After seeking guidance from Shoghi Effendi, Auntie Victoria transferred "the management and welfare of our Fellowship and the Gardens of 'Abdu'l-Baha" to the National Spiritual Assembly. Shoghi Effendi further counseled her:

"Concentrate on . . . [the Temple] and think of nothing else. Consult frequently the American National Assembly as to the best and most effective measures for the attainment of this end. Address your splendid appeals to Assemblies both east and west, near and afar, organized and unorganized, but not to individual believers. Yours is a glorious opportunity, an immense and arduous task, a most sacred obligation, a unique and inspiring privilege. Dedicate afresh your magnificent resources to the service of this most noble Cause."

The Second Long Wait

"AUNTIE" VICTORIA BEDIKIAN
whose magazines and artwork inspired children and adults worldwide to contribute money and a wide variety of gifts to the Temple Fund

In another letter he wrote:

> "Your steadfastness and ever-increasing zeal in promoting far and near the interests of the Bahá'í Temple greatly hearten me in my work. I wish you to persevere, never to relax a moment in your determination to fulfill the great and noble mission that has been entrusted to you and for which you are so highly qualified. Never feel disheartened at the slowness of the progress of the work, for eventually all these obstacles will one by one be removed, and the glorious Temple will rear its lofty pinnacles in the heart of the great American continent."[24]

Responding to Shoghi Effendi's counsel, Auntie Victoria began producing an even greater abundance of materials. During the next several years she sent more than one hundred issues of a bulletin she named *Temple Leaflets* to communities around the world. Each issue contained colored drawings, consisting at times of small roses, and at other times of elaborate designs. The bulletin also contained quotations from the writings of Bahá'u'lláh and 'Abdu'l-Bahá, and her own words of encouragement. For children she compiled another bulletin, *Lesson Leaflets*, which contained explanations of a variety of spiritual subjects. The editors of the *Baha'i News Letter* praised her efforts and added:

> Could we all see as clearly as Mrs. Bedikian how the Baha'i Temple in its very physical construction constitutes a perfect picture, in miniature, of the new civilization so many millions passionately seek and crave, how much shorter would be this period of transition and preparation among the believers of the West![25]

Perhaps Auntie Victoria's most remarkable publication was the *Mashriqu'l-Adhkár*, issued between 1926 and 1930. Some of the priceless legacies contained in its pages are the "World Temple Unity Letters" sent to Auntie Victoria from Bahá'ís around the world. Money and gifts often accompanied the letters, including "a little doyle [doily]" from Zuffenhausen, Germany, and a "lavender bag" from Manchester, England, to "buy a wee little cement for the Blessed Temple." One letter from an unemployed school teacher in Mandalay, Burma, said:

> "If I could teach, I would have sent you some amount out of my pay, but as it is not the case I shall sew some handkerchiefs and send them to you. My eldest sister, my little niece and others will help in this work. That is all we can do for the present, but we pray and hope that our Lord will help us along and show us the way to do some greater work."

N. R. Vakil, a Bahá'í from Surat, India, wrote: " 'I have sent to-day two pounds and five shillings. . . . Please credit the Temple money in the name of my child. . . . Unfortunately, the child departed a fortnight ago at the tender age of nine months, after a sudden illness. . . .'" In one of several letters sent to Auntie Victoria, Louise Waite described a meeting of the Shasta Daisy Garden she attended in Los Angeles. The thirty children at the gathering, she reported, were "all aflame with zeal to work for the great universal Temple, and but few of them are Bahá'ís."[26]

Auntie Victoria received so many gifts for the Temple Fund that she decided to establish a company that she named the Oriocci (from Orient and Occident) Institute. She asked Edward Struven, who became the caretaker at the Temple early in 1927, to handle the disposition of these items. But the plan was not successful, perhaps because the wares were too diverse: shawls, bedroom-slipper covers, table cloths, copper pencil boxes, tea-pot covers, paintings and other art work, doilies, sachet bags, doll houses, handkerchiefs, shoe trees, and novelty umbrellas. Despite Auntie Victoria's difficulty with her company, it was but one of her many valiant efforts for the Temple. Shoghi Effendi wrote to her, "The endeavours you make, the energies you expend will bear fruit in time, I assure you, and will live to adorn the annals of God's mighty Cause."[27]

One unique gift to the Temple Fund, although not sent to Victoria Bedikian, came from a member of European royalty, Queen Marie of Rumania. The gift was an exquisite pearl and diamond brooch, set in gold and silver, that the queen had given to Martha Root in gratitude for her visits. During one of five intercontinental trips, Martha Root traveled in the last week of January 1926 to Bucharest, where she immediately sent a copy of *Bahá'u'lláh and the New Era* to Queen Marie. The queen was so awed by the book that she stayed awake until 3:00 A.M. reading it. The following day she summoned Martha Root to her palace and told her, " 'I believe these Teachings are the solution for the world's problems today!' "[28]

Martha Root subsequently visited Queen Marie on seven occasions. During one meeting in early 1928, the queen said, " 'Always you are giving gifts to others, and I am going to give you a gift from me.' "[29] Upon Martha Root's simple dress she pinned the magnificent brooch. Later that week Martha Root sent the brooch to the United States, with the queen's permission, so that it could be sold at the annual convention for the Temple Fund.

In addition to the marked increase in contributions during the final year of the Plan of Unified Action, the unity of purpose demonstrated by the American Bahá'í community became evident in other ways. Communities in the United States and Canada, as well as around the world, began corresponding more frequently. The result was a stronger sense of kinship as these communities expressed their love for one another and shared ideas and mutual encouragement for fund raising and promulgating the Bahá'í teachings. The Kenosha, Wisconsin, Assembly urged, "It is very important that we all arise with greater love and zeal than ever and complete this TEMPLE at Wilmette. The entire world needs the TEMPLE now." "To neglect it further . . . ," warned Ida Finch of the Seattle Bahá'í community, "shows that we have not loved in the right way nor sacrificed in any adequate measure."[30]

As the plan entered its final months, the Bahá'ís of Montreal, Canada, made an appeal:

The uppermost thought to convey to you must be a REALISATION of what it means to commence building the next stage of the Temple. We, who are at a distance, do not realise what this means. But the believers in Wilmette and Chicago, and the architect in particular, have had to bear for EIGHT YEARS the ridicule with which they have been faced, for OUR FAILURE to continue the building operations. . . .

Do we realise that if Shogi [sic] Effendi were to say to the Oriental believers that he desired them to build our Temple, they would so sacrifice themselves they would raise the entire sum and more. Until we have been tried as to the depth of our belief and steadfastness, he will not do this.[31]

During the early and middle 1920s Shoghi Effendi did not permit Persian Bahá'ís to contribute to the Temple because the American Bahá'ís had failed to devote themselves wholeheartedly to the project.[32] Yet the American Bahá'í community had not forgotten the past sacrifices the Persian Bahá'ís had made for the Temple. When the Bahá'ís in Iran suffered oppression once again at the hands of their Muslim countrymen, the National Spiritual Assembly championed the Bahá'ís' religious freedom and addressed a lengthy appeal to the Muslim religious leaders. "The greatest gift of God to this enlightened age is the knowledge of the oneness of mankind," wrote the National Assembly. Noting that "religious teachings are the source of all human ideals, and the motive for all human action," they pleaded for "peace in the realm of religion" as a prerequisite for "peace among the nations." The Muslim clergymen were enjoined to foster "the ideal of fellowship and love" rather than to "justify separation and strife in the realm of belief."[33] It is impossible to know the Muslim response, but the appeal set a precedent for other appeals in the decades to follow.

There were several other notable accomplishments during the Plan of Unified Action, including major expansion in the operation of the Green Acre Bahá'í School in Eliot, Maine, and the establishment of a second school in Geyserville, California, during the summer of 1927.* That same year the National Spiritual Assembly prepared its Declaration of Trust, which made it

---

*Another accomplishment in 1927 was the incorporation of the National Spiritual Assembly. Shortly after incorporating, the National Assembly established a Temple Trusteeship that enabled the title to the Temple property to be transferred on 13 November 1928 from the Bahai Temple Unity to the Temple Trustees. For all practical purposes the transfer terminated the existence of the Bahai Temple Unity, but its charter was legally maintained. The charter's

the first national Bahá'í institution to codify the principles governing Bahá'í administration. The Declaration of Trust, wrote Shoghi Effendi in 1927, is " 'a worthy and faithful exposition of the constitutional basis of Bahá'í Communities in every land. . . . This document, when correlated and combined with the set of by-laws . . . will serve as a pattern to every National Bahá'í Assembly. . . .' "[34]

Teaching activity during the plan also increased as many Bahá'ís, following Martha Root's example, traveled both within and beyond the borders of Canada and the United States. One effective teaching effort was launched in 1926 when the National Spiritual Assembly organized the World Unity Conferences. The conferences were held in different large cities each month and coincided with the meetings of the National Spiritual Assembly. Their purpose was to create " 'a deeper understanding and stronger spirit of cooperation between peoples' " irrespective of their " 'political, economic and religious affiliations.' "[35] Although the results were at first disappointing, soon the conferences attracted prominent scientists, educators, statesmen, and religious leaders as attendees and sometimes participants.

As significant as the World Unity Conferences were, the "most vigorous and effective assertion of the Bahá'í teachings made in North America" during the 1920s was the organization of Race Amity Conventions. 'Abdu'l-Bahá had encouraged conventions to promote interracial fellowship, for He felt, according to Horace Holley, that the race problem was "the most serious menace to American civilization . . . unless solved by the power of true religion." The first Race Amity Convention was held in Washington, D.C., in May 1921, and conventions were held in subsequent years in Springfield, Massachusetts; New York; Philadelphia; and other cities. Each convention was well planned and advertised, bringing together thousands of blacks and whites for "the removal of friction between the races."[36]

Although the Bahá'í teachings were also promoted at occasional public

---

maintenance proved vital years later when, following the death of an early Bahá'í, it was discovered that her will was made in favor of the Bahai Temple Unity.

The existence of the Temple Trustees meant that the National Spiritual Assembly did not make decisions directly on Temple matters. In order to consult on the Temple project, the National Spiritual Assembly would adjourn its meetings and reconvene as the "Temple Trustees for the Benefit of the National Spiritual Assembly of the Bahá'ís of the United States and Canada." The Trustees kept separate minutes and annually elected their own officers, although the officer roster was usually identical with that of the National Assembly. Since major decisions of the Trustees were approved by the National Spiritual Assembly, and since only the National Assembly communicated with Shoghi Effendi, there has been no attempt in this book to distinguish between the two agencies lest such a distinction prove confusing.

meetings and Bahá'í Holy Day observances in Foundation Hall, the hall was normally closed due to the interior's dismal appearance. In early 1928 the National Spiritual Assembly made plans to spend $10,000 for further improvement of the interior. Shoghi Effendi was very anxious for the improvements to occur, not only because he wanted the building suitable for public meetings, but also because he felt it would help rekindle " 'heroic, sustained and self-sacrificing' " efforts to resume construction.[37] The work was completed in time for the 1928 annual convention, which Shoghi Effendi called the "Inauguration Ceremony" of the hall. To mark the occasion he sent a gift of "exquisite tokens of 'Abdu'l-Bahá—three rugs which for some years have been laid in the Holy Tomb on Mount Carmel."[38]

The convention opened on Thursday evening, 26 April, in Foundation Hall, marking the first convention held in the hall. As the delegates entered the circular, inner hall, they were greeted by banks of green palms and flowering plants. The three Persian carpets, bathed in soft light, lined the walls, and baskets filled with roses flanked the conference table at the front. Louise Waite remembered, "One felt upon entering it that its Holy atmosphere and beauty must effect [sic] and inspire all who attended this great Convention."[39]

After several tablets and prayers of Bahá'u'lláh were read and chanted, Corinne True stepped forward. During Mrs. True's pilgrimage in 1928 'Abdu'l-Bahá's sister, Bahíyyih Khánum, had given her a large package of tea and a bottle of attar of rose to be used at the inauguration ceremony. Mrs. True conveyed the love of Bahíyyih Khánum to the assembled Bahá'ís and then personally served each a cup of the special tea. Parvene Bagdadi, the young daughter of Dr. Zia Bagdadi, anointed each delegate with the attar of rose, the rare fragrance of which soon filled the huge room. "Words cannot describe the spiritual radiance which illumined the faces of all," Louise Waite observed, "nor of the happiness that was manifested as old friends met once more in this Holy Spot."[40]

The inauguration ceremony was particularly significant to the Bahá'ís in 1928 because of an event on the other side of the world that saddened them. Near the time that Foundation Hall was opened to the public, the Ashkhabad Temple was expropriated by the Soviet government in enforcement of a law designed to assume control of all religious edifices. It was the building of the Ashkhabad Temple that had given the early Chicago Bahá'ís the idea for building a Temple of their own. "For the time being it would seem the torch of the Cause must be held aloft here," the Spiritual Assembly of Chicago wrote, "until in the wisdom of God it shall blaze anew in the heart of Asia!"[41]

The Second Long Wait

During the first quarter of 1929 Shoghi Effendi expressed his concern that little time remained in which to raise the remaining funds for the superstructure. " 'He, as well as some of the other friends who are motivated by a great force of faith,' " a letter from the Holy Land said, " 'believe firmly that God's miracles will not fail to perform their wonders and at the very eleventh hour the full sum will be collected.' "[42]

On 25 October 1929 the Bahá'ís might have found that miracle as they read these words penned by Shoghi Effendi:

> Moved by an impulse that I could not resist, I have felt impelled to forego what may be regarded as the most valuable and sacred possession in the Holy Land for the furthering of that noble enterprise which you have set your hearts to achieve. With the hearty concurrence of our dear Bahá'í brother, Ziaoulláh Asgarzadeh, who years ago donated it to the Most Holy Shrine, this precious ornament of the Tomb of Bahá'u'lláh has been already shipped to your shores, with our fondest hope that the proceeds from its sale may at once ennoble and reinforce the unnumbered offerings of the American believers already accumulated. . . .[43]

The "precious ornament" that Shoghi Effendi donated to the Temple Fund was a magnificent silk carpet. Commonly called a palace carpet, it had been commissioned by the emir of Bukhara and was considered "one of the most exquisite pieces ever woven in Persia." The weaver had lived in the Khurasan province of Persia and had been renowned as "the most expert weaver in that country."[44] Into the carpet he wove a pattern that resembled a rose garden: "Beautifully sustained floral motives in crimsons and browns occupy the center on a field of rich ivory. The fine and characteristic border is of dark and very rich coloring, a fine dark crimson being predominant, enriched with a beautiful pale blue."[45]

Because of the Bolshevik Revolution the carpet was never delivered to the emir. Shortly after the end of the First World War, Ziaoulláh Asgarzadeh purchased the carpet from a group of merchants in Persia and undertook an arduous journey to present the carpet to 'Abdu'l-Bahá:

> After many weary weeks the pilgrim finally reached Haifa and carried the carpet to the Pilgrim House on Mt. Carmel, adjacent to the Tomb of the Báb, where it was spread on the floor. When 'Abdu'l-Bahá came to the house He immediately inquired of the caretaker whose carpet that was, and upon being told, He said

that so valuable a work of art should not be on the floor where it might become soiled. . . . The pilgrim then told 'Abdu'l-Bahá that the carpet had been brought for Him and He replied that so beautiful a gift should be placed in the Shrine of Bahá'u'lláh, and that He would place it there Himself.

A few days later 'Abdu'l-Bahá, accompanied by His visitors and a few local Bahá'ís, rode the train from Haifa to Akka. There 'Abdu'l-Bahá bade the older Bahá'ís to complete the short journey to the Shrine of Bahá'u'lláh in a carriage He had arranged for them, "while He, Himself rode the white donkey and the younger friends walked." During the trip Ziaoulláh Asgarzadeh offered some chocolate to 'Abdu'l-Bahá, which He shared with the others. They then began to sing. "I never felt so happy in my life as then when singing in the presence of the Master," wrote Mr. Asgarzadeh, "and I am sure all the others felt the same way. After we reached Bahjí we had dinner and then 'Abdu'l-Bahá spread the carpet in the Holy Shrine, and thus my hope was realized."[46]

The carpet remained in the Shrine until Shoghi Effendi had it shipped to the United States in 1929. There he hoped it would be purchased by a Bahá'í. "Its value," said a circular describing the carpet, "has been established at the sum of $20,000, at which figure offers will be considered . . . but no offer from a non-Bahá'í will be accepted until those interested among the believers have been given full opportunity to acquire the rug for the Cause."[47]

Shoghi Effendi's hope was diminished by the stock-market crash in New York during the latter half of October. Not only was it difficult to find a buyer for the carpet, but suddenly the $85,000 still needed had to be acquired in the midst of an economic crisis unparalleled in the history of the nation, and growing worse daily. The Bahá'ís, however, heeded Shoghi Effendi's appeals. The level of contributions, rather than diminishing, increased; the amounts were small, but the number of Bahá'ís contributing rose dramatically. By January 1930 the sum needed had shrunk to $44,000, and by February only $12,000 was still required. At last a headline on page one of the *Baha'i News Letter,* March 1930, proclaimed: "Temple Construction Fund Completed: Raising of Required Sum of $400,000 Meets Conditions Laid Down by Shoghi Effendi in 1925 for Resumption of Temple Construction."[48]

For the 1930 annual convention, held the following month, the National Spiritual Assembly arranged a victory ceremony. On top of a three-foot-high platform, extending from the speaker's table toward the center of Foundation Hall, lay the beautiful carpet. To the Bahá'ís gathered in Wilmette, Shoghi Effendi cabled:

Delegates and visitors at the annual Bahá'í convention, Foundation Hall, 25–27 April 1930. The silk rug on the platform was taken from the Shrine of Bahá'u'lláh and given to the Temple by Shoghi Effendi. Earlier he had given the carpets hanging on the wall.

"Convey assembled delegates expression profound gratitude, heartfelt congratulations their heroic achievement. May speedy construction entire edifice usher in era unprecedented triumphs beloved Faith as promised by 'Abdu'l-Bahá.

"America's sustained, glorious sacrifice will assuredly endow rising edifice with such spiritual potencies as shall excite wonder, admiration all peoples. Befittingly inaugurate resumption Temple construction. Consecrated carpet need neither be sold nor returned. Dedicated as permanent ornament first Mashriqu'l-Adhkár of the West."[49]

The carpet would become a lasting reminder to the Bahá'ís that their perseverence would empower them to succeed. Meeting the financial goal of the Plan of Unified Action now enabled them to turn their thoughts toward the lofty dome—a dome that would bring their dream closer to long-awaited fulfillment.

Chapter Fourteen
SKYWARD

ALTHOUGH preliminary structural and engineering plans had been prepared by Major Burt in 1921 as a condition for Wilmette's issuance of a construction permit, these plans were far from adequate, and lack of funds during the 1920s had prevented their completion. When funds were finally available, the Bahá'ís had lost the creative genius of Major Burt, who had died in July 1928. Several Bahá'í architects and engineers donated a great deal of time, particularly in mid-1929, to determine the most practical way of constructing the Temple.[1]

One of the difficulties that caused concern was that certain building methods and materials suitable for the realization of the unusual design still needed to be perfected. Allen McDaniel, an engineer and member of the Temple Advisory Board and of the National Spiritual Assembly since 1925, told the delegates at the 1929 convention about a conversation that had taken place shortly after Foundation Hall was completed:

> "I remember talking this matter over quite in full one day . . . with the late Major Burt . . . and Major Burt said at that time, 'Mr. McDaniel, this is a remarkable problem. . . . [It] is fortunate that you are unable to proceed with the construction of this Temple at this time, because I have a feeling that as the years roll by you will find that the construction of this Temple is a matter of growth. It is a matter of growth of our knowledge of construction, our knowledge of materials, which is rapidly developing.' "

What was impractical ten years before, continued Allen McDaniel, was now possible because of advances made with concrete. Consultation with several experts in the federal government, the Portland Cement Association, and the Concrete Institute confirmed a recommendation made by Major Burt in 1921 that concrete would be a viable building material. In March 1930 the National Spiritual Assembly negotiated with Allen McDaniel's company, The Research

ALLEN McDANIEL
a member of the National Spiritual Assembly of the Bahá'ís of the United States and Canada for twenty-one years and its chairperson from 1926 to 1934. He also served as project engineer while the Temple's superstructure was being constructed and its outside ornamentation installed.

Service of Washington, D.C., "to complete the necessary structural and engineering plans, to prepare specifications leading to the awarding of contracts, to supervise the construction and see to it that work is properly performed in the most economical and efficient manner."2

The Bahá'ís had always assumed that the $400,000 raised during the Plan of Unified Action would be used to construct only the first story of the building, including the ornamentation. Yet building the Temple in sections, as was often done by religious organizations, would require constructing "a temporary roof at considerable expense." "This roof structure," Allen McDaniel wrote, "would be removed and scrapped when further funds became available to build the second story. And so on until the dome was erected to crown the entire building." Mr. McDaniel and his partner, Dr. Frederick Newell, conceived instead a radical, "epoch-making" technique for building the entire structural-steel and reinforced-concrete superstructure all at one time. "Such a building would have the form and proportions of the finished Temple, would be entirely enclosed, and would constitute the form to which the surface ornamentation—comprising the architectural design—would be subsequently applied."3

The plan to erect the entire superstructure, thus avoiding the cost of the temporary roofs, was approved. By early August 1930 all plans and specifications, consisting of hundreds of blueprints, were complete. Bids were requested from a select group of widely known construction firms, and nine bids were received, ranging in amounts from $345,000 to $437,000. The National Spiritual Assembly signed a contract with the lowest bidder, the George A. Fuller Company, on 27 August 1930.[4]

The controversy that had surrounded Louis Bourgeois was forgotten. At the convention in April 1930 he was called to the podium, where he "received a veritable storm of applause which completely overcame him." Although his health had been failing for several months, he refused to stop his work on the Temple. In late July the National Spiritual Assembly telegrammed several Bahá'í communities: "Mr. Bourgeois precariously ill. National Assembly suggest[s] immediate special meeting friends for prayers for recovery."[5] For a time his condition improved. But on Wednesday, 20 August 1930, at the age of seventy-four, Louis Bourgeois died.

The next day an article appeared in the *New York Times* that announced: "Louis J. Bourgeois, Architect, Dead: Designer of Bahá'í Temple Is Stricken as Fondest Hope Nears Fulfillment":

> Chicago, Aug. 20 (AP).—Louis Jean Bourgeois, architect and sculptor, died last night when about to have his fondest dream fulfilled. He had hoped to live long enough to see work begun next month on the Bahá'í Temple he started many years ago.[6]

The funeral service, held the following day, was conducted by Albert Windust. Several months later, on 19 December, there would be memorial services held in Foundation Hall and in other major Bahá'í centers throughout North America.

Shortly after Louis Bourgeois' death, in early September 1930, the Fuller Company began erecting a giant crane that would lift the steel columns onto the foundation. "Steelworkers, carpenters, masons, sheet-metal workers, plumbers, [and] electricians" were among the scores of workers assembled. Allen McDaniel, in his book about the building of the Temple, was impressed by the fact that "Jew and Gentile, Protestant and Catholic, Occidental and Oriental; men of various races, religions and regions worked together as a harmonious family in a common cause."[7]

Addressing the workmen on the first day, Mr. McDaniel described the unique nature of the project and tried to impart Louis Bourgeois' vision. In

Skyward

View of Foundation Hall showing the crane that would lift the steel beams of the Temple superstructure into place, 8 October 1930

addition, each man was given a colored picture of the design. The workers then went about their tasks, according to Mr. McDaniel, in "a spirit of co-operation and pride":

> Many of the workmen spoke of having had their Temple pictures framed and hung on the walls of their homes. No accidents occurred on the job, and even the structural erectors . . . carried on their hazardous operations uneventfully, under what became known on the job as "The Spell of the Temple."

Later Allen McDaniel's partner, Dr. Newell, reported to the National Spiritual Assembly:

Skyward

Steel beams in place for the main level of the Temple, 23 October 1930. In the foreground are concrete forms for the main-level arches.

A most notable feature is the smoothness and quietness of the operations, resulting from the working out of carefully considered plans matured during the past few years. It is comparable to the flowering of the century plant, apparently dormant, but which almost over night puts out beautiful blossoms.

Like Solomon's Temple, there is no . . . confusion. Every piece of steel has fitted exactly into place. . . .[8]

But it was not long before trouble slowed the work of the diligent crew: The contractor had difficulty with accurate construction of the massive wood formworks for the curved arches and pylons. It was decided that they needed to lay a "templet, or full-size pattern" over the top of the foundation "to determine

The concrete work nearing completion at the main level, 14 November 1930. Being installed are steel beams for the gallery and clerestory, and the first steel sections of the dome.

accurately the location of the corner pylons and the true size and curvature of the first-story arches."⁹ The templet was then moved to a level area on the ground, where the formwork arches could be built up from it. Some inaccuracies in the formworks appeared, nevertheless, resulting in slight variations in the dimensions of the nine sides of the Temple. Although not noticeable to the eye, the variations created minor problems when the ornamentation was applied years later.

Enough of the steel framework was erected within the first two weeks of construction that it was necessary to raise the crane to the gallery level. Two weeks later it was raised to the dome level. Once the steel was in place at each of the levels, the wood formworks were attached and tons of concrete poured inside them. The "exceptional nature of the work" attracted many curious

Skyward

The completed steelwork for the dome, 30 December 1930. Concrete forms for the gallery are being installed. Concrete work at the main level has been completed.

onlookers each day. As the building arose and as the wooden formworks were stripped away to reveal the hardened concrete, the visitors were awed by the curved "lines and warped surfaces . . . in every part of the structure" and marveled at the arches that were "horizontal as well as vertical."[10]

The unusually mild weather throughout the fall and early winter of 1930–31 allowed the project to move forward smoothly and significantly ahead of schedule. Then disaster struck. On the morning of 15 January 1931, while the Temple watchman was reportedly asleep, the Chicago area was buffeted by high winds. Even though the weather had turned much colder, concrete had been poured into formworks for portions of the upper part of the gallery and the floor of the clerestory. Strange-looking stoves called "salamanders," used to keep the concrete from freezing, were sitting around the edge of a seventy-two-foot-wide wooden platform, suspended from the dome and adjacent to the clerestory floor.¹¹ Scattered about the platform were several pieces of equipment and wooden crates containing most of the aluminum and glass for the watershed to be erected inside the dome's steel framework. Suddenly smoke could be seen pouring out of the southwest side of the building. Huge tarpaulins covering the drying concrete had blown over the salamanders and caught fire. Within a few minutes the entire upper portion of the Temple was a blazing inferno, fed by the scaffolding and wooden forms for the concrete. The *Chicago Evening American* reported that

> Fire apparatus from Wilmette and Evanston responded. Frozen mains and hydrants cut the pressure of the water so that firemen were powerless to reach the full height of the temple and the flames blazed furiously.
> Among those who witnessed the fire were Mrs. Alice DeLongpre Bourgeois, widow of the architect. . . .
> Mrs. Bourgeois watched the conflagration from a window in her studio home across the street from the temple. She was visibly affected by the fire which threatened to ruin the climax of her husband's lengthy career. . . .¹²

The Chicago Tribune reported that thousands of people gathered to watch the firemen contend with the fire. Two men, the Temple watchman and one of the firemen, received serious injuries during the mishap. A growing area pride in the building was revealed by an Evanston newspaper account:

> Fighting against a sheeting of *slippery* ice and at the expense of a broken leg and a wrenched back or two, Evanston firemen joined in the battle against the blaze which recently damaged the Baha'i temple in Wilmette. When the Wilmette council offered to pay the Evanston firemen they refused. "The pleasure," replied the gallant chief speaking through the city clerk, "was all ours."¹³

The Bahá'í world reeled under the shock as cablegrams carried the news across the nation and beyond to distant lands. The damage, however, proved to be relatively minor. In addition to lost glass and equipment, it was necessary to replace the clerestory floor and repair other concrete sections. Neither the structural steelwork nor the dome sustained any damage.

Insurance covered the loss, which totaled $50,000. In fact, the fluctuating value of the dollar allowed the contractor to realize some savings, part of which were returned to the National Spiritual Assembly, as specified in the contract.

Skyward

Chicago Evening American *newspaper photograph of the fire at the Temple during the early morning hours of 15 January 1931. The fire began when tarpaulins covering the fresh concrete were ignited by small stoves that kept the concrete from freezing.*

Skyward

The main level of the Temple following the fire on 15 January 1931. Much of the debris, including aluminum and glass for the dome, had fallen nearly one hundred feet from the clerestory.

This, coupled with other money-saving measures used during construction, allowed the Bahá'ís to save approximately $30,000 and to accomplish considerable ventilation and electrical work not originally contracted for. As a result of the fire, the National Spiritual Assembly discovered that there was no insurance coverage on Foundation Hall. "It seems almost miraculous," wrote Allen McDaniel, "that not even one drop of water entered the Temple Foundation Hall, in spite of the fact that tons of water were poured on the building for several hours during the morning of the fire."[14]

Another outcome of the fire was a new surge of publicity for the Bahá'í Faith, sparked in part by the wide distribution in daily newspapers of photographs and stories of the blaze. Several Chicago newspapers featured stories, often on the front page, of the fire and the history of the Faith; and articles continued to be printed for several days. One Bahá'í noticed that

> Everyone asks with the greatest concern and friendliness regarding the outcome of the fire and they express themselves as feeling relieved when they learn that the damage is slight and the progress will not be definitely hindered. Comments in the public press have been most sympathetic . . . so that one cannot help but feel that this [fire] brought with it an outburst of sympathy that should be most heartening to the friends of the Cause everywhere.
>
> The meetings at the Temple foundation hall . . . are being well attended, the audiences of mostly strangers, generally numbering between one hundred fifty to two hundred people every Sunday, many of whom have signified their intention to join study classes. . . .[15]

Because weather conditions soon became favorable and the workers remained in high spirits, the fire did not significantly affect the construction schedule. Within a few weeks the workers poured concrete for the clerestory and completed assembling the nearly one hundred thousand pieces of steel and aluminum for the dome framework and watershed. More than nineteen thousand square feet of glass were then installed throughout the building.

Three weeks after the fire, on 3 February 1931, Corinne True once again set out for the Holy Land aboard the steamship *Empress of France*. Although nearly seventy years old and no longer directly involved in the administrative affairs of constructing the Temple, her enthusiasm and support for the project had never waned. In 1929 she built a home in Wilmette, five blocks from the Temple. When construction reached the clerestory level, she could see the building from her bedroom window. Her home became a mecca for Bahá'í travelers, and she is still warmly remembered by those who experienced her gentle and kind nature, and her warm and loving hospitality. She had a unique quality, eulogized one Bahá'í, of "continuously doing little things at a telling moment which made the act live forever in the heart of the recipient."[16]

Corinne True took several photographs with her to Haifa so that Shoghi Effendi could see the progress of the construction work. "The Temple was the subject of much conversation and its unusually quick progress praised . . . ," she recorded in her notes of the trip. "The Guardian expressed deep regret that Mr. Bourgeois could not have lived to have seen this work done."[17]

One of Corinne True's greatest joys in traveling to Haifa was renewing her

The Temple's superstructure nearing completion, 2 March 1931. All fire damage had been repaired.

friendship with Bahá'u'lláh's daughter Bahíyyih Khánum, the Greatest Holy Leaf. During the 1920s Bahíyyih Khánum became the most important woman in the annals of the Bahá'í Faith. It was she to whom 'Abdu'l-Bahá had entrusted His Will and Testament. It was she who announced to the Bahá'í world that 'Abdu'l-Bahá had appointed Shoghi Effendi as Guardian of the Bahá'í Cause. It was she who became a fortress of strength and support for young Shoghi Effendi during the early years of his Guardianship. In spring 1922, when Shoghi Effendi became ill and nearly collapsed because of the continuing emotional strain of 'Abdu'l-Bahá's death, it was she who served as the head of the worldwide Bahá'í community until his return from a rest in Switzerland.

During the final years of Bahíyyih Khánum's life, her greatest hope and "fondest desire" was to see the work on the Temple pushed forward vigorously.

The completed superstructure of the Bahá'í Temple, 28 April 1931. More than nineteen thousand square feet of glass had been installed in the building.

"The Greatest Holy Leaf, now in the evening of her life," wrote Shoghi Effendi to the American Bahá'ís in 1929, "with deepening shadows caused by failing eye-sight and declining strength swiftly gathering about her, . . . [yearns] to hear as the one remaining solace in her swiftly ebbing life the news of the resumption of work on an Edifice, the glories of which she has, from the lips of 'Abdu'l-Bahá, Himself, learned to admire."[18] Thus the Temple was the primary focus of conversation between Corinne True and Bahíyyih Khánum as they once more spent many peaceful hours together. When it was time to leave, Corinne True felt an even greater sadness than on her other pilgrimages, for she suspected that she would never again have the privilege of being in the presence of the Greatest Holy Leaf.

Skyward

The dedication of the completed superstructure, 1 May 1931. The circular pattern on the floor was a glass skylight that provided light for Foundation Hall. In the early 1940s the skylight was removed.

By 27 April 1931 the Temple superstructure was essentially complete, " 'strikingly impressive in its position and in its broader outlines,' " reported The Research Service, " 'drawing favorable remarks from thousands of individuals who pass it daily.' " " 'In these broad outlines,' " the report continued, are exemplified " 'the ideals which inspired the men and women who strived for its erection.' "[19]

Four days later, on 1 May, the twenty-third annual convention opened in Foundation Hall. It was a wondrous and emotional moment for the Bahá'ís as they reached the Temple grounds and beheld for the first time the mammoth superstructure. "To separate the spirit of the convention from the atmosphere of the Temple is impossible," remarked one Bahá'í. "Could anyone look at it for the first time without a sense of its meaning, without a spiritual uplift?" Shortly after the convention began a cablegram from Shoghi Effendi was read:

> "The Greatest Holy Leaf joins me in requesting delegates assembled under Mashriqu'l-Adhkár's sacred dome convey all American believers expression our heartfelt congratulations, boundless joy, profound gratitude practical completion superstructure glorious edifice. Fervently appeal all associated this holy enterprise, consummate their achievement by upholding whatever manner national representatives may deem necessary for provision exterior ornamentation. Inestimable blessing shall crown America's sustained, self-sacrificing endeavor."[20]

During the mid-afternoon of 1 May the Bahá'ís gathered in the bare upstairs auditorium to dedicate "this universal Temple to prayer and the praise of God." Appointed readers spoke from halfway up the ungainly stairs that led to the gallery. As "hearts overflowed with joy and gratitude," the immense auditorium reverberated with the words of Bahá'u'lláh, the Báb, and 'Abdu'l-Bahá. It was exactly nineteen years to the day when 'Abdu'l-Bahá had placed the dedication stone in the hole dug by representatives from many countries. "Thus for the first time in history," wrote one Bahá'í, "the praises of God dawned from a universal house of worship in America, this Temple where all religions blend into one religion, where all races are one race, where all creeds and prejudices are destined to vanish."[21]

But the Temple was far from complete. Even its skyward climb would not be over until the nine majestic ornamental ribs towered above the new dome. The day the building would stand finished seemed almost as remote as it had twenty-eight years earlier. Many of the Bahá'ís attending the dedication must have wondered about the new difficulties they would surely encounter in the years or maybe even decades ahead.

Chapter Fifteen

THE MASTER CRAFTSMAN

On 31 May 1931, four weeks after the convention and the dedication of the superstructure of the Temple, Shoghi Effendi again urged the Bahá'ís to resume construction as quickly as possible. " 'When the structure shall be completed,' " he declared, " 'a new era will be inaugurated in the history of the Cause' " in the United States. Inspired by Shoghi Effendi's appeals and by what was sensed as a "new spirit among the believers" resulting from the completion of the superstructure, the National Spiritual Assembly, in June 1931, launched a second Plan of Unified Action.¹ The primary objective of the plan was to amass $425,000 over a three-year period to provide for the ornamentation of the Temple's exterior. The National Assembly intended to issue contracts for various phases of the work as funds became available. They also requested every Bahá'í community to devote all Nineteen Day Feasts* during the three years "to the subject of the Temple" and "to make this collective effort the central point" of Bahá'í activity.²

Three months later, in an editorial in *Bahá'í News*, the National Spiritual Assembly again reminded the Bahá'ís of Shoghi Effendi's desire to see the work on the ornamentation accomplished as quickly as possible; only when the Temple was fully completed, the Assembly reiterated, would its real influence be realized. "Nothing short of continued self-sacrifice can achieve this end. . . . [The] present financial depression should be regarded both as a *challenge* and *opportunity to prove the reality and potency of our faith.*"³

In the same editorial the National Spiritual Assembly praised the sixteen hundred Western Bahá'ís for their sacrifices during the final days of the first

---

*The Nineteen Day Feast is a gathering held by each local Bahá'í community at the beginning of each nineteen-day Bahá'í month. The Feast consists of a devotional program, discussion of matters affecting the entire community, and fellowship.

Plan of Unified Action. The Temple, "an enterprise which had languished for nearly ten years...," the National Assembly wrote, "suddenly arises as a phoenix from the ashes of apparent defeat...." What had caused "these moths of weakness and inaction" to become "powerful, soaring, achieving falcons"? the Assembly asked, referring to the Bahá'ís themselves. How had a group that had lacked audaciousness been transformed into one that was bold and self-assured? *"Unity* of *purpose,"* it claimed, *"unity* of *action;* the *stirring* to *sacrifice;* the *consciousness* of *Faith* in our *Guardian's assurances,* and the *increased power* of *devotion* and *prayer."* Yet the National Assembly warned the Bahá'ís to resist being satisfied with this partial achievement. "Shall we," it asked, "permit ourselves gradually to relax into a somnolent state ever again?"[4]

The depression continued to affect, directly or indirectly, nearly all Bahá'ís. Many Local Spiritual Assemblies found themselves providing relief not only for destitute Bahá'ís but for others in their communities as well. Contributions were so meager that the National Spiritual Assembly was not able to establish the new construction fund for the ornamentation or to meet general operating expenses. On 10 October 1931, in an "unprecedented action," the National Spiritual Assembly telegraphed every Local Spiritual Assembly in the United States and Canada: " 'Dire emergency. National Fund requires immediate contributions, notify all believers.' "[5]

Five days later the National Assembly told the Bahá'ís that it was not only in need of operating capital but was faced with "the fact that $10,000 is immediately needed to safeguard the Temple structure during the coming winter. *What we want to impress upon every loyal believer is that the Temple Trustees have been forced to place contracts for heating installation... without having that amount in the treasury....*"[6]

Although the funds necessary to meet the contractual obligations were soon gathered, a building fund had still not been started by the following February. The National Spiritual Assembly continued trying to inspire the Bahá'ís through frequent reports and appeals. Shoghi Effendi also sought to stimulate the Bahá'ís and attempted to set an example of regular giving by pledging a contribution of ninety-five dollars each month through the duration of the new Plan of Unified Action. He continued to write letters and, at times, chastised the Bahá'ís for their inaction. In March, for example, he wrote, "I grieve, beyond words, to learn of the scanty response of the friends.... I am acutely conscious of the unprecedented character of the depression under which you labor. I am fully aware of the sacrifices you have already made, and realize

The Master Craftsman

the urgent need of allaying the burden which weighs so heavily on some of the poor and distressed believers. But I realize also the uniqueness of the opportunity which it is our privilege to seize and utilize."7

In other letters he tenderly encouraged the Bahá'ís. On 21 March 1932, in a lengthy letter that provided insight into a variety of spiritual subjects, Shoghi Effendi closed by addressing the "pressing claims" of the Temple:

> my voice is once more reinforced by the passionate, and perhaps, the last, entreaty, of the Greatest Holy Leaf, whose spirit, now hovering on the edge of the Great Beyond, longs to carry on its flight to the Abhá Kingdom, and into the presence of a Divine, an almighty Father, an assurance of the joyous consummation of an enterprise, the progress of which has so greatly brightened the closing days of her earthly life.

In the letter's last paragraph Shoghi Effendi made reference to the enormous Century of Progress Exposition being built at that time along three miles of Lake Michigan's shoreline to celebrate Chicago's one hundredth birthday in 1933. He expressed to the Bahá'ís the hope that the "multitudes" of people who would come to Chicago to see the fair could, "as a result of your sustained spirit of self-sacrifice, be privileged to gaze on the arrayed splendor of . . . [the Temple's] dome—a dome that shall stand as a flaming beacon and a symbol of hope amidst the gloom of a despairing world."8

Shoghi Effendi's desire to finish the dome by spring 1933 sparked renewed interest among the Bahá'ís and inspired an outpouring of funds from the fifty-five delegates and one hundred visiting Bahá'ís gathered at the 1932 convention. An Evanston newspaper reported that almost $30,000 was contributed as Bahá'ís "removed the jewels from ears, necks, wrists and fingers. . . ."9 One necklace was reportedly worth several thousand dollars. It was also noted that Dr. Zia Bagdadi contributed a Persian coin that had been given him by 'Abdu'l-Bahá.

Shortly before the convention the National Spiritual Assembly had received a report on anticipated costs and construction time for the dome: It would take six months to prepare the molds, at a cost of $30,000, and another six months and $120,000 to cast and erect the ornamental panels. Even though the National Spiritual Assembly had only $10,000 available for construction (not the $30,000 reported in the newspapers), it decided in June to begin the ornamentation of the Temple dome immediately. "Otherwise the time required on construction would make it impossible to complete the dome by the date, June 1, 1933, fixed by the Guardian."[10]

That decision resulted in the signing of a contract on 6 June 1932 with plaster and concrete specialist John Joseph Earley, from the Washington, D.C., area. The choice of concrete for the ornamentation was made after several materials, including limestone, granite, terra cotta, sandstone, tile, brick, cast iron, aluminum, and bronze, had been evaluated during the 1920s. Even marble, which would have required decades to carve, had been considered.[11]

The use of concrete had at first been discouraged. H. Van Buren Magonigle, the architect who addressed the 1920 Bahai Temple Unity convention, strongly disapproved of concrete and told the delegates:

> I think a re-enforced concrete building pure and simple is the most repellant object imaginable. . . . Re-enforced concrete does not weather at all, it merely gets dirty, and it has no beauty of surface, it has no translucence of surface, and it is an exceptionally ugly color. It is almost impossible to get anything but an ugly color, and if it is painted it looks worse than it did before.[12]

Yet according to John Earley's biographer Frederick Cron, Mr. Earley recognized that "concrete also had a beauty of its own."[13] By removing the outside layer of gray cement paste that held the aggregate particles together, he discovered that the splendor of those particles is revealed to the eye. His pioneering efforts to develop and then promote the use of architectural concrete and, later, of concrete mosaics and precast concrete panels, launched a revolution in the construction industry that has still not ended.

Two separate committees, appointed by the National Spiritual Assembly "to investigate the matter of material adapted to the external decoration," recommended John Earley to do the work. In explaining the decision, the National Spiritual Assembly noted that he "has perfected a process which the late Louis G. [sic] Bourgeois . . . considered by far the best for the carrying out of his unique plan. . . ." "The model prepared by Mr. Earley a few years ago and since then exposed to the weather on the Temple grounds," the National Assembly continued, "has perfectly met the test. Moreover, specific requests made to other firms for an estimate of cost have brought no satisfactory result. . . . [In] Mr. Earley we have a creative genius and an experienced, conscientious craftsman whose skill and whose enthusiasm fit him ideally for the task. . . ."[14]

The Master Craftsman

JOHN JOSEPH EARLEY
pioneer of architectural concrete, whose Temple ornamentation was his "crowning achievement"

John Earley's company, the Earley Studio, had been founded in the early 1890s by his father, James Farrington Earley. James Earley was an Irish immigrant descended from three generations of ecclesiastical artists and stone carvers; he became a sculptor well known throughout the eastern seaboard of the United States. His most famous work was the "Buffalo" nickel, commissioned by the United States Mint. For more than a decade the Earley Studio had provided beautiful, imaginative carvings for several churches and buildings.

John Earley assumed control of the studio after the death of his father in 1906 and altered its activity from stone masonry to plaster and stucco work. One of his earliest contracts was to remodel the interior of the White House during Theodore Roosevelt's first term as president.

In 1914 John Earley became closely allied with the United States Bureau of Standards shortly after that agency undertook a series of research projects to determine methods for increasing the durability of stucco, the most common covering for concrete. Armed with the knowledge gained from these experiments, he accepted a contract in the nation's capital to stucco the masonry work of an elaborate park being constructed in a new residental section known as Meridian Hill. He and his associates cast a sample section of the wall, but the United States Fine Arts Commission criticized the gray color of the stucco for being drab and uninteresting. Seeking a method to beautify the staircases, balustrades, and reflecting pools, he tried to eliminate the stucco by imitating Italian pebble mosaics, formed by pressing small stones into newly poured concrete before it hardened. Yet it was questionable whether the resulting finished surfaces could withstand the cold winters.

A new and radical approach for solving the problem then occurred to John Earley. He cast another small section of the wall and, before the concrete had completely dried, he removed the wooden molds, a process known as "stripping the forms."[15] Using wire brushes, he then scraped away the sand and cement covering the larger pebbles in the concrete mixture. The yellow-brown color of the pebbles from the Potomac River used in almost all concrete in the Washington, D.C., area gave the wall a warm, tan appearance instead of the cold gray. Not only was the wall beautiful, but it proved to be highly durable. The masonry work in Meridian Hill Park, completed in 1919, stands today in nearly perfect condition.

During the years that followed, the Earley Studio was commissioned to ornament many other structures, most of which are also still in excellent condition. Famous among them are Chicago's Fountain of Time, cast in 1922 on part of what had been the Midway Plaisance of the 1893 Columbian Exposition; the Shrine of the Sacred Heart in Washington, D.C., abundantly rich in the vibrant colors of John Earley's concrete mosaic decorations; the massive recreation of the Greek Parthenon, completed in 1925 in Nashville, Tennessee; the stunning beauty of the mosaic ceilings in the United States Department of Justice building; and the Polychrome House, constructed in Silver Spring, Maryland, in 1934. The latter was the first prefabricated concrete structure from which tens of thousands of the world's office buildings, apartments, and other structures formed of precast concrete sections are descended. During nearly thirty years of being involved with innovative projects, John Earley gained a reputation as "the world's foremost expert on the practical aspects of concrete making," wrote Frederick Cron. "Under his direction the Earley Studio executed works of such unusual complexity and beauty that they have never been equalled."[16]

At the annual convention of the American Concrete Institute in 1933, John Earley described the beginning of his relationship with the Bahá'ís:

The Master Craftsman

"Twelve years ago, last August [1920], two gentlemen came to my studio in Washington. They came unexpectedly and they brought with them only the photograph of a plaster model. They had been sent by a mutual friend, an engineer, deeply interested in the work being done with concrete by this studio, who suggested that we might offer a solution for their problem. One of these gentlemen was Mr. Louis Bourgeois, an architect, and the most unusual personality I have met in that profession. . . . the photograph which they brought was of a Temple, the most exotically beautiful building I have ever seen. It came up out of the earth like the sprout of some great plant bursting out to life and growth.

"Mr. Bourgeois explained that he was the architect of the building and a member of the Bahá'í Faith who believe themselves to be the children of a new era, who believe that they have received a new Manifestation. It soon became clear that this Temple was the dream of Mr. Bourgeois' life, that all his hopes and ambitions were centered in it, and that he believed himself to have been inspired to design a temple unlike any other in the world, so that it might be the symbol of a new religion in a new age. At that moment he was anxiously seeking a material with which to build it and someone with the ability to understand his work and the skill to execute it. He left with me the photograph, after autographing it. I have it still. It marks the beginning of the project for me.

"In the time which intervened between this meeting and the death of Mr. Bourgeois about two years ago [1930], there developed between us an interesting and instructive friendship. We studied this temple with all its ramifications of form, of treatment and of meaning as a preparation for the time when work on it would be begun. It was strange, in a way, that we of the studio should have given so much thought to it. We had no authority to do so and as a matter of fact we were not commissioned to do the work until this summer just past. But somehow it always seemed to be our work. We understood it, we had the material and were equipped to do it. The architect was interesting to us and we to him. And then there was the job itself, a thing to fascinate the imagination. A temple of light with a great pierced dome through which by day the sunlight would stream to enlighten all within and through which by night the Temple light shone out into a darkened world. When at night we look into the sky we see only the stars but could we see the orbits of the stars how wonderful it would be. Great curves intertwining in weird perspective. Ovals, circles, and vesicas of endless variety twisted and woven into some great cosmic fabric. This is the theme of the dome, the courses of the stars woven into a fabric. But this is not all, interwoven with the courses of the stars . . . are the tendrils of living things, leaves, and flowers, because no symbol of creation would be complete without a symbol of life. Lifted above the dome are nine great ribs, nine aspirations that mount higher than the courses of the stars. I wonder after all if it was strange that we of the studio should have given so much thought to this project?"[17]

When Shoghi Effendi learned that the National Spiritual Assembly planned to begin work on the dome immediately and that it had negotiated a contract with the Earley Studio, he cabled that the National Assembly's decision was "fraught with incalculable consequences."[18] He conveyed the delight of the Greatest Holy Leaf and stated that they both were fervently praying that the American Bahá'ís would not relax their determination to complete the Temple swiftly.

Thirty-five days later, on 15 July 1933, a message arrived from Shoghi Effendi that brought great sorrow to the American Bahá'ís and, indeed, to all Bahá'ís throughout the world. Bahíyyih Khánum, the Greatest Holy Leaf, the eldest daughter of Bahá'u'lláh, had died. " 'I for my part,' " cabled Shoghi Effendi, " 'bewail sudden removal . . . my sole earthly sustainer, the joy and solace of my life.' " He announced that " 'so grievous a bereavement' " necessitated cancellation of all Bahá'í festivities for nine months, and he instructed that a memorial service be held at the Temple. In a subsequent cable he told the sorrow-stricken Bahá'ís in North America not to allow their resolve to be thwarted by the Greatest Holy Leaf's death; for the Temple was the enterprise upon which she had " 'centered her brightest hopes.' " " 'Might not this present grief . . . ,' " he cabled them on 8 August, " 'release such forces as will ensure speedy completion . . . Mashriqu'l-Adhkár, . . . administration's mighty bulwark, . . . symbol of its strength and harbinger . . . its promised glory.' "[19]

Although work progressed rapidly, John Earley had to cope with several difficult problems. Louis Bourgeois had never provided engineering plans for his final designs of the exterior ornamentation, nor had he determined any method for attaching the ornamentation to the steel superstructure. What existed was a series of drawings, some of which depicted " 'the most extraordinary full-sized details' " of the ornamentation. The largest drawing, showing the face of the immense ribs, measured ninety feet. Another drawing, depicting a panel in the field of the dome, was seventy feet long.* Shortly after meeting Louis Bourgeois in 1920, John Earley had been able to observe him create some of these drawings:

---

*The longest roll was 109 feet, but it contained several drawings.

The Master Craftsman

"Each of these drawings was made in one piece in a loft building on La Salle Street in Chicago where Mr. Bourgeois stretched out on the floor a great sheet of paper and with his pencil tied to the end of a long stick he drew in great sweeps, in a manner never to be forgotten, the interlacing ornament of the dome. One line through another, under and over, onward and upward until the motif was completed. Never have I seen a greater feat of draftsmanship nor a more interesting draftsman than Mr. Bourgeois. Most surprising of all perhaps is the approximation to accuracy which he maintained in these great drawings in spite of the disadvantages under which he worked. He was obliged to stand on the drawing which he was making and his only view of the whole was from the top of a step ladder."[20]

Another problem John Earley and his associates faced was maintaining the theme of the ornamentation while assuring that the decoration did not detract from the silhouette of the building.

"Were we to treat the exterior surface of the dome so that the perforations were too large they would destroy the architectural continuity. Were they too small they would not appear to be perforations. If the surface were simply perforated without further treatment the decoration would be inadequate, the theme would be lost, there would be no pathways of the stars nor movements of living things. All this must be modelled into the surface of the dome with care and good judgment, so that at no place will the intertwining of this complicated grille escape from the configuration of the hemisphere. The interior surface of the dome is the subject of another group of considerations. If the solids between the perforations are too large the dome will appear as a dark surface spotted with bright dots. It would be like looking into a colander. If the solids be too thin, the light which enters will seem to bend around them and the bright spots will resolve into a confused blur. The pattern would be lost. And so with time and the greatest of care every ornamental detail must be adjusted to the unity of the architecture and the sequence of the story, as words are made to tell a story in the cadence of a poem."[21]

John Earley and his staff needed to devise methods that would allow the craftsmanship to be both practical and economical, yet produce concrete panels that would effectively convey Louis Bourgeois' intricate conception. The man responsible for translating the artistic to the practical was John Earley's partner, Basil Gordon Taylor.[22] At the studio he built a full-sized, wooden replica of a

The Master Craftsman

Wooden replica at the Earley Studio, Rosslyn, Virginia, of a one-ninth section of the Temple dome. The carved models were attached to verify the accuracy of their curvature.

portion of the dome's mammoth steel framework. Only a one-ninth section was required since the dome would consist of nine identical triangular arcs divided by nine identical ribs. Mr. Earley recalled:

> "Now for the first time, we faced reality and were able to see the relation between the existing steel structure and a proposed concrete covering. All other relations of form such as that between the area of the concrete dome and its thickness; the relations of length, height and width in the great ribs, and curve of the rib up over the arc of the dome, all such ceased to be concepts and became experiences. The question whether this dome should be poured in place as a continuous fabric or precast and set, ceased to be a question. It was immediately apparent to practical judgment that a perforated concrete shell such as this dome, if cast as a continuous fabric attached to and supported by steel members, would tear itself to pieces in its first drying."[23]

The Master Craftsman

Construction at the Earley Studio of a steel-rod core for one ornamental panel for the Temple

Tests showed that concrete consisting of quartz, sand, and portland cement had the plasticity necessary to create the intricate designs and a durability greater than most concrete and many types of stone. Two types of quartz were selected to achieve the desired beauty of the panels: crystalline quartz that was mined near King's Creek, Spartanburg, South Carolina; and opaque or opalescent quartz that came from Monita, Virginia. The quartz was crushed, screened to an exact size, and mixed with sand and cement to form an extremely white architectural concrete. Seven hundred forty-three tons of quartz were used in creating the ornamentation for the exterior of the dome.

To make each panel even stronger, an intricate reinforcement system of steel rods was designed. By using stainless steel for the connecting system that would attach the ornamentation to the steel dome, the builders were able to minimize future rust damage.

The Master Craftsman

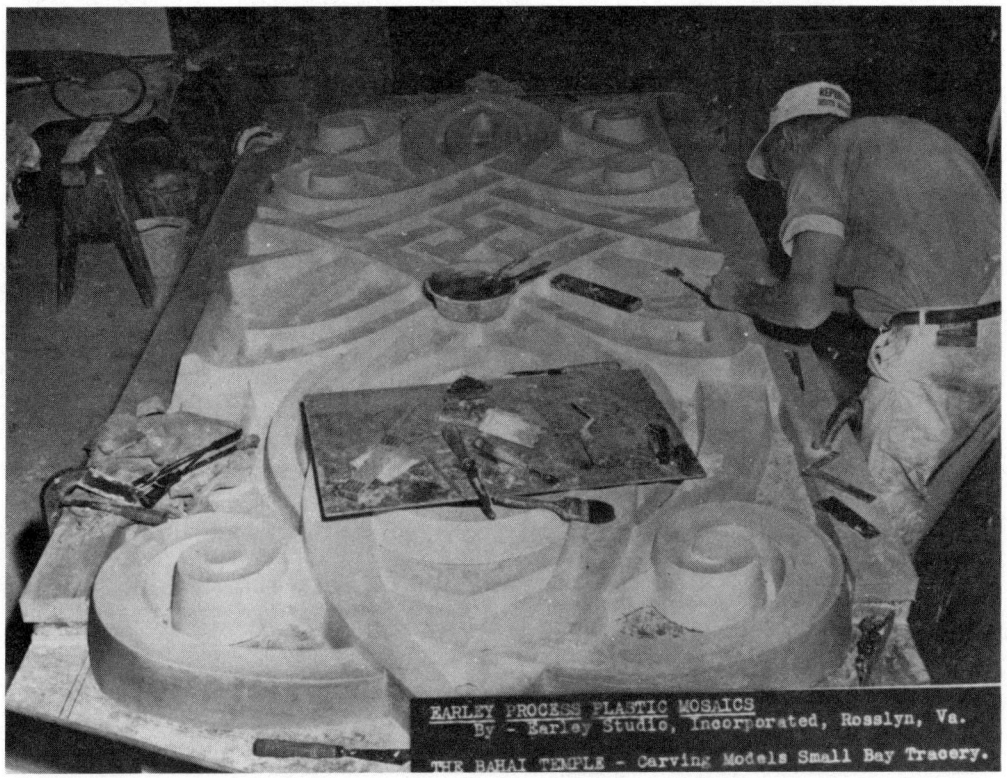

An Earley Studio craftsman carving the model for one section of the Temple ornamentation

As each problem was solved, John Earley's affection for the project increased. " 'Each decision,' " he said, " 'affords a new thrill and stirs our interest to the highest point. It is a project for which we feel that the best is none too good.' " A sign, erected atop one of the buildings at the Rosslyn, Virginia, division of the studio, reflected the pride he felt: "THE BAHA'I TEMPLE DOME, WILMETTE, ILL.: THE MOST ELABORATE CONCRETE STRUCTURE IN THE WORLD."[24]

By the beginning of August, two months after John Earley was awarded the dome contract, he completed the necessary planning and organizational work. The first step in producing the hundreds of panels was to take sections of Louis Bourgeois' drawings and redraw them onto huge slabs of modeling clay. A model for each section was then meticulously carved. Each model was the basis for constructing a mold from which the corresponding section of orna-

The Master Craftsman

The model for the base of the ribs of the Temple at the clerestory level

mentation would be produced. Since the building is nine sided, at least nine panels of ornamentation would be cast from each mold. Half of the sections in the dome were replicated twenty-seven times; hence only twenty-four molds were required to produce the 388 panels for the dome and ribs. The studio sculptor, Leander Wiepert, became so enamored with the project that he insisted on carving all of the clay models without assistance.

The clay model for the lowest level of ornamentation on the dome was completed by mid-August, and a template of that section was shipped to Wilmette and attached to the dome to ensure that both the model and Basil Taylor's one-ninth wooden replica of the dome matched perfectly with the actual building. As Mr. Wiepert finished each clay model, another worker used it to construct a plaster mold. A plaster model, more rigid than the clay model, was cast from the plaster mold. Each plaster model was then attached to the wooden replica of the dome to guarantee the accuracy of the fit.

After each plaster model was accepted, the artisans cast another plaster

The Master Craftsman

The concrete mixture for the Temple ornamentation being poured into a completed mold at the Earley Studio. At least nine panels of ornamentation could be cast from each mold.

mold, whose function was described as being similar to "grandmother's cake tin."[25] Each mold was lined with a thin zinc coating and then shellacked so that it would withstand repeated usage. By hand the workers filled the molds with the mixture of portland cement, sand, and quartz that would become the actual ornamental panel.

After the mixture for the first panel had set for approximately eighteen hours, the nearly dry experimental cast was removed from the mold. The workmen leaned the cast vertically against posts and, using wire brushes and a dilute acid, removed the soft surface mortar to expose the quartz. Although they had successfully executed this process "hundreds of times" before on other jobs, they encountered trouble. "The green concrete of the fragile, perforated casting," explained Frederick Cron, "was not strong enough to hold up its own weight, and a number of ominous cracks appeared during the wire brushing."[26] John Earley immediately began testing several variations to the process and overcame the trouble by making a slight change in the formulation of the concrete.

The Master Craftsman

Workmen at the Earley Studio using small steel brushes and dilute acid to wash away the outer layer of cement and reveal the beautiful quartz aggregate

The production of the panels was an immense task; the wire brushing alone would, by the time the building was completed, consume thousands of man-hours. Once each panel was cast and cleaned, it was cured for several days in a huge humidity chamber. Following additional air drying in the studio yard, each panel was carefully inserted into a protective wooden frame before beginning the seven-hundred-mile trip west to Wilmette on a railroad flatcar.

The work at the studio, however, started to fall behind schedule in late 1932 because the terms of the contract had called for construction to "proceed as rapidly as permitted by funds in hand," and the National Spiritual Assembly was behind in its payments. In December 1932 the National Assembly, attempting to achieve every possible economy, terminated its operating budget. Requests from committees for funds were considered on an individual basis and then only when there was an urgent need. The National Assembly told the Bahá'ís that these actions demonstrated "how important . . . [it] considers it to subordinate all activities to the needs of the Temple Fund until the dome has been completed."[27] Another method the National Assembly employed for motivating individuals was to calculate the cost of each ornamental panel and then issue fund updates every two weeks. In this way each community could keep track of the additional number of panels represented by the funds received during a given period.

Enthusiasm was also enkindled once more in Bahá'í communities worldwide, and accounts of sacrifices in other lands began appearing in the *Bahá'í News*. The community of Poona, India, for example, resolved to sacrifice as much as possible for the project and managed to collect $1,800. One Bahá'í in Poona was very poor and, although struggling to repay a burdensome debt, was also trying to save a small amount of money to buy a blanket to protect him from the "severity of the cruel nights of winter." Once the community began its fund drive, however, he immediately gave his savings for the Temple, "joyfully deciding . . . to endure the long wintry nights even as before, without a cover over him, with but cheerless plank under him."[28]

Another sacrifice, made by a Bahá'í in Java, was recounted by Keith Ransom-Kehler, a noted Bahá'í teacher and world traveler:

> Just as the ship was about to sail, he said to me very earnestly: "I have no money. All my salary goes to the support and education of my family. The only thing I have of any value is my watch. We are told of the vital importance of the Mashriqu'l-Adhkár to the world of humanity, therefore we Bahá'ís must strain every nerve for its completion." Unstrapping his watch—ordinarily considered a necessity to any business man—he handed it to me with a radiant smile.

Mrs. Ransom-Kehler also told of three "ardent friends" in Mazindaran, Iran, who contributed their gold earrings, and of a Bahá'í woman in Tehran who, inspired by several meetings held in the city for the Temple, "gave a new chuddar (outer wrap) belonging to her recently deceased mother, as the only article of worth that she possessed."[29]

Yet despite these sustained and sacrificial efforts, contributions to the project were inadequate. By 1 May 1933 only $46,000 had been raised. The completion date had already slipped to the end of November, and it appeared it would slip further. The building's skyward climb seemed thwarted again.

Chapter Sixteen

THE TEMPLE'S BEAUTY EMERGES

WHEN THE delegates arrived at the Temple on 1 June 1933 for the twenty-fifth annual convention, only eight panels had been received in Wilmette, and only one of these had been installed on the building. The delegates were gripped with disappointment and a sense of failure, and consulted extensively about the problems of securing the funds to continue the ornamentation. Convention-reporter Charlotte Linfoot recorded that by the second day of the convention "the friends began to bring in not only contributions in cash but also some of the most precious gifts which have yet found their way into the archives." Among the items were a lock of Bahá'u'lláh's hair, around which He had written a prayer; a handkerchief and comb that had belonged to 'Abdu'l-Bahá; prayer beads that had been used by the Greatest Holy Leaf; and two rubies. "Other gifts similar to these, each of priceless value to the Bahá'ís, rings and other articles sacrificed by those who had nothing else to give," continued to be received throughout the sessions.[1] Nearly $10,000 was contributed.

In June the National Spiritual Assembly was able to make a payment of $15,000 to John Earley, and in July, another payment of $18,000. The National Assembly cabled Shoghi Effendi on 19 July: " 'Temple work proceeding full schedule without interruption. . . . All making supreme effort.' "[2] On 28 August the first railroad car filled with several dozen panels of ornamentation left the Earley Studio. Five days later a second shipment left. Attached to the sides of each railcar were huge banners that proclaimed: "THE BAHAI TEMPLE DOME, WILMETTE ILL."

Upon arrival at a railway siding a few miles from the Temple, the panels were transferred to trucks and transported to the construction site. There a crane, which had been erected on top of the dome, lifted the panels into position. When the first full shipment arrived at the end of the first week in September, several Bahá'ís gathered to read prayers. The only person known for

The Temple's Beauty Emerges

Completed sections of the Temple-dome ribs loaded on a railroad car for transportation to Wilmette, Illinois. The first full shipment arrived at the Temple site in early September 1933.

certain to have been present, and who read a prayer during the service, was a young woman, Mary Maxwell, the daughter of May and Sutherland Maxwell. A few years later Mary Maxwell would become the wife of Shoghi Effendi and would, as his representative, dedicate the completed Temple in 1953.

By the end of September, 260 of the 388 panels had been constructed. Seventy-six of these had already been installed on the dome. On the twenty-sixth of that month, however, the National Spiritual Assembly again sent a special letter to all Local Spiritual Assemblies telling them that contributions were inadequate. The National Assembly declared it was "unable to believe that the friends will permit any failure in this the greatest of all present Bahá'í obligations" and assured the Bahá'ís that the dome ornamentation would be completed during November. By the end of September, the National Assembly noted, $18,000 would be needed, of which "we are still short $7,500, due to be paid by October first." The National Assembly also dispelled the rumor that "any deficit in the fund has been guaranteed by certain individuals."[3]

The Temple's Beauty Emerges

Unloading panels for the Temple dome at a railroad siding near the Wilmette Temple site

The community apparently had been strained to its psychological, if not its material, limits. In addition to contributing to the Temple and to fulfilling other financial demands, Bahá'ís in America were sending thousands of dollars for the purchase of land surrounding the Bahá'í sacred shrines on Mount Carmel. By 31 October, when $18,000 was due for the work performed at the Earley Studio that month, there was only $6,000 in the treasury. On 2 November Shoghi Effendi cabled: "Appeal hard pressed American believers heed this my last passionate entreaty not suffer slightest interruption Temple construction dim magnificence their epochmaking enterprise...." If the Bahá'ís would redouble their efforts, he promised to grant a "one year's respite" once the dome was finished.[4]

Shoghi Effendi's appeal succeeded in intensifying further the American

The Temple's Beauty Emerges

A rib section being guided into position on the dome of the Temple

Bahá'ís' efforts, but the result was still not adequate. The financial conditions worsened when the original construction estimate of $150,000 was exceeded by nearly $29,000, despite numerous economy measures devised by John Earley. The main reason for the overrun was that the original estimate only provided for completing the mammoth ribs to the base of the dome instead of to the base of the clerestory nineteen feet below. Constructing the entire ornamental rib system, however, ultimately saved money. The estimate also failed to provide for the installation of the furring system, the metal beams to which the dome ornamentation was attached. In addition, labor costs had risen considerably during 1933 because of regulations issued by the National Recovery Administration, part of the United States government's program to overcome the depression. Had Shoghi Effendi's original goal of 1 June 1933 been met, the Bahá'ís would have saved several thousand dollars because the regulations were put into effect after that date. Even though contributions during the ten-month period from May 1933 through February 1934 came within a few dollars of reaching $142,000—"a truly impressive assertion of the capacity of the believers"—the National Spiritual Assembly was forced to borrow $10,000 from a local bank to meet its contractual obligations.[5]

On 4 March 1934 the last panel was attached to the dome. The most complex aspect of decorating the Temple was, at last, complete. "Overjoyed epochmaking achievement," cabled Shoghi Effendi. "Intense gratitude. Ardently supplicating still mightier evidences American believers exemplary stewardship Faith of Bahá'u'lláh."[6]

Fortuitously, the Century of Progress Exposition had been so successful, apparently serving as a temporary diversion from the frustrations of the continuing depression, that the exposition's organizers decided to extend its operation into 1934. Fair goers could now travel north to Wilmette and gaze on the dome's beauty, which, according to Dr. Rexford Newcomb, dean of the College of Fine and Applied Arts at the University of Illinois, was "not matched by any domical structure since the construction of Michelangelo's dome on the Basilica of Saint Peter in Rome."[7]

Finding the idea of a one-year respite repugnant, and encouraged by "increasing expressions from believers all over the country" to proceed immediately with work on the clerestory, the National Spiritual Assembly had cabled Shoghi Effendi in January 1934 for permission to begin the $36,400 project. They planned to negotiate a contract that would again let them pay for the work over several months. " 'Heartily welcome proposal,' " replied Shoghi Effendi. " 'Additional sacrifices entailed clerestory ornamentation will add further laurels to crown already won American believers and hasten fulfillment long cherished expectations.' "[8]

On 22 May, less than three months after the completion of the dome, the first railroad car containing ninety-seven panels for the clerestory left the Rosslyn, Virginia, plant. Although installation began in mid-June, the studio work was slowed in July by a three-week strike of the District of Columbia plasterers' union. The strike, however, did not adversely affect the cost of the work at the studio.

Raising funds for the nineteen-foot-high clerestory proved no less frustrating than in the past. The only reason inadequate contributions did not impede progress was that John Earley was "carrying the entire expense" of the work.

"Whatever has been done . . . to date," the National Spiritual Assembly wrote, "represents his sacrifice and not ours."9

By September the National Assembly had been able to make only a single payment of $1,000 against the more than $15,000 it owed the Earley Studio at that time. It also still owed $7,500 on the bank loan. On 14 September the National Assembly sent an urgent telegram to all Local Spiritual Assemblies: "We have reported to Shoghi Effendi Temple construction will be stopped September twenty-second unless we have assurance that fifteen thousand can be paid before October first."10 Yet another surge provided $12,000, and John Earley agreed to continue working. But the frustrating history of rises and relapses of interest among the Bahá'ís again repeated itself when, in early January 1935, the National Assembly had to secure a second $10,000 loan.

The notion of pay-as-you-go had been a colossal failure. Shoghi Effendi directed that future contracts could not be negotiated "unless the entire sum required for the contract has already been collected." "Economic conditions, both within and without the Cause," he noted, "are nowadays too unstable to allow us to undertake any extensive scheme before insuring its uninterrupted and successful prosecution."11

The Bahá'ís were again disheartened in the late summer of 1934 when the dome's luminous beauty was marred by some of the terrible dust storms reaching Chicago. A drought had devastated the Midwest that year, and strong winds, laden with top soil, impregnated the soil into the new concrete, darkening it significantly. Although there was an attempt to clean the dome in 1942, it was not until the early 1970s, when the exterior was chemically washed and sandblasted, that the discoloration was reduced enough to escape notice.

Despite many difficulties during the early 1930s, a transition of great significance occurred with respect to the national Bahá'í community's collective priorities. Sharing the tenets of the Bahá'í Faith with interested individuals had always been a high priority to the Bahá'ís; but a relatively few individuals had been responsible for the early expansion of Bahá'í communities in the Western Hemisphere. These communities were almost completely independent of each other until a national identity began to emerge following the formation of the Bahai Temple Unity in 1909. Because the Temple Unity's primary reason for existing was to construct a place of worship, the Temple was identified with the Temple Unity's efforts to coordinate the collective activities of the American Bahá'í community. Teaching, meanwhile, remained associated with individual or local community efforts.

The division of priorities was further accentuated by the manner in which the Bahai Temple Unity organized its budget. Before the integration of all national financial activities into a National Bahá'í Fund in the early 1920s, there had been essentially a Temple Fund and a Teaching Fund. Individuals often had been uncertain about which was more important, and a sense of competition had existed in the minds of many Bahá'ís.

The Bahai Temple Unity's efforts to unify activities had been greatly expanded by the National Spiritual Assembly under the guidance of Shoghi Effendi. But not until the Temple's superstructure had been completed in 1931 did Shoghi Effendi begin to emphasize the need for the American Bahá'í community to balance its interest and energies between its teaching activities and the Temple project, the "twin outstanding activities" of the Bahá'ís in America.[12]

As the clerestory ornamentation was nearing completion—a severe winter prevented the work's being finished until July 1935—Shoghi Effendi took the transition of priorities a step further by appealing to the Bahá'ís to " 'lend immediate, unprecedented impetus' " to the arena of teaching. Only through unrelenting concentration on " 'this paramount issue,' " he noted, could the Bahá'ís ensure the eventual completion of the Temple.[13]

On 26 and 27 October 1935 the National Spiritual Assembly held a special "National Meeting" at the Temple to commemorate the completion of the dome unit (dome, ribs, and clerestory) and to consult on ways to advance the Faith. Although the conference led to several meetings between the National Assembly and the local Bahá'í communities, and although there was a marked increase in individual teaching, the National Assembly wrote in its 1935–36 annual report that the year had been "a period of spiritual incubation, of a turning inward to the life of the soul."[14] The event that contributed most to the "spiritual incubation" was the publication of *Gleanings from the Writings of Bahá'u'lláh*, Shoghi Effendi's translation into English of passages from the most important of Bahá'u'lláh's writings. Many of these passages, which provided new and deeper insight into the Bahá'í teachings, had not previously been available.[15]

The year of reflection and rejuvenation proved to be vital for the task that lay ahead. The National Assembly was inspired by Shoghi Effendi's continuing appeals for a teaching program "unexampled in its scope and sustained vitality."[16] Emboldened by his appeal to ponder 'Abdu'l-Bahá's Tablets of the Divine Plan, which called for the speedy establishment of the Faith in every state in the union and in every republic in the Americas, and reassured by the 1936 delegates' pledged support, the National Spiritual Assembly formulated the most far-reaching teaching plan in the history of the Bahá'í Faith. It appointed both a National Teaching Committee and ten regional teaching committees. These committees were charged with a number of tasks, including coordinating intercommunity conferences; providing teaching assistance to local communities; and recruiting and coordinating Bahá'ís who were willing to travel and teach throughout the continent. The National Spiritual Assembly also appointed an Inter-America Committee to develop plans to establish Bahá'í communities in Mexico, Central America, the Caribbean, and South America.

Yet all of this activity was but a prelude to a bolder and more audacious advance in 1937. Shoghi Effendi, capitalizing on the active organizational effort during the previous year, not only demanded that the Bahá'ís "intensify their teaching work a thousandfold" but again focused their attention on the Temple. The American Bahá'í community should "resume with inflexible determination," he cabled, "exterior ornamentation of entire structure" and "formulate feasible Seven Year Plan to assure success Temple enterprise."[17]

The salient feature of the Seven Year Plan was the raising of $350,000 for the Temple Fund. The construction work was to be done in successive stages as funds became available. Coupled with this goal was an expanded version of the previous year's teaching plan, formulated to achieve by the end of the seven years Shoghi Effendi's objective of establishing the Faith in each state and province in the United States and Canada, as well as in each country of the Western Hemisphere.

The opening weeks of the plan were marked at first by exultation as Siegfried Schopflocher pledged $100,000 to the Temple project, as he had in 1929. Later the Bahá'ís were beset by extreme sadness and dismay as Heinrich Himmler, head of Adolf Hitler's secret police, ordered on 9 July 1937 the dissolution of all Bahá'í administrative institutions in Germany. Undaunted, the American Bahá'ís pressed forward with their plans. A technical committee was appointed by the National Spiritual Assembly to investigate alternatives for proceeding with the exterior ornamentation, including the possibility of using a company other than the Earley Studio.[18] But the committee's unanimous decision was the same as in the past: Only the Earley Studio could successfully complete the project. After a productive conference with John Earley to study construction costs, the committee informed the National Spiritual Assembly that $145,000 would be needed to ornament the gallery. Shoghi Effendi, apparently anxious to see a swift resumption of the work, relaxed his restrictions regarding full funding and permitted the signing of a contract as soon as the Temple Fund had half of the required amount. The new contract was signed on 5 October 1937.

When the delegates arrived at the thirtieth annual convention in late April 1938, they were greeted with a flurry of activity at the Temple site. Eighty-three completed panels had already arrived from Rosslyn, as well as reinforcing steel, molds, and a variety of equipment. Fifty-four thousand pounds of sand and crushed quartz had also arrived, for some of the ornamentation had to be cast directly onto the building rather than at John Earley's Rosslyn plant.

Three events made the thirtieth annual convention particularly memorable. The first was the visit of Lidja Zamenhof of Poland, daughter of the inventor of Esperanto, which many Bahá'ís believed would become the universal language called for by Bahá'u'lláh. Lidja Zamenhof, who was a Bahá'í, came to the United States as the guest of the National Spiritual Assembly and spent more than a year traveling throughout the country, where she visited Bahá'í centers, spoke at Bahá'í proclamations, and taught Esperanto.

The second event involved Grace Robarts Ober, a well-known Bahá'í teacher whose friends numbered in the hundreds. During 'Abdu'l-Bahá's visit in 1912 Grace Ober had traveled ahead to each city He visited to arrange for accommodations. When He arrived, she acted as both housekeeper and hostess, "always ready for the constant stream of guests from morning to night." For years a staunch supporter of the Temple project, Grace Ober had once driven five hundred miles in 1932 to pray in the bare auditorium. Of that experience she wrote that there was no way to describe the spiritual power "that reaches down to the depth of heart and soul."[19]

On Saturday morning, 1 May, the third day of the 1938 convention, the delegates were shocked and saddened when they received a cablegram from Shoghi Effendi informing them of the death of Munírih Khánum, 'Abdu'l-Bahá's wife. It was reported that as Grace Ober entered Foundation Hall for the afternoon session, she remarked that she wished she could be in heaven to witness the reunion between 'Abdu'l-Bahá and His now-departed wife. After a session filled with reports of teaching activities throughout Canada and the United States, Harlan Ober, Grace's husband and chairman of the convention, called upon his wife to describe her teaching activities in Toronto, Canada, and Louisville, Kentucky.

> As she stood before the assemblage one sensed an almost unearthly radiance flowing from her. She looked unbelievably young and fresh and beautiful....

> There was a resonance and a ring in her voice which swept her audience to spiritual heights. Through her poured a mighty challenge and a resounding call for pioneer teachers to arise and take the Cause of Bahá'u'lláh to all parts of America. . . .
>
> As she finished her talk she grasped the table with her left hand, and raising her right arm as high as her fingers could reach, in a characteristic gesture of victory or farewell, she cried out in a triumphant voice, (or was it, perhaps, a call for help to a Higher World) "Yá-Bahá'u'l-Abhá!" Then she sank into a chair on the platform.

Nearly unconscious, Grace was helped from the room by her husband and another Bahá'í who was a physician. The delegates were informed shortly afterward that she was extremely ill, and a request was made for healing prayers. A few minutes later a second plea was made for prayers, "and again that loving group of friends besought the favor of God on her behalf." More minutes passed. Finally, a member of the National Spiritual Assembly came to the podium and, in a voice trembling with sadness and dismay, announced that Grace Ober had died. The Bahá'ís, "with breaking hearts," prayed for her spiritual progress "throughout all the Worlds of God."[20]

The sorrow over her passing was tempered by a happier moment, the presentation to the delegates of a gift from Shoghi Effendi to the American Bahá'ís as a token of his gratitude. The gift, given on Shoghi Effendi's behalf by Amelia Collins, was a lock of Bahá'u'lláh's hair, " 'arranged' " and " 'preserved' " by the " 'loving hands' " of the Greatest Holy Leaf. Shoghi Effendi cabled that the gift was to " 'rest beneath dome of Temple.' "[21]

By November, when work had to be terminated because of the cold winter weather, the gallery ornamentation was ahead of schedule and nearly complete. Only the upper portions of the nine pylons remained to be ornamented. In addition, sufficient funds were available to negotiate a $21,000 contract for the hand-carved models for the first floor; this work could be done at the Rosslyn studio during the winter. When this information was cabled to Shoghi Effendi on 29 November, he responded: "Delighted. Unbounded gratitude." Later that same day he cabled his decision to contribute one thousand pounds sterling in the name of the Greatest Holy Leaf as a token of her gratitude for the Bahá'ís' response to her last appeal for the Temple Fund. He announced that the fund, still under the umbrella of the National Fund, "from now on will bear her name and be consecrated" to her memory.[22]

Shoghi Effendi continued throughout the remainder of the Seven Year

Right: *A dome panel being lowered into position, 21 September 1933.* Below left: *The completed dome, finished on 4 March 1934, and completed clerestory, finished 29 June 1935.* Below right: *The gallery faces and pylons nearing completion, summer 1939*

Left: *The completed dome, clerestory, and gallery, July 1939.* Below left: *The lower portion of a main-level pylon being washed with acid, April 1940. The main-level and gallery pylons were cast in place from molds shipped from the Earley Studio.* Below right: *Installation of main-level facings, April 1941*

The Temple's Beauty Emerges

Construction of the eighteen circular steps that would surround the Temple, summer 1942. The casting took place in the upstairs auditorium.

Plan to urge a "proper balance" between the Temple project and the teaching work—one should never be allowed to "preponderate over the other." He helped the American Bahá'ís understand that the primary role of the Temple for years to come was closely linked with the teaching work; thus he reaffirmed that the Temple and teaching work were not mutually exclusive:

> Superb and irresistible as is the beauty of the First Mashriqu'l-Adhkár of the West, majestic as are its dimensions, unique as is its architecture, and priceless as are the ideals and the aspirations which it symbolizes, it should be regarded, at the present time, as no more than an instrument for a more effective propagation of the Cause and a wider diffusion of its teachings. In this respect it should be viewed in the same light as the administrative institutions of the Faith which are

The Temple's Beauty Emerges

Foundations in place to receive the 972 sections of the steps of the Temple, July 1942

designed as vehicles for the proper dissemination of its ideals, its tenets, and its verities.[23]

By the end of the second year of the Seven Year Plan, great strides had been made in the teaching work. Local Spiritual Assemblies had increased from seventy-two to eighty-eight, and Bahá'ís resided in 190 cities that had no Bahá'ís at the beginning of the plan. In addition, extensive teaching efforts were under way in Argentina, Chile, Cuba, Mexico, The Philippines, and Uruguay.

On 31 July 1939 the gallery was completed. The final cost was $126,250, nearly $19,000 less than the original estimate. At the same time the National

The Temple's Beauty Emerges

Spiritual Assembly negotiated a $10,000 contract with the Earley Studio to complete the lower third of the first-floor pylons by 31 December.

A few weeks before the termination of the gallery phase of the project, the National Spiritual Assembly announced that on 1 October it would transfer the National Bahá'í Secretariat from West Englewood, New Jersey, to the studio Louis Bourgeois had built across the street from the Temple at 536 Sheridan Road in Wilmette. On 4 July Shoghi Effendi sent his congratulations and commented on the import of that decision:

> To the far-flung Bahá'í communities of East and West, most of which are being increasingly proscribed and ill-treated, and none of which can claim to have had a share of the dual blessings which a specially designed and constructed House of Worship and a fully and efficiently functioning Administrative Order invariably confer, the concentration in a single locality of what will come to be regarded as the fountain-head of the community's spiritual life and what is already recognized as the mainspring of the administrative activities, signalizes the launching of yet another phase in the slow and imperceptible emergence, in these declining times, of the model Bahá'í community—a community divinely ordained, organically united, clear-visioned, vibrant with life, and whose very purpose is regulated by the twin directing principles of the worship of God and of service to one's fellowmen.

When the move was completed, he cabled on 3 October: "Hail historic act signalizing auspicious conjunction" of the two agencies, the "twin foci" of a "steadily evolving American Bahá'í community life."[24]

With the National Bahá'í Secretariat now working in the precincts of the Temple, a contract was signed in May 1940 to ornament three of the nine faces of the main story. Because each main face contained a different quotation from the writings of Bahá'u'lláh, models for each of these sections had to be made separately. An extra casting of one of the panels from directly above the windows was made and given as a gift to Shoghi Effendi in Haifa, where the panel was placed at the entrance to one of the gardens near the Shrine of the Báb. By mid-summer the main-story pylons were completed, and the contract for the six remaining faces was signed at the end of August 1940.

As the entire main level neared completion during the latter part of 1941, the National Spiritual Assembly received some astonishing news: It did not possess clear title to the Temple property. Documents verifying payment for the portion of the land purchased from Silas Crandall in 1909 had never been

The completed exterior of the Bahá'í Temple, finished on 8 January 1943

properly recorded, even though the Bahai Temple Unity had paid an attorney to take care of the matter. The oversight emerged when an attempt was made to exchange additional land with the village of Wilmette to allow for the further reduction of the sharp curve of Sheridan Road adjacent to the Temple property.

The Temple's Beauty Emerges

A lawyer was retained by the National Spiritual Assembly to investigate the matter and prove that the land had been paid for. Several long-time Bahá'ís were approached in an attempt to learn exactly how the property had been acquired. "Strange as it may seem," the lawyer reported, "none of them could recall how this was done. . . ."[25] The lawyer then tried to locate records through the bank that had handled the original transactions but "found that that organization had failed many years ago"; its records were no longer attainable. Next the lawyer contacted the attorney who was originally retained by the Bahai Temple Unity, but he was "in his nineties, and is unable to give any help." In desperation, a search was made for Silas Crandall, "but that party can not [sic] be found."[26] At that point the lawyer asked advice from the Chicago Title and Trust Company and was told to provide financial records of the Bahai Temple Unity proving that the land had been paid for. But the records before 1915, which would have contained the needed receipts, could not be found. Finally, the attorney submitted the only records that were available—the financial reports printed in various issues of *Star of the West* magazine. Based on these alone, clear title was issued.

In March 1942 the final contract was signed for the eighteen circular steps that would completely surround the Temple and symbolize the Báb's first eighteen disciples. The work was delayed, however, because John Earley had been contracted by the War Department to undertake some emergency war construction projects. In mid-May the casting of the steps began inside the upstairs auditorium, from where they were moved into place by a portable hoist. A total of 972 sections were cast, which, if laid end to end, would extend a distance of two miles. "War conditions involving increased labor wage rates, the necessity of working the force six days a week, with double pay for the sixth day, increased freight rates, higher liability and social security insurance rates and other factors" combined to raise the cost of the steps from the original estimate of $30,000 to $51,700, one of the largest percentage cost overruns in the history of the project.[27]

On 8 January 1943, two months shy of the fortieth anniversary of the launching of the project, and nearly seventeen months ahead of schedule, the exterior ornamentation was completed. "Heart aglow with pride, love, gratitude for superb achievement," cabled Shoghi Effendi. "The Concourse on high is jubilant. Myself bow head in joyous, reverent recognition of prodigious accomplishment which deserves to rank among the outstanding enterprises" during the ministry of 'Abdu'l-Bahá "and the most signal victory won" since 'Abdu'l-Bahá's death.[28]

The Temple's Beauty Emerges

With the exterior ornamentation now in place, the American Bahá'ís had weathered one of the most challenging periods in the development of their community. They were undaunted by the prospects of facing several more years fraught with problems in order to complete the Temple's interior. For the moment they had achieved their goals—and they would triumph again.

Chapter Seventeen

THE FAME OF THE TEMPLE SPREADS

FROM THE moment the completed superstructure was opened to visitors following the dedication ceremony in May 1931, and as the exterior ornamentation was subsequently constructed and attached to the building, the fame of the Temple grew rapidly. The first intense interest during the thirties was sparked by a Bahá'í exhibit at Chicago's Century of Progress Exposition, 1933–34. The exhibit was located in a prominent place in the center of the Hall of Religions and featured a model of the Temple made by Louis Voelz of Kenosha, Wisconsin. It was installed during the first week in September 1933, the same week the first full shipment of panels for the dome arrived at the Wilmette construction site, eight miles north of the exposition grounds.

Exposition officials estimated that more than ten thousand visitors a day passed the model. Seventy-five thousand pamphlets on the Bahá'í Faith were distributed. Scores of people attended numerous lectures presented in the same building. Many more traveled to Wilmette to view the partially clad dome and to attend lectures in Foundation Hall.

It was Louis Voelz's model that later inspired the National Spiritual Assembly to commission several plaster models of the Temple, each twenty-seven inches wide and twenty-three inches high. Produced by John Earley, these models, as well as photographs and drawings of the Temple, were displayed in places as diverse as the Canadian National Exposition in Toronto and the American Furniture Company in Albuquerque; Orchestra Hall in Chicago and Keen's Flower Shop in Phoenix; the Universal Atlas Portland Cement Company headquarters in New York City and the Sears-Robarts Store in Atlanta; the City Hall in San Francisco and the Turner Art Galleries in Denver. One of the models was sent to Shoghi Effendi and placed on display for visitors to the Bahá'í World Center.

In 1939 the National Teaching Committee acquired six of the models and arranged for them to be displayed in thirty-seven locations in the United States and Canada. The committee reported that the models produced the "most outstanding methods of publicizing the Faith, and teaching both directly and indirectly.... Indeed, we have found, that even before the completion of the Temple, the Master's promises that 'the Temple would become the first and most important teacher' has become fulfilled."[1]

One of the models was displayed at the 1939–40 New York World's Fair, attended by forty-five million visitors. "Millions of people" were reportedly captivated by the model, and two hundred thousand pieces of free literature were distributed.[2] At the 1939 Golden Gate International Exposition in San Francisco, a creation of the Works Progress Administration, more than six hundred thousand people viewed one of the models, and literature in excess of sixty thousand pieces was given away.

At times the fame of the Temple was spread in rather unusual ways, such as when it was featured in a May 1937 episode of "My Diary: Chickie Chalmers," a newspaper serial appearing regularly in *Chicago's American*. In one episode Chickie and her boyfriend, Gil, took a drive north along the shore of Lake Michigan until they reached the Temple. Upon seeing it, Chickie exclaimed:

> Oh, what a beautiful building ... all filigree with a lacy dome. We stopped there and went inside. Gil said he'd always wanted to see it, anyway.
>
> It was cold and bare and unfinished ... a little disappointing. Pretty soon, though, a grand old man in breeches and boots came up and asked us what we wanted, and then proceeded to explain all about the place.

The article recounted salient aspects of the lives of Bahá'u'lláh and 'Abdu'l-Bahá, mentioned Louis Bourgeois and his basic architectural concepts, and then helped perpetuate a false rumor, apparently inspired by the problems with the water that was encountered when building the caissons:

> Below the bed rock they found a sea of quicksand, a heavy, magnetic mass, pulling everything which came within its scope.
>
> The swell old man said he considered this symbolic of the Baha'i faith, that it attempts to draw believers of all kinds to a common ground. Christians, Jews, Mohammedans and Buddhists may worship here.
>
> It was a treasure trove ... the building and the old man. We were fascinated for an hour while he spun stories of pilgrimages and martyrdom and sacrifices to the ideal. We left, promising to come back to a Sunday service some day.[3]

The Fame of the Temple Spreads

Another unusual reference to the Temple appeared in a comic series entitled "Inspector Post and His Junior Detective Aides." For several editions this syndicated comic strip recounted Inspector Post's search for, and capture of, a gang of Oriental thieves who had stolen "the fabulous jewels" from the Temple.[4] The author's idea was possibly inspired by Louis Bourgeois' original design for the dome's interior ornamentation, which called for the symbols of various world religions, found on the outside, lower-level pylons, to be duplicated within the thirty-six repetitive slices of the dome's ornamentation. Mr. Bourgeois' specifications called for each symbol to be inlaid with glass colored like rubies, diamonds, emeralds, topaz, sapphires, and amethysts.

Birds also promoted the building. For decades flocks of purple martins, about twice the size of sparrows, had gathered in the Evanston area each year during the late summer. They perched on telephone wires, fences, and electric poles for several weeks before beginning their annual migration to South America. When the dome was finished, however, the holes in the ornamentation apparently created a marvelous sanctuary, as did the large space between the concrete panels and the dome's glass watershed; for thousands of birds began gathering there each year. Photographs of the birds enjoying their summer resting place appeared annually for several years in most area newspapers.

Periodically, advertisements capitalized on the Temple. A cartoon ad for Pure Oil, for example, showed a couple driving past the building, which, the woman noted, was one of the most famous sights in the area. The man agreed but responded that a Pure Oil gas station was a more welcome sight when his car needed attention. Other publicity was more complimentary, such as articles about the project appearing in prestigious publications issued by Bell Telephone and United States Steel.[5]

As the exterior ornamentation progressed, a growing sense of pride among Wilmette residents became increasingly obvious. When the *Wilmette Life* was notified that workers were beginning to ornament the gallery, the newspaper reported its "unfeigned pleasure" with the development. After noting that "many misgivings were voiced" when construction began in 1920, the newspaper commented:

> It was freely predicted when the basement was constructed and fitted up as a temporary place of worship, that it would so remain year after year, a blot upon the attractive entrance to the New Trier villages over Sheridan road.... [But] the public gradually gained confidence that the project, on the original plans, would eventually be completed....

The Fame of the Temple Spreads

Postage-stamp cancellation, used in Wilmette, Illinois, during National Air Mail Week, 15–21 May 1938

No one has been more appreciative of the patience of north shore villagers and the cooperation of municipal authorities, than the Baha'is themselves. Always when asking concessions or grants, it was with the calm assurance that generosity would not be imposed upon, and that the work of construction would go forward as rapidly as available funds would permit. Never has there been a violation even of a verbal agreement with constituted authority.

While the north shore is warm in its congratulations to the Baha'is on the progress they are making, the north shore is itself to be congratulated upon the site selected for this magnificent temple of worship.[6]

When National Air Mail Week was celebrated in 1938 to mark the twentieth anniversary of airmail service in the United States, Wilmette Postmaster Herbert O'Connell chose a cancellation-stamp design that depicted an airplane flying over the Temple. Over four thousand letters from Wilmette received the special postmark during the seven-day period. More items were mailed from Wilmette per capita than anywhere else in Illinois. The reason was that Bahá'ís throughout the United States and Canada, excited by the special cancellation, sent more than two thousand packages and letters to be mailed by fellow Bahá'ís residing in Wilmette. The Wilmette Bahá'ís also sent Shoghi Effendi a special greeting, signed by each member of the community and pledging "to strive as never before" to help finish the Temple.[7] In response to the special postal cancellation, the National Spiritual Assembly sent a mailing to all Local Spiritual Assemblies in order to give them a copy of it.

The Fame of the Temple Spreads

The incident that perhaps reflects most strongly the deepening bond between the Temple and the citizens of Wilmette occurred during the early months of the Second World War. At that time airplane pilots, as part of their advanced training, flew "dead reckoning" practice missions from the naval air base in nearby Glenview to old freighters on Lake Michigan. Wooden flight decks had been built atop the freighters to simulate aircraft carriers. The standard flight plan required each pilot, unaided by instrumentation, to fly from the air base to the Temple, where the pilot would get his bearings and then head east over the water. Many of these young men took great delight in flying as close as possible around the Temple, known on military maps as "Point Oboe."[8] Several local residents were horrified, fearing that one of the planes would crash and devastate Wilmette's great treasure. Public pressure prompted the village president, Harry Kinne, to send a written appeal to the commanding officer of the air base. Shortly thereafter, the pilots began keeping a respectable distance from the building.

Interest in the Temple by the media, coupled with growing use of the media by Bahá'ís, resulted in several thousand people's coming to the Temple each year. Radio advertisements helped attract individuals and groups, and newspaper advertisements increased attendance at public meetings. Contacts were made with travel agencies and transportation companies, of which several began distributing literature on the Temple that was provided free by the Bahá'ís. Literature was also made available in several hotels. Field representatives of the Chicago Chamber of Commerce distributed Temple brochures to companies throughout the United States who were considering holding conventions in Chicago. Articles in travel magazines were solicited by the Bahá'ís, but the information printed was not always completely correct; *Highway Traveler* magazine, for example, claimed that the Temple was a duplicate of the Taj Mahal.[9]

By 1940 tours of the Temple had become quite popular. Among the groups who visited that May, for example, were apprentice seamen from the Great Lakes Naval Training Station. During the war years several thousand sailors stationed at the training facility visited the Temple through tours sponsored by the YMCA of Waukegan, Illinois. Other visitors included two groups of high-school students from Muncie and Trafalgar, Indiana; the Bohemian Women's Club of Chicago; the Women's Club of Waukegan; youth from St. Luke's Episcopal Church, Evanston; children from the Third Unitarian Church, Chicago; members of the Chicago YWCA's Beacon Club; delegates attending the Illinois Federation of Women's Clubs convention; a WPA Adult Education Tour sponsored by the Chicago Board of Education; and a psychology class from the National College of Education in Evanston.

Although many visitors were attracted by the uniqueness of the building, many more came because of rumors old and new. One popular story reported that the curving lines in the dome represented sacred snakes that were kept in secret rooms in Foundation Hall. Another misconception, inspired by the huge amount of glass in the building, identified the Bahá'ís as sun worshipers. A third rumor stated that if a person were to travel to the opposite side of the earth, they would find a duplicate Temple. Were this to be true, that Temple would be in the middle of the Indian Ocean.

In the 1920s visitors had been greeted and guided through Foundation Hall primarily by the resident custodians. But as the number of visitors increased, it became imperative that Bahá'ís serve as volunteer guides. Shoghi Effendi supplied guidelines for this unique service. Soon guiding became a major aspect of the teaching efforts of Bahá'ís in Chicago, Evanston, Wilmette, and other communities in the greater Chicago area. "The Temple is the easiest place in the world" to share Bahá'u'lláh's teachings, wrote Gertrude Struven, a Wilmette Bahá'í involved with the guiding program. Bahá'ís serving as guides "gain invaluable experience in meeting all races, creeds, nationalities; high and low, rich and poor, religious, un-religious, enthusiastic and apathetic, educated and ignorant; angry ones, blind, seeing and indifferent."[10]

In the same article, published in 1939, Mrs. Struven recounted several experiences with visitors. One gentleman from Turkistan came to Chicago just to see the building. " 'I saw a picture of this Temple in my country,' " he said, " 'and made up my mind immediately that I was going to see that Temple. And here I am!' " Another visitor, a woman from Wilmette who could see the building from her home, arrived at the Temple in an agitated state one day shortly after the first ornamental panels were attached to the dome. "When she comprehended that they were covering the glass inner dome, she said in real dismay, 'What! You don't mean to tell me you are going to cover my beautiful, grey bubble?' " One Sunday morning a family from California visited the Temple because the train conductor told them to be sure to see the building. "This happens to be quite a regular thing," Mrs. Struven observed. "Hotel clerks, train dispatchers, ticket agents, taxi drivers and bus drivers" all told travelers to see the Temple.[11]

Groups of area children visited the Temple often, for they were attracted by the areas of the building that provided "intriguing and tempting recreation," such as the concrete slope that existed before the circular stairs were installed.

The Fame of the Temple Spreads

When some boys were caught one afternoon scampering about the tar-covered slope, they were "pleasantly surprised" when, instead of being reprimanded, they were invited to see the inside of the building, including the boilers and Louis Bourgeois' model. "They became interested in it all," wrote Mrs. Struven. "They have even returned later and brought more boys and introduced us as 'their friends.' "[12]

That many who visited were affected by a spiritual potency of the unfinished building was confirmed by the growing popularity of the weekly public meetings. By the mid-1930s it was not uncommon to have 200 to 300 people attend the lectures each Sunday. Even during the winter as many as 100 would be present. One meeting in 1941 had an audience in excess of 650. Through the years dozens of Bahá'ís spoke at these meetings, among them Horace Holley, Mountfort Mills, Martha Root, Siegfried Schopflocher, Corinne True, and Albert Windust.

The enthusiasm for the lectures was so great that for a time two were held each Sunday. A significant portion of the audiences attended more or less regularly. To assist those who wanted to study Bahá'u'lláh's teachings, a reference library was established in the building. Many people enrolled in study classes held at the Temple and also in several nearby communities.

Interest in the Temple persisted in many places throughout the world, due not only to the enthusiasm of numerous Bahá'í communities but, even more important, to the efforts of Martha Root. Throughout the 1930s she had never ceased her travels. The list of prominent personages with whom she spoke grew year by year at a rapid rate: King Haakon of Norway; King Faisal of Iraq; Princess Elizabeth of Greece; President Edvard Beneš of Czechoslovakia; Prince Muḥammad-'Alí of Egypt; the maharajas of Benares, Patiala, and Travancore; Dr. Nicholas Butler, president of Columbia University; Tawfíq Rushdí Bey, the foreign minister of Turkey; Dr. Erling Eiden, archbishop of Sweden; Dr. K. Ichiki, minister of the Japanese Imperial Household; Baron Yoshiro Sakatani, member of the House of Peers of Japan—these are but a few of the names on that long list. On more than one occasion Martha Root discovered that the person whom she was interviewing did indeed know of the existence of the Bahá'í Faith—because he or she had heard of the Temple.

Martha Root gave countless lectures and interviews, often several in a single day. When her articles, or articles written about her, appeared in newspaper after newspaper, in city after city, in nation after nation, they were often accompanied by pictures of herself, 'Abdu'l-Bahá, and Louis Bourgeois' large model of the Temple. She found repeatedly that she could use the building as a means to interest people in what she had to say.

In 1937 Martha Root visited the Temple for the last time. She wrote shortly afterward that it "is the most spiritually beautiful building I have ever seen. I shall remember it here and in all the worlds of God. I had not dreamed it could be so celestial, so beautiful." Recalling her work with the Ideas Committee in 1920, she acknowledged, "How thrilling to have had a part, even a small part, in its being 'brought into reality.' "[13]

The increasing publicity brought to the Temple by persons such as Martha Root served to widen the growing awareness of the Bahá'ís' endeavors around the globe. Their worldwide community was not only expanding according to the wishes of 'Abdu'l-Bahá, but it was coming closer to the realization of another of His dreams—the completion of the first Bahá'í Temple in the West. With the exterior ornamentation proudly in place, it was time for the Bahá'ís to celebrate. And celebrate they did.

Chapter Eighteen
THE FINAL YEARS

AT EXACTLY two hours and eleven minutes after sunset on 22 May 1944 the second century of the Bahá'í Faith began. Major commemorations for this centennial anniversary were planned in Shiraz, Iran (birthplace of the Bahá'í Faith), and in India, Egypt, England, Iraq, Palestine (Israel), and the United States, where activities were scheduled to take place at the Temple in Wilmette from 19 through 24 May.

The Bahá'ís of the Western Hemisphere had more to celebrate than the Centenary and the completion of the Temple's exterior. The year 1944 was the fiftieth anniversary of the establishment of the Bahá'í Faith in the West. It also marked the conclusion of the Seven Year Plan, the success of which, wrote Shoghi Effendi, far exceeded "the most sanguine hopes of its ardent promoters." "Within so short a period, during such troublous years, such exploits were achieved as will forever illuminate the pages of Bahá'í history."[1]

In addition to the Temple exterior's being completed almost one and a half years early, the goal of having Bahá'ís residing in every American state and Canadian province had been achieved, and the United States and Canada boasted nearly twice the number of Local Spiritual Assemblies than they had seven years earlier.* Local Spiritual Assemblies had also been formed in fourteen Latin American countries; the other countries in Latin America possessed active Bahá'í groups. This raised to sixty the number of countries in which the Bahá'í Faith had been established.

More than sixteen hundred Bahá'ís—including a third of all "Bahá'ís in the United States, its outlying possessions, and Canada," and Bahá'ís from Argentina, Bolivia, Brazil, Chile, Colombia, Costa Rica, Cuba, Ecuador, El

---

*For a Local Spiritual Assembly to be formed, there must be at least nine Bahá'ís residing in a specific locality (town, city, unincorporated area).

The Final Years

The Bahá'í Temple illuminated with temporary floodlights for the 22 May 1944 dedication of the building, which took place during the fiftieth anniversary of the establishment of the Bahá'í Faith in the West and the beginning of the second Bahá'í century

Salvador, Guatemala, Haiti, Honduras, Jamaica, Mexico, Nicaragua, Panama, Paraguay, Peru, Santo Domingo (Dominican Republic), Uruguay, and Venezuela—gathered at Wilmette for the Centenary celebration.[2] It was an incredible feat considering the difficulties posed by the Second World War.

Local newspaper coverage of the celebration was extensive. The 18 May issue of the *Evanston Review*, for example, devoted seven separate articles and more than 130 column inches to the Centenary. Noting in one article that "Few Evanstonians will find cause to quarrel with their [Bahá'í] vision of world unity," the newspaper affirmed:

The Final Years

> The north shore from the start has been proud that it was chosen as the site of a world shrine of this religion. The Baha'i House of Worship is unquestionably one of the most beautiful pieces of architecture on this continent. It gives unique character to the Wilmette and Evanston skyline.
>
> From this background of goodwill that has extended back through many years, Evanstonians this week join in extending welcome to the pilgrims who have traveled many miles to the graceful white dome that marks the center of their religion.[3]

Local radio stations were also intrigued by the gathering and aired numerous reports and interviews with prominent Bahá'ís. WCFL, Chicago, conducted a live broadcast from the Grand Ballroom of the Stevens Hotel during the Centenary banquet, held as part of the celebration.

Preparations at the Temple had been extensive. For the first time the outside of the building was illuminated at night by temporary but powerful floodlights. The light made the building seem "fragile and light," reported Marzieh Gail, well known to Bahá'ís for her translations, essays, and biographies and to readers at large for her colorful books on the Middle Ages, the Renaissance, and the Victorian era. "It almost drifts; it seems only to have settled, the way a butterfly will settle."[4] Preliminary landscaping had also been completed around the building, the parking facilities expanded, and Foundation Hall completely renovated. All exposed steel throughout the building had been painted, primarily through the efforts of caretakers John Junius, Edward Struven, and Carl Hannen, the latter two of whom had retired from their positions in 1943 after years of faithful service. In the upstairs auditorium several temporary loudspeakers had been installed, and a thousand chairs had been arranged in a large circle.

One of the speakers at the first session, held downstairs during the evening of 19 May, was Harry Kinne, president of the Wilmette village board, who welcomed the visiting Bahá'ís. During his speech Mr. Kinne remarked:

> "When people ask me Where's Wilmette? I tell them: if you want to locate Wilmette, just locate the Bahá'í Temple. There's where Wilmette is. . . .
>
> ". . . You good people are welcome. Please feel welcome. And if you violate any little regulations or ordinances, please see Mr. Wolff (The Village Manager) or myself (laughter) and we'll pardon you—because we know you wouldn't do anything but what you'd think would be all right."[5]

Each day was filled with numerous activities and presentations.[6] Not only were there many talks by Bahá'ís but also by prominent individuals who were not Bahá'ís, including Dr. Harry Allen Overstreet, an educator and author from New York; Earl Reed, a Chicago architect and educator; Dr. Raymond Frank Piper, a noted authority on comparative religions; and Philip Leonard Green, author of several books on Latin America, including *Our Latin American Neighbors* and *Pan American Progress*.

At 9:40 P.M. on 22 May the Bahá'ís gathered quietly in the auditorium to mark the moment when a century earlier the Báb had proclaimed His spiritual mission, and to dedicate once again the Mother Temple of the West. Marzieh Gail recorded her impressions of that historic event:

> we walked up the white path in the darkness, up the steps through one of the nine great portals. The vast space beneath the Dome was packed with Bahá'ís. I wished the Guardian could have been here to see them; to see all these souls across the earth, who have grown out of the words that the Báb spoke in Shíráz a hundred years ago tonight.
>
> . . . I looked behind me and saw faces pressed against the glass—people on the steps outside, peering in and wondering. I can't explain how happy the people inside were; I had never felt an audience like this.[7]

Following the devotional readings the Bahá'ís participated in what was perhaps the most meaningful of all the week's activities: One by one the Bahá'ís were able to view a portrait of the Báb, the Prophet-Forerunner of the Faith. The portrait had been sent to America by Shoghi Effendi for this great gathering. Again Marzieh Gail recalled:

> The lines formed slowly; after each one had looked at the Face of the Báb, he left by a portal of the Temple; I could see the shadows of the people moving on the great Temple windows as they went. . . .
>
> People were talking unobtrusively as they streamed away in the darkness. Over the dark bridge, on the Canal, I stopped and looked back. . . . There was the lit Temple, rising above us. And I felt, thinking of the Portrait of the Báb being there—in this, His setting—as if He had come home somehow. And I felt relieved, as if at last the peoples of the western hemisphere could hear Him say, as the first believer heard Him, long ago in Shíráz: "Enter therein in peace, secure."[8]

The Final Years

Several hours later, during the second day of Centenary activities in Haifa, Shoghi Effendi unveiled a model for a beautiful superstructure to be built over the Shrine of the Báb. Designed by Sutherland Maxwell, the superstructure would comprise an arcade of columns surrounding all four sides of the Shrine, above which would rise a dome resting on an intermediate octagonal story. Amatu'l-Bahá Rúḥíyyih Khánum (née Mary Maxwell), the wife of Shoghi Effendi, wrote that

> This concept was pursuant with the wishes of 'Abdu'l-Bahá who had desired that the building should be surmounted by a dome. But not one stone of the stones blessed by his tears and labours should ever be removed. His structure was the core, sacred and precious beyond the embellishments of art, and it was now to be enclosed in a shell of beauty befitting the station and glory of the beloved Martyr-Herald of our Faith, and yet revealing the original building on all sides.[9]

Although the arcade and octagon were designed in accordance with 'Abdu'l-Bahá's directives, the graceful clerestory with its eighteen windows memorializing the first eighteen disciples of the Báb—and the magnificent dome rising above the clerestory—were based on Sutherland Maxwell's original design for the Wilmette Temple.* Once again the history of the two buildings was intertwined.

Although numerous teaching activities continued unabated in the months following the Centenary celebration, the Bahá'ís felt the need to prepare more widespread campaigns to develop Bahá'í institutions and attract more members to the Faith. These future exertions, predicted Shoghi Effendi, would "eclipse the most shining victories" of the Seven Year Plan. In February 1945 the National Spiritual Assembly announced that it was devising a "unified national campaign" to release "the latent powers of the entire Bahá'í community" and to coordinate the community's "collective capacity for carrying the Message [of Bahá'u'lláh] to a larger portion of the public and with increased force."[10]

By November the National Assembly, supported by seven of its major committees working in close collaboration with each other, was ready to launch a series of major public meetings in eleven "key" cities. Also planned was a "great network" of teaching activities "to serve a large number of other cities and towns." The public meetings and teaching activities were to be assisted by unprecedented "newspaper advertising, publicity, radio, free literature, displays

---

*See p. 91.

and public relations material."¹¹ The effort was so effective that by the time of the national convention in 1946, new groups of Bahá'ís had been formed in twenty-nine locations, and twenty-three other localities now had at least one Bahá'í.

If November 1945 was a happy time of expansion, it was also a time of great sadness. While inspecting work on a project in Washington, D.C., John Earley suffered a massive stroke and died several days later on 25 November. His presence in the concrete industry would be sorely missed, for in 1934 John Earley had received the American Concrete Institute's highest award in recognition of his development of architectural concrete. Two years later he had received the American Institute of Architect's prestigious Craftsmanship Medal. In 1938 he had been elected president of the American Concrete Institute, "bringing to that office for the first time the viewpoint of the craftsman and fabricator of concrete rather than that of the scientist and engineer." His last great project, begun in 1936 during the two-year hiatus between the finishing of the Temple's dome unit and the starting of the gallery, had been the ornamentation of the 128-foot-high, octagonal Thomas Alva Edison Memorial Tower in Menlo Park, New Jersey. Yet, in spite of John Earley's many accomplishments and numerous, revolutionary building projects, Frederick W. Cron, the chronicler of his career, claims that the lacy, dream-like fabric of concrete that Mr. Earley wove about the Temple was his "crowning achievement."¹²

The final push to complete the Temple had its beginnings at the 1946 convention. Shoghi Effendi announced, in a cable to the delegates, that the "two year respite well earned" by their communities' "colossal effort" during the Seven Year Plan, had ended and that the time had come for the inauguration of the "second Seven Year Plan." There would be four objectives: further expansion and consolidation of the Faith in the Americas, involving a multiplication of Bahá'í centers and "bolder proclamation" of the Faith to people everywhere; the formation of a separate National Spiritual Assembly in Canada and one each in Central and South America; the initiation of "systematic teaching activity" in the "wartorn, spiritually famished European continent"; and the completion of the Temple's interior by 1953.¹³

The National Spiritual Assembly was confronted with a severe handicap in initiating work on the interior. Louis Bourgeois had made small working drawings for the inside of the building, which the National Assembly purchased from his wife following his death. But he had never completed the full-scale drawings of the plans he had designed during the last two years of his life. In addition, there were several aspects of his plan that were both complex and

The Final Years

costly: the jewel-like dome; small rooms occupying eight of the perimeter bays; stained-glass ceilings for the eight rooms; and huge, ornamental metal doors for each of the nine main entryways. Another problem was the imposing, ugly staircase that occupied the ninth bay.

Shoghi Effendi instructed the National Spiritual Assembly to "adhere as much as possible" to Louis Bourgeois' design. "Any modifications should be in the nature of eliminating or simplifying—and only when absolutely necessary. . . ." He also recommended that the eight rooms around the perimeter of the auditorium be eliminated to increase seating capacity, and he stipulated that the seats in the main part of the auditorium should face toward Akka. He authorized the elimination of as many of the nine entrances as might prove necessary and further instructed that any material, including wood, should be used that would enhance the acoustical quality of the auditorium.[14]

In July 1946 the National Spiritual Assembly authorized Allen McDaniel, who was no longer a member of the National Assembly, to conduct a preliminary study of Louis Bourgeois' interior design. Assisted by John Kennedy and a Mr. Pompilio—architectural draftsmen who had worked with the Earley Studio during the planning of the exterior ornamentation—Mr. McDaniel provided the National Assembly with sketches of possible simplifications that conformed to Shoghi Effendi's instructions.

The National Assembly also appointed a Technical Committee comprised of two of its own members, Horace Holley and George Latimer, as well as Edwin Eardley, Doris Holley, Carl Scheffler, Otto Smeskel, and Clarence Ullrich. The committee's purpose was to study the problems involved in developing a satisfactory design. The National Assembly, at its October meeting, voted to allow the Technical Committee to have Allen McDaniel's sketches modified since they "did not fully express a plan for the interior. . . ." The committee was further directed to consult an outside architect. Earl H. Reed, a Chicago architect who had addressed the Bahá'ís at the 1944 Centenary celebration, was commissioned to prepare a second scheme based on the original Bourgeois design, and Allen McDaniel was directed to continue developing his own recommendations. Both were instructed to give attention not only to the ornamentation but also to the lighting, heating, ventilation, plumbing, and acoustics.[15]

One consultant to both studies was Dr. Paul E. Sabine, director of the Riverbank Laboratories in Geneva, Illinois, and the leading acoustical authority in the United States at the time. He accepted the task because he felt the Temple "offers a very interesting technical problem" and because he was "very sympathetic to the particular aims of the Faith."[16]

The Final Years

Louis Bourgeois' elaborate interior design for one of the Temple's windows. Before his death in 1930 at the age of seventy-four, Mr. Bourgeois had only been able to make small working drawings for the inside of the Temple. Nevertheless, the drawings provided a starting point for several alternative versions by other architects during the 1940s.

The Final Years

The two completed designs were submitted to the National Spiritual Assembly in March 1947 and were immediately forwarded to Shoghi Effendi. The most striking differences between the two plans were the treatments of the dome (the McDaniel plan adopted Mr. Bourgeois' concept of having the dome perforated to let the sunlight through while the Reed plan did not) and the seating (the Reed design called for "sloping, banked seats under the gallery, forming a bowl arrangement").[17] Louis Bourgeois' jewel-like dome, separate rooms, stained-glass ceilings, metal grilles over the windows, and metal doors were eliminated in both designs. Also abandoned were more than five hundred incandescent light fixtures and a huge searchlight in the dome. The searchlight would have sent skyward an intense beam that would have been broken by the ribs into nine segments.

Earl Reed estimated his design would cost $850,000 to build. Allen McDaniel submitted an estimate of $500,000, but several items provided by Mr. Reed, including an elevator and draperies, were omitted in Mr. McDaniel's cost figures. On 11 April 1947 a secretary wrote on Shoghi Effendi's behalf that Shoghi Effendi favored Mr. McDaniel's plans "as they are more economical and incorporate many ideas of Mr. Bourgeouis [sic], chiefly the idea of a perforated dome," which he considered "in spite of certain technical drawbacks, such as danger of leakage, to be essential and a feature not to be abandoned." He did not object to the sloping seats, provided this arrangement did not add significantly to the total cost, the ceiling of which he set at $650,000. He also conveyed through his secretary that "although he approves of the modified ornamentation concept of Mr. McDaniel, he feels, in a few instances, he has departed too much from the original, and the homogeneity of Bourgeouis' [sic] design is lacking." He suggested that several of the elements of the Reed plan should be incorporated into the McDaniel design.[18]

When it was discovered that Mr. Reed's elevated seating would cost more than $200,000 because of the additional steel support system that would be required, the idea was abandoned. The National Spiritual Assembly contracted with Allen McDaniel to prepare new drawings that incorporated the rest of Shoghi Effendi's recommendations.

In 1947 the Technical Committee was dissolved because it had fulfilled the tasks assigned to it. The National Assembly then formed a Temple Construction Committee consisting of four National Assembly members—Amelia Collins,

Opposite: *Allen McDaniel's design for the interior ornamentation of the Temple. It attempted to simplify Louis Bourgeois' original conception but was later abandoned.*

The Final Years

Paul Haney, Philip Sprague, and Edna True. The main difference between the two committees was that the new one was empowered to review all business agreements related to the Temple. Among the committee's assignments was to identify individuals qualified to prepare the many detailed architectural and engineering drawings that would be necessary once Allen McDaniel had completed his work on the revised preliminary drawings.

At its June 1947 meeting the National Assembly received a list of several possible architects and architectural firms. The architect who interested the National Assembly most and who had been "strongly recommended by practically all technical people consulted" was Alfred P. Shaw of the Chicago firm Shaw, Naess and Murphy.* Among the many prominent structures designed by Alfred Shaw are the Chicago Merchandise Mart, the Field Building, and the interior of the Chicago Museum of Science and Industry.[19]

During its June 1947 meeting the National Assembly consulted with Robert McLaughlin, a Bahá'í who was a noted architect in the New York area and who a short time later would be appointed director of the School of Architecture at Princeton University. Mr. McLaughlin felt that it was not necessary to hire an architect; a "good draftsman" could produce the working drawings and specifications necessary to negotiate contracts for the actual construction. But he strongly advised the National Assembly that it needed "a building committee of well qualified persons as their representatives."[20] Acting on this recommendation, the National Assembly appointed a Technical Advisory Board to work with the Temple Construction Committee. The members of the new board were Allen McDaniel, Robert McLaughlin, and Edwin Eardley, a Bahá'í who worked for one of Detroit's leading architectural firms, for whom he prepared cost analyses on construction projects.

In July the National Assembly devoted much of its meeting to determining whether the task of final preparation should be assigned to Messrs. Kennedy and Pompilio, as recommended by the Technical Advisory Board, or to Alfred Shaw. Although it seemed more expeditious to hire Messrs. Kennedy and Pompilio given their familiarity with the design, the minimum fee required by the two men was $13,000 higher than Mr. Shaw's estimated fee. Hence a contract was signed with Mr. Shaw on 4 August 1947.

The general consensus among the members of the National Spiritual

---

*During the time the National Assembly was considering Alfred Shaw for preparing the final drawings of the interior, Mr. Shaw left his partners and formed a new architectural and engineering firm—Shaw, Metz and Dolio.

The Final Years

Assembly was that the McDaniel plan was the "final modification of the Bourgeois design." It was, therefore, made clear to Alfred Shaw that "no further alterations in the architectural concept of the interior could be made. . . ." Yet Paul Haney expressed concern "as to whether from an artistic point of view the flow of design as conceived by Mr. Bourgeois has been fully preserved." When the National Assembly attempted to clarify this point with Robert McLaughlin, he suggested that "Mr. Shaw should be given an opportunity to work out his own interpretation of the carrying out of the Bourgeois theme. . . ."[21]

By November 1947 Alfred Shaw had submitted several preliminary sketches, but the Technical Advisory Board was not satisfied with the results. Modifications in the sketches during the next several weeks prompted the board to recognize that Mr. Shaw's work was beginning to show "the freedom of expression and graceful flow of line in which Bourgeois excelled." Yet Mr. Shaw proposed that the first two levels of the auditorium be combined and that the clerestory not be visible from the interior. This was strongly rejected by the Technical Board. After two more months of work by Mr. Shaw, Robert McLaughlin informed the National Assembly on behalf of the Technical Board that the design was evolving "into a very distinguished interior" that would be "completely homogeneous with the best of the exterior." Mr. McLaughlin told the National Assembly a few months later that he "did not know of another architect in the country of Mr. Shaw's professional standing and reputation who would have been as cooperative in sublimating himself to the conditions and directions under which it was necessary for him to work."[22]

Alfred Shaw was also successful in integrating elements of architectural styles that had become popular since the death of Louis Bourgeois. Thirty-six of the seventy-two concrete piers supporting the dome were converted into ornamental columns that taper inward toward the bottom, rather than tapering outward, as many types of masonry columns had done for centuries. "In so doing," wrote Robert McLaughlin, the tapered columns "register as surface treatment and not as massive masonry."[23] Similar columns can be found in Frank Lloyd Wright's Johnson Wax Administration Building in Racine, Wisconsin, a noted example of the simple and economical Streamline Moderne style that evolved during the 1930s. In the Temple's light fixtures and provision for indirect lighting in the alcoves, Mr. Shaw also incorporated elements of Art Deco, popularized during the late twenties.

On 4 and 6 May 1948 Shoghi Effendi approved Alfred Shaw's design and instructed that construction contracts be placed as quickly as possible.[24] The George A. Fuller Company, general contractor for the superstructure in 1930–

The Final Years

31, was again hired to do the interior work. This decision was based on the company's familiarity with the building and their willingness to accept a contract for three years at a flat fee of $25,000, an arrangement Mr. Shaw and the Technical Advisory Board felt to be most advantageous for the National Assembly.

Modifications to the design, however, were not yet complete. Alfred Shaw wanted to study his plans in three dimensions by having several portions of the ornamentation made into models. Arrangements were made in June 1948 to have these models done by the Earley Studio, which was still in business.* But the studio was involved in so many projects that it was unable to begin the modeling quickly enough. Thus the work was reassigned to an architectural sculpturing studio, Rochette and Parzini, in New York City. After Mr. Shaw studied the models, he made several changes in the design "in the interest of better flow and vitality of the ornamental motifs."[25]

When projected building costs exceeded the goal of $650,000, several economy measures were studied, including the elimination of the new stairway to the gallery and the substitution of rubber tile for terrazzo flooring. Shoghi Effendi vetoed these recommendations and "reluctantly" approved a new maximum expenditure of $750,000.[26]

For reasons of cost, it was at first decided that ornamental plaster would be used instead of the Earley Studios' architectural concrete; the Bahá'ís felt that as much as $40,000 could be saved in material and labor. Yet the Earley Studio, armed with the knowledge gained from a decade of experience with the building, was able to submit a bid $12,000 lower than the one for ornamental plaster. Hence the National Assembly decided in favor of the Earley Studio in January 1949. This delighted everyone since it was felt that architectural concrete was "preferable to plaster as to appearance, durability, cleanliness and permanence."[27]

While work on the ornamentation progressed, the Fuller Company removed the original staircase on the southwest side of the Temple auditorium and constructed a much smaller and more beautiful one on the northeast side. The temporary wooden entry doors were replaced with simple glass and metal

---

*Providentially, only weeks before John Earley's death he had sold the studio for one dollar to his lifetime partner, Basil Taylor.

Opposite: *Alfred Shaw's modified design for the interior of the Temple. The ornamentation proposed for the inside of the gallery arches was not implemented.*

The Final Years

The unfinished interior of the Temple auditorium a few years before the ornamentation was installed. The stairway on the left was removed and a more beautiful one built on the other side of the auditorium.

The Final Years

Panels of interior ornamentation being installed on the main level of the Temple auditorium

ones, and large panels of plate glass were substituted for the crosshatched windows throughout the main level. Half of the concrete piers supporting the upper levels of the building were reduced in width and rounded to accept the tapered ornamental surfacing.

Following installation of the metal ducting for the heating and ventilation systems, the Fuller Company constructed ceilings in each of the alcoves. Alfred Shaw had incorporated into each ceiling two graceful ogee curves that converge at the top into a straight line. Acoustical plaster was used in both the gallery and clerestory ceilings to help reduce sound reverberation.

The first railroad car containing sections of the concrete tracery for the interior left the Earley Studio on 8 July 1949. The panels were installed first at the base of the main-floor level and then, level by level, covered the interior walls and dome. The work proceeded smoothly and was not even interrupted

The Final Years

Interior ornamentation of the dome of the Temple nearing completion, March 1951

by a second fire connected with the Temple project, this time at the Earley Studio.

After the war the studio had ceased employing a night watchman. But in mid-February 1950 Basil Taylor inexplicably decided to employ a watchman again. One week later, during the evening of 22 February, the watchman noticed a bright glow toward the back area of the studio grounds. Running out into the yard, he discovered in flames some piles of old lumber and a large shed near the rear woodworking building. By the time the fire department arrived, the north wall of the studio's main building was starting to blaze. Fortunately, the flames were extinguished quickly, and the damage proved minimal. " 'If the fire had not been detected promptly,' " wrote Allen McDaniel, " 'the loss would have . . . resulted in a delay of at least 6 months in the work of the Temple ornamentation.' "[28]

The Final Years

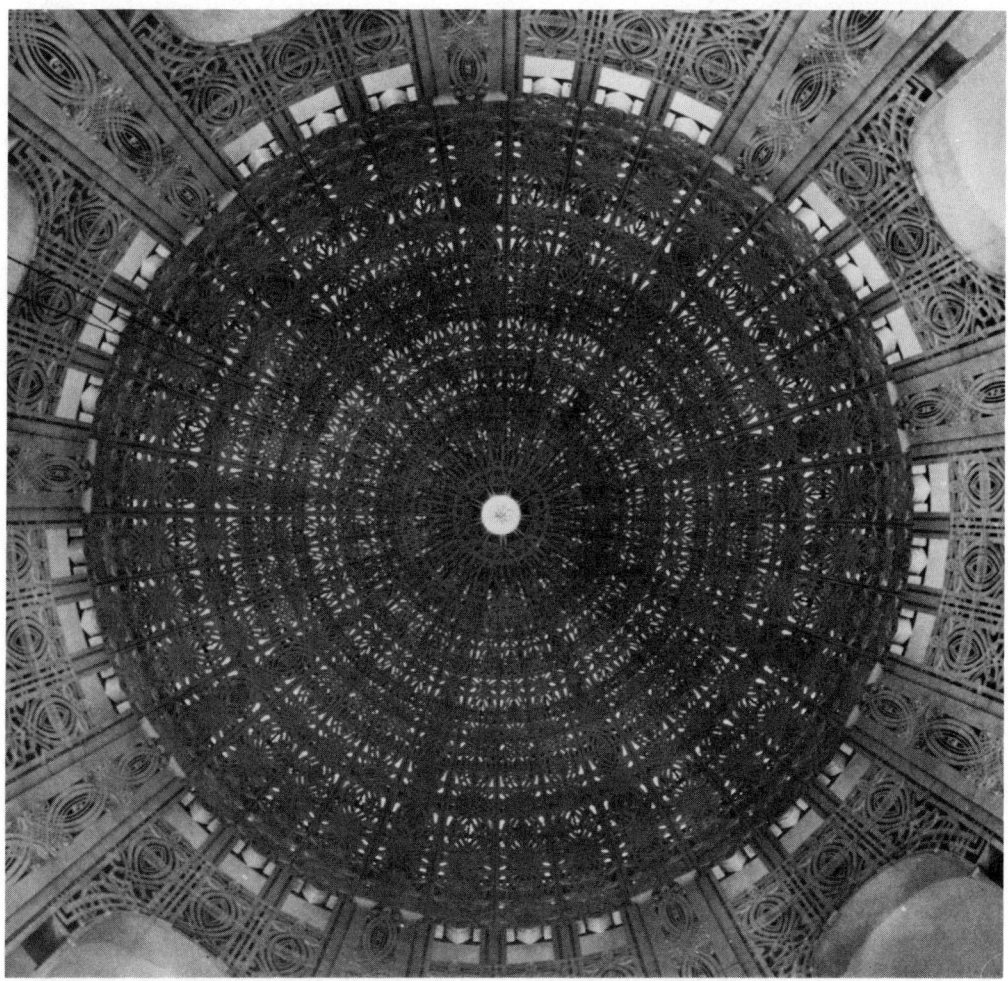

The interior of the dome of the Temple, virtually completed, June 1951

The last shipment of ornamentation left Rosslyn, Virginia, on 20 March 1951. Two weeks later the last of the 2,457 interior panels was lifted to the top of the dome and locked in place. Only five years of the second Seven Year Plan had passed, and much more than the Temple's ornamentation had been achieved by the Bahá'ís of the world. Already more than twenty-five hundred Bahá'í centers existed in 106 countries and dependencies. Bahá'í literature had been translated into more than eighty languages. The National Spiritual Assem-

Interior ornamentation at the gallery and dome levels

bly of Canada had been formed, and the National Assemblies for Central and South America were about to come into existence. Bahá'ís representing twenty-two countries had attended teaching conferences in Europe, where efforts met

The interior of the main level of the Temple auditorium, with ornamentation and lighting installed. The Bahá'í symbols over each arch were later removed at the instruction of Shoghi Effendi.

with steady success. Despite periodic deficits in 1948–49, which necessitated suspending all Bahá'í school programs and the publication of the magazine *World Order*, the Bahá'ís in the United States and Canada sustained the cost of

The Final Years

finishing the Temple's interior. They also contributed more than $50,000 to the construction of the Shrine of the Báb, the columned arcade of which was already complete.

Nevertheless, Shoghi Effendi's continuing plea was to " 'redouble your efforts.' " The Temple, he directed, could not be officially opened until 1953. Although the Bahá'ís could use the auditorium "just exactly the same way as they have been doing during the past few years," neither could they hold frequent services nor could they invite the public to meetings in the auditorium.[29] The auditorium could, however, continue to be inspected by visitors.

Several items still had to be completed inside the building, including the installation of draperies and 1,191 chairs, and the laying of a terrazzo floor. In addition, a plan needed to be developed for the gardens. A Temple Landscape Committee was appointed by the National Spiritual Assembly, and in spring 1951 several landscape architects were invited to submit designs and cost estimates.[30] The criterion for the design was based in large measure on 'Abdu'l-Bahá's directives, made decades earlier, that there be nine gardens, each with a fountain. Furthermore, the gardens were to be separated by nine avenues that lead to a circular walkway.

Louis Bourgeois' original concept for the gardens included nine illuminated fountains, the water of which would flow into a central basin that faced Akka. From the basin the water would cascade forty feet down into Lake Michigan. Mr. Bourgeois had also designed a small harbor with steps that led alongside the waterfall and up to the gardens. Such a concept apparently did not seem practical to the Bahá'ís in 1951.

Five new plans were submitted, one with an estimated cost of more than $860,000. The design the Landscape Committee recommended, however, would cost a more reasonable $250,000. It was the creation of Hilbert E. Dahl of Frankfort, Kentucky, who, while residing in Illinois in the 1930s, had served with his wife as a guide at the Temple. He had conceived his first design for the gardens in 1938. The National Spiritual Assembly approved the Dahl design on 6 July 1951. A little over a month later, on 17 August, Shoghi Effendi ratified their decision.[31]

"The evolution of a garden setting for such an architectural composition taxed the capacity of several waste baskets," noted Hilbert Dahl in an article he wrote for *Landscape Architecture* magazine. At the base of the eighteen circular stairs, he explained, was to be a circular terrace, the outer edge of which would be divided into nine incurving sections. "With a garden nestled into the arms of

The Final Years

Clearing the land around the Temple in preparation for the installation of the gardens designed by Hilbert E. Dahl, 4 September 1952

each incurving terrace section, the rhythm of the alternating curved faces of the structure [the Temple] appears carried into the garden setting with appropriate gradation."[32]

Mr. Dahl designed the nine gardens to be similar yet allow for some variation in the details. The gardens would be almost circular, enclosed on either side by an avenue of Chinese juniper trees. Beautiful and varied flowers would be highlighted in two crescent-shaped beds in each garden. Planted between the beds would be a grassed area that would widen toward the Temple and surround a circular pool measuring nineteen feet in diameter. Visitors could walk around the nine gardens on a circular walkway and approach the Temple by way of nine raised walks, each leading to a short flight of stairs. " 'The

The Final Years

Planting Chinese junipers that would line the nine approach walks to the Temple

gardens are arranged and planted with simple dignity,' " wrote Mr. Dahl, " 'restrained in treatment but with a touch of color and softness of texture which will give them a gardenesque feeling of peaceful and quiet loveliness.' "33

The George A. Fuller Company was again hired to serve as general contractor in developing the nearly five acres of grounds. The project was divided into two stages. The terrace, stairs, walkways, and most of the trees and shrubs were installed during the first stage, completed in late 1952. The second stage, involving the installation of lighting and the construction of the pools, would not be finished until after the dedication in 1953.

On 1 November 1951, three months after the National Spiritual Assembly had accepted Hilbert Dahl's design, Corinne True celebrated her ninetieth birthday. She had journeyed to the Holy Land seven times during the nearly fifty years of the Temple project, and she longed to make one final pilgrimage

The Final Years

Newly planted rows of Chinese junipers, 17 September 1952

to the heart of the Bahá'í world. When Shoghi Effendi learned of her wish, he asked her to come in October 1952, at which time she would be his only guest—a privilege rare and unique. She was not destined, however, to arrive in Haifa as merely a pilgrim; for on 28 February 1952 she received a second cablegram from Shoghi Effendi that brought some astonishing news: "Moved convey glad tidings your elevation rank Hand Cause. Appointment officially announced public message addressed all National Assemblies. May sacred function enable you enrich record services already rendered Faith Bahá'u'lláh."[34]

With her appointment as Hand of the Cause of God, a station of which she would never have considered herself worthy, Corinne True was singled out as one of the most distinguished Bahá'ís in history. The rank Hand of the Cause of God was conferred only by Bahá'u'lláh, 'Abdu'l-Bahá, and Shoghi Effendi upon Bahá'ís they felt to be most qualified to protect the Faith and promote the

The Final Years

spread of its teachings. Only a handful of Bahá'ís had been the recipients of this great honor.

The trip to Haifa would be arduous for Corinne True. Two of her daughters, Katherine and Edna, cabled Shoghi Effendi for permission to accompany their mother and care for her. Making the trip in stages, they spent a week in Paris and a second one in Switzerland. Shoghi Effendi was also in Switzerland and returned to Haifa only the day before their arrival. With him were the newly completed plans for the Ten Year Crusade, a global teaching campaign that would be launched in conjunction with the dedication of the Temple. When Mrs. True arrived, she found Shoghi Effendi on fire with anticipation of the great victories that were destined to be won.

Shoghi Effendi devoted his time and love almost exclusively to Mrs. True. They spent endless hours conversing, and he constantly took delight in her incredibly accurate memories of the early days of the Faith in America. As was often his custom, he placed Corinne True at the head of the dinner table and sat on her right. Even during dinner they were often oblivious to the rest of those present. One Bahá'í from the United States, who was working for Shoghi Effendi at that time, remarked that he had never seen Shoghi Effendi respond to anyone the way he did to Mrs. True.

One evening Shoghi Effendi arrived early for dinner, which caused the Trues to rush to finish dressing.[35] When Mrs. True entered the dining room, Shoghi Effendi approached her with a radiant and somewhat impish smile. He said that he recalled she had worked a great deal to promote the Temple project and asked her if this was correct. Thinking he was quite serious, she responded affirmatively. He then said he thought she had been involved with raising money for the Temple and wondered if this was also correct. Somewhat puzzled, she again responded affirmatively. The smile on his face broadening even further, he held forth an object and said that under the circumstances he felt she should have a small gift.

Corinne True reached forward and tenderly grasped the purse that 'Abdu'l-Bahá had used throughout His visit to the United States in 1912. Tears streamed down her cheeks as she reverently touched its worn leather to her forehead. Shoghi Effendi, his eyes filled with love and admiration, impatiently urged her to open one of the pockets. Inside she found a five-dollar gold piece bearing the date 1907, the year of her first pilgrimage. That coin was one of ten she had brought with her as a gift to 'Abdu'l-Bahá from the Women's Assembly of Teaching.

Shortly after Corinne True left Haifa, Shoghi Effendi compiled a booklet

The Temple gardens, as seen from the corner of Sheridan Road and Linden Avenue, December 1952

of statistical and comparative information on the Faith in preparation for the Ten Year Crusade. One section lists "Dates of Historical Significance: 1844–1952." The extreme importance Shoghi Effendi attached to the Temple project is indicated by the fact that five of the forty-nine historic events chosen by him to be included in the list involve various stages in the fifty-year struggle to raise the Mother Temple of the West: the first American Bahá'í convention in March 1909, 'Abdu'l-Bahá's laying of the dedication stone in May 1912, the beginning of the construction of the building in December 1920, the completion of the exterior ornamentation in 1943, and the completion of the interior in 1952.[36]

As the finishing touches were being applied to the building, Bahá'ís began

The Final Years

to anticipate eagerly the beginning of the 109th Bahá'í year in March 1953; for it would mark the start of another yearlong observance, the centenary celebration of the commencement of Bahá'u'lláh's prophetic mission. Early in 1952 Shoghi Effendi announced that during the centenary celebration four Bahá'í intercontinental teaching conferences, the first ever held, would be convened in Africa, America, Europe, and Asia to inaugurate the "long anticipated intercontinental stage" in the evolution of Bahá'í administrative institutions.[37] The second of these conferences, involving all republics of North and South America, was scheduled to be held in Chicago and Wilmette as part of a week-long American Jubilee Celebration, 29 April–6 May 1953. Among the events included in the celebration would be the forty-fifth annual convention and—fifty years and two months after the Chicago House of Spirituality launched the project—the fifth and final dedication of the Temple.

Chapter Nineteen
THE DEDICATION

EVERYTHING was ready. Gone were the workmen, the scaffolding and concrete forms, the ladders, the hammers, and other tools that had given birth to a brilliant architectural gem. Throughout the newly planted gardens, rows of Chinese junipers swayed gently in the breeze. The inside of the huge auditorium was flooded with streams of light, falling on the rich red upholstered chairs, the terrazzo floor, and the white ornamental panels with their rose-colored backgrounds and their bold, sweeping lines. Where once could be seen only cold, unadorned concrete and steel, now the eye could delight in graceful curves, weaving over and about one another as they reach upward toward the apex of the dome.[1]

On the opening day of the American Jubilee Celebration, 29 April 1953, the last of the events that had created a special bond between the Wilmette Temple and the Shrine of the Báb took place. Shoghi Effendi, cabling the Bahá'ís assembled in Chicago, joyously announced the initiation of the final construction phase of the Shrine. In a ceremony earlier that day he had laid the first forty-four of the twelve thousand guilded tiles that would cover the building's dome. During that ceremony he had also reverently placed beneath the tiles a piece of ceiling plaster from the cell of the castle of Máku, located in the Azerbaijan Mountains in northwest Iran near the Turkish border, where the Báb had been imprisoned for nine months in 1847–48. Although the date for the dedication ceremonies in Wilmette had been chosen far in advance, Shoghi Effendi had not intended to begin tiling the dome at the same time, for he did not initially know that the work on the Shrine would have progressed as far as it had. But in August 1951 he had cabled that the deteriorating international situation impelled him to contract immediately for the cutting of the stone for the octagon and dome sections of the structure.

The Jubilee week began in North America with the Bahá'í annual conven-

The Dedication

tion, held at Chicago's Medinah Temple. The most distinguished visitor at that gathering was Shoghi Effendi's wife, Amatu'l-Bahá Rúḥíyyih Khánum, who had read a prayer at the Temple site in 1933 when the first shipment of ornamentation for the exterior had arrived. Now twenty years later, she received a tumultuous welcome upon her arrival. Responding to the ovation, she said:

> Friends, if you are moved, I don't think it is at all comparable to how much I am moved. I have come from our Beloved Shoghi Effendi. He would have been very happy to be here himself with you but, as you know, he has so much work, so many guests, so many burdens, it is quite impossible for him to come himself, and so he gave me this inestimable bounty of coming as his representative and seeing you all. . . .
>
> When I was a little girl, I always said that I knew almost all the people of my Faith in America, because we could get them all into a relatively small room. . . . But to think that now in the United States there are so many Bahá'ís, that they are so active and that they are really the torch-bearers of the Cause of Bahá'u'lláh all over the world, it is just unbelievable, and it is a great privilege to be here with you today. . . .
>
> When he [Shoghi Effendi] looked forward to this great Centenary, his thoughts were particularly concentrated on the gathering of the American Bahá'ís, because he felt that the dedication of the great House of Worship of the West and the crusade that we are now embarking on, all these things converging here in Chicago . . . , make it the most important of all our events during this Holy Year.[2]

Rúḥíyyih Khánum then read a message from Shoghi Effendi, which said in part:

> My soul is uplifted in joy and thanksgiving at the triumphant conclusion of the second Seven Year Plan immortalized by the brilliant victories simultaneously won . . . in Latin America, in Europe and in Africa—victories befittingly crowned through the consummation of a fifty year old enterprise, the completion of the first Mashriqu'l-Adhkár of the western world. . . . I am impelled . . . to pay warmest tribute to the preeminent share which the American Bahá'í Community has had in the course of over half a century in proclaiming His Revelation, in shielding His Cause, in championing His Covenant, in erecting the administrative machinery of His embryonic World Order, in expounding His teachings, in translating and disseminating His Holy Word, in despatching the messengers of His Glad-

The Dedication

Hundreds of people awaiting one of the four dedication services for the Bahá'í Temple, 1–2 May 1953

Tidings, in awakening Royalty to His Call, in succoring His oppressed followers, in routing His enemies, in upholding His Law, in asserting the independence of His Faith, in multiplying the financial resources of its nascent institutions and, last but not least, in rearing its Greatest House of Worship. . . .[3]

On the afternoon of the third day of the Jubilee, 1 May, the Bahá'ís traveled to the Temple for a private dedication and simple service commemorating 'Abdu'l-Bahá's visit and laying of the dedication stone in 1912. Later that evening the Bahá'ís and several hundred residents of Chicago's northern suburbs gathered in the auditorium of the New Trier High School in nearby Winnetka to hear about the history, architecture, and purpose of the Temple. This was one of four large public meetings held during the Jubilee week at which lectures

The Dedication

The Hand of the Cause of God AMATU'L-BAHÁ RÚḤÍYYIH KHÁNUM dedicating the Bahá'í Temple on behalf of Shoghi Effendi, 2 May 1953. "This House of Worship, now opening wide its doors to people of all creeds, of all races, of all nations and of all classes, is dedicated to the three fundamental verities animating and underlying the Bahá'í Faith—the Unity of God, the Unity of His Prophets, the Unity of Mankind."

were delivered by well-known Bahá'ís—Rúḥíyyih Khánum, Horace Holley, Robert McLaughlin, and Allen McDaniel—and also by noted guest speakers, including Dr. Paul Hutchinson, editor of the influential Protestant periodical *Christian Century*, and Norman Cousins, president of the United World Federalists and editor of the *Saturday Review of Literature*.

The public dedication of the Temple was held the following afternoon, 2 May. The sky was overcast; but the weather was hardly noticed by the great number of people who stood silently and waited, filling the Temple steps, the entrance walkway, and even the sidewalk beyond. The morning had been filled with a flurry of activity as the readers participating in the dedication and the members of a Northwestern University choir had endured a lengthy rehearsal in the auditorium so that cameras and recording equipment could capture perfectly this historic event.

The Dedication

A capacity audience at one of the three public dedication services held on 2 May 1953

Shortly before the service began, Corinne True, now ninety-one years old, arrived at the Temple. One of her daughters recalled:

> I have never seen her so affected by anything as she was by the fact that she was going to the dedication. As she approached the Temple everyone stopped her wanting to speak to her, but she couldn't. She did not weep, but she could not speak. She could hardly raise her head. It was a tremendously moving moment. It was like carrying a load for a very long time, and then, suddenly, the load was lifted. At that moment it was reality.[4]

As the doors were opened and people filed in quietly, reporters made their way to the gallery, where they stood on wooden chairs and peered over the edge at the crowd below. An array of microphones stood in front of the lectern, which was flanked by huge bouquets of red roses. In the front rows sat thirteen of the eighteen living Hands of the Cause of God. Nearby sat almost all of the Bahá'ís still living who had been present at the dedication ceremony in 1912.

The Dedication

Radio and television personality William Sears, a Bahá'í who later became a Hand of the Cause of God, wrote, "Every moment inside that dome of exquisite beauty and majesty . . . was enriched by memories of the love and sacrifice that had raised this jewel of God."[5]

The ceremony opened when the voices of the choir, hidden from sight in the gallery, filled the auditorium with music. Then Rúḥíyyih Khánum stepped to the lectern to begin speaking:

> "On behalf of the Guardian of the Faith of Bahá'u'lláh, I have the great honor of dedicating this first Mashriqu'l-Adhkár of the Western World to public worship.
>
> ". . . this House of Worship, now opening wide its doors to peoples of all creeds, of all races, of all nations and of all classes, is dedicated to the three fundamental verities animating and underlying the Bahá'í Faith—the Unity of God, the Unity of His Prophets, the Unity of Mankind.
>
> "I greet and welcome you on behalf of the Guardian of our Faith within these walls, and invite you to share with us the words recorded in the Sacred Scriptures which we believe to be repositories of the eternal and fundamental truths revealed by God in various ages, for the guidance and salvation of all mankind."[6]

After asking the audience to rise, Rúḥíyyih Khánum read a prayer by Bahá'u'lláh that Shoghi Effendi had selected for the dedication. "As the address of the Dedication ended," wrote Williams Sears,

> a quiet settled over the assembled throng. Through the doorway to the East could be seen the blue waters of Lake Michigan rushing toward the Temple in great white waves, bowing and prostrating themselves upon the sand. Through the doors to the South were visible the throngs of people streaming toward the Temple. The clouds, which had threatened to shut out the sun, parted and down through the glass dome came the flooding sunlight as the first of the Holy Books was opened.

Passages were read from the Bahá'í writings, the Qur'án, and the Old and New Testaments. The dedication ended with the choir's singing "From The Sweet-Scented Streams," a prayer by Bahá'u'lláh set to music by Charles Wolcott, head of the music department for Metro-Goldwyn-Mayer.[7]

The dedication service was conducted three times, the 1,191 seat auditorium being filled for each. Hundreds more had to be turned away. It is estimated that, in addition to the Bahá'ís, twenty-seven hundred people attended or attempted to attend the service.

During the following afternoon, 3 May, more than twenty-three hundred Bahá'ís from thirty-three countries returned to the Temple to view a sacred gift sent by Shoghi Effendi. The day was again cold and windy, and people huddled together on the steps for warmth, enduring a wait that for some lasted up to five hours. As each person entered through the glass doors, Rúḥíyyih Khánum anointed them with attar of rose, as 'Abdu'l-Bahá had frequently done in 1912. At the opposite side of the auditorium the Bahá'ís slowly and quietly passed by two tables. On the first rested a portrait of the Báb, a gift from Shoghi Effendi to the Temple in 1944. On the second was Shoghi Effendi's gift for the Jubilee—a colored portrait of Bahá'u'lláh when He was a young man.

Numerous congratulatory messages were received by the National Spiritual Assembly, several from prominent public leaders. One message came from Justice William O. Douglas of the Supreme Court of the United States:

"The Bahá'í House of Worship at Wilmette, Illinois, is a structure of great beauty, as millions who have seen it know. But perhaps not so many realize its symbolic significance. It teaches the essential unity of mankind under one God, irrespective of the various sects and creeds that give expression to the various faiths. There is a basic wholeness among people the world around. There are spiritual ties that unite them in the brotherhood of man. . . . The important thing is recognition of the essential unity of mankind under one God. That is a force which cuts across politics, trade routes, racial groupings the world around. It can be made a powerful moral force in the practical affairs of the world if there is a dedication to the cause—the kind of dedication that went into the long and difficult task of constructing the Bahá'í House of Worship at Wilmette."[8]

Abba Eban, ambassador of Israel to the United States, cabled:

"On occasion of dedication of Bahá'í House of Worship I wish to convey to you sincere greetings and congratulations of State of Israel. Israel people and government, harboring in their country the Bahá'í spiritual Center, have always cherished cordial, friendly relations with Guardians [sic] of that Center and all Bahá'ís. Ideals of peace and brotherliness underlying Bahá'í Faith are dear and sacred to Israel, ancient and revived alike."[9]

Dr. Marcus Bach of the University of Iowa, a world-renowned author, wrote that it was his " 'earnest hope that men of every belief and race may catch the spirit and power inherent in the Bahá'í cause and that this day of dedication will hasten the dawn of concord and direct the eyes of nations toward the light of brotherhood and peace.' "[10]

Further praise came from Thurgood Marshall, director and counsel of the National Association for the Advancement of Colored People's Legal Defense and Education Fund, and later a Supreme Court justice. The Bahá'ís, he said, offered " 'full religious fellowship to all without distinctions based upon race and color. . . .' " The executive director of the NAACP, Roy Wilkins, wrote that " 'Our poor world is in great need of the deep faith and sincere and unostentatious practices of the Bahá'ís.' "[11]

Educators, clergymen, and numerous other well-wishers also sent moving messages. Dr. E. A. Burtt of Cornell University stated that the dedication was " 'a notable occasion in the history and progress of religion in the United States.' " Ruth Bryan Rhode, former United States ambassador to Denmark, expressed the hope that " 'the beauty of the edifice and its symbolism [would] carry inspiration in wider and wider circles around our troubled earth.' " Dr. Raymond Frank Piper of Syracuse University found the Temple to be " 'a unique and magnificent achievement in the history of the world's religions and cultures because it embodies, in incomparable, compelling, and unforgettable beauty, the glorious ideal of the enlightened and creative unity of religions. . . .' "[12]

The media demonstrated considerable interest in the dedication and Jubilee celebration, as it had during the Bahá'í Centenary in 1944. Five hundred fifty-seven newspapers in 397 cities carried articles, including the *Washington Post, Seattle Times, Boston Advertiser, Cincinnati Enquirer, Louisville Courier-Journal, Indianapolis Times, Albuquerque Tribune, Minneapolis Star, Los Angeles Times,* and *Detroit News.* Both the *Chicago Daily News* and the *Chicago Tribune,* as well as newspapers in Milwaukee, provided extensive coverage of the Jubilee week activities; the *Tribune* featured a colored photograph of the Temple on the front page of its Sunday picture section.[13] Throughout the Jubilee week three major railroads serving Chicago—the Rock Island; the Chicago, Milwaukee and St. Paul; and the Sante Fe—distributed to all Chicago-bound passengers booklets that pictured the Temple on the cover and featured an article on its history.

Universal International covered the dedication in its Universal Newsreel, released through film exchanges in thirty-one cities and thirty-eight foreign countries. The film showed various views of both the inside and outside of the Temple, as well as of a group of Bahá'ís walking up the circular steps. Other publicity included a series of thirteen radio programs that was broadcast in

The Dedication

The Bahá'í Temple, Wilmette, Illinois, shortly after its dedication, 2 May 1953

The Dedication

many cities and beamed by the World Wide Broadcasting Corporation to Europe, the Near East, and Latin America. Fifty television stations and numerous radio stations nationwide aired programs related to the dedication.

The eight days of activities surrounding the dedication came to a close all too soon. One of the dedication's participants, Marzieh Gail, returned to Wilmette shortly before sunset on the final day. "The Temple had taken on the color of old lace," she recalled. "Birds were darting and calling in and out of the intricacies of the dome." On the steps below, children were playing, and in the gardens mechanical sprayers watered the grass. The young trees, standing "as uncertain as a newborn colt," cast their reflection upon the wet walkways. "It was one of those twilights when the dead seem to return and to remember us again. Certainly this place, which so many of our dead spent much of their lives to build, must draw them back. The living had all gone away, but I knew they never would be very far from here."[14]

Though the long history of constructing the Temple was at an end, a new saga was beginning. The "flaming beacon" at last stood ready to receive the citizens of the world.[15]

Chapter Twenty
EPILOGUE

WHEN THE eleven men of Chicago's 1903 House of Spirituality read the account of the Temple construction in Ashkhabad and discussed building one of their own, they probably did not comprehend the significance of their decision. 'Abdu'l-Bahá's response to their petition—that the building of a Temple was "the greatest affair and the most important matter to-day"—may even have baffled them, for their knowledge of Bahá'u'lláh's teachings was still rudimentary.[1] Eight decades later it is clear why 'Abdu'l-Bahá attached such importance to the Temple. The project forced the few Bahá'í communities in existence in America in 1903 to look beyond the requirements of their local affairs and to focus their time, energy, and resources on a nationwide effort that produced, as essential by-products, a national administrative structure and several systematic plans for spreading Bahá'í beliefs.

Many of the early Bahá'ís saw in the immense project only the raising of a building. But at least some of them appreciated the value of organizing as a national community. "ORGANIZATION is the base of UNITY and of all accomplishment," wrote Thornton Chase in 1910.[2] His tireless efforts in nurturing the Chicago House of Spirituality, even after his move to California, provided an example to Bahá'ís at a time when organization was deemed neither necessary nor appropriate.

Corinne True also appreciated the necessity of pooling talent and resources. She recognized that the Chicago community's initial reluctance to enlist the help of other communities was the "limitation which rendered us powerless." Her response was to champion, with 'Abdu'l-Bahá's guidance, the formation of the Bahai Temple Unity, which would place responsibility for the Temple work in the hands of elected representatives from across the country. Thus she helped lay the foundation for the National Spiritual Assembly—the successor to the Bahai Temple Unity Executive Board. "In reality this [Temple project] marks the beginning of our nationality," Corinne True wrote in the early days of the

Epilogue

project. It soon became apparent, however, that more than a national identity was being forged. Only two decades later, in 1927, the National Spiritual Assembly of the Bahá'ís of the United States and Canada would adopt a Declaration of Trust that would become, according to Shoghi Effendi, a " 'worthy and faithful exposition of the constitutional basis of Bahá'í Communities in every land' " and would " 'serve as a pattern to every National Bahá'í Assembly. . . .' "3

In the nearly five decades between the petition of the House of Spirituality and the planting of the last rows of junipers, the project required the unremitting dedication of a still relatively small group of adherents to the new religion. Many Bahá'ís—Corinne True, Louis Bourgeois, and Victoria Bedikian among them—devoted a major portion of their lives to the Temple. Others made material sacrifices, large and small. The winter blanket foregone in India; the pennies from a handkerchief sold in Persia; the dimes and nickels from blacks in the South, "very poor and sometimes very old"—these are the sacrifices that will inspire Bahá'ís for generations.4

'Abdu'l-Bahá had specifically counseled the Bahá'ís of the East to send their contributions to America, for He wished it to become known " 'throughout the universe that the Bahais of the East and West are as members of one household and the children of the one Lord.' "5 As early as 1909 the resources of Bahá'ís in both hemispheres were being collected to build the Wilmette Temple. "We have learned an entirely new aspect of the Cause . . . ," wrote the National Spiritual Assembly in 1925, "its unshakeable bond of unity extending from Assembly to Assembly, from nation to nation, from race to race; and its unique capacity for combining many loyalties into one common purpose. . . ."6 The finished Temple stands today as evidence of what that bond of unity can achieve.

'Abdu'l-Bahá predicted that upon the Temple's completion " 'the spirit of teaching [the Faith] . . . will permeate to all parts of the world.' "7 Although it had taken 109 years (1844–1953) to establish the Faith in 128 countries, that number was increased by 50 during the twelve months immediately following the 1953 dedication of the Temple. By 1963 the Faith had been established in 259 countries, more than twice the number before the dedication, and the number of National Spiritual Assemblies had been increased from twelve to

Opposite: *The Bahá'í Temple, Wilmette, Illinois. 'Abdu'l-Bahá's hope was that "all religions, races and sects" would "come together within its universal shelter" and "that the proclamation of the oneness of mankind" would "go forth" from its hallowed precincts.*

Epilogue

fifty-six. Today (1984), in the 209 independent nations, dependent territories, and overseas departments around the globe, as they are now calculated by The Universal House of Justice, there are 135 National Spiritual Assemblies.

The Wilmette Temple's destiny as the " 'mother,' " a " 'sample for the coming centuries,' " has also been confirmed.[8] Two Temples were finished in 1961, one near Kampala, Uganda, and another near Sydney, Australia. Three years later the first Temple in Europe was dedicated on the outskirts of Frankfurt, West Germany. In 1972 the Bahá'ís opened the doors of a fifth Temple, situated on a hill overlooking Panama City. Two other Temples are currently under construction in India and Western Samoa, and Temple sites have been purchased in many locations around the world.

Visitors to the Wilmette Temple during the thirty years since its dedication have numbered more than 4,300,000 people, ten times the recorded number who visited during the three decades the building was under construction. They have come from nearly every nation on earth. Some have become Bahá'ís, helping to expand to nearly 114,000 the number of localities in which Bahá'ís reside worldwide. Others come again and again, drawn by the spirit of welcome that lowers the barriers of race, nationality, and creed. Through a growing number of programs for the public, the Temple continues to be a major vehicle for promoting the Bahá'í teachings, particularly in the United States. On 23 May 1978 special recognition was given to the Temple when the United States government listed it in the National Register of Historic Places.

The Wilmette Temple's ultimate purpose, however, is still in its infancy. For in the future this and all Temples will each serve as the core of an indispensable institution of the Bahá'í Faith, the Mashriqu'l-Adhkár, or "dawning place of the mention of God." Surrounding each Temple and completing the Mashriqu'l-Adhkár will be educational, social, and humanitarian facilities that will "afford relief to the suffering, sustenance to the poor, shelter to the wayfarer, solace to the bereaved, and education to the ignorant."[9] These facilities will be arenas in which the finest fruits of humankind's science and technology as well as its spiritual understanding and insight can be utilized. A home for the aged, completed in 1958, is the first of the humanitarian facilities built in the vicinity of the Wilmette Temple.

Today the Temple provides the "place of meeting" that 'Abdu'l-Bahá hoped would be "conducive to unity and fellowship" for all humanity.[10] Beneath its dome people of all religions come together regularly to worship, without clergy or ritual, and to hear sacred writings from the world's Holy Books read and sung. Staff members of the national administrative center of the Faith in the

United States also gather there often, singly and in groups, to derive inspiration for the discharge of their responsibilities.

Shoghi Effendi has stated that the building of the Temple in Wilmette was the "crowning achievement" of the Bahá'ís during the first Bahá'í century. It is the hope of Bahá'ís that buildings such as the Temple and its surrounding dependencies will continue to grow in their service to humanity, for only then will the Temple become a haven for all humankind. Already many people are reaping the fruits of the labors of early Bahá'ís such as Thornton Chase, who, in 1908, had a remarkably clear vision of the role of the Temple:

> There is little doubt that, wherever it may be, a Bahai community will grow up about it, care for it, and meet in it often, and occasionally it will be the point of gathering for large assemblies and for visiting friends from the whole world. Of course there will be other Temples in Chicago and elsewhere, but this First one in America will, as long as it stands[,] be a sort of shrine and Dawning Place of Worship for the beloved everywhere.[11]

APPENDICES

Appendix One
The Bahá'í Faith

THE BAHÁ'Í FAITH, an independent world religion, was founded by Mírzá Ḥusayn 'Alí (1817–92), known as Bahá'u'lláh, the "Glory of God." The Bahá'í Faith's origins are intimately linked with the Bábí Faith, founded in Persia (Iran) in 1844 by Mírzá 'Alí-Muḥammad (1819–50), known as the Báb, or "Gate." The Báb announced that He was not only the founder of an independent religion, but the herald of a new and far greater prophet or messenger of God, Who would usher in an age of peace for all mankind. In 1863 Bahá'u'lláh declared that He was the One prophesied by the Báb.

Bahá'u'lláh's teachings quickly brought Him into conflict with the Persian government and the Muslim clergy, and He was exiled from Iran to various places within the Ottoman Empire. In 1868 He was sent as a prisoner to the fortress city of Akka in the Holy Land, in the vicinity of which He passed away in 1892. In His will He appointed 'Abdu'l-Bahá (1844–1921), His eldest son, to succeed Him in leading the Bahá'í community and in interpreting the Bahá'í writings. 'Abdu'l-Bahá in turn appointed His eldest grandson, Shoghi Effendi (1897–1957), as His successor, the Guardian of the Cause and authorized interpreter of the Bahá'í teachings. Today the affairs of the Bahá'í world community are administered by The Universal House of Justice, the supreme elected council of the Bahá'í Faith.

The central teachings of the Bahá'í Faith are the oneness of God, the oneness of religion, and the oneness of mankind. The fundamental principles proclaimed by Bahá'u'lláh are that religious truth is not absolute but relative; that Divine Revelation is a continuous and progressive process; that all the great religions of the world are divine in origin; and that their missions represent successive stages in the spiritual evolution of human society. Since Bahá'u'lláh teaches that the purpose of religion is the promotion of concord and unity and that religion is the foremost agency for the achievement of peace and orderly progress in society, the Bahá'í writings provide the outline of institutions necessary for the establishment of peace and world order. These include a world federation or commonwealth, with executive, legislative, and judiciary arms; an

Appendix 1

international auxiliary language; a world economy; a mechanism for world intercommunication; and a universal system of currency, weights, and measures.

The Bahá'í writings also provide specific guidance that helps Bahá'ís (followers of Bahá'u'lláh) fulfill the basic purpose of human life—knowing and worshiping God and "carrying forward an ever-advancing civilization"—while they strive to bring about the unity of mankind, world peace, and world order. For example, the Bahá'í writings call for the fostering of a good character and the development of spiritual qualities such as honesty, trustworthiness, compassion, and justice. These are achieved through prayer, meditation, and work done in the spirit of service to humanity—all expressions, for Bahá'ís, of the worship of God. In the pursuance of the Bahá'í principle of the organic oneness of humanity, the Bahá'í writings call for the eradication of prejudices of race, creed, class, nationality, and sex. They call for the systematic elimination of all forms of superstition hampering human progress and the achievement of a balance between the material and spiritual aspects of life, both of which rest on an understanding of the principles of an unfettered search for truth and of the harmony of science and religion as two facets of truth. They encourage the development of the unique talents and abilities of every individual, through the pursuit of knowledge and the acquisition of skills; for the practice of a trade or profession is required not only for personal satisfaction but also for the enrichment of society as a whole. They call for the full participation of both men and women in all aspects of community life, including the elective and administrative processes and decision making, in implementation of the Bahá'í principle of equal opportunities, rights, and privileges for both sexes. They call for the fostering of the principle of universal compulsory education.

Excellent selections of Bahá'u'lláh's writings can be found in *Gleanings from the Writings of Bahá'u'lláh*, trans. Shoghi Effendi, 2d ed. (Wilmette, Ill.: Bahá'í Publishing Trust, 1976), and *Prayers and Meditations*, trans. Shoghi Effendi (Wilmette, Ill.: Bahá'í Publishing Trust, 1938). In the *Kitáb-i-Íqán: The Book of Certitude* (trans. Shoghi Effendi, 2d ed. [Wilmette, Ill.: Bahá'í Publishing Trust, 1950]) Bahá'u'lláh explains the evolution of religion through the successive prophets of God and clarifies some of the allegorical and abstruse passages of Jewish, Christian, and Muslim scriptures.

Many of Bahá'u'lláh's teachings are discussed and interpreted by 'Abdu'l-Bahá in His *Some Answered Questions*, comp. and trans. Laura Clifford Barney, 5th ed. (Wilmette, Ill.: Bahá'í Publishing Trust, 1981). The talks 'Abdu'l-Bahá gave while traveling through North America in 1912 are compiled in *The Promulgation of Universal Peace: Talks Delivered by 'Abdu'l-Bahá during His Visit to the United States and Canada in 1912*, comp. Howard MacNutt, 2d ed. (Wilmette, Ill.: Bahá'í Publishing Trust, 1982).

Surveys of Bahá'u'lláh's writings between 1853 and 1868 can be found in Adib

Taherzadeh's *The Revelation of Bahá'u'lláh: Baghdád 1853-63* (Oxford: George Ronald, 1974) and *The Revelation of Bahá'u'lláh: Adrianople 1863-68* (Oxford: George Ronald, 1977). The life of Bahá'u'lláh is described in detail by H. M. Balyuzi in *Bahá'u'lláh: The King of Glory* (Oxford: George Ronald, 1980) and the life of the Báb in *The Báb: The Herald of the Day of Days* (Oxford: George Ronald, 1973). A third biography by Mr. Balyuzi, *'Abdu'l-Bahá: The Centre of the Covenant of Bahá'u'lláh* (London: George Ronald, 1971), recounts the life of 'Abdu'l-Bahá. The authoritative history of the first century of the Bahá'í Faith is Shoghi Effendi's *God Passes By*, rev. ed. (Wilmette, Ill.: Bahá'í Publishing Trust, 1974).

For general introductions to the Bahá'í Faith see J. E. Esslemont, *Bahá'u'lláh and the New Era: An Introduction to the Bahá'í Faith*, 4th rev. ed. (Wilmette, Ill.: Bahá'í Publishing Trust, 1980); Horace Holley, *Religion for Mankind* (London: George Ronald, 1956; Wilmette, Ill.: Bahá'í Publishing Trust, 1966); and John Ferraby, *All Things Made New: A Comprehensive Outline of the Bahá'í Faith* (London: Bahá'í Publishing Trust, 1975).

Appendix Two
Ashkhabad, the City of Love

ASHKHABAD is located in the desert plain of western Turkistan near the foothills of the Elburz Mountains. Translated into English, Ashkhabad means "the City of Love." Turkistan was part of the Persian Empire until the 1880s, when the Russians gained control of the area and selected Ashkhabad as the area's governmental seat. Ashkhabad was soon transformed from a village of a few scattered tents and mud huts into a thriving city. The construction of the Transcaspian Railway allowed the area also to develop into an important trade center.

The growing city attracted many immigrants, including large numbers of Bahá'ís and Muslims. The Bahá'ís became an integral part of the community, with many working as masons and construction workers. Many others became successful as importers.

Although the hatred of the Muslims for Bahá'ís never diminished, it did not affect the Bahá'í community of Ashkhabad until 1889. As the initial act of what was apparently intended to be a brutal and systematic attack on the entire Bahá'í community, a group of Shí'ah Muslims hired two assassins to murder a prominent Bahá'í, Ḥájí Muḥammad-Riḍáy-i Iṣfahání, in the middle of the bazaar. The brutal deed was cheered on by some five hundred Muslims. The Russian authorities responded swiftly, arresting all who were involved. A trial was conducted by a military commission, sent from Saint Petersburg by Czar Alexander III. The authorities found the two assassins and their four accomplices guilty of murder, sentenced the assassins to death, and ordered their accomplices to be taken to Siberia. Moments before the execution, a reprieve was granted the two assassins as a result of the intervention of the Bahá'ís. The incident gave the Bahá'ís a great deal of prestige and resulted in Russia's granting official recognition to the Bahá'í Faith; Russia was the only nation at that time to recognize the Bahá'ís in this way. The Bahá'ís' intervention also prepared the way for the construction of schools, a library, a medical clinic, and the Bahá'í Temple in Ashkhabad.[1]

During the early years of 'Abdu'l-Bahá's ministry, interest in building the first Bahá'í Temple had been kindled in many countries throughout the Middle East. 'Abdu'l-

Ashkhabad, the City of Love

Bahá decided that Ashkhabad would be the site for the first Temple. He sent Ḥájí Mírzá Muḥammad-Taqí, also known as Jináb-i-Afnán, to coordinate the historic undertaking. A first cousin of the Báb, Jináb-i-Afnán was a close childhood friend of the Báb's and often played games with Him. It was for Jináb-i-Afnán's father, the Báb's uncle, that Bahá'u'lláh wrote the Kitáb-i-Íqán. Jináb-i-Afnán sacrificed not only his time and energy but also his wealth to build the Ashkhabad Temple.

In the latter part of 1902 trenches were dug, and the foundation for a nine-sided structure was begun. Shortly thereafter General Krupatkin, governor-general of Turkistan, laid a cornerstone for the building on behalf of the czar of Russia. Even though contributions were received from Bahá'ís in Persia and other nearby countries, as well as from other cities in Russia, it was the tireless efforts of the local Bahá'ís that made completion of the project possible. Many thousands of stones were carried by hand to the site from the surrounding countryside. Month after month the masons labored to raise the Temple's walls. When finished, it was nearly five stories high, towering above every other structure in Ashkhabad.

Located in the heart of the city, the Temple sat amid luxurious gardens bordered by four tree-lined avenues. Its main entrance, facing the Holy Land and flanked by minarets, was two stories high and opened into a graceful rotunda, which was crowned by a hemispherical dome of exquisite beauty. Two series of balconies, or loggias, surrounded the rotunda and opened out upon the verdant gardens. At the four corners of the gardens were two Bahá'í schools, a medical dispensary, and an inn for travelers. The Ḥaẓiratu'l-Qúds, or Bahá'í administrative headquarters, was located near the Temple, and farther back stood a utilities building and a small residence for the gardener.

By the time of the Bolshevik Revolution in 1918 the population of the Bahá'í community in Ashkhabad had reached about four thousand. Persian Bahá'ís had also settled in many other Russian cities. In the years immediately following the revolution there was no apparent opposition to the Faith. But in 1922 " 'the official gazette of the Soviet government published an article in which it said that the Bahá'ís were turning the thoughts of the Russian youth from Bolshevism to their own religion and beliefs (and) consequently their efforts should be stopped.' "[2] Although some inconveniences were experienced following the appearance of the article, little open hostility occurred until 1926, when Bahá'ís in Moscow were detained and questioned. Their books and papers were confiscated, and in some cases their homes and other property were seized.

In 1928 the first Bahá'ís in Ashkhabad were arrested. The government severely restricted the activities of the Spiritual Assembly, suspended their publications, and confiscated their mail. In the late summer of that year the government decreed that all

Appendix 2

places of worship inside the Soviet Union were henceforth the property of the government. For three months the Temple's doors were barred. Local newspapers carried government-placed advertisements offering to rent the building. The Temple was reopened only after the Bahá'ís agreed to sign a costly rental contract.

Calm settled over the Bahá'í communities of the Soviet Union. The lease on the Temple was renewed in 1933. Two years later the government announced that religious structures were to be returned to their original owners, provided that specified major repairs for each of those structures could be completed by their respective religious communities within six months. Bahá'ís throughout the Soviet Union sacrificed their few remaining possessions to pay for the extensive repairs required on the Temple. Work was completed before the deadline, and ownership was transferred back to the community.

The Bahá'ís resumed their public meetings, which were soon being conducted twice weekly. A large sign was placed at the entrance to the Temple that proclaimed the principles of the Faith in four languages. The great hall in the Ḥaẓiratu'l-Qúds again overflowed with Bahá'ís on holy days and other special events, and melodious chanting and lyrical music filled the air. The reprieve, however, was short-lived:

> "On the eve of February 5, 1938, all the members of the Local Spiritual Assembly of 'Ishqábád [Ashkhabad], and a great number of the Friends were arrested by order of the authorities and that same night the houses of the Friends were searched, and all Tablets, Bahá'í records and other articles were confiscated. Some of the women, more active than the rest in Bahá'í administrative affairs, were also led away to prison."[3]

For one last time the Temple was seized. A Soviet law was enforced that required a religious community to consist of at least fifty members in order to maintain a place of worship. The Bahá'í population of Ashkhabad, once numbering in the thousands, had fallen below the minimum. "According to recently received information," the National Spiritual Assembly of the Bahá'ís of Iran reported, "the Soviet Government has taken over the Temple, has turned it into an art gallery, and is keeping it in its original condition. For there are no longer any Bahá'ís in 'Ishqábád."[4]

The Temple, however, was not destined to be used for any purpose other than that for which it had been constructed. In 1948 a series of earthquakes devastated much of Ashkhabad and badly damaged the Temple. Although the central rotunda remained standing, it was weakened by heavy rains and began to endanger the nearby houses. In order to ensure the safety of Ashkhabad's citizens, the government ordered the Temple razed in 1963. That same year The Universal House of Justice wrote to Nikita Khrushchev, leader of the Soviet Union, and requested that the land be converted into a public park and that a marker be erected explaining the importance of the site to all Bahá'ís. The letter was never answered.

Even though Bahá'í communities throughout the Soviet Union suffered hardship and persecution for several years, that country will be remembered fondly by Bahá'ís of future generations. For it was the Russian minister to Persia who left no stone unturned to establish Bahá'u'lláh's innocence and secure His release from prison in 1853. Furthermore, it was in the Soviet Union that Bahá'ís erected their first Temple. Yet far more was accomplished in Ashkhabad than the building of a Temple: Through the construction of ancillary institutions such as schools and a hospice, the Bahá'ís of Ashkhabad developed the institution of the Mashriqu'l-Adhkár to a degree never before attained, thereby giving the Bahá'í world an example invaluable to the present and the future.

Appendix Three

Brief Biographies of Some Bahá'ís Associated with the Temple Project

3.1 / Dr. Zia Mabsut Bagdadi

Dr. Zia Bagdadi's family became followers of the Báb before the Báb's execution in 1850. Dr. Bagdadi's father and grandfather both traveled extensively with Ṭáhirih, the only woman among the Báb's first eighteen disciples.

Both the names Zia (Light) and Mabsut (Happy) were given by Bahá'u'lláh to Dr. Bagdadi after his birth in 1882. As a small child, Dr. Bagdadi once had the joy of visiting Bahá'u'lláh at Bahjí. " 'Here He used to hold my hand while walking to and fro in His large room, revealing Tablets, chanting the prayers with the most charming and melodious voice. . . .' "[1]

In 1907 Dr. Bagdadi opened the first tuberculosis clinic in Alexandria, Egypt. Two years later he traveled to the United States to further his medical training. In 1911 he joined the staff of *Star of the West* magazine and in 1912 became the editor of the magazine's Persian section. That year he also accompanied 'Abdu'l-Bahá during portions of His journey throughout America.

Dr. Bagdadi was elected to the Executive Board of the Bahai Temple Unity in 1918. In March 1921 he became the first Bahá'í resident of Wilmette, Illinois, where he lived two blocks from the Temple site. Along with Corinne True and Louis Bourgeois, Dr. Bagdadi monitored the construction of Foundation Hall on almost a daily basis. He later moved to Augusta, Georgia, and died there in April 1937.[2]

3.2 / Albert H. Hall

The son of a minister, Albert H. Hall was born in July 1858 in Alexandria, Ohio. When he was fifteen, his family moved to Minnesota. He studied at the University of Minnesota and later went to Washington, D.C., for further studies at what is now known as George Washington University. After graduating, he returned to Minnesota, where he practiced law in Minneapolis for the next thirty-six years. During that time he handled more than thirty-five hundred cases. To his colleagues he was " 'primarily and essentially the poor man's lawyer; no client was too mean, nor was his cause too small . . . [It] made no difference whether the client had funds, or even prospects of receiving them, and it seemed as though the less the prospect of getting a fee, the more generously he gave of his brilliant mind and indefatigable energy. . . .' "[3] Mr. Hall shared the story of the Bahá'í Faith with most of his colleagues and clients.

Albert Hall served on the Executive Board of the Bahai Temple Unity from 1910 to 1914. He was nearly sixty-two years old when the annual convention of 1920 was held in New York. Although he had suffered from poor health for nearly a year and had been warned by his physician not to travel, he was determined to be present when the Temple design was selected. By the time he returned home, his illness had become critical. He died less than two weeks later.[4]

3.3 / Alfred Eastman Lunt

Born on 12 February 1878, Alfred Eastman Lunt learned of the Bahá'í Faith while attending law school at Harvard University. He became a Bahá'í in 1905 at the age of twenty-seven and during the next three decades became one of the foremost champions of the Faith in America. Although he was a diligent and effective teacher of Bahá'u'lláh's message, his involvement with the development of Bahá'í administration will endure as his most important contribution. He was a member of Boston's Bahá'í governing council from its inception. With few exceptions he was elected each year by that community as one of its delegates to the national Bahá'í convention, where he often served as chairman.

Alfred Lunt was elected to the Bahai Temple Unity Executive Board each year from 1913 to 1924 and, with the exception of two years, served on the National Spiritual Assembly from its inception until his death in 1937. His exceptional abilities as a lawyer were instrumental in guiding the Temple project through several difficult stages in the late 1910s and 1920s.

At Alfred Lunt's passing Shoghi Effendi wrote that his absence created " 'a void in both the teaching and administrative fields, which few of our present day believers can fill.' " " 'He was the living embodiment of such a rare combination of qualities as few can display and none can surpass.' "[5]

3.4 / Allen B. McDaniel

Allen B. McDaniel was born on 5 September 1879 in Exeter, New Hampshire. He attended the Massachusetts Institute of Technology and graduated in 1901 with a

Appendix 3

degree in architectural engineering. In 1915, while working at the Champaign-Urbana campus of the University of Illinois, Allen McDaniel became a Bahá'í. He served on the National Spiritual Assembly for twenty-one years and was its chairman from 1926 to 1934. He represented the National Assembly at meetings with officials of both the United States and foreign governments.

Allen McDaniel's most noted contribution, however, was his devotion of technical knowledge and experience to the Temple project for more than three decades. During more than half that period he also provided the services of his engineering consulting firm, The Research Service, at significantly reduced fees.

In 1952, at the age of seventy-three, Allen McDaniel wrote *The Spell of the Temple*, a book that shares many of his experiences in helping to build the Temple. Although the book has flaws in its historical accuracy, it helped spread the fame of the Temple. Mr. McDaniel died on 18 December 1965 at the age of eighty-six.[6]

3.5 / William Sutherland Maxwell

During the first two decades of this century William Sutherland Maxwell, known to Bahá'ís as Sutherland, and his brother, Edward, owned the largest architectural office in their native Canada and built many of Canada's most famous landmarks. Just before launching his successful practice, Sutherland Maxwell studied in Paris. There he met May Bolles, an American who had recently become a Bahá'í and had been a member of the first group of Americans to visit 'Abdu'l-Bahá. In 1902 the couple was married in London. They returned to Canada, where May Maxwell became the first Bahá'í to live in that country. It was not until 1909, when they were visiting 'Abdu'l-Bahá, that Mr. Maxwell became a Bahá'í.

During the next three decades Sutherland Maxwell was busy with area Bahá'í activities and with his career. Among his professional achievements was his being named a fellow to both the Royal Institute of British Architects and the Royal Architectural Institute of Canada.

In 1937 Sutherland Maxwell's daughter, Mary, was married to Shoghi Effendi. Three years later May Maxwell died of a heart attack shortly after arriving in Buenos Aires on a teaching trip. Following her death Shoghi Effendi invited Mr. Maxwell to live in Haifa. A few months after his arrival Shoghi Effendi gave him the task of designing the superstructure for the Shrine of the Báb.

During the late 1940s Sutherland Maxwell's health began to fail, and he suffered several major illnesses. In the summer of 1951 he traveled to Montreal for a visit but was not able to return to Haifa. That winter Shoghi Effendi appointed him a Hand of the Cause of God. He died shortly afterward in March 1952.[7]

3.6 / Mountfort Mills

Mountfort Mills, a graduate of Harvard Law School, was one of the most distinguished of the early American Bahá'ís. He served as the first president of the Bahai Temple Unity and the first chairman of the National Spiritual Assembly of the Bahá'ís of the United States and Canada. He played an historic role in the development of Bahá'í administration when he prepared the final draft of the Declaration of Trust and By-Laws adopted by the National Assembly in 1927.

Mountfort Mills also performed invaluable international services for the Faith. The most historic of his accomplishments involved one of the most sacred Bahá'í holy places, the house in which Bahá'u'lláh had resided during His exile in Baghdad. Agitation by members of the Muslim clergy resulted in the house's being seized by the Iraqi government in 1922. After six years of unsuccessful legal battles to regain control of the property, the National Spiritual Assembly of Iraq appealed to the League of Nations. At the direction of Shoghi Effendi, Mountfort Mills traveled to Baghdad to study the case and meet with King Faisal. There Mr. Mills gained assurances that the decision of the League would be upheld. Later he prepared the petition that was presented to the League and that resulted in a favorable verdict for the Bahá'ís. In April 1949 Mountfort Mills, the " 'distinguished and international champion,' " died in New York after forty-three years as a member of the Bahá'í Faith.[8]

3.7 / Charles Mason Remey

Charles Mason Remey was one of the earliest Bahá'ís of Washington, D.C., and an active member of that community. During the early 1900s he traveled extensively outside the United States. Among the numerous Bahá'í communities he visited was Ashkhabad, Turkistan. He provided the first written account for the West of the completed Temple at Ashkhabad.

In addition to his architectural designs for the Wilmette Temple, Mason Remey designed a house for visiting pilgrims that was built in Haifa during 'Abdu'l-Bahá's lifetime. In the 1950s he designed the International Bahá'í Archives building, which Shoghi Effendi built near the Shrine of the Báb. Mason Remey also designed the Temples in Sydney, Australia; Kampala, Uganda; and Temples for Tehran and Haifa, which have not yet been built.

In 1951 Shoghi Effendi appointed Mason Remey both a Hand of the Cause of God and the president of the International Bahá'í Council, created by Shoghi Effendi as the forerunner to The Universal House of Justice. When Shoghi Effendi died in 1957 without having appointed a successor, Mason Remey claimed to be that successor. As a

Appendix 3

result, his fellow Hands of the Cause, who provided the leadership for the worldwide Bahá'í community for six years after Shoghi Effendi's death, removed Mason Remey from membership in the Bahá'í Faith.

3.8 / Siegfried Schopflocher

Siegfried Schopflocher was born in 1877 in Germany. Although raised in an orthodox Jewish family, he abandoned his religion's customs after graduating from school and became an agnostic. He moved to Canada and became a successful business entrepreneur. Several years later he learned of and accepted the Bahá'í Faith.

The Temple was not the only Bahá'í enterprise that received the wholehearted support of Siegfried Schopflocher. Green Acre, located in Eliot, Maine, and the oldest Bahá'í school in America, needed extensive repairs in the early 1920s. Mr. Schopflocher provided for this work and purchased several important properties in the vicinity of the school to allow for its expansion.

Mr. Schopflocher frequently traveled internationally for his business. On many of these trips he also carried out important assignments for Shoghi Effendi. He served for several years on the National Spiritual Assembly of the United States and Canada until, in 1948, the National Spiritual Assembly of Canada was formed as an independent administrative agency. Mr. Schopflocher served on the Canadian institution for the remainder of his life and was instrumental in gaining government recognition for it.

On 29 February 1952 Siegfried Schopflocher was appointed a Hand of the Cause of God by Shoghi Effendi. Mr. Schopflocher died in July 1953, three months after attending the dedication of the Temple in Wilmette, Illinois.[9]

3.9 / Louise R. Waite

Music and poetry dominated the life of Louise R. Waite, who was born on 14 November 1867. Her earliest letters to 'Abdu'l-Bahá, dated 1902, contained verses she had written. He gave her the name Shahnaz (Melody), encouraged her to write even " 'more beautiful compositions,' " and told her that " 'thy poetry will forever be read in the Spiritual Meetings. . . .' "[10] She also wrote many songs that were sung by Bahá'ís throughout the world.

The Temple became one of many themes found in her compositions. Several of her hymns were published in *Baha'i Hymns of Peace and Praise,* and twenty of them were also published in early volumes of *The Bahá'í World.*[11] Four of these hymns dealt with the Temple, and one of them, the "Temple Song" (see pp. 266–67), became extremely popular among the Bahá'ís.

In March 1915 Louise Waite and her husband, Edgar, moved from Chicago to California. As a Bahá'í she was extremely active in Los Angeles and served for several terms on that community's Spiritual Assembly. She also belonged to many clubs and was a member of various writers' groups for women. This activity continued until 27 May 1939 when she died quietly in her sleep.[12]

3.10 / Roy C. Wilhelm

The members of Roy C. Wilhelm's family were deeply religious, but very independent thinkers. His maternal grandmother was convinced the return of Christ was at hand and frequently counseled the family to watch for signs of that great event. Roy Wilhelm's mother first learned of the Bahá'í Faith from a friend and embraced the new religion in the late 1890s. Born on 17 September 1875, Roy Wilhelm was at first unimpressed with the Bahá'í Faith, but he accepted it in 1907 while accompanying his mother on a visit to 'Abdu'l-Bahá's home.

One of the earliest contributions of Mr. Wilhelm was his making available inexpensive literature on the Faith, for there was little available at the time. Copies of his compilations, known as "Big Ben" and "Little Ben," eventually numbered in the hundreds of thousands and were used extensively by Bahá'ís. As head of the family-owned coffee business he always included some carefully selected excerpt from the Bahá'í writings in his company's advertisements. When he was on business trips he constantly introduced people to the Faith and gave away pamphlets and booklets.

Among Roy Wilhelm's strongest characteristics were his honesty and integrity. 'Abdu'l-Bahá trusted him implicitly and frequently sent him letters and cablegrams for forwarding to other individuals and groups. 'Abdu'l-Bahá's last communication to America was sent to Mr. Wilhelm, as was the cablegram from the Greatest Holy Leaf announcing 'Abdu'l-Bahá's passing.

Roy Wilhelm served for several years as a member of the Bahai Temple Unity Executive Board. He was also elected every year to the National Spiritual Assembly from its inception until 1946 when, at the age of seventy-one, he retired. He was treasurer of the National Assembly for fifteen years.

Roy Wilhelm died in December 1951. Shoghi Effendi, noting his " 'saintliness, indomitable faith,' " and " 'outstanding services,' " posthumously named him a Hand of the Cause of God.[13]

3.11 / Albert R. Windust

Born in Chicago in March 1874, Albert R. Windust was a sickly child. He was not able to attend school until the fifth grade, and his formal education ended eighteen months later when his mother became ill and died. Barely fourteen years of age, he became an apprentice in a printing firm. Here his knowledge of the contemporary world rapidly expanded, for every magazine article and book he helped assemble was read and reread. An active Methodist, his inquisitive and questioning nature soon placed him at odds with many Christian theological beliefs. In 1898 he learned of the Bahá'í Faith and was soon a member.

In addition to his involvement with the Temple, Albert Windust performed many valuable services for the Faith. He helped form the Bahá'í Publishing Society and was responsible for an early printing in English of *The Hidden Words*, one of Bahá'u'lláh's most important works. On behalf of the Chicago House of Spirituality Mr. Windust began collecting and preserving letters from 'Abdu'l-Bahá; this work laid the foundation for today's National Bahá'í Archives. He later assembled those letters for publication under the title of *Tablets of Abdul-Baha Abbas*. He was also instrumental in publishing the first five volumes of *The Bahá'í World*, volume one of which appeared in 1926.[14] The accuracy of these books is due primarily to his conviction that nothing short of perfection was tolerable for any Bahá'í publication.

All of these contributions, however, pale when compared to his creation in 1910 of *Star of the West* magazine, the first international Bahá'í news organ. For more than twelve years Albert Windust and his only partner, Gertrude Buikema, handled all phases of preparation, printing, and distribution of the magazine to subscribers around the world.

Late in 1952 Albert Windust became quite ill but refused to admit it. Although in need of a doctor's care, he stubbornly forbade it, for he was determined to be in Wilmette for the dedication of the Temple. After weeks of suffering he achieved his goal. Shortly after the dedication he collapsed and remained in a coma for five days. He survived and recovered after two operations. At eighty years of age he resumed his Bahá'í activities and returned to work on a limited basis. He lived for three more years until March 1956.

Appendix Four
Tables and Other Miscellaneous Information

4.1 / Signators of the Petition to 'Abdu'l-Bahá, 7 March 1903

Arthur S. Agnew	Henry L. Goodale	Byron S. Lane	Chester I. Thatcher
Rufus H. Bartlett	Oscar S. Hinckley	George Lesch	Albert R. Windust*
Thornton Chase	Charles Ioas*	Charles Scheffler	

*Drafters of the petition

4.2 / States Where 1906 Petition Signators Resided

Alabama	Idaho	Minnesota	Oregon
Arizona	Illinois	Missouri	Pennsylvania
California	Indiana	New Hampshire	Rhode Island
Colorado	Iowa	New Jersey	Texas
Connecticut	Maine	New Mexico	Vermont
Florida	Massachusetts	New York	Washington
Georgia	Michigan	Ohio	Wisconsin

4.3 / Some Individuals Present at the Meeting in Chicago to Discuss the Temple Project, 26 November 1907

Thornton Chase	Chicago, IL	L. A. Lehmann	Spokane, WA
Aura Crable	Chicago, IL	Fannie Lesch	Chicago, IL
Ellen Davies	Chicago, IL	George Lesch	Chicago, IL
Mirza Enayat'u'llah		Susan I. Moody	Chicago, IL
Ameen'u'llah Fareed	Chicago, IL	Charlotte Morton	Milwaukee, WI
Cecilia M. Harrison	Chicago, IL	Andrew J. Nelson	Racine, WI
Henrietta (Emogene) Hoagg	Oakland, CA	Gus Sand	Muskegon, MI
Bernard M. Jacobsen	Kenosha, WI	Charles E. Sprague	Chicago, IL
Louis Keller	Chicago, IL	Esther (Nettie) Tobin	Chicago, IL
Luella Kirchner	Chicago, IL	Corinne True	Chicago, IL
Byron S. Lane	Bangor, MI		

Appendix 4

4.4 / Delegates to the First Bahai Temple Unity Convention and the Cities They Represented, 20–23 March 1909

Arthur S. Agnew	Chicago, IL	Marie L. Hooper	Dixon, IL
D. D. Babcock	Seattle, WA	Charles Ioas	Lawrence and Bangor, MI
John Bosch	San Francisco, Oakland, Los Angeles, and Pasadena, CA; Honolulu, HI	Bernard M. Jacobsen	Kenosha, WI
		L. A. Lehmann	Spokane, WA
		Mrs. Charles L. Lincoln	Brooklyn, NY
		Mrs. A. W. Meafoy	Cleveland, OH
Annie T. Boylan	New York, NY	John Harrison Mills	Buffalo, NY
Mrs. A. M. Bryant	Denver, CO	Mountfort Mills	New York, NY
Thornton Chase	Clyde, IL	Susan I. Moody	Chicago, IL
John S. Crowley	Boston, MA	Charlotte Morton	Milwaukee, WI
A. M. Dahl	Philadelphia, PA	Howard MacNutt	New York, NY
John Deremo	Fruitport, MI	Mrs. Howard MacNutt	Brooklyn, NY
Sophia Englehorn	Portland, OR	Andrew J. Nelson	Racine, WI
Mrs. L. W. Foster	Clyde, IL	Mary Lesley O'Keefe	Walla Walla and Spokane, WA
Edward C. Getsinger	Washington, DC		
Charles H. Greenleaf	New York Mills, MN	Anna L. Parmerton	Cincinnati, OH
		John C. Peterson	Seattle, WA
Emma Erskine Hahn	New York, NY	Charles Mason Remey	Washington, DC
Albert H. Hall	Minneapolis, MN	Cora W. Renner	Sandusky, OH
C. S. Hargis	Genoa Junction, WI	Edward D. Struven	Baltimore, MD
		Benjamin R. Taylor	Cincinnati, OH
William H. Hoar	Jersey City and North Hudson, NJ	Corinne True	Chicago, IL
		Marie A. Watson	Sugar Grove, PA

4.5 / Constitution of the Bahai Temple Unity

9

HE IS GOD!

"We, the Bahai Assemblies of North America, in unity convened at the City of Chicago, to the end that we may advance the Cause of God in this western hemisphere by the founding and erection of a Temple with service accessories dedicated to His Holy Name, and devoted in His love to the service of mankind, do hereby adopt the following constitution:

Article I.

"We acknowledge God as the Source and Preserver of our Unity, revealed to us through the Manifestation of His Glory in Baha'o'llah and declared by the beloved Servant of God and man, Abdul-Baha.

Article II.

"The name of this Unity shall be Bahai Temple Unity.

Article III.

"The object of this Unity shall be to acquire a site for and erect and maintain thereon a Bahai Temple or Mashrek-el-Azkar, with service accessory buildings, at Chicago, Ill., in accordance with the declared wish of Abdul-Baha.

Article IV.

"The powers of this Unity shall abide in the several Bahai Assemblies, now and hereafter comprising it, and shall be exercised through one representative chosen by each established Assembly, to serve for the term of one year. If more than one Assembly shall exist or be established in any city or local municipality, such Assemblies shall unite in the one representative, except the following, which shall each select two representatives: New York (Borough of Manhattan), Chicago and Washington. New York (Borough of Brooklyn) shall select one representative.

Article V.

"The affairs of this Unity shall be managed by an Executive Board of nine members to be selected by open ballot in convention, or written assent by mail, and whose term of office shall be one year. From their number the Executive Board shall select a President, a Vice-President, a Secretary, a Financial Secretary and a Treasurer.

"The two Secretaries and the Treasurer shall constitute the Temple Treasury, in which name, by joint action, they shall receive, deposit, invest and disburse all funds of this Unity, under the direction of the Executive Board, and until incorporation, as herein provided, shall hold as Trustees the property of this Unity.

Article VI.

"The annual meeting of this Unity shall be held on the 20th day of March, at the place selected by the Executive Board; at the same time and place shall be held the annual meeting of the Executive Board. All other meetings shall be upon call or at stated periods as fixed by the Executive Board.

Article VII.

"The local seat of this Unity shall be the City of Chicago, Ill., where an office shall be established and maintained until the erection of the Temple.

Article VIII.

"The Executive Board shall have power, in their discretion, to incorporate this Unity under the Religious Incorporation Act of Illinois, or such other state as they may select.

Article IX.

"This constitution may be amended at any annual meeting of the Unity, or by mail, but only upon assent of at least two-thirds of the component Assemblies to such proposed amendment, and not until it shall be recommended by at least two-thirds of the Executive Board, and thirty days' written notice thereof shall be given to all the Assemblies before action."

Appendix 4

4.6 / Some Individuals Present at the Initial Ground-Breaking Ceremony, and the Cities They Represented, 1 May 1912

'Abdu'l-Bahá 'Abbás		
C. H. Allen		Akron, OH
Mrs. C. H. Allen		Akron, OH
August Anderson		Kenosha, WI
Mrs. August Anderson		Kenosha, WI
Herbert Anderson		Chicago, IL
Siyyid Asadu'lláh		
Willard H. Ashton	Delegate	Rockford, IL
Mrs. Willard H. Ashton		Rockford, IL
Dr. Zia Bagdadi	Alternate	Chicago, IL
Helene Bagge	Alternate	Muskegon, MI
Alice W. Bailey		Minneapolis, MN
Ella M. Bailey	Alternate	San Francisco, CA
Dr. Pauline Barton-Peeke	Delegate	Cleveland, OH
Alice R. Beede	Delegate	Montclair, NJ
Walter Bohanan		
John D. Bosch		Geyserville, CA
Annie T. Boylan	Delegate	New York, NY
Mrs. Russell L. Booker	Delegate	Akron, OH
Russell L. Booker	Alternate	Akron, OH
Rev. C. Burchart		Bangor, MI
Lucy Burt		
A. P. Chapman		St. Louis, MO
Mrs. A. P. Chapman		St. Louis, MO
Josephine Clark	Delegate	Denver, CO
Harriet M. Cline	Delegate	Tropico, CA
Claudia Coles		Washington, DC
Ella G. Cooper		Oakland, CA
Alice A. Davidson		Cleveland, OH
Mrs. Paul K. Dealy	Delegate	Fairhope, AL
Georgiana Dean		Fairhope, AL
John Deremo		Fruitport, MI
Mrs. John Deremo		Fruitport, MI
Dr. Frederick W. D'Evelyn	Delegate	San Francisco, CA
Edwin H. Eardley		Baltimore, MD
Beatrice D. Eardley		Baltimore, MD
Mrs. H. Emmel	Alternate	Baltimore, MD
Ida A. Finch	Alternate	Seattle, WA
Barbara Fitting		Boston, MA
Mrs. Thomas W. Fleming		
Mrs. Julius Fraser	Delegate	Fruitport, MI

Tables and Other Miscellaneous Information

Lua Getsinger		San Francisco, CA
Charlotte Gillen	Delegate	Seattle, WA
H. Goodale		Kenosha, WI
Mrs. H. Goodale		Kenosha, WI
Helen S. Goodall		Oakland, CA
Walter Goodfellow	Alternate	Jersey City, NJ
Minnie E. Graham		Cleveland, OH
Charles Greenleaf		Chicago, IL
Louis G. Gregory	Delegate	Washington, DC
Albert H. Hall	Delegate	Minneapolis, MN
Joseph H. Hannen		Washington, DC
Pauline Knobloch Hannen	Delegate	Washington, DC
Mrs. C. S. Hargis	Delegate	Genoa Junction, WI
Rosa Harman		Kenosha, WI
Dr. Homer S. Harper	Alternate	Minneapolis, MN
Irene C. Holmes	Alternate	Montclair, NJ
Marie Hooper		
Rene Hooper		
Leroy Ioas		
Dr. Ardeshir Behram Irani		
Bernard M. Jacobsen	Delegate	Kenosha, WI
Ghodsieh (Qudsíyyih) Khánum-i-Ashraf		
Albert C. Killius	Delegate	Spokane, WA
Mrs. Albert C. Killius	Alternate	Spokane, WA
Luella Kirchner	Alternate	Chicago, IL
Genevieve Kraai		
Mrs. Byron S. Lane	Delegate	Bangor, MI
Byron S. Lane	Alternate	Bangor, MI
J. H. Latimer	Delegate	Portland, OR
Mrs. J. H. Latimer	Alternate	Portland, OR
Josephine Locke		Los Angeles, CA
Sophie Loeding		Chicago, IL
Elfie Lundburg		Chicago, IL
Mr. Luxmore		Akron, OH
Lillian E. McClellan		Cleveland, OH
Washington McCormick	Delegate	Everett, WA
Mrs. Washington McCormick	Alternate	Everett, WA
Louisa Mathew	Delegate	London, England
A. F. Matthisen		
Mountfort Mills	Delegate	New York, NY
Charlotte Morton	Delegate	Milwaukee, WI
Elizabeth Muther	Delegate	Honolulu, HI
Andrew J. Nelson	Delegate	Racine, WI
Augusta Nelson		
Peter Nelson		

Appendix 4

Dr. W. F. Nutt	Delegate	Chicago, IL
Harlan F. Ober	Delegate	Boston, MA
Mr. Packman		Kenosha, WI
Mrs. Packman		Kenosha, WI
Annie L. Parmerton	Delegate	Cincinnati, OH
Olof Pary	Delegate	New York Mills, MN
Mrs. Olof Pary		New York Mills, MN
Mrs. M. E. Powell		Baltimore, MD
Ella F. Priday		Cleveland, OH
Elsbeth Renwanz		
Mary Revell	Delegate	Philadelphia, PA
Grace Robarts	Alternate	Buffalo, NY
Martha L. Root	Delegate	Pittsburgh, PA
Sigurd Russell	Delegate	Los Angeles, CA
Dr. Myrta P. Sandoz		
Mrs. Edward L. Struven	Delegate	Baltimore, MD
Mrs. Howard Struven		Washington, DC
Adele Stuber		Cincinnati, OH
Mihtar Ardi<u>sh</u>ír Bahrám Surú<u>sh</u>		
Mrs. C. M. Swingle		Cleveland, OH
Benjamin F. Taylor		Cincinnati, OH
Hazel Tomlinson		
Corinne True	Delegate	Chicago, IL
Valíyu'lláh Varqá		Tehran, Persia
Mr. Vaughn		
Eldon Voelz		
Louis J. Voelz		Kenosha, WI
Mrs. Louis J. Voelz		Kenosha, WI
Voelz children		Kenosha, WI
Henrietta C. Wagner	Delegate	Pasadena, CA
Louise Waite		Chicago, IL
Mary Emily Walker	Delegate	Muskegon, MI
Ernest Walter		
Lillian Walter		
Cora Watson		Cincinnati, OH
Roy C. Wilhelm	Delegate	Ithaca, NY
Marie Wilson		Boston, MA
Dr. Clement Woolson	Delegate	St. Paul, MN
Leona A. Woolson		St. Paul, MN

4.7 / Architects Who Prepared Designs for the Bahá'í Temple

Louis Bourgeois*	West Englewood, NJ
Charles E. Brush*	Chicago, IL

Tables and Other Miscellaneous Information

L. S. Buffington	Minneapolis, MN
Charles L. Lincoln*	New York, NY
William Sutherland Maxwell*	Montreal, Canada
Myron Potter*	Cleveland, OH
Charles Mason Remey*	Washington, DC
Fred J. Woodward*	Washington, DC

*Designs displayed at the 1920 convention

4.8 / Individuals Present at the Temple Site When Boring for Bedrock Commenced on 24 September 1920

Arthur S. Agnew	L. P. Hummel*	Dr. John Osenbaugh
G. C. Ayers*	Mrs. C. Ioas	Arna True Perron
Alice Bourgeois	Louis P. Keller	Carl Scheffler
Louis Bourgeois	Mrs. G. Kuhlman	Ida B. Slater
John E. Christensen	Leona Leadroot	William F. Slater
Mrs. E. G. Foster	Mary Lesch	Esther (Nettie) Tobin
F. France (foreman)*	Effie L. Lobdell	Albert R. Windust
Mrs. H. Gale	Christine Loeding	Henry S. Zenner*
Maude C. Houser	Kokab H. A. MacCutcheon	

*Employees of the S. B. Geiger Artesian Well Contractor Company

4.9 / Some Public-Meeting Speakers in Foundation Hall in the 1930s and 1940s

Arthur S. Agnew	Horace Holley	Ruth Moffett
Agnes Alexander	Marion Holley	Harlan Ober
Elsie Austin	Flora Hottes	Robert Pettet
Dr. Zia Bagdadi	Leroy Ioas	Edris Rice-Wray
Dorothy Baker	Monroe Ioas	John Robarts
Countess Gita Barry-Orlova (Russia)	Beatrice Irwin	Martha Root
	Howard Colby Ives	Carl Scheffler
Helen Bishop	Mabel Ives	Siegfried Schopflocher
Drs. Mariette and Stanley Bolton (Australia)	Ali-Kuli Khan	William Sears
	Fannie Knobloch	Mamie Seto
Matthew Bullock	George Latimer	Philip Sprague
William Kenneth Christian	Charlotte Linfoot	Corinne True
Stanwood Cobb	Margery McCormick	Katherine True
Pearl Easterbrook	Allen McDaniel	Marjorie Ullrich
Nellie French	Loulie Mathews	Albert Vail
Marzieh Gail	Nina Matthisen	Louise Waite
Louis Gregory	Edwin Mattoon	Sarah Walrath
John Haggard	Mountfort Mills	Albert Windust
Carl Hannen		

4.10 / "Temple Song"—Words and Music by Louise R. Waite

266

Reprinted from *The Bahá'í World: A Biennial International Record, Volume IV, 1930–1932,* comp. National Spiritual Assembly of the Bahá'ís of the United States and Canada (New York: Bahá'í Publishing Committee, 1933), pp. 535–36.

Appendix 4

4.11 / Temple Statistics

Total cost of construction	$2,613,012
Area of Temple property	6.97 acres
Seating capacity of auditorium	1,191
Chief dimensions of Temple	
Height from floor of Foundation Hall to pinnacle of dome ribs	191 feet
Height from floor of auditorium to pinnacle of dome ribs	164 feet
Height from floor of auditorium to apex of inside dome	138 feet
Height of Foundation Hall	27 feet
Diameter of Foundation Hall	202 feet
Height of auditorium main level (to base of gallery)	36 feet
Height of gallery	46 feet
Height of clerestory	19 feet
Height of inside dome	37 feet
Height of outside dome	46 feet
Diameter of inside dome	72 feet
Diameter of outside dome	90 feet
Height of ribs above outside dome	17 feet
Depth of caissons	120 feet
Diameter of circular platform at top of outside steps	152 feet
Height of main-story pylons	45 feet
Area of glass in auditorium	19,500 sq. feet

4.12 / Inscriptions Appearing Above the Nine Temple Entrances (from the Writings of Bahá'u'lláh)

"The earth is but one country and mankind its citizens."
"The best beloved of all things in My sight is Justice—turn not away therefrom if thou desirest Me."
"My love is My stronghold—he that entereth therein is safe and secure."
"Breathe not the sins of others so long as thou art thyself a sinner."
"Thy heart is My home—sanctify it for My descent."
"I have made death a messenger of joy to thee—wherefore dost thou grieve?"
"Make mention of Me on My earth that in My heaven I may remember thee."
"O rich ones on earth—The poor in your midst are My trust—guard ye My trust."
"The source of all learning is the knowledge of God—exalted be His Glory."

4.13 / Inscriptions Appearing Inside the Nine Interior Alcoves (from the Writings of Bahá'u'lláh)

"All the Prophets of God proclaim the same faith."
"Religion is a radiant light and an impregnable stronghold."
"Ye are the fruits of one tree and the leaves of one branch."

Tables and Other Miscellaneous Information

"So powerful is unity's light that it can illumine the whole earth."
"Consort with the followers of all religions with friendliness."
"O Son of Being! Thou art My lamp and My light is in thee."
"O Son of Being! Walk in My statutes for love of Me."
"Thy Paradise is My love; thy heavenly home is reunion with Me."
"The light of a good character surpasseth the light of the sun."

4.14 / Visitor Statistics, 1932–82

Although several thousand people visited Foundation Hall before the construction of the superstructure, and although the building was formally opened on 1 May 1931, the earliest records of attendance still in existence start in July 1932. Before the formal opening of the upstairs auditorium in 1953, the visitor count was made at the entrance to Foundation Hall. This count, however, did not include attendance at the meetings held on Sunday afternoons. Since the building's completion, the count represents only those visitors who enter the upstairs auditorium. Many people do not visit both levels; however, the number of people who go downstairs and not upstairs is very small.

Despite signs of welcome, many visitors assume they are not permitted inside the building; thus they remain in the gardens and cannot be counted. The total number of visitors—those who have been counted, those who came before July 1932, and those who have only visited the gardens—may number as high as six or seven million.

Year	Year Total	Cumulative Total
July 1932–July 1937	67,312	67,312
August 1937–December 1938	24,903	92,215
1939	15,600	107,815
1940	16,822	124,637
1941	12,466	137,103
1942	13,455	150,558
1943	15,760	166,318
1944	17,107	183,425
1945	26,558	209,983
1946	32,584	242,567
1947	25,720	268,287
1948	23,169	291,456
1949	24,859	316,315
1950	22,297	338,612
1951	40,149	378,761
1952	46,215	424,976
1953	99,839	524,815
1954	105,963	630,778
1955	100,120	730,898
1956	91,433	822,331

Appendix 4

Year		
1957	89,646	911,977
1958	98,895	1,010,872
1959	88,947	1,099,819
1960	92,783	1,192,602
1961	92,657	1,285,259
1962	98,841	1,384,100
1963	105,034	1,489,134
1964	117,141	1,606,275
1965	117,296	1,723,571
1966	125,678	1,849,249
1967	134,703	1,983,952
1968	153,022	2,136,974
1969	156,117	2,293,091
1970	202,234	2,495,325
1971	213,636	2,708,961
1972	195,210	2,904,171
1973	185,067	3,089,238
1974	191,136	3,280,374
1975	186,100	3,466,474
1976	192,261	3,658,735
1977	178,006	3,836,741
1978	180,720	4,017,461
1979	167,830	4,185,291
1980	191,770	4,377,061
1981	202,827	4,579,888
1982	206,766	4,786,654

4.15 / Present-Day Administration of the Temple

Since the dedication of the Temple in 1953, the National Spiritual Assembly has experimented with various organizational methods for accommodating the growing numbers of persons visiting the Temple for the varied activities taking place there. Today the Temple is administered by a committee appointed annually by the National Spiritual Assembly. This committee, which receives no remuneration, is assisted by a small full-time, salaried staff that oversees all the activities occurring during the more than forty-six hundred hours the building is open each year (52.5% of the total hours in the year). It also coordinates several hundred Bahá'í volunteers who donate their time as guides and teachers, devotional-program readers and coordinators, public-meeting speakers and chairpersons, choir members, tour leaders, hospitality hosts and hostesses, and members of various planning committees and task forces.

As part of its ongoing assessment of how to serve better the interests of visitors to the Temple, the committee has recently approved architectural plans to renovate the downstairs visitors' center. The committee also continues to refine existing programs and to develop new ones that meet the needs of Bahá'ís and visitors alike. Information about devotional programs and other meetings can be obtained by contacting the activities office at the Bahá'í Temple.

NOTES

NOTES

Chapter One / Prologue

1. See appendix 1, "The Bahá'í Faith."
2. Chase to Dr. Seyid El Abedeen, 15 April 1903, personal papers of Edna M. True.
3. Azmellah Mahdi to unidentified recipient in the Holy Land, 13 Ramazan 1320 A.H. [13 December 1902], personal papers of Edna M. True. See appendix 2, "Ashkhabad, the City of Love."
4. Allen B. McDaniel, "Building the Temple: A Historical Record of the Bahá'í Universal House of Worship at Wilmette, Illinois" [paper prepared for the celebration of the fiftieth anniversary of the Temple project], 1951, pp. 2–3, National Bahá'í Archives, Wilmette, Ill.; Rufus H. Bartlett to Mírzá Asadu'lláh, 9 March 1903, personal papers of Edna M. True. See appendix 4.1, "Signators of the Petition to 'Abdu'l-Bahá, 7 March 1903."
5. 'Abdu'l-Bahá to unidentified "Members of the Spiritual Meeting" [of Chicago?], trans. 30 May 1903, in *Tablets Revealed by Abdul-Baha in Reference to the Erection of the Mashrek-el-Azkar (the Bahai Temple of Worship)*, personal papers of Edna M. True; 'Abdu'l-Bahá to Chicago House of Spirituality, trans. 2 July 1903, in *Tablets Revealed by Abdul-Baha*, personal papers of Edna M. True. (Since authoritative translations of these letters have not yet been made, the letters are to be considered only as historic documents.—ED.)

In addition to numerous statements 'Abdu'l-Bahá would write regarding the Temple, He would also compose two prayers for the project:

> O God, my aim, my hope! With hearts full of longing and breasts full of yearning, we beg of Thee and we supplicate at the threshold of Thy might to raise the Mashriqu'l-Adhkár in Chicago, in the most speedy manner. Make its basis firm and its structure enduring, suffer its pillars to remain unshakable and make its columns of the steel and iron of firmness. Glorify its servants, beautify the characters and make the worshippers beloved. Suffer its nightingales to sing "Yá-Bahá'u'l-Abhá" and warble the praises of our

Lord, the Most Supreme. Make its men the standards unfolded on the mountains of the world, and its women the sanctified angels of the tabernacle of the world! ('Abdu'l-Bahá, "Temple Prayer," *Bahá'í News*, no. 58 [Jan. 1932], p. 8.)

O God! O God! We implore Thee with throbbing heart and streaming tears to aid each one who strives in the erection of the house of the Lord wherein Thy Name is mentioned at morn and eventide.

O Lord, send down Thy benediction on whosoever serves this edifice and aids in the upraising of this Temple for the unity of all sects and religions. Confirm him in every good deed among mankind; open the doors of riches and wealth unto him; and make him an inheritor of the treasures of the Kingdom which perish not; cause him to be a sign of giving unto the people; uphold him by the sea of Thy bounty and generosity which forever surges with the waves of Thy grace and favor.

Verily, Thou art the Generous, the Bountiful, the All-Glorious!

('Abdu'l-Bahá, "Prayer for the Temple," *Baha'í News*, no. 126 [June 1939], p. 2.) (Since authoritative translations of these prayers have not yet been made, the prayers are to be considered only as historic documents.—ED.)

Chapter Two / The Bahá'í Faith Comes to America

1. Stephen Longstreet, *Chicago 1860–1919* (New York: David McKay Co., 1973), pp. 272–73, 290.
2. United States State Department, quoted in Garreta Busey, "The Bahá'í Faith Comes to America," in *The Bahá'í Centenary* (Wilmette, Ill.: Bahá'í Publishing Committee, 1944), p. 78.
3. Unidentified contemporary account, quoted in Busey, "Bahá'í Faith Comes to America," p. 79.
4. Busey, "Bahá'í Faith Comes to America," p. 80; unidentified delegates to the World's Parliament of Religions, quoted in Busey, "Bahá'í Faith Comes to America," pp. 80–81.
5. Henry H. Jessup, "The Religious Mission of the English-Speaking Nations," in *The World's Parliament of Religions*, ed. Rev. John Henry Barrows, 2 vols. (Chicago: The Parliament Publishing Co., 1893), II, 1125–26.

The distinguished Orientalist Edward Granville Browne, a professor at Pembroke College, Cambridge, England, was one of the few Westerners who met Bahá'u'lláh (in April 1890). The details of that meeting are recorded in ['Abdu'l-Bahá], *A Traveller's Narrative: Written to Illustrate the Episode of the Báb*, trans. Edward G. Browne (New York: Baha'i Publishing Company, 1930), pp. xxxix–xli. For additional information about Bahá'u'lláh see H. M. Balyuzi, *Bahá'u'lláh: The King of Glory* (Oxford: George Ronald, 1980).

Rev. Jessup later met 'Abdu'l-Bahá in 1900. In his account of that meeting he demonstrates his contempt for the Bahá'í Faith. (See Moojan Momen, ed., *The Bábí and Bahá'í Religions, 1844–1944: Some Contemporary Western Accounts* [Oxford: George Ronald, 1981], p. 317.)

6. Shoghi Effendi, *The World Order of Bahá'u'lláh*, 2d rev. ed. (Wilmette, Ill.: Bahá'í Publishing Trust, 1974), p. 71. For additional information about Shoghi Effendi, see Rúḥíyyih Rabbani, *The Priceless Pearl* (London: Bahá'í Publishing Trust, 1969).

The Faith had been mentioned previously in the United States in several newspapers and magazines, the earliest known article appearing in the January 1846 issue of the *Eclectic Magazine of Foreign Literature, Science and Art* (p. 142). But these early articles were directed at describing the barbaric treatment of the Bábís, forerunners of the Bahá'ís, rather than introducing the teachings of Bahá'u'lláh. (See Momen, *Bábí and Bahá'í Religions*, p. 4.)

The Faith came to the attention of the United States government as early as 1867 when a group of Bahá'ís from Baghdad sent a petition to the Congress through the United States consul general at Beirut. The document described the history of the Faith, the martyrdom of the Báb, the Prophet-Forerunner of the Bahá'í Faith, and the persecutions inflicted upon Bahá'u'lláh, although He was not mentioned by name. The closing of the petition said in part: "Consequently we unanimously agreed to report and inform the Congress of the Republic, of the state of that wise man, that God may prepare for him relief and acquittal, and that you may help and find out a way to deliver that oppressed person from under tyranny and oppression." (Petition from the Persian Reformers, 16 March 1867, Record Group 59, "General Records of the Department of State," microfilm file T367, reel 5, National Archives, Washington, D.C.) The petition was delivered to William H. Seward, secretary of state under Andrew Johnson. The fate of the petition remains unknown.

7. 'Abdu'l-Bahá, quoted in Shoghi Effendi, *God Passes By*, rev. ed. (Wilmette, Ill.: Bahá'í Publishing Trust, 1974), p. 275.

8. See appendix 3 for brief biographies of some of the earliest Bahá'ís in the United States. The author is indebted to Robert Stockman, author of a forthcoming book on the early history of the Bahá'í Faith in North America, for clarifying the details about Ibráhím Khayru'lláh.

9. William P. Collins, "Kenosha: The history of the second Bahá'í community in the United States," *Bahá'í News*, no. 553 (Apr. 1977), p. 2.

10. Ibid., pp. 3–4. 'Abdu'l-Bahá probably did not review the entire book, for some of it was never translated into Arabic.

Ibráhím Khayru'lláh was reported to have suggested that he should be made the " 'Chief of the Cause in America,' " to which 'Abdu'l-Bahá replied: " 'We have no chiefs, we are all servants at the Holy Threshold, and I am the Servant of the servants.' " (Albert Windust, "The Bahá'í Faith in America to 1912," *World Order*, 11 [Nov. 1945], 247.)

11. Albert Windust to unidentified recipient, n.d., Albert Windust Papers, National Bahá'í Archives, Wilmette, Ill.
12. Carl Scheffler, "Thornton Chase: First American Bahá'í," *World Order*, 11 (Aug. 1945), 152.
13. 'Abdu'l-Bahá, quoted in Shoghi Effendi, *God Passes By*, p. 257.
14. Chase to 'Abdu'l-Bahá, 27 February 1904, Thornton Chase Papers, National Bahá'í Archives, Wilmette, Ill.
15. Ibid.
16. Ibid.
17. Shoghi Effendi, *God Passes By*, p. 260.
18. Chase to Dr. Seyid El Abedeen, 15 April 1903, personal papers of Edna M. True; Arthur Agnew, untitled reminiscences, n.d., Arthur Agnew Papers, National Bahá'í Archives, Wilmette, Ill.; Scheffler, "Thornton Chase," p. 154.
19. Chase to Albert Windust (copy), 16 November 1910, Chase Papers. During the early years of the twentieth century, before the Bahá'ís in the Western Hemisphere had developed an understanding of the purpose of Bahá'í institutions, many believed that organizing the affairs of the Faith would diminish its potency and that religion was meant to apply solely to the individual, not to a collective community.
20. 'Abdu'l-Bahá, *Tablets Revealed by the Master Abdul Beha Abbas*, trans. Mirza Ali Kuli Khan (Chicago, 1901), pp. 4–5; 'Abdu'l-Bahá to unidentified Persian Bahá'í, date unknown, quoted with editorial comment in *Bahai News*, 1, no. 9 (20 Aug. 1910), 11.

Chapter Three / Mother of the Temple

1. Corinne True's acceptance of the Bahá'í Faith occurred in 1899, as verified by her own hand. (See her Historical Record Card, National Bahá'í Archives, Wilmette, Ill.) It has been assumed erroneously that her Persian teachers were the same teachers 'Abdu'l-Bahá had sent to the United States after the defection of Ibráhím Khayru'lláh; however, the first of these teachers, Ḥájí 'Abdu'l-Karím-i-Ṭihrání, actually did not arrive in New York until May 1900. Mrs. True may have met Mr. Khayru'lláh, although he was out of the country for an extended period of time in 1899. It is also possible that she met Anṭún Ḥaddád, another Syrian Bahá'í in the United States before the turn of the century.
2. 'Abdu'l-Bahá, *Tablets of Abdul-Baha Abbas*, 3 vols. (New York: Bahai Publishing Society, 1909–16), I, 85–86.
3. Ibid., I, 86.
4. Corinne True and her family continued to reside each summer in Michigan, where she helped to nurture Bahá'í communities in Grand Rapids, Muskegon, Grand Haven, and Fruitport.

5. 'Abdu'l-Bahá, *Tablets*, I, 87.
6. Ibid., I, 88.
7. True to Mrs. Charles Lincoln, 20 May 1908, tape recording of Mrs. Charles Lincoln correspondence, National Bahá'í Archives, Wilmette, Ill.; 'Abdu'l-Bahá, *Tablets*, I, 96–97.
8. Windust to Mírzá Aḥmad Sohráb, 8 November 1911, *Star of the West* Papers, National Bahá'í Archives, Wilmette, Ill.

Chapter Four / Corinne True Goes to Akka

1. For additional information about Albert Windust see appendix 3.11.
2. Thornton Chase to George Winterburn, 8 January 1905, Thornton Chase Papers, National Bahá'í Archives, Wilmette, Ill. For additional information about Louise Waite see appendix 3.9.
   The amount of $103 appears on a receipt issued by Corinne True to Louise and Edgar Waite on 6 December 1906. After the 1904 concert the funds had been loaned to the Chicago House of Spirituality, which then returned the money two years later for deposit in the Temple Fund of the Women's Assembly of Teaching. Since the 10 January 1905 minutes of the House of Spirituality state that $101.50 was realized from the concert, the additional $1.50 may have been from interest accrued during the interim.
3. True to Mrs. Charles Lincoln, 20 May 1908, tape recording of Mrs. Charles Lincoln correspondence, National Bahá'í Archives, Wilmette, Ill.
4. True to Windust, 26 November 1906, Chicago House of Spirituality Records, National Bahá'í Archives, Wilmette, Ill.; Chicago House of Spirituality, Minutes, 17 November 1906, Chicago House of Spirituality Records; Lesch to Kenosha Bahai Men's Board, 31 December 1906, Chicago House of Spirituality Records.
5. True to Chicago House of Spirituality, 16 November 1906, Chicago House of Spirituality Records; Women's Assembly of Teaching to unidentified American Bahá'í communities, 13 December 1906, personal papers of Edna M. True. See appendix 4.2, "States Where 1906 Petition Signators Resided."
6. Corinne True, *Notes Taken at Acca* (Chicago: Bahai Publishing Society, 1907), pp. 12–13. The German Templar Colony had been established in 1868 by a German Adventist sect in expectation of the return of Christ, an event they believed would occur on Mount Carmel. Over the doors of their homes, school, and church were inscriptions saying "Der Herr ist Nahe" (The Lord is near).
7. Thornton Chase, *In Galilee* (Chicago: Bahai Publishing Society, 1907), pp. 20–21; Shoghi Effendi, *God Passes By*, rev. ed. (Wilmette, Ill.: Bahá'í Publishing Trust, 1974), p. 186.
8. True, *Notes Taken at Acca*, p. 18; True to Helen Goodall, 3 June 1907, Helen S. Goodall Papers, National Bahá'í Archives, Wilmette, Ill.

9. 'Abdu'l-Bahá, *Tablets of Abdul-Baha Abbas*, 3 vols. (New York: Bahai Publishing Society, 1909–16), I, 94.

10. True, *Notes Taken at Acca*, pp. 20–21. It has been reported that in her later years Mrs. True elaborated on the moment when 'Abdu'l-Bahá identified the scroll. After grasping it, He held it high and exclaimed, " 'This, this is what gives me great joy.' " ('Abdu'l-Bahá, quoted in Honor Kempton, "Corinne Knight True," in *The Bahá'í World: An International Record, Volume XIII, 1954–1963*, comp. The Universal House of Justice [Haifa: The Universal House of Justice, 1970], p. 847.)

11. True, *Notes Taken at Acca*, p. 21; Gertrude Buikema to Roy Wilhelm (copy), 29 July 1908, personal papers of Edna M. True.

12. Arna True Perron, interview with author, Claremont, Calif., December 1972.

13. Ibid.

14. Corinne True, "Address to The Bahai Assembly," Chicago, Ill., 10 November 1907, personal papers of Edna M. True; True to Lincoln, n.d., tape recording of Lincoln correspondence.

15. Ella Goodall Cooper, "Bahiyyih Khanum—An Appreciation," *Bahá'í Magazine*, 23 (Oct. 1932), 203.

16. Corinne True to unidentified recipient, 4 April 1907, personal papers of Edna M. True.

17. Edna M. True, interview with author, Wilmette, Ill., 25 September 1975; Corinne True, "Memories of 'Abdu'l-Bahá," tape recording, 30 April 1951, personal papers of Edna M. True.

18. Arna True Perron, interview with author, Claremont, Calif., December 1972. The stones bore a Bahá'í symbol that represents the relationship of God to man through His Prophets.

19. Corinne True to unidentified recipient, 4 April 1907, personal papers of Edna M. True.

20. True to Goodall, 3 June 1907, Goodall Papers; True to Lincoln, n.d., tape recording of Lincoln correspondence.

Chapter Five / The Search

1. Carl Scheffler to Edna and Katherine True, and Arna True Perron, 6 June 1961, personal papers of Edna M. True.

2. Carl Scheffler, "Thornton Chase: First American Bahá'í," *World Order*, 11 (Aug. 1945), 156.

3. 'Abdu'l-Bahá, quoted in Arthur S. Agnew, *Table Talks at Acca* (Chicago: Bahai Publishing Society, 1907), pp. 22–23. (Because this statement was conveyed verbally, it does not have the authority of a signed letter in an approved translation.—ED.)

4. Corinne True, "Notes of Mrs. Corinne True," n.d., personal papers of Edna M. True.

5. Chicago House of Spirituality, Minutes, 15 June 1907, Chicago House of Spirituality Records, National Bahá'í Archives, Wilmette, Ill.

6. Chicago House of Spirituality, Minutes, 30 June 1907, Chicago House of Spirituality Records; Chicago House of Spirituality to True, 29 July 1907, Chicago House of Spirituality Records.

7. Corinne True, "Brief History of the Mashriqu'l-Adhkar in America to 1915," in *Bahá'í Year Book, Volume One, 1925–1926*, comp. National Spiritual Assembly of the Bahá'ís of the United States and Canada (New York: Bahá'í Publishing Committee, 1926), p. 67.

8. Corinne True, quoted in Minutes of meeting held in the home of Mr. and Mrs. M. A. True, 26 November 1907, pp. 1–3, Bahá'í Temple Unity Records, National Bahá'í Archives, Wilmette, Ill. The common belief that the meeting took place on Thanksgiving Day, celebrated yearly in the United States, was probably a misunderstanding of the reference to "thanksgiving" in this statement. Thanksgiving Day in 1907 was celebrated on the fourth Thursday, 28 November, just as it is at the present time.

See appendix 4.3, "Some Individuals Present at the Meeting in Chicago to Discuss the Temple Project, 26 November 1907."

9. Byron Lane, quoted in Minutes of meeting at True home, 26 November 1907, pp. 11–12, Bahá'í Temple Unity Records; Hall to True (copy), 18 November 1907, Thornton Chase Papers, National Bahá'í Archives, Wilmette, Ill. For additional information about Albert Hall see appendix 3.2.

10. Thornton Chase, quoted in Minutes of meeting at True home, 26 November 1907, pp. 16–17, Bahá'í Temple Unity Records.

11. Dr. Ameen'u'llah Fareed, quoted in Minutes of meeting at True home, 26 November 1907, pp. 18, 5–6, Bahá'í Temple Unity Records.

12. Bernard Jacobsen, quoted in Minutes of meeting at True home, 26 November 1907, p. 10, Bahá'í Temple Unity Records.

Chapter Six / Nettie Tobin's Stone

1. ['Abdu'l-Bahá], "Utterances of Abdul-Baha upon the Mashrak-el-Azkar," *Star of the West*, 6 (19 Jan. 1916), 134.

2. [Chicago] House of Spirituality of Bahais to unidentified "Friends of God in the Light of EL-ABHA, throughout America," 19 December 1907, author's personal papers.

3. Bahai Assembly of Washington, D.C., to unidentified "Bahais of America," March 1908, author's personal papers.

4. The lineage of Archange's father, François, is unclear, for there was an Indian of the same name at the same time who was chief of a united band of Potawatomies, Ottawas, and Chippewas. Archange lived as an Indian until her marriage.

5. George D. Bushnell, *Wilmette: A History* (Wilmette, Ill.: Wilmette Bicentennial Commission, 1976), p. 112.

6. 'Abdu'l-Bahá to Corinne True (copy), trans. July 1908, personal papers of Edna M. True. (Since an authoritative translation of this letter has not yet been made, the letter is to be considered only as an historic document.—ED.) During the observance Mattie Watson, one of the members of the Women's Assembly of Teaching, read a poem she had written. The fate of the nine stones is unknown.

7. ['Abdu'l-Bahá], "Utterances," p. 135.

8. Mírzá Asadu'lláh to unidentified Bahá'ís in America (copy), 4 June 1908, personal papers of Edna M. True. In later years Nettie Tobin's finances improved slightly. Around the end of the 1920s the Trues moved from Chicago to Wilmette. During that move, when emptying the drawers of the old sewing-machine cabinet Mrs. Tobin had used, Edna True found dozens of receipts for the nickels, dimes, and quarters that Mrs. Tobin had contributed to the project.

9. According to Corinne True, Mr. Gray, the neighbor, helped Nettie Tobin select the stone and encouraged her to take one that was perfectly shaped. Since the stone has a large section missing, and since photographs taken in 1912 show the corner missing when 'Abdu'l-Bahá was at the site, Corinne True's account is puzzling. The stone could have been broken in transit, although it seems likely Mrs. True would have noted it. Likewise, if the stone was broken after it arrived at the site, some record of the accident should exist. Yet something had to be wrong with the stone in the first place for it to be rejected by the builders. Perhaps Mr. Gray felt that the stone was perfectly symmetrical rather than a perfect rectangle.

10. According to Corinne True, Mírzá Mazlúm was "a servant in the home of an Oriental Governor when they brought in a number of Bahai prisoners, whom they beat cruelly and then martyred before his eyes. Seeing this, he said to himself, I too am a Bahai because my Holy Book foretells that these things would happen." (Corinne True, undated notes, p. 8, personal papers of Edna M. True.)

11. In 1894 the Chicago, Milwaukee and St. Paul Railroad extended its Chicago line through Evanston to Third Street and Maple Avenue, two blocks south of Linden Avenue. Five years later the Bluff City Electric Railway (later known as the North Shore Line), originating in Waukegan, pushed south from Highland Park into Wilmette. The tracks paralleled the Chicago and North Western line along Green Bay Road to Greenleaf Avenue, where they turned east past Fourth Street and then south to Linden Avenue. There the line interconnected with the Chicago, Milwaukee and St. Paul tracks one block south at Laurel Avenue. In 1907 the Chicago, Milwaukee and St. Paul leased its tracks to the Northwestern Elevated Railway, which eventually became part of the Chicago Transit Authority. The North Shore Line, running north from Linden Avenue, was abandoned in 1955.

12. Based on Corinne True, undated notes, pp. 3–7, personal papers of Edna M. True.

13. Chase to Mrs. A. M. Bryant (copy), 2 October 1908, Thornton Chase Papers, National Bahá'í Archives, Wilmette, Ill.

14. Ps. 118:22. The stone sent by 'Abdu'l-Bahá was in the possession of Mrs. Harrison Dyers (Asseyeh Allen) of Washington, D.C., for many years. In 1953 it was used as a ceremonial stone in the New History Society Library, New York City, built by a group of former Bahá'ís who had renounced the Bahá'í Faith.

Chapter Seven / Birth of the Bahai Temple Unity

1. 'Abdu'l-Bahá to Corinne True (copy), trans. 19 June 1908, personal papers of Edna M. True. (Since an authoritative translation of this letter has not yet been made, the letter is to be considered only as an historic document.—ED.)

2. True to Mrs. Charles Lincoln, n.d., tape recording of Mrs. Charles Lincoln correspondence, National Bahá'í Archives, Wilmette, Ill.

3. [Chicago] House of Spirituality of Bahais to unidentified "Beloved Friends in America," n.d., author's personal papers; True to Lincoln, n.d., tape recording of Lincoln correspondence. See appendix 4.4, "Delegates to the First Bahai Temple Unity Convention and the Cities They Represented, 20–23 March 1909."

4. The Báb, the Prophet-Forerunner of the Bahá'í Faith, gave to His followers a new calendar based on the solar year. The first day of the year, Naw-Rúz (the Persian name for New Year's Day) is on 21 March, the time of the vernal equinox.

5. Bahai Temple Unity, Proceedings of the Bahai Temple Convention, 22–23 March 1909, p. 1, Bahá'í Temple Unity Records, National Bahá'í Archives, Wilmette, Ill.

6. 'Abdu'l-Bahá to 1909 convention delegates, n.d., quoted in Bahai Temple Unity, Proceedings of the Bahai Temple Convention, 22–23 March 1909, p. 1, Bahá'í Temple Unity Records. (Since an authoritative translation of this letter has not yet been made, the letter is to be considered only as an historic document.—ED.)

In January 1909 Thornton Chase requested 'Abdu'l-Bahá to send a letter to the assembled delegates. Nevertheless, 'Abdu'l-Bahá's letter arrived before Mr. Chase's reached Akka. (Chase to Mírzá Moneer [Munír] Zaine, 19 January 1909, Thornton Chase Papers, National Bahá'í Archives, Wilmette, Ill.)

7. Shoghi Effendi, *God Passes By*, rev. ed. (Wilmette, Ill.: Bahá'í Publishing Trust, 1974), p. 276. See appendix 4.5, "Constitution of the Bahai Temple Unity."

8. True to unidentified recipient, 10 April 1909, Helen S. Goodall Papers, National Bahá'í Archives, Wilmette, Ill.

9. 'Abdu'l-Bahá, quoted in Shoghi Effendi, *God Passes By*, p. 276. Shoghi Effendi, in the same book, recounted the moment when 'Abdu'l-Bahá laid to rest the remains of the Báb. " 'Abdu'l-Bahá had the marble sarcophagus transported with great labor to the vault prepared for it, and in the evening, by the light of a single lamp, He laid

within it, with His own hands—in the presence of believers from the East and from the West and in circumstances at once solemn and moving—the wooden casket containing the sacred remains of the Báb and His companion. When all was finished, and the earthly remains of the Martyr-Prophet of S͟hírázwere, at long last, safely deposited for their everlasting rest in the bosom of God's holy mountain, 'Abdu'l-Bahá, Who had cast aside His turban, removed His shoes and thrown off His cloak, bent low over the still open sarcophagus, His silver hair waving about His head and His face transfigured and luminous, rested His forehead on the border of the wooden casket, and, sobbing aloud, wept with such a weeping that all those who were present wept with Him. That night He could not sleep, so overwhelmed was He with emotion" (Shoghi Effendi, *God Passes By*, p. 276).

Thornton Chase, after hearing of 'Abdu'l-Bahá's achievement, wrote in a letter to a friend: "I stood again in spirit at that sacred spot on the Mountain of beauty, and my heart went down into that chamber with the Beloved. Oh! How I do long to be near Him! . . . That great event in history . . . shall draw forth millions of kindred tears in the years to come." (Chase to Mírzá Moneer [Munír] Zaine, 9 September 1909, Thornton Chase Papers, National Bahá'í Archives, Wilmette, Ill.)

Chapter Eight / The Ceremony

1. For additional information about Albert Hall and Mountfort Mills see appendices 3.2 and 3.6 respectively.
2. *Chicago Examiner*, 18 May 1909.
3. Early in 1910 the Executive Board reported that "Harmonious and mutually helpful co-operation has been effected with the village council of the Village of Wilmette and the officers of The Sanitary District of Chicago, as a result of which arrangements have been consummated in an agreement (now in the process of being carried out), whereby the alley running through our tract, and Greenleaf Avenue on its northern boundary, will be vacated; and in return the Unity will convey, and dedicate to public use, land for Sheridan Road through part of our triangular tract formerly lying north of Greenleaf Avenue. This permits a greatly improved line for Sheridan Road, curving in a graceful line to the north and west at our eastern and northern boundary and across the bridge over the Drainage canal. The agreement also contemplates the granting to the Sanitary District Board of some additional width it needs for its abutments, in return for which we acquire a greater width to our tract at points that clear up and straighten our westerly line leaving us a somewhat enlarged tract of symmetrical outline." (Bahai Temple Unity to unidentified "Bahais and Friends in the Cause of God," n.d., author's personal papers)
4. Honore Jaxon, "Brief Report to Date on Site Negotiations," *Bahai News*, 1, no. 4 (17 May 1910), 26.

5. "Record of the Second Annual Convention of Bahai Temple Unity, held April 25 and 26, 1910," *Bahai News*, 1, no. 4 (17 May 1910), 12; True to Helen Goodall, 29 June 1909, 23 January 1911, Helen S. Goodall Papers, National Bahá'í Archives, Wilmette, Ill.

6. Chase to Albert Windust, 29 April 1908, *Star of the West* Records, National Bahá'í Archives, Wilmette, Ill. By 1915 contributions had also been received from Ireland, Italy, South Africa, Brazil, New Zealand, Mauritius, and the Isle of Pines.

7. 'Abdu'l-Bahá to "his honor Ameen," trans. 19 April 1910, quoted in "Record of the Second Annual Convention," p. 14; 'Abdu'l-Bahá to "the beloved of God in America" [delegates to the 1910 annual Bahá'í convention], trans. 18 March 1910, quoted in "Record of the Second Annual Convention," pp. 8–9. (Since authoritative translations of these letters have not yet been made, the letters are to be considered only as historic documents.—ED.)

8. True to Goodall, 29 June 1909, Goodall Papers.

9. Louise R. Waite, *Words of Abdul-Baha In regard to the Mashrak-el-Azkar in Chicago* (n.p., 1909), author's personal papers. (Because this statement was conveyed verbally, it does not have the authority of a signed letter in an approved translation.—ED.)

10. True to Goodall, 2 March 1911, Goodall Papers. (Because this statement was conveyed verbally, it does not have the authority of a signed letter in an approved translation.—ED.)

11. ['Abdu'l-Bahá], "Tablet to the American Friends from Abdul-Baha," *Star of the West*, 2, no. 4 (17 May 1911), 7.

12. ['Abdu'l-Bahá], "Tablet from Abdul-Baha," *Star of the West*, 2, no. 13 (4 Nov. 1911), 3.

13. True to Goodall, 2 March 1911, 25 February 1910, Goodall Papers.

14. 'Abdu'l-Bahá, quoted in Howard MacNutt, "Introduction to 1922 Edition," in 'Abdu'l-Bahá, *The Promulgation of Universal Peace: Talks Delivered by 'Abdu'l-Bahá during His Visit to the United States and Canada in 1912*, comp. Howard MacNutt, 2d ed. (Wilmette, Ill.: Bahá'í Publishing Trust, 1982), p. xv.

15. "Program, Bahai Temple Unity Convention, April 27, to May 2, 1912," *Star of the West* Records; *Chicago Daily News*, 30 April 1912, 29 April 1912; Mírzá Maḥmúd-i-Zarqání, "Kitáb-i-Badáyi'u'l-Áthár: Diary of 'Abdu'l-Bahá's travels in Europe and America, written by His secretary," TS, entry for 29 April 1912, National Bahá'í Archives, Wilmette, Ill.

16. The report on the land was presented by Bernard Jacobsen, secretary of the Executive Board: "After numerous interviews a price of $17,000 was finally agreed upon. Mr. Conrad originally wanted $65 per foot for this ground and required $7,000 cash and $5,000 per year until paid. We felt that this was more than we could carry, so the proposed plan for the use of the grounds were laid before him and he finally agreed to give us our present terms of $17,000,—$5,000 cash, $3,000 per year, at 5% interest

until paid. This gave us a saving in interest and a longer term to pay the balance, which was a decided advantage for the Unity.

"Mr. Conrad became so enthused with the object of our institutions that he has since then offered us the use of the $3,000 which we are to pay him in September as a loan for the purchase of other grounds if desired. The spirit of good-will has followed all of our transactions with these people. . . .

"Then there is another piece of property owned by Mr. Yost, which lies north and adjacent to the piece we bought from Mr. Conrad and consists of about 140 feet frontage on Sheridan Road. Several meetings have been held with Mr. Yost, but his price is exorbitant at present. Therefore, we have decided to let this matter rest until some future time" (Bernard M. Jacobsen, "Record of the Fourth Annual Convention of Bahai Temple Unity: Chicago, April 27th—May 1st, 1912," *Star of the West*, 3, no. 5 [5 June 1912], 4).

Mr. Yost's property was later purchased by Benjamin Marshall, a noted architect who designed the Drake and Blackstone hotels in Chicago and the Orrington Hotel in Evanston. In 1921 Marshall spent more than one million dollars constructing one of the most fabulous residences ever built in the Chicago area, complete with a fifth-century Chinese temple and a glassed-in tropical garden, the trees and shrubs for which required a five-car train to transport. In 1936 the mansion was purchased by Nathan Goldblatt. Several years later, as real estate taxes soared, he offered the property to the village of Wilmette as a gift. The offer was rejected, and the mansion was torn down in 1950 following a fire that did extensive damage to the structure. The 2.6 acres of land were purchased by the National Spiritual Assembly of the Bahá'ís of the United States for fifty thousand dollars. The ornamental iron gates leading to the lakeside parking lot are the only remaining evidence of Marshall's magnificent creation.

17. For additional information about Dr. Zia Bagdadi see appendix 3.1.
18. *News of the Nation*, 2 July 1890.
19. 'Abdu'l-Bahá, *Promulgation*, pp. 67–68.
20. Joseph H. Hannen, "The Public Meetings of the Fourth Annual Convention of Bahai Temple Unity: Chicago, April 27th–May 2d, 1912," *Star of the West*, 3, no. 4 (17 May 1912), 32.
21. 'Abdu'l-Bahá, *Promulgation*, p. 65.
22. The "Temple Song" can be found on pages 266–67.
23. See appendix 4.6, "Some Individuals Present at the Initial Ground-Breaking Ceremony, and the Cities They Represented," 1 May 1912.
24. Mírzá Aḥmad Sohráb, "Abdul-Baha at the Grave of Thornton Chase," *Star of the West*, 3, no. 13 (4 Nov. 1912), 15.
25. *Chicago Daily News*, 1 May 1912.
26. Honore J. Jaxon, "Dedication of the Mashrak-el-Azkar Site," *Star of the West*, 3, no. 4 (17 May 1912), 5–6.
27. 'Abdu'l-Bahá, *Promulgation*, pp. 71–72.

28. Louise R. Waite, "My Visits With, and Instructions From, Abdul Baha While He was in Chicago, from April 30 to May 6, 1912," *Star of the West* Records.

29. Ibid.

30. Jaxon, "Dedication," p. 7; Mardíyyih Nabíl Carpenter, "Commemoration of the Twenty-Fifth Anniversary of 'Abdu'l-Bahá's Visit to America," in *The Bahá'í World: A Biennial International Record, Volume VII, 1936–1938*, comp. National Spiritual Assembly of the Bahá'ís of the United States and Canada (New York: Bahá'í Publishing Committee, 1939), p. 219.

Chapter Nine / The First Long Wait

1. Edna M. True, interview with author, Wilmette, Ill., 25 September 1975.

2. 'Abdu'l-Bahá, paraphrased by Corinne True, True to Goodall, 29 December 1913, Helen S. Goodall Papers, National Bahá'í Archives, Wilmette, Ill. (Because this statement was conveyed verbally, it does not have the authority of a signed letter in an approved translation.—ED.)

3. Corinne True, undated notes, personal papers of Edna M. True.

4. "Record of the Second Annual Convention of Bahai Temple Unity, held April 25 and 26, 1910," *Bahai News*, 1, no. 4 (17 May 1910), 17; 'Abdu'l-Bahá, paraphrased by Roy Wilhelm, in Martha L. Root, "Pot-Pourri of Convention Fragrances," *Star of the West*, 8 (20 Aug. 1917), 116. (Because this statement was conveyed verbally, it does not have the authority of a signed letter in an approved translation.—ED.)

5. Bernard M. Jacobsen, "Report of Fifth Annual Convention of the Bahai Temple Unity," *Star of the West*, 4 (1 Aug. 1913), 139.

6. Roy Wilhelm, quoted in Jacobsen, "Report of Fifth Annual Convention," p. 133; Alfred Lunt, Claudia S. Coles, Roy C. Wilhelm, Corinne True, and Edna McKinney, "Plan Adopted for Ways and Means," *Star of the West*, 4 (1 Aug. 1913), 146.

7. *News Items of 1914–15: Devoted to the Interests of Mashrek El Azkar Work and Workers* (n.p., n.d.), author's personal papers.

8. 'Abdu'l-Bahá to Ella G. Cooper, trans. 22 March 1913, quoted in *News Items of 1914–15*. (Since an authoritative translation of this letter has not yet been made, the letter is to be considered only as an historic document.—ED.)

9. True to Goodall, 18 September 1913, Goodall Papers.

10. 'Abdu'l-Bahá to unidentified recipient (cablegram), date unknown, quoted in Corinne True, "6th Bahai Temple Unity Convention, 1914," TS (copy), *Star of the West* Records, National Bahá'í Archives, Wilmette, Ill.; True, "6th Bahai Temple Unity Convention, 1914"; True to *Star of the West*, n.d., *Star of the West* Records.

11. ['Abdu'l-Bahá], "Last words of Abdul-Baha concerning the Mashrak-el-Azkar," *Star of the West*, 6 (19 Jan. 1916), 149. The following is a breakdown of the total purchase price of the Temple site (from *Star of the West*, 6 [19 Jan. 1916], 150–51):

Purchase Price:

Original two lots (purchased in 1908 by the Chicago House of Spirituality):	$ 2,000.00
Main Tract:	32,500.00
Lakeshore Tract:	17,000.00
Taxes and Assessments (through fiscal year ending 27 April 1914):	4,747.05
Interest:	4,761.62
Expenses (lawyers, filing fees, etc.):	<u>2,707.46</u>
Total:	$63,716.13

12. 'Abdu'l-Bahá, quoted in Mírzá Aḥmad Sohráb, "The World is at the Threshold of a Most Tragic Struggle," *Star of the West*, 5 (27 Sept. 1914), 164–65. (Because this statement was conveyed verbally, it does not have the authority of a signed letter in an approved translation.—ED.)

13. 'Abdu'l-Bahá, quoted in "The Main Sessions of the Convention: A Digest from the Minutes," *Star of the West*, 7 (13 July 1916), 60. (Because this statement was conveyed verbally, it does not have the authority of a signed letter in an approved translation.—ED.)

14. Executive Board of the Bahai Temple Unity, "Foreword," *Star of the West*, 6 (19 Jan. 1916), 132.

15. "The Main Sessions of the Convention: A Digest from the Minutes," *Star of the West*, 7 (13 July 1916), 66; 'Abdu'l-Bahá to Wilhelm (copy), 27 December 1916, personal papers of Edna M. True. (Since an authoritative translation of this letter has not yet been made, the letter is to be considered only as an historic document.—ED.)

16. "Copy of Resolution Unanimously Adopted by the Executive Board of Bahai Temple Unity[,] August 16, 1917 at Green Acre, Eliot, Me.," TS, personal papers of Edna M. True. Green Acre Bahá'í School is one of the permanent educational institutions of the Bahá'í Faith in the United States. The site was visited by 'Abdu'l-Bahá during His visit to America in 1912.

17. *News Items of 1914–15*; Corinne True, "Mashrak-el-Azkar: 'The Spiritual Foundation,' " *Star of the West*, 5 (8 Sept. 1914), 153.

18. Williams to Corinne True, 17 November 1919, personal papers of Edna M. True.

19. Bahai Temple Unity to [Joseph?] Hannen (copy), 3 November 1911, personal papers of Edna M. True; "Record of the Fourth Annual Convention of Bahai Temple Unity," *Star of the West*, 3, no. 5 (5 June 1912), 4.

20. Alfred Lunt to Bahai Temple Unity, 6 October 1916, personal papers of Edna M. True; Bahai Temple Unity, Minutes, 3 May 1916, Bahá'í Temple Unity Records, National Bahá'í Archives, Wilmette, Ill.

21. Alfred Lunt to Bahai Temple Unity, 6 October 1916, personal papers of Edna M. True.

22. After being named "Ouilmette Park," the park was later called "Washington Park." In August 1955 it was renamed "Gillson Park" in honor of patent attorney Louis K. Gillson, the Wilmette Park District's first president.

23. ['Abdu'l-Bahá], "Words of Abdul-Baha to the Bahais Regarding Their Attendance at the Panama-Pacific International Exposition in San Francisco," *Star of the West*, 5 (19 Jan. 1915), 265.

24. John A. Britton, quoted in "Ceremonies at the Official Reception given to the International Bahai Congress by the Directorate of the Panama-Pacific International Exposition in Festival Hall, Exposition Grounds, Saturday, April 24, 1915, 10 a.m.," *Star of the West*, 6 (17 May 1915), 27–28.

25. Dr. Frederick W. D'Evelyn, quoted in "Ceremonies at the Official Reception," p. 29.

26. Bahai Temple Unity, Minutes, 25 April 1915, Bahá'í Temple Unity Records; Louis G. Gregory, "The Teaching Campaign—News from the South," *Star of the West*, 7 (19 Jan. 1917), 170. For additional information about Louis Gregory see Gayle Morrison, *To Move the World: Louis G. Gregory and the Advancement of Racial Unity in America* (Wilmette, Ill.: Bahá'í Publishing Trust, 1982).

27. 'Abdu'l-Bahá, *Tablets of the Divine Plan: Revealed by 'Abdu'l-Bahá to the North American Bahá'ís*, rev. ed. (Wilmette, Ill.: Bahá'í Publishing Trust, 1977). Eight letters were written in March and April 1916; but only five reached America that year, at which time they were printed in *Star of the West* in September. The remaining three letters, along with six others written in February and March 1917, remained in the Holy Land until after the First World War. They were first presented to the American Bahá'ís at the 1919 annual Bahai Temple Unity convention held in New York between 26 and 30 April.

In one of his books H. M. Balyuzi described the timelessness of 'Abdu'l-Bahá's instructions in the Tablets of the Divine Plan: "before 'the proclamation of the oneness of humanity' could be raised to all the world 'systematically and enthusiastically', the Administrative Order had first to be developed as an instrument of collective teaching—a tremendous labour of sixteen years initiated by the Guardian of the Faith [Shoghi Effendi] after 'Abdu'l-Bahá's passing—so that by 1937 the first stage in fulfilling the Tablets of the Divine Plan could be inaugurated in the First Seven Year Plan of the American Bahá'í community. Since then, the launching of a number of teaching plans of limited scope in all continents, and the undertaking of two successive world-encompassing projects in which the Bahá'ís of the whole world have participated, have revealed the potentialities of the master-plan which the mind of 'Abdu'l-Bahá conceived in those years of sorrow and stress. [As of 1984 there have been four projects.] But much still lies in the lap of the future, for the Tablets of the Divine Plan are no less than 'Abdu'l-Bahá's charter for the teaching of the Faith of Bahá'u'lláh throughout His Dispensation." (H. M. Balyuzi, *'Abdu'l-Bahá: The Centre of the Covenant of Bahá'u'lláh* [London: George Ronald, 1971], pp. 424–25)

Notes to Pages 75–77

28. 'Abdu'l-Bahá to Root, trans. 10 January 1919, quoted in "Tablets of Abdul-Baha recently revealed," *Star of the West*, 10, no. 2 (9 Apr. 1919), 30. Although the original translation included the words "wide-reaching consequences," the authoritative translation for this phrase is "great results." For more details about Martha Root's work see M. R. Garis, *Martha Root: Lioness at the Threshold* (Wilmette, Ill.: Bahá'í Publishing Trust, 1983).

Chapter Ten / The Quest for a Design

1. While living in West Englewood, Louis Bourgeois was commissioned by Roy Wilhelm to create plans for a structure that became known as the "Evergreen Cabin." It was near the site where this cabin would later be erected that 'Abdu'l-Bahá had conducted the famed Unity Feast in 1912.

For additional information about Roy Wilhelm see appendix 3.10.

2. Based upon Françoise Gaudet-Smet, "Un Oncle Mystérieux Devenu Bâtisseur du Temple des Bahaïs," *Perspectives*, 15 (19 May 1973).

3. It has been suggested that Louis Bourgeois designed several Gothic cathedrals while in France. This seems doubtful. He was married in May 1879, and his wife bore three children before her death. Therefore, the earliest he could have become a widower was during the first part of 1882. Since it is certain he was in Chicago by 1886, this leaves a maximum of four years for his collaboration with his cousin, his advanced studies in Paris, and his extended travels throughout Europe and the Middle East. Thus he would have had little time for architectural work. Perhaps as part of his training in Paris he executed one or two designs from which buildings were later erected.

4. "Architectural Romance of Bahai Temple Told by Los Angeles Engineer in Book," *Southwest Builder and Contractor* (6 Nov. 1925), 42. After his arrival in the United States in 1886 Mr. Bourgeois worked for such noted Chicago architectural firms as Burnham & Root and Holabird & Roche. He also opened an office on LaSalle Street, Chicago, with an architect named Mr. Ostling. During the first year of the partnership Mr. Ostling became ill and retired, leaving Mr. Bourgeois to carry on the infant business. He designed several houses throughout the city in addition to Saint Cecilia Church at the corner of 45th Street and Atlantic Avenue. He moved to Omaha, Nebraska, after winning a competition for designing a bank. Later he returned to Chicago and formed a second partnership with Jules de Horvath. They jointly designed the Savoy Hotel at the corner of 30th Street and Michigan Avenue. Sometime during the mid-1890s Mr. Bourgeois moved to San Francisco, where he helped design twenty-one buildings for the San Francisco Fair. He then spent the next four to five years in Los Angeles. He moved to New York during the latter part of 1901.

5. L. B. Pemberton, *A Modern Pilgrimage to Palestine* (Philadelphia: Dorrance, 1925), p. 79; Louis Bourgeois, quoted in "An Architect Who Was Inspired By The Stars," *Washington Post*, 11 July 1920.

6. Pemberton, *Modern Pilgrimage*, p. 79. Just to the west of Portland, Oregon, overlooking the Columbia River at Crown Point State Park, is a structure known as "Vista House." Designed by Edward Lazarus and built in 1916–17, the building possesses several architectural similarities with the Bahá'í Temple in Wilmette, including its circular base, pylons at the first and second levels, and the basic outlines of the main door and windows. But Vista House is much smaller, eight sided, and devoid of Louis Bourgeois' lacy ornamentation. Although a connection between the two architects has not been established, it appears likely that some sort of relationship did exist.

7. Roy Wilhelm, statement penned on photo-mailer packet, Roy C. Wilhelm Papers, National Bahá'í Archives, Wilmette, Ill. (Because 'Abdu'l-Bahá's statement was conveyed verbally, it does not have the authority of a signed letter in an approved translation.—ED.)

8. "Death Cuts Short Architect's Record of Great Baha'i Project," *Wilmette Life*, 12 December 1930.

9. Ibid.

10. Ibid. For additional information about Alfred Lunt see appendix 3.3.

11. "Death Cuts Short Architect's Record."

12. Ibid.

13. Ibid.

14. Bourgeois to Shahnaz [Louise] Waite (handwritten copy), 23 September 1920, author's personal papers; "Death Cuts Short Architect's Record." The garden in West Englewood was used by 'Abdu'l-Bahá for prayer and meditation during His visit in 1912.

15. "Death Cuts Short Architect's Record."

16. Allen B. McDaniel, "The Temple of Light," in *The Bahá'í World: A Biennial International Record, Volume IX, 1940–1944*, comp. National Spiritual Assembly of the Bahá'ís of the United States and Canada (Wilmette, Ill.: Bahá'í Publishing Committee, 1945), p. 175.

17. "Death Cuts Short Architect's Record."

18. Ibid.

19. Ibid.

20. Ibid.

21. Ibid.

22. Daniel Burnham, quoted in Chicago Convention and Tourism Bureau, 1979 Annual Report, p. 16.

23. The author is indebted to Roy Solfisburg of the architectural firm Holabird and Root for his assistance in identifying the architectural styles represented in the Temple design.

24. Bourgeois to Waite, 23 September 1920, author's personal papers. Louise Waite, the early Chicago Bahá'í who had arranged the 1904 fund-raising concert, later wrote a poem that expressed the symbolism of the Temple's bell silhouette:

Bell of the Temple of Love and Unity,
From realms above your clarion tones now ring;
Calling aloud to all humanity
Awake! Arise! and with the angels sing,
Glory to God and His Eternal Plan,
Come to the Temple of the Brotherhood of Man!

Bell of the Temple of Peace enduring,
Softly your tender tones fall on the air,
Calling the hearts of men to Love's true union,
Calling to worship in God's Temple fair.
Glory to God and His Eternal Plan,
Come to the Temple of the Brotherhood of Man!

Bell of the Temple, Unseen Reality,
Yet thy clear tones by inner ear is heard.
Bell of the Temple of wondrous beauty,
Founded upon God's Manifested WORD!
Glory to God and His Eternal Plan,
Come to the Temple of the Brotherhood of Man!

(Louise Waite, "The Temple Bell," *Reality*, 2 [Nov. 1920], 30)

25. Remey to National Spiritual Assembly of the Bahá'ís of the United States and Canada, 26 February 1925 and 9 September 1929, National Spiritual Assembly of the Bahá'ís of the United States and Canada Records, National Bahá'í Archives, Wilmette, Ill.

26. See R. Jackson Armstrong-Ingram's forthcoming thesis "Song, Gender, and Symbol in the Mashriqu'l-Adhkár in Wilmette, Illinois" (Queens University, Belfast) for a discussion of similarities between Louis Bourgeois' designs and those of other architects. See also Charles Mason Remey, *Mashrak-el-Azkar* (Chicago: Bahai Publishing Society, 1917).

27. "Death Cuts Short Architect's Record."

28. Mary Hanford Ford, "The Bahá'í Temple," in *The Bahá'í World (Formerly: Bahá'í Year Book): A Biennial International Record, Volume III, 1928–1930*, comp. National Spiritual Assembly of the Bahá'ís of the United States and Canada (New York: Bahá'í Publishing Committee, 1930), p. 150.

Chapter Eleven / Day of Decision

1. Bahai Temple Unity Executive Board to unidentified "Bahai Assemblies of America," 18 February 1920, personal papers of Edna M. True.

2. Mountfort Mills, quoted in Louis Gregory, "Twelfth Annual Mashrekol-Azkar Convention and Bahai Congress," *Star of the West*, 11 (17 May 1920), 59.

3. Corinne True, quoted in Gregory, "Twelfth Annual Mashrekol-Azkar Convention," p. 65.

4. The procedural framework of the convention had always been complex and, in retrospect, somewhat peculiar. Attempts had been made periodically to improve the process, but things still remained cumbersome. One example was the seating of delegates. Each year a Credentials Committee was formed to certify each delegate before they were officially recognized. While this task was being executed, the unofficial delegates would choose a temporary chairman and secretary and would listen to unofficial reports submitted by various permanent committees. After the report of the Credentials Committee, a permanent chairman and secretary would be announced by a committee that had been selected previously to choose them. All of the reports then would be ratified by the "official" delegates.

Another peculiar aspect of the convention was that communities often elected delegates who did not reside within their jurisdiction. Although fifty-eight delegates were seated at the New York convention, they represented sixty-four cities. (In 1919 one delegate had represented eight communities.) The factors contributing to this practice were several. Members of small communities often did not possess the funds necessary to permit travel to the conventions; some communities felt that none of their members possessed the qualifications necessary to be effective delegates; and certain Bahá'ís had a charisma that caused communities to choose them, irrespective of who was available locally.

In conventions before 1920 each delegate had been granted one vote for each community they represented. Sometimes this resulted in a single individual's wielding considerable influence. The Executive Board, attempting to minimize the potential of that influence in the selection of the Temple design, submitted a resolution asking that each delegate be limited to one vote only. The issue was vigorously debated throughout most of the morning session as motions and amendments to motions were offered and rejected. At last it was decided that the present and all future conventions would adhere to the one-person-one-vote concept. Within a few years the practice of electing delegates from outside a community was also abandoned.

5. 'Abdu'l-Bahá, quoted in "Twelfth Annual Mashrekol Azkar Convention, N.Y. City, 1920," transcript, pp. 51–53, National Bahá'í Archives, Wilmette, Ill. (Because this statement was conveyed verbally, it does not have the authority of a signed letter in an approved translation.—ED.)

The financial report given at the convention stated that $174,433.72 was available to initiate construction. $154,000 of this, however, was held as certificates and war bonds.

6. Louis Bourgeois, quoted in "Twelfth Annual Convention," transcript, pp. 75, 73, 76.

7. Ibid., p. 77.

Notes to Pages 89–95

8. "Report of Twelfth Annual Mashrekol-Azkar Convention Held in New York City, April 26th–29th, 1920," *Star of the West*, 11 (27 Sept. 1920), 178. For additional information about William Sutherland Maxwell and Charles Mason Remey see appendices 3.5 and 3.7 respectively.

A listing of architects who prepared designs for the building can be found in appendix 4.7.

9. Mountfort Mills, quoted in "Twelfth Annual Convention," transcript, pp. 114, 123.

10. H. Van Buren Magonigle, quoted in "Twelfth Annual Convention," transcript, pp. 120, 123–25.

11. Ibid., pp. 124–26. It was widely reported that Mr. Magonigle had said, " 'This is the first new idea in architecture since the thirteenth century' " (H. Van Buren Magonigle, quoted in Louis J. Bourgeois, *The Bahai Temple: Press Comments, Symbolism* [Chicago: Louis J. Bourgeois, 1921], p. 7). Mr. Magonigle repeatedly denied having made the statement, and the convention transcript gives no indication that he ever expressed such a sentiment.

During the 1930s Mr. Magonigle served as the chairman of the advisory board of architects for the Temple. Several years later he wrote: " 'Mr. Bourgeois has conceived a Temple of light, to which structure as usually understood is to be conceded visible support eliminated so far as possible and the whole fabric to take on the airy structure of a dream. It is a large envelope enshrining an idea, the idea of light; a shelter of cobweb interposed between earth and sky, struck through and through with light, light which will partly consume the forms and make of it a thing of faery.' " (H. Van Buren Magonigle, quoted in Louis G. Gregory, "Twenty-Second Annual Convention," *Baha'i News*, no. 41 [May 1930], p. 5)

12. Corinne True, quoted in "Twelfth Annual Convention," transcript, p. 182. (Because 'Abdu'l-Bahá's statement was conveyed verbally, it does not have the authority of a signed letter in an approved translation.—ED.)

13. "Report of Twelfth Annual Convention," pp. 187–88.

14. Charles Mason Remey and Mountfort Mills, quoted in "Twelfth Annual Convention," transcript, pp. 222, 228. The selection of the Temple design took place on the same day that 'Abdu'l-Bahá was knighted in recognition of His herculean efforts to care for and feed countless people during the First World War: " 'Today in the presence of the Bahais, the notables of the country, the leaders of all religions, while the English soldiers were saluting and the military music was playing, the Master received the highest gold medal sent by the King of England. It was a very happy occasion.' " ("The Knighting of Abdul-Baha," *Star of the West*, 11 [31 Dec. 1920], 266)

15. Bourgeois, *Bahai Temple*, p. 14; Peyton Boswell, "Bahai Temple Strikes New Art Note," *New York American*, 23 May 1920, reprinted in *Star of the West*, 11 (5 June 1920), 83–84.

16. "An Architect Who Was Inspired By The Stars," *Washington Post*, 11 July 1920. This article was syndicated and appeared in several newspapers.

The statement regarding 'Abdu'l-Bahá's move to Chicago was probably a misunderstanding by the interviewer, or perhaps by the Bahá'ís being interviewed, about 'Abdu'l-Bahá's hoped-for return to the United States to lay an actual cornerstone. It is reminiscent of another misunderstanding in late 1911, fostered by many Bahá'ís, including Corinne True, who believed that 'Abdu'l-Bahá would bring with Him the sacred remains of Bahá'u'lláh to be reburied beneath the Temple.

17. Bourgeois, *Bahai Temple*, pp. 16–17.

18. Ibid., pp. 5–6.

19. Jináb-i-Fáḍil-i-Mázindarání, quoted in "Bahai Congress held by the Bahai Temple Unity for the presentation of the Universal Principles of Unity and Peace and the Thirteenth Annual Mashreq'ul-Azkar Convention, Banquet Hall, Ninth Floor, Auditorium Hotel, Chicago, April 23–27, 1921," transcript, p. 133, National Bahá'í Archives, Wilmette, Ill. Jináb-i-Fáḍil performed numerous invaluable services for the Bahá'í Faith. On one occasion he performed an heroic mission for 'Abdu'l-Bahá that is credited with saving the lives of thousands of Persian Bahá'ís.

20. Louise Waite, "The Temple of the Mashriqu'l-Adhkar" [unpublished lessons on the Bahá'í Faith], lesson 12, part 3, p. 6, author's personal papers.

21. "The Cleansing of the Earth During the Millennium," *Leaves of Healing* (21 May 1921), 137.

22. Root to unidentified "Beloved Brothers and Sisters," 6 December 1920, Albert Windust Papers, National Bahá'í Archives, Wilmette, Ill. The "Hands of Service" program was the same program created years earlier in Washington, D.C., where Bahá'ís provided manual labor for other Bahá'ís and then contributed their wages to the Temple project.

23. Root to unidentified recipients, 21 August 1921, author's personal papers.

24. *Japan Times and Mail*, 16 February 1921, quoted in Bourgeois, *Bahai Temple*, p. 8; Gertrude Harris to unidentified recipient, 1 June 1920, Albert Windust Papers; Bourgeois, *Bahai Temple*, p. 8; Ford to unidentified recipient, quoted in "Bulletin #2, July 1920, Issued by the Teaching Committee appointed by the Delegates to the Convention," Albert Windust Papers.

25. Bourgeois, *Bahai Temple*, pp. 7–8.

26. Ibid., p. 8; Ford, "Bulletin #2."

27. Waite, "Temple of the Mashriqu'l-Adhkar," p. 7. The design for the Chicago Tribune Building, built between 1922 and 1925, and located across the street from the Wrigley Building, also resulted from a design competition. Louis Bourgeois submitted a design that, although not chosen, was sufficiently interesting to receive prominent newspaper coverage.

28. Waite, "Temple of the Mashriqu'l-Adhkar," p. 7.

Notes to Pages 101–08

Chapter Twelve / The Agony of Victory

1. Mountfort Mills, quoted in "Bahai Congress held by the Bahai Temple Unity for the presentation of the Universal Principles of Unity and Peace and the Thirteenth Annual Mashreq'ul-Azkar Convention, Banquet Hall, Ninth Floor, Auditorium Hotel, Chicago, April 23–27, 1921," transcript, p. 4, National Bahá'í Archives, Wilmette, Ill.
2. 'Abdu'l-Bahá, quoted in "Bahai Congress," p. 4. (Because this statement was conveyed verbally, it does not have the authority of a signed letter in an approved translation.—ED.)
3. 'Abdu'l-Bahá, quoted in "Twelfth Annual Mashrekol Azkar Convention, N.Y. City, 1920," transcript, p. 52, National Bahá'í Archives, Wilmette, Ill. (Because this statement was conveyed verbally, it does not have the authority of a signed letter in an approved translation.—ED.)
4. Louis Bourgeois, quoted in *The Bahai Centenary 1844–1944*, comp. National Spiritual Assembly of the Bahá'ís of the United States and Canada (Wilmette, Ill.: Bahá'í Publishing Committee, 1944), p. 129.
5. Bahai Temple Unity Executive Board to 'Abdu'l-Bahá (cablegram), [August 1920?], quoted in "Bahai Congress," pp. 79–80.
6. 'Abdu'l-Bahá to Bahai Temple Unity Executive Board (cablegram), [August 1920?], quoted in "Bahai Congress," p. 80; 'Abdu'l-Bahá to Corinne True, date unknown, quoted in "Bahai Congress," p. 80. (Since an authoritative translation of this letter has not yet been made, the letter is to be considered only as an historic document.—ED.)
7. Louis Bourgeois, quoted in Louis G. Gregory, "The Thirteenth Mashreq'ul-Azkar Convention and Bahai Congress," *Star of the West*, 12 (17 May 1921), 78–79. 'Abdu'l-Bahá returned to Haifa shortly after Louis Bourgeois' departure and hung the drawings of the "Mother Ma<u>sh</u>riqu'l-A<u>dh</u>kár," a title He gave the Temple, in the two rooms of the Shrine of the Báb used by visiting Bahá'ís for meditation.
8. Helen Burt Potteiger to author, 16 September 1982, author's personal papers.
9. Alfred Lunt, quoted in "Bahai Congress," pp. 83–84.
10. Ibid., p. 85; "Wilmette Fights Proposed $1,500,000 Bahai Temple," *Chicago Herald and Examiner*, 20 January 1921; 'Abdu'l-Bahá, paraphrased by Alfred Lunt in "Bahai Congress," p. 86. (Because 'Abdu'l-Bahá's statement was conveyed verbally, it does not have the authority of a signed letter in an approved translation.—ED.)
11. Alfred E. Lunt, "The Open Forum," *Wilmette (Ill.) Lake Shore News*, 4 February 1921.
12. "Board Asks Details and Facts of Bahais," *Wilmette (Ill.) Lake Shore News*, 4 February 1921; Lunt, "Open Forum."
13. Corinne True, quoted in "Bahai Congress," p. 270; Bahai Temple Unity Executive Board to unidentified "Bahai Assemblies of the United States and Canada," n.d., personal papers of Edna M. True.

14. Bahai Temple Unity Executive Board to unidentified recipients, [ca. 1921], p. 2, personal papers of Edna M. True.

15. According to Louis Bourgeois, a group of New York philanthropists who wanted to build the Temple in Fort Washington Heights had offered him $17,000 for the model.

The Executive Board paid $8,000 to Major Burt, $6,416.85 to various draftsmen, and $1,632.86 for miscellaneous expenses. Added to the $50,000 fee for Louis Bourgeois and the $6,500 expenditure for the Temple model and the Haifa trip, the amount is $72,549.71.

16. Louis Bourgeois, quoted in "Bahai Congress," p. 333. One indication of the number of architectural drawings required for the building is that during an eleven-month period between 1921 and 1922, Louis Bourgeois and his two draftsmen prepared seventy-nine detailed engineering drawings, of which sixty-one were elaborate illustrations of various sections of the exterior ornamentation.

17. Mr. Patzer, quoted in "Bahai Congress," pp. 334–35.

18. Mountfort Mills, quoted in "Bahai Congress," pp. 272, 273; Horace Holley, quoted in "Bahai Congress," pp. 348–49; Grace Krug, quoted in "Bahai Congress," pp. 357–58.

19. Alfred Lunt, quoted in "Bahai Congress," p. 83.

20. 'Abdu'l-Bahá to William Henry Randall, trans. 19 December 1920, Original Translations of Tablets of 'Abdu'l-Bahá, National Bahá'í Archives, Wilmette, Ill. (Since an authoritative translation of this letter has not yet been made, the letter is to be considered only as an historic document.—ED.)

21. During an extended period of heavy rains in 1914, the stone's weight caused it to sink through the mud. Several weekends were spent digging in order to relocate the stone. If it had been placed originally at the exact center of the property, routine calculations would have located it quickly.

22. [Edward?] Kinney, quoted in "Bahai Congress," pp. 97–98.

23. Major Henry Burt, quoted in "Bahai Congress," p. 100.

24. Bahai Temple Unity Executive Board to unidentified recipients, n.d., p. 2, personal papers of Edna M. True.

25. Bahai Temple Unity Executive Board to unidentified recipients, n.d., p. 3, personal papers of Edna M. True.

26. Bahai Temple Unity Executive Board to 'Abdu'l-Bahá, date unknown, quoted in Bahai Temple Unity Executive Board to unidentified recipients, n.d., p. 5, personal papers of Edna M. True.

27. *The Memorial Services of Abdul-Baha on Mount Carmel, Palestine: Account From Letters and Newspapers*, trans. Dr. Zia Bagdadi (Chicago, 1921), pp. 4, 6.

28. [Albert Windust], "The night has come," *Star of the West*, 12 (12 Dec. 1921), 245–46.

29. Laborers and cement workers were paid $.72 per hour; carpenters, $1.00 per

hour; and structural-steel setters, $1.10 per hour.

30. Dr. Zia Bagdadi to Bahai Temple Unity Executive Board, 9 February 1922, personal papers of Edna M. True. For additional information about Dr. Zia Bagdadi see appendix 3.1.

Alfred Anderson and his wife and daughter lived in a structure on the Temple grounds that had been erected as a storage shed during the construction of Foundation Hall. During the winters it was often impossible to heat the shed even to fifty degrees.

31. Albert Vail, "First Meeting in the Bahai Temple," *Star of the West,* 13 (Sept. 1922), 132. The Báb had been executed publicly by firing squad in Tabriz, Persia, on 9 July 1850.

32. Bahai Temple Unity to unidentified "Beloved Friends of the American and Canadian Assemblies," [summer 1922], personal papers of Edna M. True; Bahai Temple Unity to unidentified "Beloved Friends of the Bahai Assemblies of the United States and Canada," 21 October 1922, personal papers of Edna M. True.

Chapter Thirteen / The Second Long Wait

1. 'Abdu'l-Bahá, *Will and Testament of 'Abdu'l-Bahá* (Wilmette, Ill.: Bahá'í Publishing Trust, 1944). For additional information about Shoghi Effendi see Rúḥíyyih Rabbani, *The Priceless Pearl* (London: Bahá'í Publishing Trust, 1969).

During the final, perilous months before the Young Turks Revolution in 1908, 'Abdu'l-Bahá concealed His Will and Testament within the same metal cylinder that Corinne True had used to carry the petition for the Temple to the Holy Land in 1907.

2. Shoghi Effendi, *God Passes By,* rev. ed. (Wilmette, Ill.: Bahá'í Publishing Trust, 1974), p. 333.

3. Shoghi Effendi, *Bahá'í Administration: Selected Messages 1922–1932,* 7th rev. ed. (Wilmette, Ill.: Bahá'í Publishing Trust, 1974), p. 54. In order to protect the completed foundation from being damaged by winter weather, temporary heating units needed to be installed and several leaks repaired. Since there was no money left in the Temple Fund, it was necessary to borrow $10,000 to do the work. Some bills went unpaid for more than a year.

4. [National Spiritual Assembly of the Bahá'ís of the United States and Canada], "The Mashriqu'l-Adhkar," *Baha'i News Letter,* no. 3 (Mar. 1925), p. 3.

5. Shoghi Effendi to National Spiritual Assembly of the Bahá'ís of the United States and Canada (cablegram), 10 February 1925, quoted in "Mashriqu'l-Adhkar," p. 3. The exchange rate for ninety-five pounds sterling in 1925 was slightly less than five hundred dollars.

Even though contributions were far from adequate, it should not be construed that everyone was uncaring. There were many individuals throughout this period who made significant efforts to support the work. Some Bahá'í children, known as "Bahai Juniors," and residing primarily in Canada and the United States, contributed "Temple

Banks" that totaled more than $1,100 in slightly more than one year. ("Our Temple Banks," *Magazine of The Children of the Kingdom,* 4 [Sept. 1923], 92)

6. True to Temple Committee, 13 February 1925, quoted in "Mashriqu'l-Adhkar," *Baha'i News Letter,* no. 5 (May–June 1925), p. 5. The letter was written by Corinne True at Shoghi Effendi's direction while she was visiting him in Haifa. Shoghi Effendi then approved the letter.

7. Ibid.

8. National Spiritual Assembly of the Bahá'ís of the United States and Canada to unidentified "Assemblies of the United States and Canada," 14 August 1924, personal papers of Edna M. True. Louis Bourgeois lived in the studio for the remainder of his life. Lengthy negotiations were required following his death to purchase the studio from his wife.

9. Mr. Millar, quoted in "References to the Bahá'í Faith," in *The Bahá'í World: A Biennial International Record, Volume IV, 1930–1932,* comp. National Spiritual Assembly of the Bahá'ís of the United States and Canada (New York: Bahá'í Publishing Committee, 1933), pp. 234–35. In addition to designing the studio, Mr. Bourgeois designed a house for the Temple caretaker to replace the abominable shed in which Alfred Anderson had been living. The 1925 convention voted a $3,000 appropriation to build the house at 112 Linden Avenue. (The actual cost of construction was $4,898.37.) Several years later the building was converted into administrative offices, which housed the Secretariat of the National Spiritual Assembly until November 1980.

Louis Bourgeois gave frequent lectures on the Temple to both Bahá'í and non-Bahá'í audiences. One lecture so inspired a gathering of New York Bahá'ís that they pledged $8,223 to the Temple that evening.

Mr. Bourgeois was also very active in the Wilmette Bahá'í community. When the first Spiritual Assembly was formed in that community in 1927, he was elected its chairman.

The first Bahá'ís to live in Wilmette were Dr. Zia and Mrs. Zeenat Bagdadi, who moved there in March 1921. Although the growth of the community was slow, there were twenty-two adult believers by 1937, four of whom became Bahá'ís through their attraction to the Temple.

10. "A Plan of Unified Action," *Baha'i News Letter,* no. 39 (Mar. 1930), p. 4.

11. *A Plan of Unified Action to Spread the Baha'i Cause Throughout the United States and Canada, January 1, 1926–December 31, 1928* (Green Acre, South Eliot, Maine: National Spiritual Assembly [of the Bahá'ís of the United States and Canada], 1925), pp. 6, 15.

12. Ibid., pp. 7, 8.

13. "Shoghi Effendi's Endorsement of Plan of Unified Action," *Baha'i News Letter,* no. 39 (Mar. 1930), p. 4.

14. *Baha'i News Letter,* no. 12 (June–July 1926), p. 1.

15. "Correspondence with the Guardian," *Baha'i News Letter,* no. 15 (Jan. 1927), p. 3.

16. "Questions Referred to the National Assembly," *Baha'i News Letter*, no. 18 (June 1927), p. 10.

17. Shahnaz [Louise] Waite, "Report of the 20th. Baha'i Convention Held in Chicago, April 26th—to 30th, 1928," TS, p. 5, author's personal papers.

18. "Mr. and Mrs. Collison Visit Pacific Coast Assemblies," *Bahá'í News Letter*, no. 30 (Mar. 1929), p. 7.

19. Lorol Schopflocher to Emma Rice, 1962, Emma Rice Papers, National Bahá'í Archives, Wilmette, Ill.

20. "Siegfried Schopflocher," in *The Bahá'í World: A Biennial International Record, Volume XII, 1950–1954*, comp. National Spiritual Assembly of the Bahá'ís of the United States (Wilmette, Ill.: Bahá'í Publishing Trust, 1956), p. 664. For additional information about Siegfried Schopflocher see appendix 3.8.

Contrary to today's strict confidentiality regarding the sources of contributions to the various Bahá'í funds, it was common, particularly at the yearly conventions, to make information available regarding individual gifts. The practice of publishing contribution lists was later abandoned.

21. 'Abdu'l-Bahá, "Tablet from Abdul-Baha to Victoria Bedikian," *Star of the West*, 12 (8 Sept. 1921), 170.

22. The worldwide scope of the "Fellowship Gardens" is evident from the following partial listing, gleaned from Victoria Bedikian's magazine *Mashriqu'l-Adhkár*:

The Garden of Compassion, Port Said, Egypt
The Garden of Roses, Papeeti, Tahiti
The Arcadia Garden, Pretoria, South Africa
The Garden of Books, Geneva, Switzerland
The Cherry Garden, Tokyo, Japan
The Garden of Glad Tidings, Shanghai, China
The Garden of Loving Service, Melbourne, Australia
The Educational Garden, Budapest, Hungary
The Garden of Faith, Southampton, England
The Garden of Licht (Light), Zuffenhausen, Germany

23. Doris Ebbert and Olga Finke, "Victoria Bedikian, 1879–1955," in *The Bahá'í World: An International Record, Volume XIII, 1954–1963*, comp. The Universal House of Justice (Haifa: The Universal House of Justice, 1970), p. 884.

24. "Letter from Mrs. Victoria Bedikian," *Baha'i News Letter*, no. 13 (Sept. 1926), p. 3; Shoghi Effendi to Victoria Bedikian, dates unknown, quoted in "Messages from Our Guardian to Auntie Victoria," *Mashriqu'l-Adhkár*, (Apr. 1928), p. 28.

25. "Mrs. Bedikian Publishes Bulletin on Temple," *Baha'i News Letter*, no. 15 (Jan. 1927), p. 8.

26. "Plan for United Action: Letters from Friends," *Mashriqu'l-Adhkár*, no. 4 (Oct. 1926), pp. 2–3; "World Temple Unity," *Mashriqu'l-Adhkár* (Apr. 1928), p. 22; "Plan for

United Action," p. 3; "World Temple Unity Letters," Ma<u>sh</u>riqu'l-A<u>dh</u>kár, no. 5 (Apr. 1927), pp. 7–8.

27. "Messages from Our Guardian," p. 28. In the late 1940s Victoria Bedikian, now widowed, resolved to undertake an extended trip to visit and encourage Bahá'í communities. Over a period of many months she made four trips by bus to every corner of the United States. She suffered a severe heart attack late in 1952, which prevented her from attending the dedication of the Temple. Nevertheless, she continued her inspiring letters and drawings until the final day of her life, 3 June 1955. Memorial services for her were held in several countries.

28. Marie, Queen of Rumania, quoted in Martha L. Root, "Queen Marie of Rumania," in *The Bahá'í World: A Biennial International Record, Volume VI, 1934–1936*, comp. National Spiritual Assembly of the Bahá'ís of the United States and Canada (New York: Bahá'í Publishing Committee, 1937), p. 580.

Bahá'u'lláh and the New Era, written by Dr. J. E. Esslemont, is an introduction to the Bahá'í Faith. The first draft of the book was reviewed in 1919 by 'Abdu'l-Bahá, who made several recommendations for improving the text. When the revision was completed, Dr. Esslemont returned the book to 'Abdu'l-Bahá for final editing. 'Abdu'l-Bahá was able to revise four chapters before His death in 1921. The book has been reprinted numerous times and translated into fifty-eight languages. For a recent edition see J. E. Esslemont, *Bahá'u'lláh and the New Era: An Introduction to the Bahá'í Faith*, 4th rev. ed. (Wilmette, Ill.: Bahá'í Publishing Trust, 1980).

29. Marie, Queen of Rumania, quoted in Shoghi Effendi, *God Passes By*, p. 394. The brooch, two wings studded with diamonds, and with a huge pearl in the center, had been a gift to Queen Marie from royal relatives in Russia. It was purchased at the 1928 annual convention by Willard Hatch, a Bahá'í from Los Angeles. In 1931 he took the brooch to Haifa and presented it to Shoghi Effendi as a gift to the International Bahá'í Archives.

A few months after first meeting Martha Root in 1926, Queen Marie wrote a testimony that was published in several newspapers in Canada and the United States. In it she stated: "If ever the name of Bahá'u'lláh or 'Abdu'l-Bahá comes to your attention, do not put their writings from you. Search out their Books, and let their glorious, peace-bringing, love-creating words and lessons sink into your hearts as they have into mine" (*Toronto Daily Star*, 4 May 1926, reprinted in Marie, Queen of Rumania, "Open Letters of Queen Marie of Rumania," in *The Bahá'í World [Formerly: Bahá'í Year Book]: A Biennial International Record, Volume II, 1926–1928*, comp. National Spiritual Assembly of the Bahá'ís of the United States and Canada [New York: Bahá'í Publishing Committee, 1928], p. 174). On another occasion she wrote: " 'The Bahá'í teaching . . . is like a wide embrace gathering together all those who have long searched for words of hope. It accepts all great Prophets gone before, it destroys no other creeds and leaves all doors open. Saddened by the continual strife amongst believers of many confessions and wearied of their intolerance towards each other, I discovered in the

Bahá'í teaching the real spirit of Christ so often denied and misunderstood: Unity instead of strife, Hope instead of condemnation, Love instead of hate, and a great reassurance for all men.'" (Marie, Queen of Rumania, quoted in Shoghi Effendi, *The World Order of Bahá'u'lláh: Selected Letters*, 2d ed. [Wilmette, Ill.: Bahá'í Publishing Trust, 1974], p. 93)

30. Kenosha [Bahá'í] Assembly to unidentified "Beloved brothers and sisters," 12 December 1927, personal papers of Edna M. True; Ida Finch to unidentified "Beloved Bahai Friend," 21 November 1927, personal papers of Edna M. True.

31. Montreal Temple Committee to unidentified "Co-Workers for the Temple," 28 July 1928, personal papers of Edna M. True.

32. One prominent Western Bahá'í, in a letter written shortly after returning from a trip to the Holy Land, noted that Shoghi Effendi had said "that the Persian Baha'is were eager to assist in the construction of the Temple, but that he will not permit them (to contribute again), until America has shown her willingness to sacrifice. The Persians would give everything they have." (Marion Yazdi to Corinne True, 27 October 1928, personal papers of Edna M. True)

33. National Spiritual Assembly of the Bahá'ís of the United States and Canada to unidentified "heads of Islam," 21 March 1928, personal papers of Edna M. True.

34. Shoghi Effendi, quoted in National Spiritual Assembly of the Bahá'ís of the United States and Canada to unidentified "Local Spiritual Assemblies of the United States and Canada," 23 March 1928, personal papers of Edna M. True. See also National Spiritual Assembly of the Bahá'ís of the United States, *Declaration of Trust and By-Laws of the National Spiritual Assembly of the Bahá'ís of the United States/By-Laws of a Local Spiritual Assembly*, rev. ed. (Wilmette, Ill.: Bahá'í Publishing Trust, 1975).

35. "World Unity Conferences in Cleveland and Boston," *Bahá'í News*, no. 15 (Jan. 1927), p. 5. In November 1927, after sponsoring twenty-two conferences, the National Spiritual Assembly decided to sever its official connection with the conferences. The conference committee was disbanded, and a group of Bahá'ís, including two members of the National Spiritual Assembly, formed the World Unity Foundation to carry on the work.

36. Horace Holley, "Survey of Current Bahá'í Activities in the East and West," in *The Bahá'í World (Formerly: Bahá'í Year Book): A Biennial International Record, Volume II, 1926–1928*, comp. National Spiritual Assembly of the Bahá'ís of the United States and Canada (New York: Bahá'í Publishing Committee, 1928), p. 21; 'Abdu'l-Bahá, paraphrased by Horace Holley, in Holley, "Survey of Current Bahá'í Activities," p. 22; Gayle Morrison, *To Move the World: Louis G. Gregory and the Advancement of Racial Unity in America* (Wilmette, Ill.: Bahá'í Publishing Trust, 1982), p. 132. The annual celebration of racial accord that the conventions first promoted, Race Unity Day, is still observed by Bahá'ís in the month of June.

37. Shoghi Effendi to National Spiritual Assembly of the Bahá'ís of the United States and Canada (cablegram), date unknown, quoted in "National Assembly Letter

No. 1, 1928–1929," *Baha'i News Letter*, no. 24 (June 1928), p. 3. In 1928 the first Foundation Hall Program Committee was established by the National Spiritual Assembly. The members of the first committee were: Corinne True, chairman; Shelley Parker, secretary; Sarah Walrath, treasurer; William Slater; and Willis Hilpert. Statistics for the year 1929–30 include: average attendance—61; average new faces—21; largest attendance—105.

Concerning the use of Foundation Hall, Shoghi Effendi directed that " 'The meetings in the Temple Foundation Hall should be primarily devotional in character, and any addresses delivered there must be of a strictly Bahá'í character. The Teachings must be referred to, quoted, explained and amplified, and if non-Bahá'í subjects are referred to, they should be considered in the light, and in confirmation of, Bahá'í principles and teachings. We must preserve the identity and purity of the Faith, without restricting it to a rigid and exclusive dogma.' " ("Guardian's Instructions Concerning Meetings in Foundation Hall," *Baha'i News Letter*, no. 33 [July 1929], p. 4)

38. "Announcement of the Twentieth Annual Convention of American Bahá'ís," *Baha'i News Letter*, no. 22 (Mar. 1928), p. 1. Two of the carpets were sent by Shoghi Effendi in the care of Lorol Schopflocher, and a third was transported by Dr. and Mrs. William Slater, who accompanied Corinne True to Haifa in 1927. Three additional carpets, two of which were transported by Philip Sprague, were sent in 1929. Shoghi Effendi directed that these carpets were to hang in the Temple and were never to be walked upon or sold.

39. Waite, "Report of the 20th. Baha'i Convention," p. 1.

40. Ibid., p. 3.

41. Spiritual Assembly of the Bahá'ís of Chicago to unidentified "Baha'i friends throughout America," 9 April 1929, personal papers of Edna M. True.

42. Shoghi Effendi, paraphrased by Ruhi Afnan, quoted in "Wilmette, Illinois," *Baha'i News Letter*, no. 31 (Apr. 1929), p. 8.

43. Shoghi Effendi, "The Spiritual Significance of the Mashriqu'l-Adhkar," *Baha'i News Letter*, no. 36 (Dec. 1929), p. 1. Shoghi Effendi's letter of 25 October was not the first announcement of his intentions to send the carpet. On 25 April he had cabled: "Am sacrificing the most valuable ornament Bahá'u'lláh's Shrine in order consecrate and reinforce collective endeavours American believers speedily to consummate Plan Unified Action" (Shoghi Effendi to Horace Holley [National Spiritual Assembly of the Bahá'ís of the United States and Canada] [cablegram], 25 April 1925, Original Letters of Shoghi Effendi, microfilm reel 8, National Bahá'í Archives, Wilmette, Ill.). And three days later: "Soon shipping silken carpet . . . Bahá'u'lláh's Shrine as crowning gift on altar of Bahá'í sacrifice." ("The Guardian's Message to the Convention," *Baha'i News Letter*, no. 32 [May 1929], p. 3)

44. Nellie S. French, "A Glorious Gift—From A Shrine To A Shrine," in *The Bahá'í World: A Biennial International Record, Volume IV, 1930–1932*, comp. National Spiritual Assembly of the Bahá'ís of the United States and Canada (New York: Bahá'í

Notes to Pages 140–44

Publishing Committee, 1933), p. 208. An emir is an Arabic title designating a provincial governor, prince, or dynast in parts of Asia and Africa.

Bukhara, located today in the central region of the Uzbek Soviet Socialist Republic, was founded in the first century. The city, an important crafts and trade center, was captured by Arabs in 709. The Mangit dynasty, established in 1868, was overthrown by the Soviet Union in 1920.

    45. George Spendlove, "The Guardian's Contribution to the Temple Fund," *Baha'i News Letter*, no. 38 (Feb. 1930), insert. The Shrine of Bahá'u'lláh, where the palace carpet lay for many years, is located next to the mansion of Bahjí, northeast of Akka. Bahá'u'lláh lived in the mansion for approximately twelve years until His passing in 1892. The Shrine is the place to which Bahá'ís turn when reciting certain daily prayers.

    46. French, "Glorious Gift," pp. 208, 210. The specific reasons that prevented delivery of the rug to the emir of Bukhara are not known, but there was probably much unrest and turmoil resulting from the Bolshevik Revolution.

    47. Spendlove, "Guardian's Contribution."

    48. "Temple Construction Fund Completed," *Baha'i News Letter*, no. 39 (Mar. 1930), p. 1. The treasurer's office issued an unprecedented 1,631 individual receipts between 1 April 1929 and 31 March 1930.

    49. Shoghi Effendi to National Spiritual Assembly of the Bahá'ís of the United States and Canada (cablegram), date unknown, quoted in Louis G. Gregory, "Twenty-Second Annual Convention," *Baha'i News*, no. 41 (May 1930), p. 2.

Chapter Fourteen / Skyward

    1. Although the architectural drawings (as differentiated from the structural and engineering drawings) were completed by Louis Bourgeois in the early 1920s, several details had to be added later by the engineers. Mr. Bourgeois also developed plans for large, low-lying structures adjacent to the Temple that could later be covered by the gardens. His idea was that the structures could be used for constructing and storing the Temple ornamentation. Serious consideration was given to the proposal because some thought the structures eventually could serve as parking garages for cars—and airplanes.

    2. Allen McDaniel, quoted in "Convention Minutes," *Baha'i News Letter*, no. 34 (Oct. 1929), p. 4; F[rederick] H. Newell, "Agreement with Research Service, Inc.," *Baha'i News Letter*, no. 39 (Mar. 1930), pp. 7–8. For additional information about Allen McDaniel see appendix 3.4.

    3. Allen B. McDaniel, "Building the Temple: A Historical Record of the Bahá'í Universal House of Worship at Wilmette, Illinois" [paper prepared for the celebration of the fiftieth anniversary of the Temple project], 1951, p. 68, National Bahá'í Archives, Wilmette, Ill. Dr. Frederick Haynes Newell, born in March 1862, received a degree in engineering from the Massachusetts Institute of Technology in 1885. As part of the

United States Geological Survey Team he participated in the preparation of several congressional bills, including the Reclamation Act of 1902. From 1907 to 1914 he served as director of the Reclamation Service, a bureau of the Department of the Interior, where he was responsible for settling thousands of families on reclaimed land. For his work with reclamation, President Theodore Roosevelt lauded him as " 'a public servant of whom it is the bald and literal truth to say that by his service he has made all good American citizens his debtors' " (Theodore Roosevelt, quoted in "Frederick Haynes Newell," in *The National Cyclopaedia of American Biography, Volume XXIII* [New York: James T. White, 1933; Ann Arbor, Mich.: University Microfilms, 1967], p. 162).

After spending several years as the head of the Civil Engineering Department of the University of Illinois, Dr. Newell formed a partnership with Allen McDaniel in 1924 and organized The Research Service, an engineering consulting firm. Among the firm's projects, in addition to the Temple, were water conservation projects in Pennsylvania and Virginia, rural electrification in Virginia, and control, conservation, and utilization of flood waters in the Mississippi Basin.

Dr. Newell was a member of the United States Land Commission, the United States Inland Waterways Commission, and the National Advisory Board for fuels and structural materials. He founded the American Association of Engineering and was affiliated with a host of other societies. He died in Washington, D.C., in July 1932.

4. The structural plans for the superstructure were prepared by Benjamin B. Shapiro, a structural engineer in Chicago who had also prepared the plans for Foundation Hall under the direction of Major Burt.

The contract with the George A. Fuller Company included all materials and labor for the erection of the structural-steel framework and concrete walls and for the installation of doors, window frames, glass, and related hardware. One of the provisions of the contract with the Fuller Company was that Foundation Hall had to remain usable during construction. The steel framework was erected by the Overland Construction Company of Chicago, one of more than two-dozen subcontractors working on the project.

A separate bid was sought for electrical work, plumbing, steam fittings, ventilation, and piping. The lowest bid was $108,000. Since there were insufficient funds to cover the second contract, much of this work had to be postponed.

5. Louise Waite, "22nd Baha'i Convention—Held in Temple Foundation Hall," p. 15, author's personal papers; National Spiritual Assembly of the Bahá'ís of the United States and Canada to Spiritual Assembly of the Bahá'ís of Chicago (telegram), 30 July 1930, quoted in Spiritual Assembly of the Bahá'ís of Chicago to Mrs. Edward Struven, 30 July 1930, Wilmette Bahá'í Archives, Wilmette, Ill.

6. "Louis J. Bourgeois, Architect, Dead," *New York Times,* 21 August 1930, reprinted in *Baha'i News,* no. 44 (Sept. 1930), p. 2.

7. Allen Boyer McDaniel, *The Spell of the Temple* (New York: Vantage Press, 1953), p. 57.

8. Ibid., pp. 57–58; F[rederick] H. Newell, "Temple Progress," *Baha'i News*, no. 47 (Jan. 1931), p. 5.

9. McDaniel, *Spell of the Temple*, p. 58.

10. Ibid.

11. The origin of the term *salamander*, referring to a type of heater, dates from the mid-1600s. It was named after a spirit that supposedly lived in fire.

12. "$50,000 Fire in Temple," *Chicago Evening American*, 15 January 1931.

13. *Evanston Shoppers' Review*, 2 February 1931.

14. Allen B. McDaniel, "Report on the Fire at Baha'i Temple," *Baha'i News*, no. 48 (Feb. 1931), p. 5.

15. Carl Scheffler to unidentified "Bahais of the United States and Canada," 5 February 1931, personal papers of Edna M. True. Photographers from three Chicago area newspapers (the *Chicago Tribune*, the *Chicago Evening American*, and the *Herald and Examiner*) reached the Temple site during the latter stages of the fire.

16. Honor Kempton, "Corinne Knight True," in *The Bahá'í World: An International Record, Volume XIII, 1954–1963*, comp. The Universal House of Justice (Haifa: The Universal House of Justice, 1970), p. 847.

17. Corinne True, "Trip to Haifa: 1931," unpublished notes, p. 5, personal papers of Edna M. True.

18. Shoghi Effendi, "The Spiritual Significance of the Mashriqu'l-Adhkar," *Baha'i News Letter*, no. 36 (Dec. 1929), p. 1.

19. McDaniel, "Building the Temple," p. 74.

20. Bertha Hyde Kirkpatrick, "Dedication of the Temple," in *The Bahá'í World: A Biennial International Record, Volume IV, 1930–1932*, comp. National Spiritual Assembly of the Bahá'ís of the United States and Canada (New York: Bahá'í Publishing Committee, 1933), p. 206; Shoghi Effendi to National Spiritual Assembly of the Bahá'ís of the United States and Canada (cablegram), date unknown, quoted in Louis G. Gregory, "The Annual Convention," *Baha'i News*, no. 52 (May 1931), p. 1.

21. Kirkpatrick, "Dedication of the Temple," p. 208.

Chapter Fifteen / The Master Craftsman

1. Allen McDaniel, "The Building of the Temple," *Bahá'í News*, no. 53 (July 1931), p. 3.

2. National Spiritual Assembly of the Bahá'ís of the United States and Canada, "A New Plan of Unified Action," *Bahá'í News*, no. 53 (July 1931), p. 4.

3. National Spiritual Assembly [of the Bahá'ís of the United States and Canada], "The Temple—'Talisman' of Unity," *Bahá'í News*, no. 55 (Sept. 1931), pp. 2–3.

4. Ibid.

5. National Spiritual Assembly of the Bahá'ís of the United States and Canada

to unidentified "Local Spiritual Assemblies" (telegram), 10 October 1931, quoted in National Spiritual Assembly [of the Bahá'ís of the United States and Canada], "Urgent Appeal from the National Spiritual Assembly," *Bahá'í News*, no. 56 (Oct.–Nov. 1931), p. 1.

6. National Spiritual Assembly [of the Bahá'ís of the United States and Canada], "Urgent Appeal," p. 1.

7. Shoghi Effendi (letter written on his behalf) to National Spiritual Assembly of the Bahá'ís of the United States and Canada, with postscript in Shoghi Effendi's own handwriting, 14 March 1932, Original Letters of Shoghi Effendi, microfilm reel 8, National Bahá'í Archives, Wilmette, Ill.

8. Shoghi Effendi, "The Golden Age of the Cause of Bahá'u'lláh," *The World Order of Bahá'u'lláh: Selected Letters*, 2d ed. (Wilmette, Ill.: Bahá'í Publishing Trust, 1974), pp. 67–68.

9. "Baha'i Followers Donate Jewels to Fund for Temple," *Evanston News-Index*, 2 May 1932.

10. Temple Trustees, "Report of Temple Trustees for the Benefit of the National Spiritual Assembly of the Bahá'ís of the United States and Canada for the Year 1931–32," *Bahá'í News*, no. 62 (May 1932), p. 9; National Spiritual Assembly [of the Bahá'ís of the United States and Canada], "Letter from the National Spiritual Assembly," *Baha'i News*, no. 64 (July 1932), p. 1.

11. A Materials Committee, consisting of Major Henry J. Burt (chairman), Louis Bourgeois, Sutherland Maxwell, E. R. Boyle, and Allen McDaniel, was appointed in 1921 to study the different materials. The committee commissioned test sections of ornamentation made from cast concrete, cast stone, terra cotta, and aluminum alloy. These sections were left on the grounds for several years to check for weathering and durability. John Earley's concrete test section never showed any signs of deterioration.

12. "Twelfth Annual Mashrekol-Azkar Convention, N.Y. City, 1920," transcript, pp. 131–32, National Bahá'í Archives, Wilmette, Ill.

13. Frederick W. Cron, *The Man Who Made Concrete Beautiful: A Biography of John Joseph Earley* (Fort Collins, Colo.: Centennial Publications, 1977), p. 4.

14. National Spiritual Assembly, "Letter from National Spiritual Assembly," p. 1.

15. Cron, *Man Who Made Concrete Beautiful*, p. 9.

16. Ibid., p. 12.

17. John J. Earley, "The Project of Ornamenting the Bahá'í Temple Dome," quoted from the *Journal of the American Concrete Institute*, in *The Bahá'í World: A Biennial International Record, Volume V, 1932–1934*, comp. National Spiritual Assembly of the Bahá'ís of the United States and Canada (New York: Bahá'í Publishing Committee, 1936), pp. 287–88. According to John Earley's biographer, Frederick Cron, "The period from 1932 to 1939 was the busiest, most fruitful and creative in John Earley's entire career. Yet during this same period he found time not only to direct his own business, but also to make important contributions to the American Concrete Institute, a technical

society dedicated to improving the design and manufacture of concrete products and structures. . . ." (Cron, *Man Who Made Concrete Beautiful*, p. 59)

18. Shoghi Effendi to National Spiritual Assembly of the Bahá'ís of the United States and Canada (cablegram), 11 June 1932, Original Letters of Shoghi Effendi, microfilm reel 8.

19. "The Ascension of Bahíyyih Khánum," *Baha'i News*, no. 65 (Aug. 1932), pp. 1, 3; "The Crucial Matter," *Baha'i News*, no. 66 (Sept. 1932), p. 2.

20. Earley, "Project of Ornamenting the Dome," p. 288.

21. Ibid.

22. Associated with the business since he had been a young man, Basil Taylor had been asked by John Earley's father, just before the father's death, to remain at the studio and help John Earley carry on the work.

23. Earley, "Project of Ornamenting the Dome," pp. 289, 292.

24. Ibid., p. 292.

25. Allen McDaniel, *The Spell of the Temple* (New York: Vantage Press, 1953), p. 69.

26. Cron, *Man Who Made Concrete Beautiful*, pp. 43, 45.

27. National Spiritual Assembly, "Letter from National Spiritual Assembly," p. 1; National Spiritual Assembly [of the Bahá'ís of the United States and Canada], "Letter from the National Spiritual Assembly," *Baha'i News*, no. 70 (Jan. 1933), p. 2.

28. "Poona Baha'is' Temple Contribution," *Baha'i News*, no. 72 (Apr. 1933), p. 8.

29. "Letter from Mrs. Keith Ransom-Kehler," *Baha'i News*, no. 73 (May 1933), pp. 6–7. During 1930–32 the Bahá'ís in Iran managed to construct a $100,000 community center in Tehran. They also purchased a large tract of land in the hills overlooking Tehran as a site for a Temple. 'Abdu'l-Bahá, however, directed that they not build a Temple until the one in the United States was completed.

Chapter Sixteen / The Temple's Beauty Emerges

1. Charlotte M. Linfoot, "The Story of the Convention," *Baha'i News*, no. 75 (July 1933), pp. 3, 4.

2. National Spiritual Assembly of the Bahá'ís of the United States and Canada to Shoghi Effendi (cablegram), 19 July 1933, quoted in "Cablegram from Shoghi Effendi," *Baha'i News*, no. 76 (Aug. 1933), p. 1.

3. National Spiritual Assembly of the Bahá'ís of the United States and Canada to unidentified "Local Spiritual Assemblies," 26 September 1933, quoted in " 'The Seal of Final and Complete Victory,' " *Baha'i News*, no. 78 (Oct. 1933), p. 2.

4. Shoghi Effendi to National Spiritual Assembly of the Bahá'ís of the United States and Canada (cablegram), 2 November 1933, Original Letters of Shoghi Effendi, microfilm reel 8, National Bahá'í Archives, Wilmette, Ill.

5. National Spiritual Assembly of the Bahá'ís of the United States and Canada

to unidentified "Local Spiritual Assemblies," 17 April 1934, author's personal papers.

6. Shoghi Effendi to National Spiritual Assembly of the Bahá'ís of the United States and Canada (cablegram), 7 March 1934, Original Letters of Shoghi Effendi, microfilm reel 8.

7. Dr. Rexford Newcomb, "The Baha'i Temple—An Appreciation," *Baha'i Magazine*, 25 (Sept. 1934), p. 188.

8. "Present Status of Temple Construction," *Baha'i News*, no. 81 (Feb. 1934), p. 1; Shoghi Effendi to National Spiritual Assembly of the Bahá'ís of the United States and Canada (cablegram), date unknown, quoted in "Present Status," p. 1.

9. National Spiritual Assembly of the Bahá'ís of the United States and Canada to unidentified "Local Spiritual Assemblies," 18 September 1934, author's personal papers.

10. National Spiritual Assembly of the Bahá'ís of the United States and Canada to Ann W. Bartholomew [Spiritual Assembly of the Bahá'ís of Wilmette] (telegram), 14 September 1934, personal papers of Edna M. True.

11. Shoghi Effendi (letter written on his behalf) to National Spiritual Assembly of the Bahá'ís of the United States and Canada, 10 May 1934, Original Letters of Shoghi Effendi, microfilm reel 8.

12. Shoghi Effendi (letter written on his behalf) to National Spiritual Assembly of the Bahá'ís of the United States and Canada, 20 June 1931, Original Letters of Shoghi Effendi, microfilm reel 8.

13. Shoghi Effendi to National Spiritual Assembly of the Bahá'ís of the United States and Canada (cablegram), date unknown, quoted in National Spiritual Assembly of the Bahá'ís of the United States and Canada to unidentified "Local Spiritual Assemblies," 20 May 1935, author's personal papers.

14. National Spiritual Assembly of the Bahá'ís of the United States and Canada, "Annual Report: National Spiritual Assembly, 1935–1936," *Baha'i News*, no. 100 (May 1936), p. 3.

15. For a recent edition see Bahá'u'lláh, *Gleanings from the Writings of Bahá'u'lláh*, trans. Shoghi Effendi, 2d ed. (Wilmette, Ill.: Bahá'í Publishing Trust, 1976).

16. Shoghi Effendi, *Messages to America: Selected Letters and Cablegrams Addressed to the Bahá'ís of North America, 1932–1946* (Wilmette, Ill.: Bahá'í Publishing Committee, 1947), p. 6.

17. Shoghi Effendi (letter written on his behalf) to National Spiritual Assembly of the Bahá'ís of the United States and Canada, with postscript in Shoghi Effendi's own handwriting, 28 July 1936, Original Letters of Shoghi Effendi, microfilm reel 8; Shoghi Effendi, *Messages to America*, p. 9. On 11 April 1937 a program at the Temple marked the twenty-fifth anniversary of 'Abdu'l-Bahá's arrival in New York in 1912. Joining the Bahá'ís were members of many groups that had been addressed by 'Abdu'l-Bahá during his travels throughout the United States and Canada. In addition to Bahá'í speakers, representatives of four of the groups—the Women's International League for Peace, the

National Association for the Advancement of Colored People, the Theosophical Society of America, and Hull House—addressed the large assemblage in Foundation Hall.

18. The committee's membership included L. W. Eggleston (chairman), Frank A. Baker, E. Roger Boyle, Stuart W. French, C. Herrick Hammond, and Frank R. MacMillan. "This membership included Bahá'ís and non-Bahá'ís, business men, an architect, an engineer and builder, and the head of the research department of the Portland Cement industry." ("Temple Construction Resumed," *Baha'i News*, no. 110 [Sept. 1937], p. 2)

19. Mabel Rice-Wray Ives, "Grace Robarts Ober," in *The Bahá'í World: A Biennial International Record, Volume VIII, 1938–1940*, comp. National Spiritual Assembly of the Bahá'ís of the United States and Canada (Wilmette, Ill.: Bahá'í Publishing Committee, 1942), p. 658; Grace Ober, "Five Hundred Miles to Pray in the Temple," *Bahá'í News*, no. 59 (Feb. 1932), p. 1.

20. Ives, "Grace Ober," p. 656.

21. Shoghi Effendi to National Spiritual Assembly of the Bahá'ís of the United States and Canada (cablegram), 27 April 1938, quoted in National Spiritual Assembly of the Bahá'ís of the United States and Canada to unidentified "Local Spiritual Assemblies," 13 May 1938, author's personal papers.

22. Shoghi Effendi to National Spiritual Assembly of the Bahá'ís of the United States and Canada (cablegram), 29 November 1938, Original Letters of Shoghi Effendi, microfilm reel 8; Shoghi Effendi to National Spiritual Assembly of the Bahá'ís of the United States and Canada (cablegram), 29 November 1938, Original Letters of Shoghi Effendi, microfilm reel 8.

23. Shoghi Effendi (letter written on his behalf) to National Spiritual Assembly of the Bahá'ís of the United States and Canada, with postscript in Shoghi Effendi's own handwriting, 28 January 1939, Original Letters of Shoghi Effendi, microfilm reel 8; Shoghi Effendi, *The Advent of Divine Justice*, 3d rev. ed. (Wilmette, Ill.: Bahá'í Publishing Trust, 1969), p. 37.

24. Shoghi Effendi, *Messages to America*, pp. 23–24; Shoghi [Effendi] Rabbani, "Cablegram from Shoghi Effendi," *Bahá'í News*, no. 135 (Apr. 1940), insert, p. 3. This cablegram was sent on 3 October 1939. Twenty days later Shoghi Effendi sent perhaps his most thought-provoking message regarding the significance of the Temple, referring to it as an "Ark" that would "ride triumphant" the "tidal wave" of calamities being experienced in the world, and declaring that it would offer the "sole refuge" to a "steadily sinking civilization" (Shoghi Effendi to National Spiritual Assembly of the Bahá'ís of the United States and Canada [cablegram], 23 October 1939, Original Letters of Shoghi Effendi, microfilm reel 8).

The National Bahá'í Secretariat is part of the Ḥaẓíratu'l-Quds, the collective name for the component agencies of local and national Bahá'í administrative institutions, and the "pivot of all Bahá'í administrative activity." Shoghi Effendi, in *God Passes By*, elucidates the functions of this institution and its relationship to the Mashriqu'l-Adhkár: "Complementary in its functions to those of the Mashriqu'l-Adhkár—an edifice exclusively reserved for Bahá'í worship—this institution [the Ḥaẓíratu'l-Quds], whether local or national, will, as its component parts, such as the Secretariat, the Treasury, the Archives, the Library, the Publishing Office, the Assembly Hall, the Council Chamber, the Pilgrims' Hostel, are brought together and made jointly to operate in one spot, be increasingly regarded as the focus of all Bahá'í administrative activity, and symbolize, in a befitting manner, the ideal of service animating the Bahá'í community in its relation alike to the Faith and to mankind in general. From the Mashriqu'l-Adhkár . . . the representatives of Bahá'í communities, both local and national, together with the members of their respective committees, will, as they gather daily within its walls at the hour of dawn, derive the necessary inspiration that will enable them to discharge, in the course of their day-to-day exertions in the Ḥaẓíratu'l-Quds—the scene of their administrative activities—their duties and responsibilities as befits the chosen stewards of His Faith." (Shoghi Effendi, *God Passes By*, rev. ed. [Wilmette, Ill.: Bahá'í Publishing Trust, 1974], pp. 339–40)

25. Alan McCormick to Mr. Greenacre, 18 November 1941, National Bahá'í Archives, Wilmette, Ill.

26. Alan McCormick to Chicago Title and Trust Company, 30 January 1942, National Bahá'í Archives, Wilmette, Ill.

27. Allen B. McDaniel, "The Temple of Light," in *The Bahá'í World: A Biennial International Record, Volume IX, 1940–1944*, comp. National Spiritual Assembly of the Bahá'ís of the United States and Canada (Wilmette, Ill.: Bahá'í Publishing Committee, 1945), p. 183.

28. Shoghi Effendi, *Messages to America*, pp. 59–60. The total cost for the gallery, main level, and steps was $391,664, only about $40,000 above the original estimate of $350,000. Actually, the exterior was not technically completed until ten years later. After the interior was completed in 1952, the caps for the nine main-level and nine gallery pylons were designed, constructed, and raised into place not long before the dedication in 1953.

Chapter Seventeen / The Fame of the Temple Spreads

1. "Temple Model Exhibits," in National Spiritual Assembly of the Bahá'ís of the United States and Canada, *Annual Reports: National Spiritual Assembly of the Bahá'ís of the United States and Canada; Bahá'í Trustees; and National Committees, 1939–1940* (Wilmette, Ill.: National Spiritual Assembly of the Bahá'ís of the United States and Canada, n.d.), p. 16.

2. Ibid.

3. "My Diary: Chickie Chalmers," *Chicago's American*, 18 May 1937. Construction never went below bedrock, nor was quicksand ever encountered. There were problems in three of the caissons with water-bearing sand (see chapter 12), but there are no records indicating that the sand was incapable of supporting an object.

4. *Chicago Sunday Tribune,* 7 May 1933.
5. *Bell Telephone News* (Feb. 1937); *U.S. Steel News* (Mar. 1937).
6. "Making Progress," *Wilmette Life,* date unknown.
7. "Wilmette Leads in Air Mail Week Observation," *Wilmette Life,* 26 May 1938; Bahá'í Community of Wilmette, Ill., to Shoghi Effendi, 19 May 1938, personal papers of Edna M. True. During the late 1930s the Wilmette community grew large enough that homes were no longer adequate for community gatherings. The community wanted to use the Temple for its own meetings, but when permission was requested from Shoghi Effendi, he responded: "In consideration of the fact the Bahá'í House of Worship in Wilmette is the national property of the American Bahá'í Community, and is destined to become the national administrative headquarters of the Faith in America, it would not seem appropriate that that building or any part of the Temple edifice be used for the holding of purely local gatherings by the friends in Wilmette. Its use should be confined to such national gatherings as the Annual Convention, or any such meetings of a national character which the N.S.A. may propose to hold in the future" (Shoghi Effendi [letter written on his behalf] to Spiritual Assembly of the Bahá'ís of Wilmette, Ill. [copy], 13 May 1939, personal papers of Edna M. True). Shoghi Effendi recommended that the community rent or purchase a separate hall.
8. "The Evanston Revue," *Evanston Review,* 18 May 1944.
9. "When Baha'is Build a Temple," *Highway Traveler,* 9 (Oct.–Nov. 1937), 7.
10. Gertrude Struven, "Interesting Experiences with Temple Visitors," in *The Bahá'í World: A Biennial International Record, Volume VII, 1936–1938,* comp. National Spiritual Assembly of the Bahá'ís of the United States and Canada (New York: Bahá'í Publishing Committee, 1939), p. 436.
11. Ibid., pp. 438, 440.
12. Ibid., pp. 440–42.
13. Root to Roy Wilhelm, Horace Holley, and Mountfort Mills, 17 March 1937, Mountfort Mills Papers, National Bahá'í Archives, Wilmette, Ill.; Shoghi Effendi, *God Passes By,* rev. ed. (Wilmette, Ill.: Bahá'í Publishing Trust, 1974), p. 388.

Chapter Eighteen / The Final Years

1. Shoghi Effendi, *Messages to America: Selected Letters and Cablegrams Addressed to the Bahá'ís of North America, 1932–1946* (Wilmette, Ill.: Bahá'í Publishing Committee, 1947), p. 97.
2. Louis G. Gregory, "The Historic Thirty-Sixth Convention," *Bahá'í News,* no. 170 (Sept. 1944), p. 1.
3. "Welcome Visitors," *Evanston Review,* 18 May 1944.
4. Marzieh Gail, "Impressions of the Centenary," *Bahá'í News,* no. 170 (Sept. 1944), p. 15.
5. Ibid., pp. 10–11.

6. Bahá'í speakers in the 1944 Centenary programs included Elsie Austin, Dorothy Baker, Mrs. Charles Reed Bishop, William Kenneth Christian, Rowland Estall, Nellie French, Marzieh Gail, Horace Holley, Marion Holley, Octavio Illescas, Firuz Kazemzadeh, Eduardo Lopez, Mrs. Edward Roscoe Matthews, Dr. Fernando Nova, Alfred Osborne, Carl Scheffler, Corinne True, Albert Windust, and Hilda Yen.

Bahá'í chairpersons, readers, singers, and other program participants included Marion Anderson, Ella Cooper, Richard Crooks, Louis Gregory, Paul Haney, Emogene Hoagg, Leroy Ioas, Olivia Kelsey, Honor Kempton, Ali-Kuli Khan, George Latimer, Estaban Leyton, Charlotte Linfoot, Edwin Mattoon, Mrs. Fred Morton, Mary McClennen, Allen McDaniel, Harlan Ober, Walter Olitzki, Eli Powlas, Siegfried Schopflocher, Anthony Seto, Philip Sprague, John Charles Thomas, Edna True, and Roy Wilhelm.

7. Gail, "Impressions of the Centenary," pp. 15–16.

8. Ibid., p. 16.

9. Rúhíyyih Khánum, "The Centenary of a World Faith: 3. Centenary Celebrations in the Holy Land," in *The Bahá'í World: A Biennial International Record, Volume X, 1944–1946,* comp. National Spiritual Assembly of the Bahá'ís of the United States and Canada (Wilmette, Ill.: Bahá'í Publishing Committee, 1949), p. 154.

10. Shoghi Effendi (letter written on his behalf) to National Spiritual Assembly of the Bahá'ís of the United States and Canada, with postscript in Shoghi Effendi's own handwriting, 18 August 1944, Original Letters of Shoghi Effendi, microfilm reel 8, National Bahá'í Archives, Wilmette, Ill.; National Spiritual Assembly [of the Bahá'ís of the United States and Canada], "A National Campaign," *Bahá'í News,* no. 173 (Feb. 1945), p. 4.

11. National Spiritual Assembly [of the Bahá'ís of the United States and Canada], "The National Campaign," *Bahá'í News,* no. 177 (Nov. 1945), p. 3.

12. Frederick W. Cron, *The Man Who Made Concrete Beautiful: A Biography Of John Joseph Earley* (Fort Collins, Colo.: Centennial Publications, 1977), pp. 59, 2.

13. Shoghi Effendi to 1946 annual-Bahá'í-convention delegates (cablegram), 23 April 1946, Original Letters of Shoghi Effendi, microfilm reel 5.

14. Shoghi Effendi (letter written on his behalf) to National Spiritual Assembly of the Bahá'ís of the United States and Canada, 20 July 1946, Original Letters of Shoghi Effendi, microfilm reel 8.

15. Temple Trustees for the Benefit of the National Spiritual Assembly of the Bahá'ís of the United States and Canada, Minutes, 7 December 1946, pp. 1–2.

16. Temple Trustees for the Benefit of the National Spiritual Assembly of the Bahá'ís of the United States and Canada, Minutes, 19 January 1947, p. 2. Other people who acted as special consultants for the interior were: Dudley Blakely and Mark Tobey (color); Mary Elizabeth Hyde, Beatrice Irwin, and Clarence Welsh (lighting); Dr. Frank McMillan (concrete); Major Lenox Lohr and William A. Wolff (engineers); Edward R. Collison (contractor); Theodore Lindenberg (acoustics); Dr. Hilton Ira Jones (scientist).

Notes to Pages 208–20

17. Shoghi Effendi (letter written on his behalf) to National Spiritual Assembly of the Bahá'ís of the United States and Canada, 11 April 1947, Original Letters of Shoghi Effendi, microfilm reel 8.

18. Ibid.

19. Temple Trustees for the Benefit of the National Spiritual Assembly of the Bahá'ís of the United States and Canada, Minutes, 3–6 July 1947, p. 2.

20. Temple Trustees for the Benefit of the National Spiritual Assembly of the Bahá'ís of the United States and Canada, Minutes, 6–9 June 1947, p. 4.

21. Temple Trustees, Minutes, 3–6 July 1947, p. 7; "Report of Chairman of Temple Construction Committee: Appendix to Minutes of Temple Trustees of August 3 and 4, 1947," TS, p. 1.

22. Temple Trustees for the Benefit of the National Spiritual Assembly of the Bahá'ís of the United States and Canada, Minutes, 5–7 December 1947, p. 2; January 1948, p. 3; and 25–26 March 1948, p. 7.

23. Robert W. McLaughlin, "Architecture of the Temple Interior," in *The Bahá'í World: A Biennial International Record, Volume XI, 1946–1950*, comp. National Spiritual Assembly of the Bahá'ís of the United States and Canada (Wilmette, Ill.: Bahá'í Publishing Committee, 1952), p. 336.

24. Shoghi Effendi to National Spiritual Assembly of the Bahá'ís of the United States (cablegrams), 4, 6 May 1948, Original Letters of Shoghi Effendi, microfilm reel 8.

25. Temple Trustees for the Benefit of the National Spiritual Assembly of the Bahá'ís of the United States, Minutes, 29 July 1948, p. 2.

26. Shoghi Effendi to National Spiritual Assembly of the Bahá'ís of the United States (cablegram), 21 December 1948, Original Letters of Shoghi Effendi, microfilm reel 8.

27. Allen B. McDaniel and Paul E. Haney, "Interior Ornamentation of the Bahá'í House of Worship," in *The Bahá'í World: A Biennial International Record, Volume XII, 1950–1954*, comp. National Spiritual Assembly of the Bahá'ís of the United States (Wilmette, Ill.: Bahá'í Publishing Trust, 1956), p. 536.

28. Allen B. McDaniel, quoted in "Temple Work Protected," *Bahá'í News*, no. 230 (Apr. 1950), p. 4. Mr. Taylor and his son continued to operate the studio until December 1973, when they closed its doors for the last time.

29. Shoghi Effendi (letter written on his behalf) to Richard Nolen, 16 February 1951, quoted in " 'Redouble Your Efforts,' " *Bahá'í News*, no. 244 (June 1951), p. 1; Shoghi Effendi (letter written on his behalf) to National Spiritual Assembly of the Bahá'ís of the United States, 29 March 1951, quoted in "How We May Use the Temple," *Bahá'í News*, no. 244 (June 1951), p. 1.

30. The members of the Temple Landscape Committee were Leroy Ioas, H. Borrah Kavelin, Robert McLaughlin, and Clarence Ullrich.

31. Shoghi Effendi, quoted in Allen B. McDaniel, "Building the Temple: A Historical Record of the Bahá'í Universal House of Worship at Wilmette, Illinois" [paper

prepared for the celebration of the fiftieth anniversary of the Temple project], 1951, p. 126, National Bahá'í Archives, Wilmette, Ill.

32. Hilbert E. Dahl, *Baha'i Temple Gardens: The Landscape Setting of a Unique Architectural Monument*, reprinted from *Landscape Architecture* (July 1953), pp. 2–3.

33. Hilbert Dahl, quoted in National Spiritual Assembly of the Bahá'ís of the United States, "Landscape Plan of the Bahá'í House of Worship by Hilbert Dahl," in *The Bahá'í World: A Biennial International Record, Volume XII, 1950–1954*, comp. National Spiritual Assembly of the Bahá'ís of the United States (Wilmette, Ill.: Bahá'í Publishing Trust, 1956), p. 542.

34. Shoghi Effendi to Corinne True (cablegram), 28 February 1952, personal papers of Edna M. True.

35. At that time Shoghi Effendi was living in the house 'Abdu'l-Bahá had built at No. 7 Haparsim Street in Haifa. The Western Pilgrim House was across the street. The older Pilgrim House, built near the Shrine of the Báb during 'Abdu'l-Bahá's lifetime, was used for pilgrims from the East.

36. Shoghi Effendi, comp., *The Bahá'í Faith: 1844–1952* (Wilmette, Ill.: Bahá'í Publishing Committee, 1953), pp. 5–6.

37. Shoghi Effendi to National Spiritual Assembly of the Bahá'ís of the United States (cablegram), 29 November 1951, Original Letters of Shoghi Effendi, microfilm reel 8. The centenary celebration was the second of three "Holy Years" designated by Shoghi Effendi. As described earlier, the first Holy Year (1944) marked the beginning of the second Bahá'í century. The third Holy Year (1963) commemorated the one hundredth anniversary of Bahá'u'lláh's declaration of His mission.

Chapter Nineteen / The Dedication

1. At the dome's apex is the Arabic inscription *Ya Bahá'u'l-Abhá*. This invocation, known as the "Greatest Name," means "O Thou Glory of Glories." " 'By Greatest Name is meant that Bahá'u'lláh has appeared in God's greatest name, in other words, that He is the supreme Manifestation of God.' " (Shoghi Effendi, "The Greatest Name," *Bahá'í News*, no. 224 [Oct. 1949], p. 5)

2. "Address by Rúhíyyih Khánum to the Bahá'í Convention," *Jubilee Celebration: Bahá'ís of the United States: April 29–May 6, 1953* (Wilmette, Ill.: National Spiritual Assembly of the Bahá'ís of the United States, 1953), p. 6.

3. Shoghi Effendi, "The Guardian's Message to the Forty-Fifth Annual Bahá'í Convention," *Jubilee Celebration*, p. 5.

4. Edna M. True, interview with author, Wilmette, Ill., 25 September 1975. Corinne True died on 3 April 1961 at the age of ninety-nine.

5. William B. Sears, "The Public Dedication of the Bahá'í House of Worship," in *The Bahá'í World: A Biennial International Record, Volume XII, 1950–1954*, comp. National Spiritual Assembly of the Bahá'ís of the United States (Wilmette, Ill.: Bahá'í Publishing

Trust, 1956), p. 155. The Hands of the Cause of God present at the dedication were Amatu'l-Bahá Rúḥíyyih K͟hánum, S͟hu'á'u'lláh 'Alá'í, Dorothy Baker, Músá Banání, Amelia Collins, 'Alí-Akbar Furútan, Horace Holley, D͟hikru'lláh K͟hádem, Ṭarázu'lláh Samandarí, Siegfried Schopflocher, George Townshend, Corinne True, and Valíyu'lláh Varqá. Among others present who would later be appointed to serve as Hands of the Cause of God were Paul Haney, then chairman of the National Spiritual Assembly of the United States, and William Sears.

      6. Rúḥíyyih K͟hánum, "The Guardian's Message on the Occasion of the Dedication of the Mother-Temple of the West," in *The Bahá'í World: A Biennial International Record, Volume XII, 1950–1954,* comp. National Spiritual Assembly of the Bahá'ís of the United States (Wilmette, Ill.: Bahá'í Publishing Trust, 1956), p. 141.

      7. William B. Sears, "Public Dedication of the Bahá'í House of Worship," pp. 155–56; Charles Wolcott, "From The Sweet-Scented Streams" (Wilmette, Ill.: Bahá'í Publishing Trust, 1954). Charles Wolcott was elected to The Universal House of Justice in 1963.

      8. Justice William O. Douglas, quoted in "Messages of Greeting Received for Temple Dedication," *Jubilee Celebration,* p. 12.

      9. Abba Eban, quoted in "Messages of Greeting," p. 12.

      10. Dr. Marcus Bach, quoted in "Messages of Greeting," p. 12.

      11. Thurgood Marshall and Roy Wilkins, quoted in "Messages of Greeting," p. 13.

      12. Dr. E. A. Burtt, Ruth Bryan Rhode, and Dr. Raymond Frank Piper, quoted in "Messages of Greeting," pp. 12–13.

      13. *Chicago Tribune,* 3 May 1953.

      14. Marzieh Gail, "Jubilee at Wilmette," *Jubilee Celebration,* p. 13.

      15. Shoghi Effendi, "The Golden Age of the Cause of Bahá'u'lláh," in *The World Order of Bahá'u'lláh: Selected Letters,* 2d ed. (Wilmette, Ill.: Bahá'í Publishing Trust, 1974), p. 68.

Chapter Twenty / Epilogue

      1. 'Abdu'l-Bahá to Chicago House of Spirituality, trans. 2 July 1903, in *Tablets Revealed by Abdul-Baha in Reference to the Erection of the Mashrek-el-Azkar (the Bahai Temple of Worship)* (n.p., n.d.), personal papers of Edna M. True. (Since an authoritative translation of this letter has not yet been made, the letter is to be considered only as an historic document.—ED.)

      2. Chase to Albert Windust (copy), 16 November 1910, Thornton Chase Papers, National Bahá'í Archives, Wilmette, Ill.

      3. True to Albert Windust, 26 November 1906, Chicago House of Spirituality Records, National Bahá'í Archives, Wilmette, Ill.; True to Mrs. Charles Lincoln, n.d., tape recording of Mrs. Charles Lincoln correspondence, National Bahá'í Archives,

Wilmette, Ill.; Shoghi Effendi, quoted in National Spiritual Assembly of the Bahá'ís of the United States and Canada to unidentified "Local Spiritual Assemblies," 23 March 1928, personal papers of Edna M. True. See also National Spiritual Assembly of the Bahá'ís of the United States, *Declaration of Trust and By-Laws of the National Spiritual Assembly of the Bahá'ís of the United States/By-Laws of a Local Spiritual Assembly*, rev. ed. (Wilmette, Ill.: Bahá'í Publishing Trust, 1975).

4. Roy Williams to Corinne True, 17 November 1919, personal papers of Edna M. True.

5. 'Abdu'l-Bahá to "his honor Ameen," trans. 19 April 1910, quoted in "Record of the Second Annual Convention of Bahai Temple Unity, held April 25 and 26, 1910," *Bahai News*, 1, no. 4 (17 May 1910), 14. (Since an authoritative translation of this letter has not yet been made, the letter is to be considered only as an historic document.—ED.)

6. National Spiritual Assembly of the Bahá'ís of the United States and Canada, and the Bahá'í Temple Unity, *Mashriq'Ul-Adhkar Report: 1909–1925* (n.p., 1925), p. 4.

7. 'Abdu'l-Bahá, quoted in Shoghi Effendi, *God Passes By*, rev. ed. (Wilmette, Ill.: Bahá'í Publishing Trust, 1974), p. 351.

8. 'Abdu'l-Bahá to 1909 convention delegates, n.d., quoted in Bahai Temple Unity, Proceedings of the Bahai Temple Convention, 22–23 March 1909, p. 1, Bahá'í Temple Unity Records, National Bahá'í Archives, Wilmette, Ill. (Since an authoritative translation of this letter has not yet been made, the letter is to be considered only as an historic document.—ED.)

9. Shoghi Effendi, "The Spiritual Significance of the Mashriqu'l-Adhkár," in *The Bahá'í World: A Biennial International Record, Volume VIII, 1938–1940*, comp. National Spiritual Assembly of the Bahá'ís of the United States and Canada (Wilmette, Ill.: Bahá'í Publishing Committee, 1942), p. 511.

10. 'Abdu'l-Bahá, *The Promulgation of Universal Peace: Talks Delivered by 'Abdu'l-Bahá during His Visit to the United States and Canada in 1912*, comp. Howard MacNutt, 2d ed. (Wilmette, Ill.: Bahá'í Publishing Trust, 1982), p. 65.

11. Shoghi Effendi, *God Passes By*, p. 349; Chase to Mrs. A. M. Bryant (copy), 2 October 1908, Thornton Chase Papers, National Bahá'í Archives, Wilmette, Ill.

Appendix Two / Ashkhabad, the City of Love

1. A[nthony] A. Lee, "The Rise of the Bahá'í Community of 'Ishqábád," *Bahá'í Studies*, 5 (Jan. 1979), 2–9.

2. Unidentified Bahá'í, quoted in Horace Holley, "Survey of Current Bahá'í Activities 1928–1930: Persecution Under the Soviet Régime," in *The Bahá'í World (Formerly: Bahá'í Year Book): A Biennial International Record, Volume III, 1928–1930*, comp. National Spiritual Assembly of the Bahá'ís of the United States and Canada (New York: Bahá'í Publishing Committee, 1930), p. 35.

3. Report of the National Spiritual Assembly of the Bahá'ís of Iran, excerpted in Horace Holley, "Survey of Current Bahá'í Activities in the East and West: Persecution and Deportation of the Bahá'ís of Caucasus and Turkistan," in *The Bahá'í World: A Biennial International Record, Volume VIII, 1938–1940*, comp. National Spiritual Assembly of the Bahá'ís of the United States and Canada (Wilmette, Ill.: Bahá'í Publishing Committee, 1942), p. 87.

4. Ibid., p. 89.

Appendix Three / Brief Biographies of Some Bahá'ís Associated with the Temple Project

1. Dr. Zia Bagdadi, quoted in "Memorial Service to Dr. Zia Mabsut Bagdádí, Held in the Bahá'í House of Worship, May 8, 1937," in *The Bahá'í World: A Biennial International Record, Volume VII, 1936–1938*, comp. National Spiritual Assembly of the Bahá'ís of the United States and Canada (New York: Bahá'í Publishing Committee, 1939), p. 539.

2. This biographical sketch is based on "Memorial Service to Dr. Zia Mabsut Bagdádí," pp. 535–39.

3. "In Memoriam," quoted in "Albert H. Hall," *Star of the West*, 11 (2 Mar. 1921), p. 323.

4. This biographical sketch is based on "Albert H. Hall," pp. 322–23.

5. Shoghi Effendi, quoted in Louis G. Gregory and Harlan Ober, "Alfred Eastman Lunt," in *Bahá'í World, Vol. VII*, pp. 533, 534. This biographical sketch is based on Gregory and Ober, "Alfred Eastman Lunt," pp. 531–34.

6. This biographical sketch is based on Paul E. Haney, "Allen B. McDaniel," in *The Bahá'í World: An International Record, Volume XIV, 1963–1968*, comp. The Universal House of Justice (Haifa: The Universal House of Justice, 1974), pp. 364–65. See also Allen B. McDaniel, *The Spell of the Temple* (New York: Vantage Press, 1953).

7. This biographical sketch is based on "William Sutherland Maxwell," in *The Bahá'í World: A Biennial International Record, Volume XII, 1950–1954*, comp. National Spiritual Assembly of the Bahá'ís of the United States (Wilmette, Ill.: Bahá'í Publishing Trust, 1956), pp. 657–62.

8. Shoghi Effendi, quoted in Horace Holley, "Mountfort Mills," in *The Bahá'í World: A Biennial International Record, Volume XI, 1946–1950*, comp. National Spiritual Assembly of the Bahá'ís of the United States and Canada (Wilmette, Ill.: Bahá'í Publishing Committee, 1952), p. 510. This biographical sketch is based on Holley, "Mountfort Mills," pp. 509–11.

9. This biographical sketch is based on "Siegfried Schopflocher," in *Bahá'í World, Vol. XII*, pp. 664–66.

10. 'Abdu'l-Bahá to Louise Waite, trans. 1902, trans. 1 July 1909, Original Translations of Tablets of 'Abdu'l-Bahá, National Bahá'í Archives, Wilmette, Ill. (Since

authoritative translations of these letters have not yet been made, the letters are to be considered only as historic documents.—ED.)

11. [Louise R. Waite], *Baha'i Hymns of Peace and Praise* (n.p., 1908). Subsequent printings continued to bear the date 1908 but included additional hymns. There were at least three more printings of the book, one as late as 1927.

See also *The Bahá'í World: A Biennial International Record, Volume IV, 1930–1932*, comp. National Spiritual Assembly of the Bahá'ís of the United States and Canada (New York: Bahá'í Publishing Committee, 1933), pp. 533–40; *The Bahá'í World: A Biennial International Record, Volume V, 1932–1934*, comp. National Spiritual Assembly of the Bahá'ís of the United States and Canada (New York: Bahá'í Publishing Committee, 1936), pp. 683–89, 700; and *The Bahá'í World: A Biennial International Record, Volume VI, 1934–1936*, comp. National Spiritual Assembly of the Bahá'ís of the United States and Canada (New York: Bahá'í Publishing Committee, 1937), pp. 745–46, 748–53, 758.

12. This biographical sketch is based on Willard P. Hatch, "Sháhnaz Khánum (Mrs. Louise R. Waite)," in *The Bahá'í World: A Biennial International Record, Volume VIII, 1938–1940*, comp. National Spiritual Assembly of the Bahá'ís of the United States and Canada (Wilmette, Ill.: Bahá'í Publishing Committee, 1942), pp. 662, 663.

13. Shoghi Effendi, quoted in Horace Holley, "Roy C. Wilhelm," in *Bahá'í World, Vol. XII*, p. 662. This biographical sketch is based on Holley, "Roy C. Wilhelm," pp. 662–64.

14. See 'Abdu'l-Bahá, *Tablets of Abdul-Baha Abbas*, 3 vols. (New York: Bahai Publishing Society, 1909–1916); *Bahá'í Year Book, Volume One, 1925–1926*, comp. National Spiritual Assembly of the Bahá'ís of the United States and Canada (New York: Bahá'í Publishing Committee, 1926); *The Bahá'í World (Formerly: Bahá'í Year Book): A Biennial International Record, Volume II, 1926–1928*, comp. National Spiritual Assembly of the Bahá'ís of the United States and Canada (New York: Bahá'í Publishing Committee, 1928); *The Bahá'í World (Formerly: Bahá'í Year Book): A Biennial International Record, Volume III, 1928–1930*, comp. National Spiritual Assembly of the Bahá'ís of the United States and Canada (New York: Bahá'í Publishing Committee, 1930); *Bahá'í World, Vol. IV*; and *Bahá'í World, Vol. V*.

INDEX

INDEX

Back notes are indicated by "p.– n.–." Bold figures are used for photographs.

Abbott, Mr., 92
'Abdu'l-Bahá, 4, 4n, 29, **30**
  American visit of, 57–67
    depends on building of Temple, 56, 57
    Hull House, 58–59
    National Association for the Advancement of Colored People convention, 59
    twenty-fifth anniversary of, celebrated, 307–08 n.17
  Bahá'í Temple
    contribution to fund for, 60
    contributions from Persia encouraged, 55, 238
    Corinne True encouraged to aid, 22, 31
    drawings of, hung in Shrine of the Báb, 294 n.7
    importance of, emphasized, 22, 50–51, 59–60, 62–64, 66–67, 237, 238
    meeting with Bourgeois, 102–03
    permission sought and given for, 4–5
    prayers written for, 273–74 n.5
    refusal to suggest design preference, 88
    site of, dedicated, 60–62, **63**, 64–65
    smaller, less expensive version of Bourgeois' design asked for, 101–02, 103
    stone sent as a marker for, 48, 281 n.14
  Center of the Covenant, 70, 70 n
  charity of, 32
  comb and handkerchief of, donated to Temple Fund, 174
  death of, 114
    eulogy by Albert Windust, 115
    tributes at funeral, 114–15
  Egypt and Europe visited by, 56
  Fête Day of, 38, 38 n
  house of, in Akka, 28, **29**
  knighthood conferred upon 292 n.14
  relationship of Bahá'ís to, 30
  title of "Master" used, 12, 12 n
  sister of. *See* Bahíyyih Khánum
  sufferings of, 101
  Tablets of the Divine Plan written by, 75, 180, 287 n.27
  titles of, 12, 12 n, 70 n
  wife of. *See* Munírih Khánum
  Will and Testament of, 121, 296 n.1
Addams, Jane, 58
Agnew, Arthur, 26, 34, 52
Akka, Palestine (Israel), 28. *See also* Pilgrimage(s) to Bahá'í holy places
Alláh-u-Abhá, 52, 52 n
American Concrete Institute, 143, 163, 205
Anderson, Alfred, 118, 296 n.30
Anderson, Herbert, 64
Asadu'lláh, Mírzá, 3–5, 46
Asgarzadeh, Ziaoulláh, 140–41
Ashkhabad, 248–51. *See also* Bahá'í Temple (Ashkhabad)
Avery Brundage Company, 108–09, 119

Báb, the, 245
  portrait of, sent to America, 203, 233
  Shrine of
    the Báb's remains laid in, 52, 281–82 n.9
    contributions to, 220
    final construction phase of, begun 227
    superstructure model of, unveiled, 204
Bach, Marcus, 233–34
Bagdadi, Parvene, 139
Bagdadi, Zia, 57, 108, 122, 160
  Bagdadis move to Wilmette, 297 n.9
  biography of, 252
  recommends building supervisor, 117–18
Bahá'í Faith, 6, 105, 105 n, 245–47
Bahá'í Faith (world community of)
  growth and teaching activities of, 217–19, 237–38, 240
    'Abdu'l-Bahá's Tablets of the Divine Plan in-

Index

Bahá'í Faith (world community of) *(continued)*
  fluence, 75, 180, 287 n.27
  "intercontinental stage" in evolution of Bahá'í institutions begun, 226
  international correspondence helps unify, 3, 136
  1944 centennial commemorations of founding of, 200–05, 311 n.6
  1953 centennial commemorations of commencement of Bahá'u'lláh's prophetic mission, 226
  Shoghi Effendi lists dates of historical significance in, 225
Bahá'í Faith in America. *See also* 'Abdu'l-Bahá; Bahá'í Temple (Wilmette); New York City, New York; Shoghi Effendi; Women; Women's Assembly of Teaching
  administration and organization of, 237–38, 276 n.19, 308–09 n.24
    Bahai Temple Unity, 49–50, **51**, 52, 260–61
    Chicago House of Spirituality, 16, 17
    convention procedures before 1920, 291 n.4
    Declaration of Trust codifies principles of, 137–38
    election procedures restructured, 122
    first National Spiritual Assembly elected, 121, 122, 122 n
    National Spiritual Assembly incorporated in 1927, 137–38 n
    secretariat moved to Wilmette, 188, 308–09 n.24
    Temple linked to growth of, 237–38
    Thornton Chase helps guide early, 16, 237
    title of "Spiritual Assembly" given to local governing bodies, 129, 129 n
    women not allowed on first governing bodies, 16–17
  American Jubilee Celebration in 1953, 226
  archives of, 258
  finances of. *See also* Bahá'í Temple (Wilmette), financing of
    budget consolidated into single National Bahá'í Fund, 129–30
    contributions increase after 1928, 131–32
  first adherents of, 7
    difficulties in educating, 14, 15
    scholars help educate, 15
    taught by Ibráhím Khayru'lláh, 11, 11 n, 12
  first printed mention of, 275 n.6
  first public mention of, 7, 10–11
  growth and teaching activities of, 14–15, 24, 200
    'Abdu'l-Bahá's Tablets of the Divine Plan influence, 75, 180, 287 n.27
    expansion of, in 1930s, 180–81, 187
    first Plan of Unified Action (1925–28), 129–31, 136–38
    first Seven Year Plan (1937–44), 181, 187, 200
    fund and program for, established in 1915, 74–75
    International Bahai Congress of 1915 at Panama-Pacific Exposition, 74
    national and regional teaching committees formed, 181
    Race Amity Conventions, 138
    second Plan of Unified Action (1931–34), 158–59
    second Seven Year Plan (1946–53), 205
    Temple linked to, 186–87, 193, 237–40
    World Unity Conferences, 138
  national identity emerges, 179
  Nineteen Day Feasts, 158 n
  1944 Centenary of founding of Bahá'í Faith, 200–03, 311 n.6
  publicity concerning. *See* Publicity about and public response to the Bahá'í Temple
Bahá'í Faith in Ashkhabad, Russian Turkistan, 3–4, 248–51
Bahá'í Faith in Canada, 205
Bahá'í Faith in Germany
  administrative institutions dissolved under Hitler, 181
Bahá'í Publishing Society organized, 15–16, 258
Bahá'í Temple(s)
  Charles Mason Remey designed several, 255
  institution of, developed in Ashkhabad to high degree, 249, 251
  purpose of, 59–60, 240–41
  symbolism of, 4, 4 n, 6, 6 n
Bahá'í Temple (Ashkhabad), 3–4, 62, 64, 248–51
  expropriation of, by Soviets, 139, 249–50
Bahá'í Temple (Wilmette), **235, 239**. *See also* 'Abdu'l-Bahá; Bourgeois, Louis; Publicity about and public response to the Bahá'í Temple; Shoghi Effendi; True, Corinne
  bell shape of, 81
  birds find sanctuary in, 194
  caretaker's house built near, 297 n.9
  committees and institutions to organize and promote
    Bahai Temple Association of America proposed in 1908, 42
    Bahai Temple Unity founded in 1909, **51**, 52, 260–61
    Chicago House of Spirituality, 3–6, 17, 24–26, 36, 38, 42
    first Foundation Hall Program Committee appointed in 1928, 300–01 n.37
    House of Worship Activities Committee currently appointed annually, 270
    Ideas Committee appointed in 1920, 97–98

Materials Committee, 305 n.11
Technical Advisory Board appointed in 1947, 210–12
Technical Committee appointed in 1946, 206, 208
Temple Construction Committee formed in 1947, 208
Temple Landscape Committee, 220, 312 n.30
Women's Assembly of Teaching, 17, 25–26, 36, 38, 42
construction of *(in chronological order)*
 planning for, gains momentum in 1906, 25–26
 nationwide petition concerning, 26; 31; 259 app.4.1, 4.2
 could be done by stages, 89, 92
construction of Foundation Hall *(in chronological order)*
 building permit obtained, 104–07
 public objections to, and the Bahá'í response, 104–08
 drilling to bedrock begun, **105, 107,** 108, **109**
 flooding of caissons during, 108–09
 William Gorman killed during, 108–09
 foundation begun, 114, **116, 117, 118**
 original pilings faulty, 116–19
 difficulties with, prompt appointment of Bahá'í supervisor, 117–18
 slowness of, displeases neighbors, 122–23
 Foundation Hall improved, 123–24, **125,** 139
construction of superstructure *(in chronological order)*
 progress in concrete structures means concrete is viable material for, 143–45
 contract signed with Fuller Company, 145, 303 n.4
 superstructure begun, 145, **146, 147, 148, 149**
 smoothness of, during early stages, 146–47
 accuracy in arches and pylons difficult, 147–48
 fire during, 149–50, **151, 152,** 153
 superstructure completed and dedicated, **154, 155, 156,** 157
construction of exterior ornamentation *(in chronological order)*
 concrete ornamentation by Earley chosen for dome, 161
 methods used and difficulties with producing ornamentation, 164–72, **167, 168, 169, 170, 171, 172**
 ornamentation applied to dome, 174, 175, **175, 176, 177,** 178, **184, 185**
 ornamentation of clerestory, 178, 180, **184, 185**
 dust storm mars dome, 179

ornamentation of gallery, 182, 183, **184, 185,** 187
ornamentation of main story, 183, **185,** 188
exterior ornamentation completed, **189,** 190, 309 n.28
steps built, **186, 187,** 190
exposed steel painted, 202
construction of interior ornamentation *(in chronological order)*
 George A. Fuller Company awarded construction contract, 211–12
 Earley Studio awarded contract to produce ornamental panels in architectural concrete, 212
 original doors, staircase, and main-level windows replaced, 212, 215
 alcove ceilings constructed with acoustical plaster, 215
 interior ornamentation begun, 215, **215,** 216
 small fire does minimal damage at Earley Studio, 216
 interior ornamentation completed, 217, **217, 218, 219,** 220
cornerstone, 94, 114. See also Bahá'í Temple (Wilmette), dedication stone of *(below)*
dedication of, in 1931, 156–57
dedication of, in 1944, 200–03
dedication of, in 1953, 227–33, **229, 230, 231, 235**
 conducted three times, 232–33
 congratulatory messages, 233–34
 covered by 557 newspapers, 234
 guest speakers during week of, 230
 Hands of the Cause of God present at, 313–14 n.5
 Marzieh Gail remembers, 236
 Rúḥíyyih Khánum speaks at, 228, 232
 Shoghi Effendi's message for, 228–29
 William Sears describes, 232
dedication stone of
 'Abdu'l-Bahá lays, 60, 61–62, **63,** 64–65, 157
 'Abdu'l-Bahá sends stone marker for, 48, 281 n.14
 controversy over original location of dedication stone laid by 'Abdu'l-Bahá, 113
 lost in mud, 295 n.21
 Nettie Tobin acquires, 45–48, 280 n.9
design of, 84, **85, 86, 93.** See also Bourgeois, Louis
 'Abdu'l-Bahá and Executive Board ask for reduction in size of, 101–03
 'Abdu'l-Bahá explains elements of, 31, 62, 64, 80
 'Abdu'l-Bahá refuses to select, 88
 Bourgeois' model selected at 1920 convention, 87–92, 94

Index

Bahá'í Temple (Wilmette) *(continued)*
    colored glass specified for symbols on dome, 194, 208
    costs of various designs discussed, 89, 92
    designs submitted to 1920 convention, 88, 89, **90, 91,** 92, 94
    disunity over, in 1920s, 124
    dome praised, 178
    Executive Board invites design submissions, 80
    John Earley praises, 164–65
    Magonigle comments on, 89–92
    modifications in original, 101–03, 124, 126, 206–12
    use of small chapels misunderstood, 103
  dimensions of, 268
    measurements are multiples of nine, 83
  dome of
    colored glass originally planned for, 194, 208
    compared to Basilica of Saint Peter in Rome, 178
    dust storm mars, 179
    exterior ornamentation made for, 161, 164–72, **167, 168, 169, 172**
    exterior ornamentation put on, 174, 175, **175, 176, 177,** 178, **184, 185**
    inscription in, 313 n.1
    inspiration for, 82
    interior ornamentation of, **216, 217**
    praise for, 92, 164–65, 178
  financing of, 238
    (in chronological order)
    first contributions, 5
    concert in 1904, 24–25, 277 n.2
    contributions after Corinne True's first pilgrimage, 35
    various methods devised to raise money for land, 54–55, 57
    children contribute to, 54, 296–97 n.5
    main tract of land paid for, 67, 283–84 n.16
    uniform system of contributions adopted in 1913, 68–69
    Temple Builder's Fellowship, 69
    final payment on lakeshore property, 69
    total cost of property, 285–86 n.11
    contributions 1914–20, 71–72, 75
    drop in contributions forecast by 'Abdu'l-Bahá, 71
    Roy Williams sends money from southern blacks, 72
    'Abdu'l-Bahá's estimate about cost of Temple, 92
    Temple design changed to reduce cost, 101–02
    extra costs due to flooded caissons, 108–09
    dissension over fee of Louis Bourgeois, 110–12, 124, 126
    cost of foundation less than anticipated, 114, 119
    contributions dwindle after 1920, 119–20, 122, 124, 131
    Temple Fund incorporated into national budget, 129–30
    contributions increase after 1928, 131–32
    contributions increase after carpet from Shrine of Bahá'u'lláh is donated, 141–42
    bids taken for superstructure, 145
    difficulties with, for dome ornamentation, 158–61, 172–73, 175–78
    money needed for heating installation, 159
    special contributions made at 1933 convention, 174
    Shoghi Effendi promises respite for redoubled efforts, 176
    pay-as-you-go proves unsatisfactory for clerestory ornamentation, 178–79
    John Earley carries construction expenses, 178–79
    funds for ornamenting gallery, 181, 183, 187
    funds for ornamenting main story, 183
  financing, international contributions to, 54–55, 57, 67–69, 135–37, 238. *See also* 'Abdu'l-Bahá; Shoghi Effendi
    brooch of Queen Marie given, 136, 299 n.29
    from Burma, 135
    from England, 135
    from Germany, 135
    from India, 68, 135, 173, 238
    from Java, 173
    from Persia (Iran), 55, 68, 137, 173, 238, 300 n.32
  illumination of, **201,** 202, 222
  importance of, 113–14, 237–41
    'Abdu'l-Bahá's statements on, 22, 50–51, 59–60, 62–64, 66–67, 237, 238
    as an "Ark," 308 n.24
    important to nation and world, not just to Chicago, 35
    is "Mother Temple," 51, 240
    Shoghi Effendi emphasizes, 122, 124, 225, 241, 308 n.24
  inscription in dome of, 313 n.1
  inscriptions above entrances of, 188, 268
  inscriptions in interior alcoves of, 268–69
  interior of
    Alfred Shaw produces final plans for, 210–12, 215
    cost of, 212
    modifications in original plan of, made,

Index

205–06, 208, 210–12, **207, 209, 213, 214**
landscaping of, 202, 220–22, **221, 222, 223, 225**
   Hilbert Dahl design chosen, 220–22
   Louis Bourgeois' original concept for, 220
   some, done in 1925, 124, **125**
   submission of designs for, invited, 220
meetings held at *(in chronological order)*
   meetings held on land before building was erected, 44, **47**
   seventy-second anniversary of the martyrdom of the Báb, 119, **119**
   1928 Inauguration Ceremony of Foundation Hall, 139, **142**
   Shoghi Effendi's instructions concerning Foundation Hall, 300–01 n.37
   1931 convention and superstructure dedication, **156**, 157
   1935 commemoration of completion of dome, ribs, and clerestory, 180
   local Bahá'í meetings at Temple prohibited, 310 n.7
   1944 Centenary of founding of Bahá'í Faith, 200–03, 311 n.6
   public lectures, 198
Mírzá Asadu'lláh's letter inspires plan for, 3–5
misconceptions about. *See* Publicity about and public response to the Bahá'í Temple
National Register of Historic Places lists, 240
plaster models of. *See* Publicity about and public response to the Bahá'í Temple
poem written for, 290 n.24
prayers written for, 273–74 n.5
purpose of, 59–60, 67, 240–41
rumors about. *See* Publicity about and public response to the Bahá'í Temple
site of, **39**. *See also* Bahá'í Temple (Wilmette), landscaping of *(above)*
   'Abdu'l-Bahá approves, 45
   canal route through, changed, 54
   decision made on, 42–43
   dedication of, 60–62, **63**, 64–65
   felt to be too far from Chicago, 45
   first lots purchased in 1908, **43**, 44
   first national meeting concerning, 38–41
   history of, 44
   improvements to area around, 73, 287 n.22
   lake frontage purchased in 1912, 57, 283–84 n.16
   meetings held on, before building erected, 44, **47**
   problems with trespassers and crowds, 72–73
   roadways through, eliminated, 54, 282 n.3
   search for, 24, 36–38
   Sheridan Road route changed, 103, 189–90
   title cleared in 1941, 188–90
   total cost of, to 1916, 285–86 n.11
   twelve more lots bought in 1909, 53
song written for, 266–67
symbolism of, 6, 6 n, 89, 95
teaching activities linked to, 186–87, 193, 237–38, 240
Temple Leaflets, 134–35
Temple Trustees, 137–38 n
visitors to. *See* Publicity about and public response to the Bahá'í Temple
Bahai Temple Association of America proposed, 42
Bahai Temple Unity, **51**, 52
constitution of, 260–61
Bahá'u'lláh, 5–6, 245, 302 n.45
Gleanings published in English, 180
lock of hair and prayer of, donated to Temple Fund, 174
lock of hair of, given by Shoghi Effendi to Temple, 183
portrait of, given to Temple by Shoghi Effendi, 233
Russian minister to Persia aids, 251
some Bahá'ís thought remains of, would be buried beneath Temple, 293 n.16
Bahíyyih Khánum (Greatest Holy Leaf), 32, **33**, 154–55
death of, 165
gifts from, used at Foundation Hall Inauguration Ceremony, 139
prayer beads used by, donated to Temple Fund, 174
Bangor, Michigan, 40
Barnard, George Grey, 99
Bedikian, Victoria, 132–36, **134**, 299 n.27
Blumenstein, Paul, 79, 80
Bosch, John, 50
Bourgeois, Alice De Longpre, 77, 81, 150
Bourgeois, Louis, **78**
architectural designs of, 77, 288 nn.3, 4
   Chicago Tribune Building, 293 n.27
   church of Saint-Wenceslas, 77
   Evergreen Cabin, 288 n.1
   Permanent Court of Arbitration at The Hague, **79**, 79–80, 85
   plans for other structures near Temple, 302 n.1
   Temple caretaker's house, 297 n.9
Bahá'í activities of, 297 n.9
Bahá'í Faith accepted by, 76
Bahá'í Temple design, 80–83, 84, **85**, 85–86, 88–92, **93**, 94
   difficulties with fee for, 110–12, 124, 126
   drawings of, hung by 'Abdu'l-Bahá in Shrine of the Báb, 294 n.7

325

Index

Bourgeois, Louis *(continued)*
  influence of Charles Mason Remey on, 86
  inspiration for, 86
  inspiration for dome, 82
  John Earley praises, 164–65
  measurements are multiples of nine, 83
  meeting with 'Abdu'l-Bahá concerning, 102–03
  number of architectural drawings required for, 295 n.16
  original design modified, 101–03, 124
  ornamentation details drafted in full size, 165–66
  plaster model displayed, 89, 91–92, 98–100
  plaster model made of, 81–83, **85**
  preliminary sketches of, unsatisfactory, 80
  publicity concerning, 94–97. *See also* Publicity about and public response to the Bahá'í Temple
  service on Materials Committee, 305 n.9
  sources of main features of, 84–86, 289 n.6
  spiritual presentiments concerning, 78–79, 86
  childhood of, 76–77
  death of, 145
    premature reports of, 79
  education and travels of, 77
  studio of, near Temple site, 126–27, **127, 128,** 297 n.8
  tributes to, 128–29, 145, 164
  wives of
    first, 77, 288 n.3
    second. *See* Bourgeois, Alice De Longpre
Bouzaglo, Salomon, 115
Boyle, E. R., 305 n.11
Brittingham, Isabella, 55
Britton, John A., 74
Browne, Edward Granville, 10, 274 n.5
Brush, Charles E., 89
Burnham, Daniel, 7, 83
Burt, Major Henry J., 104, 110, 112–13, 116, 126, 305 n.11
  death of, 143
Burtt, E. A., 234

California. *See* Geyserville; Los Angeles; Oakland; Pasadena; San Francisco
Canada, Bahá'ís of
  form National Spiritual Assembly, 205, 217–18
  Montreal, 40
    appeal for recommencement of Temple construction, 136–37
Century of Progress Exposition (Chicago, 1933), 160, 178, 192

Chase, Thornton, 12, **13,** 14–16, **47,** 50, **51**
  Akka described by, 28
  called first American believer, 14
  death of, 61
  importance of international letters emphasized by, 3
  Nettie Tobin's stone does not impress, 48
  pilgrimage of, 34, 36
  role of, in organizing Bahá'í governing bodies, 16, 237
  Temple's role described by, 241
  transferred to Los Angeles, 60
Chicago, Illinois. *See also* Century of Progress Exposition; World's Columbian Exposition
  Art Institute, 8, 99–100
  Bahá'ís of
    help orphaned children, 25
    initiate petition to 'Abdu'l-Bahá, 25–26
    organize House of Spirituality, 16, 17, 24–26, 36, 38, 42–45, 49, 54
    organize Women's Assembly of Teaching, 17, 18, 22, 25–26, 35, 36, 38, 42
Chicago Sanitary District, 44, 54
  canal locks, 61
Children
  contribute to Temple Fund, 54, 296–97 n.5
  education of, 21
    Fellowship Gardens organized for, 133, 298 n.22
    Lesson Leaflets written for, 135
  orphanage for, 133
  orphaned, helped by Chicago Bahá'ís, 25
  Temple visited by, 197–98
Cole, Hills, 112
Collins, Amelia, 183, 208
Cooper, Ella, 122
Cousins, Norman, 230
Cron, Frederick, 161, 163, 171, 205

Dahl, Hilbert E., 220–22
Dealy, Paul, 46
De Longpre, Alice (later Alice De Longpre Bourgeois). *See* Bourgeois, Alice De Longpre
D'Evelyn, Frederick W., 74
Douglas, Justice William O., 233

Eardley, Edwin, 206, 210
Earley, John Joseph, 161, **162,** 163–71
  death of, 205
  expenses of Temple ornamentation carried by, 178–79
  friendship of, with Louis Bourgeois, 164
  pioneering efforts of, with concrete, 161–63, 305–06 n.17

326

Index

pride of, in erecting Temple dome, 169
Temple design praised by, 164–65
Earley Studio, 162–63, 165–72, 178, 181–82, 188, 190, 212, 215–17
Eban, Abba, 233

Fáḍil-i-Mázindarání, Jináb-i, 96, 293 n.19
Feast, Nineteen Day, 158 n
Ford, Mary Hanford, 99
Foster, Grace, 38, 50
Fuller Company, George A., 145, 211–12, 215, 222, 303 n.4

Gail, Marzieh, 202, 203
  remembers dedication of Temple, 236
Germany dissolves Bahá'í administrative institutions, 181
Getsinger, Lua, 59, 64
Geyserville, California, 137
Gillson Park, 73, 287 n.22
Goldblatt, Nathan, 284 n.16
Golden Gate International Exposition (San Francisco, 1939), 193
Goodall, Helen, 52
Gorman, William, 108–09
Greatest Holy Leaf. *See* Bahíyyih Khánum
Greatest Name
  Alláh-u-Abhá, 52, 52 n
  Yá Bahá'u'l-Abhá, 313 n.1
Green, Philip Leonard, 203
Green Acre, 137
Gregory, Louis, 75, 122
Grosse Pointe, Illinois
  chosen as Temple site, 52
  history of, 44
  meetings held on, 44–45, **47**
  purchase of Temple site, 42, **43**, 44, 53, 57, 283–84 n.6, 285–86 n.11
  recommended as Temple site, 37–38, 40–41

Hague, The, Permanent Court of Arbitration at, **79**, 80
Haifa, Palestine (Israel), **27,** 28, 277 n.6 (chap. 4). *See also* Pilgrimage(s) to Bahá'í holy places
Hall, Albert, 40, 52, 59
  biography of, 252–53
Hand of the Cause of God, 223–24. *See also* Collins, Amelia; Gregory, Louis; Haney, Paul; Holley, Horace; Maxwell, William Sutherland; Remey, Charles Mason; Root, Martha; Rúḥíyyih Khánum; Schopflocher, Siegfried; Sears, William; True, Corinne; Wilhelm, Roy
Haney, Paul, 210, 211
Hannen, Carl, 202

Harrison, Cecilia, **37,** 46, 47
Ḥaẓíratu'l-Quds, 308–09 n.24
Hoar, William, 52
Holabird and Roche, 104, 107, 126, 288 n.4
Holley, Doris, 206
Holley, Horace
  defends fee of Louis Bourgeois, 111
  serves on Technical Committee, 206
  speaks at Foundation Hall public meetings, 198
  speaks during Jubilee week, 230
Holmes, Irene, 64
Honolulu, Hawaii, 24, 50
House of Worship. *See* Bahá'í Temple
Hutchinson, Paul, 230

Illinois. *See* Chicago; Grosse Pointe; Wilmette
Iran (Persia)
  American Bahá'ís protest persecution of Bahá'ís in, 137
  contributions to American Temple from, 55, 173, 238
  forbidden in 1920s by Shoghi Effendi, 300 n.32
  Tehran Bahá'í community center built, 306 n.29
  Temple site purchased, 306 n.29
Israel (Palestine). *See* Akka; Haifa; Pilgrimage(s) to Bahá'í holy places

Jacobsen, Bernard, 41, 52
Jacobsen and Company, 82–83
Jaxon, Honore, 54
Jenkyn, Daniel, 68
Jessup, Rev. Henry H., 10, 274–75 n.5
Jináb-i-Fáḍil. *See* Fáḍil-i-Mázindarání, Jináb-i
Junius, John, 202

Kennedy, John, 206, 210
Kenosha, Wisconsin, Bahá'ís of, urge completion of Temple, 41, 136
Khayru'lláh, Ibráhím, 11–12, 275 n.10
Kinne, Harry, 196, 202
Knight, Moses Green, 18
Krug, Grace, 111–12

Latimer, George, 112, 206
Lazarus, Edward, 289 n.6
Leadroot, Leo, 46
League of Nations, 87
Lesch, George, 25
Lincoln, Charles L., 89
Linfoot, Charlotte, ix, x, xi, 174
Los Angeles, California, 50
Lunt, Alfred Eastman, 80, **106,** 113, 126
  biography of, 253

Index

Lunt, Alfred Eastman *(continued)*
   elected to first National Spiritual Assembly, 122
   response of, to newspaper opposition to Temple, 105, 106–07

MacArthur Concrete Pile and Foundation Company, 116
McCarty Brothers, 114, 118–19
McDaniel, Allen B., 143, **144,** 230, 305 n.11
   biography of, 253–54
   serves on Technical Advisory Board, 210
   works on simplifying interior design of Temple, 206, 208
McLaughlin, Robert, 210, 211, 230
Magonigle, H. Van Buren, 89–92, 292 n.11
Marie, Queen (of Rumania), 136, 299–300 n.29
Marshall, Benjamin, 284 n.16
Marshall, Thurgood, 234
Mashriqu'l-Adhkár. *See also* Bahá'í Temple
   institution of, developed in Ashkhabad, 249, 251
   meaning and function of, 4, 4 n, 6, 6 n, 240–41
Maxwell, Mary (later Rúḥíyyih Khánum). *See* Rúḥíyyih Khánum
Maxwell, May, 254
Maxwell, William Sutherland, 88, 305 n.11
   biography of, 254
   design of, for Bahá'í Temple, 89, **91**
   serves on committee to review Bourgeois' contract, 112
   Shrine of the Báb designed by, 204
Mazlúm, Mírzá, 46, 47, 280 n.10
Mills, Mountfort, 59, 87, 89, 198
   biography of, 255
   elected to first National Spiritual Assembly, 122
   pilgrimage of, 101
   president of 1909 Bahai Temple Unity Executive Board, 52
   serves on committee to review Bourgeois' contract, 112
Minneapolis, Minnesota, 40
Moses, Eaton, 76
Munírih Khánum, 27, 182
Murád, Muḥammad, 115

Naṣṣár, Ibráhím, 114
National Spiritual Assembly. *See* Bahá'í Faith in America, administration and organization of
Newcomb, Rexford, 178
Newell, Frederick, 144, 146–47, 302–03 n.3
New Thought, 15
New York City, New York
   annual Bahá'í convention of 1920 in, 87–92, 94
   Bahá'ís of
      asked to work on Chicago Temple, 42
      celebrate twenty-fifth anniversary of 'Abdu'l-Bahá's visit, 307–08 n.17
   four delegates at first Bahai Temple Unity convention, 50
   wish to build own Temple, 24
   World's Fair (1939–40), 193
Nine, symbolism of the number, 15, 15 n, 89

Oakland, California, 50
Ober, Grace Robarts, 182–83
Ober, Harlan, 182
Orphanage built by Victoria Bedikian, 133
Ouilmette, Antoinne, 44, 76
Overstreet, Harry Allen, 203

Palestine (Israel). *See* Akka; Haifa; Pilgrimage(s) to Bahá'í holy places
Panama-Pacific International Exposition (San Francisco, 1915), 74
Parmerton, Anna, 52
Pasadena, California, 50
Perron, Arna True
   'Abdu'l-Bahá's gifts to, 34
   pilgrimage of, 26, 31–32, 34
Persia. *See* Iran
Philadelphia, Pennsylvania, 40
Pilgrimage(s) to Bahá'í holy places
   by Arna True Perron, 26, 31, 32, 34
   by Arthur Agnew, 34
   by Carl Scheffler, 34
   by Corinne True, 26–35, 139, 153–55, 222–24
   by Isabella Brittingham, 55–56
   by Lorol Schopflocher, 132
   by Louis Bourgeois, 102–03
   by Louise Waite, 55
   by Mountfort Mills, 101
   by Thornton Chase, 34
Piper, Raymond Frank, 203, 234
Plan of Unified Action. *See* Bahá'í Faith in America, growth and teaching activities of
Pompilio, Mr., 206, 210
Portland Cement Association, 143
Potawatomie Indians, 44, 279 n.4
Potter, Myron, 89
Publicity about and public response to the Bahá'í Temple, 99–100, 119, 192–99, 233–34, 236
   airplanes asked not to buzz Temple, 196
   cancellation-stamp design includes Temple, 195, **195**
   individual comments
      by Abba Eban, 233
      by E. A. Burtt, 234
      by George Grey Barnard, 99

by H. Van Buren Magonigle, 89–92, 292 n.11
by Harry Kinne, 202
by John Earley, 164–65
by Justice William O. Douglas, 233
by Luigi Quaglino, 99
by Marcus Bach, 233–34
by Mozo Samuel, 99
by Raymond Frank Piper, 234
by Roy Wilkins, 234
by Ruth Bryan Rhode, 234
by Thurgood Marshall, 234
Martha Root publicizes Temple, 98, 198–99
misconceptions concerning Temple, 53
Bahá'ís are sun worshippers, 197
Bahá'u'lláh's remains to be buried beneath Temple, 293 n.16
duplicate Temple on other side of earth, 197
Foundation Hall is huge fuel tank, 123
Foundation Hall is submarine refueling depot, 123
sacred snakes, 197
sea of magnetic quicksand, 193, 309 n.3
Temple is duplicate of Taj Mahal, 196
white whale kept inside Temple, 123
opposition to Temple, 104–08
Leaves of Healing condemns Temple in 1920, 97
plaster models of Temple, 192–93
displayed at Chicago's Century of Progress Exposition, 192
model made by Louis Voelz, 192
National Spiritual Assembly commissions several, 192
publicity in newspapers and magazines, 94–97, 193–95
advertisements capitalize on Temple, 194
Asia and Europe, 96
Chicago Examiner in 1909, 53
Chicago Herald and Examiner, 104
Chicago's American includes Temple in Chickie Chalmers' serial, 193
Christian Register, 95–96
comic strip uses Temple, 194
Evanston Review, 201–02
fire of 1931 reported, 150, **151**, 152–53
557 newspapers cover 1953 dedication of Temple, 234
John O'Groat Journal, 128
Lake Shore News, 104–07
New York American praises Temple in 1920, 94–95
New York Times, 94, 145
pictures of birds nesting on Temple used in area newspapers, 194
Underwood Press, 95
Washington Post praises Temple in 1909, 95, 293 n.16
Wilmette Life praises progress made on Temple, 194–95
publicity on radio and in movie newsreels, 196, 202, 234–35
publicity through railroad companies, 234
publicity through travel agencies and Chicago Chamber of Commerce, 196
visitors to Temple, 240
area children are, 197–98
numbers of (1932–82), 269–70
tours become popular, 196–97
volunteer guides organized to handle, 73, 197
Wilmette citizens grow to appreciate Temple, 196, 202

Quaglino, Luigi, 99

Race Amity Conventions, 138, 300 n.36
Randall, William H. (Harry), 88, 112, 122
Reed, Earl H., 203, 206, 208
Religion. *See* World's Parliament of Religions
Remey, Charles Mason
biography of, 255–56
designs of, for Bahá'í Temples, 86, 88, 89, **90**
elected to first National Spiritual Assembly, 122
member of first Bahai Temple Unity Executive Board, 52
suggests modifications to Bourgeois design, 124
Research Service, The, 143–44, 156
Rhode, Ruth Bryan, 234
Root, Martha, 75, 198–99
chairperson of Ideas Committee for Temple, 97–98, 199
launches publicity project for Bahá'í Faith, 98
prominent people taught by, 198
Queen Marie, 136, 299–300 n.29
Queen Marie's brooch given to Temple Fund by, 136, 299 n.29
Rúḥíyyih Khánum (née Mary Maxwell), 175, 204, **230**
attends Temple dedication, ix, 228–30, 232–33
marriage of, 175
Rumors about Temple. *See* Publicity about and public response to the Bahá'í Temple
Russia. *See also* Ashkhabad; Bahá'í Temple (Ashkhabad)
Bahá'í Faith recognized by, 248
Bahá'u'lláh aided by minister to Persia from, 251

Sabine, Paul E., 206
Samuel, Mozo, 99

Index

San Francisco, California
  Bahá'ís represented by John Bosch at 1920 annual convention, 50
  Golden Gate International Exposition (1939), 193
  Panama-Pacific International Exposition (1915), 74
Scheffler, Carl, 34, 36, 206
Schopflocher, Lorol, 132
Schopflocher, Siegfried (Fred), 131, 132, 181, 198
  biography of, 256
  designated "Chief Temple Builder," 132
Sears, William, 232
Seattle, Washington, 40, 136
Secretariat, National Bahá'í, 188, 308–09 n.24
Seven Year Plan. *See* Bahá'í Faith in America
Shapiro, Benjamin B., 303 n.4
Shaw, Alfred P., 210–12, 215
Shoghi Effendi
  appointed Guardian of Bahá'í Faith by 'Abdu'l-Bahá's Will and Testament, 121
  the Báb's portrait sent by, to America, 203
  Bahá'í Temple
    Bahá'ís congratulated for completing superstructure of, 157
    Bahá'ís congratulated for finishing exterior ornamentation of, 190
    carpets given to, 139; 140–41; **142**; 301 nn.38, 43; 302 n.45
    finishing dome ornamentation of, encouraged, 158, 159–61
    importance of, emphasized, 122, 124, 225, 241, 308 n.24
    interior modifications suggested for, 206
    lock of Bahá'u'lláh's hair given to, 183
    message sent to dedication of, 228–29
    one thousand pounds sterling contributed toward, 183
    one year's respite promised if efforts to finish, are redoubled, 176
  booklet on Bahá'í dates of historical significance written by, 225
  comments of, on mention of Bahá'í Faith at World's Parliament of Religions, 10–11
  Corinne True and. *See* True, Corinne
  National Spiritual Assembly of the United States and Canada organized by, 121, 122, 122 n
  Plan of Unified Action supported by, 130–31
Shrine of the Báb. *See* Báb, the
Smeskel, Otto, 206
Sprague, Philip, 210
Star of the West, 129, 190, 258
Struven, Edward, 202
Struven, Gertrude, 197–98
Struven, Howard, 112
Sullivan, Louis, 86

Taj Mahal, 96
Taylor, Basil Gordon, 166–67, 212 n, 216, 306 n.22
Teaching. *See* Bahá'í Faith (world community of); Bahá'í Faith in America
Temple. *See* Bahá'í Temple
"Temple Song," words and music of, 266–67
Tobin, Esther (Nettie), **45**, 45–48, 280 nn.8, 9
True, Arna (later Arna True Perron). *See* Perron, Arna True
True, Corinne Knight, 18, **19**, 20–23, 26–35, 276 n.4
  'Abdu'l-Bahá's letters to, 20, 21, 22
  appointed Hand of the Cause of God, 223–24
  Bahá'í Faith accepted by, 20, 276 n.1
  Bahá'í Temple
    'Abdu'l-Bahá calls for her involvement with, 22
    assistance with Nettie Tobin's dedication stone for, 47
    attendance at 1953 dedication of, 231
    attendance at 1912 dedication of site of, 61, 64
    contributions solicited for, after first pilgrimage, 35
    financial secretary of first Bahai Temple Unity Executive Board, 52
    fund-raising activities for, 69
    importance of, shown to be beyond just Chicago, 35
    "Mother of the Temple," 23
    petition carried to 'Abdu'l-Bahá concerning, 26, 31
    search for a site, 36–37
  builds house near Temple in 1929, 153
  education and marriage of, 18–20
    death of children, 20–21, 26, 58
    family life, 21
  elected to first National Spiritual Assembly, 122
  instrumental in formation of Bahai Temple Unity, 49
  pilgrimages of, to Bahá'í holy places
    in 1907, 26–35
    in 1928, 139
    in 1931, 153–55
    in 1952, 222–24
    'Abdu'l-Bahá's purse given to Corinne True by Shoghi Effendi, 224
  speaks at Foundation Hall public meetings, 198
  speaks at 1920 Bahá'í congress, 87–88
  Women's Assembly of Teaching founded by, 18
True, Davis, 58
True, Edna, x, xi, 210
True, Harriet, 20
True, Kenneth, 20

Index

True, Laurence, 26
True, Moses, 19, 21, 58
True, Nathaniel, 20

Ullrich, Clarence, 206
United World Federalists, 230
Unity
   'Abdu'l-Bahá asks for, among Bahá'ís, 56
   Corinne True quotes from 'Abdu'l-Bahá concerning, 39–40
   international letters increase, 3, 136
   Temple linked to, 59–60, 89, 136, 159, 237–38

Voelz, Louis, 192

Wagner, Chris, 73
Waite, Louise, 24, 100, 139
   biography of, 256–57
   pilgrimage of, 55
   poem written by, 290 n.24
   songs written by, 60, 64, 256
   words and music to "Temple Song," 266–67
War, 'Abdu'l-Bahá's comments on, 70–71
Washington, D.C., Bahá'ís of
   propose "Bahai Temple Association of America" in 1908, 42, 49
   send delegate to first Bahai Temple Unity convention, 50
   unaware of Temple progress until 1906, 24
Watson, Marie, 76
White, Kingsley, 112
Wiepert, Leander, 170
Wilhelm, Roy, 68, 75, 76, 122
   biography of, 257
   Evergreen Cabin of, 288 n.1
Wilkins, Roy, 234
Williams, Roy, 72
Wilmette, Illinois
   Bagdadis are first Bahá'ís to live in, 297 n.9
   Bahá'ís send pledge to Shoghi Effendi, 195
   citizens of, grow to appreciate Temple, 196
   president of village board of, speaks highly of Temple, 202
   Gillson Park, 73, 287 n.22
   history of, 44
   public objects to Temple, 104–08
   village board issues building permit, 107
Windust, Albert
   'Abdu'l-Bahá eulogized by, 115
   biography of, 257–58
   comments of, on role of Bahá'í women, 22–23
   locates possible site for Temple, 24
   speaks at Foundation Hall public meetings, 198
Wolcott, Charles, 232
Women
   'Abdu'l-Bahá encourages, 17
   Albert Windust's comments on role of Bahá'í, 22–23
   excluded from first Bahá'í governing bodies, 16–17
   Temple project helped advance equality of, 49
   Widow's Quilt Fund, 54
Women's Assembly of Teaching, 17, 18, 25, 35, 36, 42
Woodward, Fred J., 89
World Federalists, United, 230
World Unity Conferences, 138, 300 n.35
World War I
   'Abdu'l-Bahá's comments on, 70–71
   communication with 'Abdu'l-Bahá difficult during, 75
World's Columbian Exposition (Chicago, 1893), 7–11. *See also* World's Parliament of Religions
World's Fair (New York, 1939–40), 193
World's Parliament of Religions (Chicago, 1893), 8–11
   Bahá'í Faith mentioned at, 10–11

Yá Bahá'u'l-Abhá, meaning of, 313 n.1

Zamenhof, Lidja, 182